Dwight Diller

Contributions to Southern Appalachian Studies

1. *Memoirs of Grassy Creek: Growing Up in the Mountains on the Virginia–North Carolina Line.* Zetta Barker Hamby. 1998

2. *The Pond Mountain Chronicle: Self-Portrait of a Southern Appalachian Community.* Edited by Leland R. Cooper and Mary Lee Cooper. 1998

3. *Traditional Musicians of the Central Blue Ridge: Old Time, Early Country, Folk and Bluegrass Label Recording Artists, with Discographies.* Marty McGee. 2000

4. *W.R. Trivett, Appalachian Pictureman: Photographs of a Bygone Time.* Ralph E. Lentz II. 2001

5. *The People of the New River: Oral Histories from the Ashe, Alleghany and Watauga Counties of North Carolina.* Edited by Leland R. Cooper and Mary Lee Cooper. 2001

6. *John Fox, Jr., Appalachian Author.* Bill York. 2003

7. *The Thistle and the Brier: Historical Links and Cultural Parallels Between Scotland and Appalachia.* Richard Blaustein. 2003

8. *Tales from Sacred Wind: Coming of Age in Appalachia. The Cratis Williams Chronicles.* Cratis D. Williams. Edited by David Cratis Williams and Patricia D. Beaver. 2003

9. *Willard Gayheart, Appalachian Artist.* Willard Gayheart and Donia S. Eley. 2003

10. *The Forest City Lynching of 1900: Populism, Racism, and White Supremacy in Rutherford County, North Carolina.* J. Timothy Cole. 2003

11. *The Brevard Rosenwald School: Black Education and Community Building in a Southern Appalachian Town, 1920–1966.* Betty J. Reed. 2004

12. *The Bristol Sessions: Writings About the Big Bang of Country Music.* Edited by Charles K. Wolfe and Ted Olson. 2005

13. *Community and Change in the North Carolina Mountains: Oral Histories and Profiles of People from Western Watauga County.* Compiled by Nannie Greene and Catherine Stokes Sheppard. 2006

14. *Ashe County: A History; A New Edition.* Arthur Lloyd Fletcher. 2009 [2006]

15. *The New River Controversy; A New Edition.* Thomas J. Schoenbaum. Epilogue by R. Seth Woodard. 2007

16. *The Blue Ridge Parkway by Foot: A Park Ranger's Memoir.* Tim Pegram. 2007

17. *James Still: Critical Essays on the Dean of Appalachian Literature.* Edited by Ted Olson and Kathy H. Olson. 2008

18. *Owsley County, Kentucky, and the Perpetuation of Poverty.* John R. Burch, Jr. 2008

19. *Asheville: A History.* Nan K. Chase. 2007

20. *Southern Appalachian Poetry: An Anthology of Works by 37 Poets.* Edited by Marita Garin. 2008

21. *Ball, Bat and Bitumen: A History of Coalfield Baseball in the Appalachian South.* L.M. Sutter. 2009

22. *The Frontier Nursing Service: America's First Rural Nurse-Midwife Service and School.* Marie Bartlett. 2009

23. *James Still in Interviews, Oral Histories and Memoirs.* Edited by Ted Olson. 2009

24. *The Millstone Quarries of Powell County, Kentucky.* Charles D. Hockensmith. 2009

25. *The Bibliography of Appalachia: More Than 4,700 Books, Articles, Monographs and Dissertations, Topically Arranged and Indexed.* Compiled by John R. Burch, Jr. 2009

26. *Appalachian Children's Literature: An Annotated Bibliography.* Compiled by Roberta Teague Herrin and Sheila Quinn Oliver. 2010

27. *Southern Appalachian Storytellers: Interviews with Sixteen Keepers of the Oral Tradition.* Edited by Saundra Gerrell Kelley. 2010

28. *Southern West Virginia and the Struggle for Modernity.* Christopher Dorsey. 2011

29. *George Scarbrough, Appalachian Poet: A Biographical and Literary Study with Unpublished Writings.* Randy Mackin. 2011

30. *The Water-Powered Mills of Floyd County, Virginia: Illustrated Histories, 1770–2010.* Franklin F. Webb and Ricky L. Cox. 2012

31. *School Segregation in Western North Carolina: A History, 1860s–1970s.* Betty Jamerson Reed. 2011

32. *The Ravenscroft School in Asheville: A History of the Institution and Its People and Buildings.* Dale Wayne Slusser. 2014

33. *The Ore Knob Mine Murders: The Crimes, the Investigation and the Trials.* Rose M. Haynes. 2013

34. *New Art of Willard Gayheart.* Willard Gayheart and Donia S. Eley. 2014

35. *Public Health in Appalachia: Essays from the Clinic and the Field.* Edited by Wendy Welch. 2014

36. *The Rhetoric of Appalachian Identity.* Todd Snyder. 2014

37. *African American and Cherokee Nurses in Appalachia: A History, 1900–1965.* Phoebe Ann Pollitt. 2015

38. *A Hospital for Ashe County: Four Generations of Appalachian Community Health Care.* Janet C. Pittard. 2015

39. *Dwight Diller: West Virginia Mountain Musician.* Lewis M. Stern. 2016

40. *The Brown Mountain Lights: History, Science and Human Nature Explain an Appalachian Mystery.* Wade Edward Speer. 2016

DWIGHT DILLER
West Virginia Mountain Musician

Lewis M. Stern

CONTRIBUTIONS TO SOUTHERN APPALACHIAN STUDIES, 39

McFarland & Company, Inc., Publishers
Jefferson, North Carolina

ALSO BY LEWIS M. STERN
AND FROM MCFARLAND

*Imprisoned or Missing in Vietnam:
Policies of the Vietnamese Government Concerning
Captured and Unaccounted for United States Soldiers,
1969–1994* (1995; softcover 2012)

*Defense Relations Between the United States and Vietnam:
The Process of Normalization, 1977–2003* (2005)

LIBRARY OF CONGRESS CATALOGUING-IN-PUBLICATION DATA

Names: Stern, Lewis M., author.
Title: Dwight Diller : West Virginia mountain musician / Lewis M. Stern.
Description: Jefferson, North Carolina : McFarland & Company, Inc., 2016 |
 Series: Contributions to Southern Appalachian studies ; 39 |
 Includes bibliographical references, discography, filmography, and index.
Identifiers: LCCN 2016011522 | ISBN 9781476664767 (softcover : acid free paper) ∞
Subjects: LCSH: Diller, Dwight. | Fiddlers—West Virginia—Biography. |
 Banjoists—West Virginia—Biography. | Old-time music—Appalachian
 region—History and criticism.
Classification: LCC ML418.D44 S7 2016 | DDC 787.2/162130092—dc23
LC record available at http://lccn.loc.gov/2016011522

BRITISH LIBRARY CATALOGUING DATA ARE AVAILABLE

© 2016 Lewis M. Stern. All rights reserved

*No part of this book may be reproduced or transmitted in any form
or by any means, electronic or mechanical, including photocopying
or recording, or by any information storage and retrieval system,
without permission in writing from the publisher.*

Front cover: Dwight Diller at a festival in West Virginia, 1973
(photograph by Carl Fleischhauer); top inset: detail of Ron Chacey's
inlay work on the peghead and fingerboard of the banjo neck built by
Dan Dagget for Dwight Diller (courtesy of Dan Dagget)

Printed in the United States of America

*McFarland & Company, Inc., Publishers
Box 611, Jefferson, North Carolina 28640
www.mcfarlandpub.com*

Table of Contents

Acknowledgments	vii
Introduction	1
One. Early Life	15
Two. Learning Music	35
Three. Playing Music	58
Four. Studying Religion	85
Five. A Life of Teaching	102
Conclusion	128
Discography and Filmography	153
Chapter Notes	159
Bibliography	188
Interviewees	196
Index	201

Acknowledgments

Writing a biography becomes an affair of the heart. Over time, the project on the West Virginia old time musician Dwight Diller seemed to have crept into every corner of my life. It occupied my attention during every waking moment for the year I spent researching and writing. Against my wife Mary's admonition to keep my weekends free for rest and recuperation from this all-consuming task, I found myself furtively making and receiving phone calls pertaining to the project, or at my desk writing from the crack of dawn until the rest of the city woke up. In effect, this became an eight-day a week job.

However, I had a lot of help.

I owe Mary A. Kiernan Stern a great deal for her forbearance, for her strong and continuous efforts to keep this project organized and on track, and for her reminders to take a deep breath. Mary brought to bear her keen sense of writing work in this new internet-driven age of information saturation, based on her own book project, and gradually prompted me to shed my devotion to index cards and manila folders in favor of a much more interactive, modern way of organizing information to make it accessible and available for this kind of project. I also owe Mary for her sage guidance, based on her decades of professional work as a clinical social worker, regarding my effort to untangle the challenges that Dwight freely acknowledged.

My son Ethan lent a consistently professional hand to the information technology issues that confronted me. Those ranged from simple things like keeping my computer operational, to file management and recovery issues including safehavening the massive audio and visual resources that I collected with the help of many contributors to the effort to build a database of Dwight's music and Dwight's music instruction.

My daughter Anna offered consistently sharp and effective editorial advice and wise recommendations about publishing in the 21st century, recognizing that all the while I was much more comfortable and familiar with life in the 20th century. She helped me understand the myriad of possibilities that had reshaped writing, and publishing, and gave me good advice on locating and navigating internet resources that were indispensable.

Many others lent a hand to this undertaking. I owe thanks to the following people:

Professors A. Donald Augsburger and George Brunk provided vivid recollections of Dwight Diller's days at Eastern Mennonite University in Harrisonburg, Virginia, and helped me understand much about the Mennonites.

Janet Burton, a dedicated first grade teacher and a creative banjo player, delved into her massive digital holdings and provided me with access to unique recordings of Dwight accumulated in her continuous search for archaic music. Janet is a good banjo friend from the massive online community called Banjo Hangout, and thus represents one of those relationships nurtured online, the sort we taught our children to avoid at all costs.

Professor Cece Conway, Department of English, Appalachian State University, Boone, North Carolina, helped me thread my way into relevant scholarship about Appalachian literature and culture, and taught me a great deal about religion in central West Virginia during the 1940s through the 1960s. Importantly, she led me to ask fundamental questions about the early festivals in West Virginia and Virginia, the nature of old time music in local communities such as Lexington, Virginia, and Durham/Chapel Hill, North Carolina, and encouraged me to hunt for recorded examples of Dwight's banjo playing in the earliest stages of his development as a musician.

John A. Cuthbert, director and curator of the West Virginia and Regional History Collection at the West Virginia University Libraries, provided guidance regarding the Thomas Brown recordings housed at West Virginia University in Morgantown.

Paul Deblois, a long-time member of the northern Virginia Friends of Old Time Banjo, generously allowed me to borrow huge chunks of his *Banjo Newsletter* collection from that publication's earliest years. Paul also worked exceptionally hard digitizing the large number of cassettes, videos, and other eccentric audio forms used to capture Dwight's music as early as the 1970s, and his teaching work at banjo retreats and workshops in the period from the 1980s to the 2000s. He did this patiently, and with a loving touch, and I appreciate his every effort.

Carl Fleischhauer, digital initiatives project manager in the Office of Strategic Initiatives, Library of Congress, provided frank, candid and consistently thoughtful observations about the Library of Congress Hammons project, the art and practice of ethnographic fieldwork, old time festivals in the 1970s including Ivydale, and his knowledge of and friendship with Dwight Diller. He also made accessible to me truly valuable documents from the American Folklife collection of the Library of Congress, and from his own private library, and shared photographs he took in the early 1970s at some of the old time music gatherings that stood as unique documents of those events. Finally, he read early portions of the text and offered critical evaluations of the trajectory of my arguments. I'm indebted to him for the time and energy he brought to all this work on behalf of this writing project.

Andrew Fults, Bates Littlehales, Chuck Lee, Ron Chacey and Dan Dagget, and Jeff Kramer offered detailed explanations of various banjo building projects they undertook for Dwight, providing details, documents and photographs that were invaluable.

Gail Gillespie, an old time music multi-instrumentalist and former editor of the *Old Time Herald*, and her musician husband Dwight Rogers, scoured their memories and personal archives for information on banjo contests in which Dwight Diller competed during the 1970s, and plumbed the depths of their encyclopedic knowledge of old time music to answer my many questions about West Virginia musical traditions and old time fiddlers.

Bobby Griffin, a 2011 recipient of the Vandalia Award, West Virginia's highest folk life honor, offered good advice and very practical recommendations on reaching out to musicians and archivists about West Virginia musical traditions and history.

Wayne Howard, the author of a four-part feature about the Hammons family of West Virginia published in the *Old Time Herald*, and a retired computer programmer and analyst, provided inspired, exceptionally artistic thinking about the preservation of regional musical traditions, the teaching of traditional banjo and fiddle music, and the evolution of old time music in contemporary times—and the role and consequences of music festivals in that process. He went to great lengths to make available to me his extremely valuable field notes from visits to the homes of Hammons family members, and copies of his personal tape recordings of Sherman, Lee, Burle and Maggie Hammons as well as unique recordings of Dwight's own music. Additionally, Wayne worked hard to help me digitize and duplicate many of the audio and visual resources that found their way to my mailbox throughout the course of this work.

John Huerta, former general counsel of the Smithsonian, avid banjo player and vintage banjo collector, long-time resident of Elkins, West Virginia, shared his recollections of the old time world in the 1970s, lent a West Coast perspective to the development of old time "scenes," and helped me make valuable connections to musicians in West Virginia.

Alan Jabbour, former director of the American Folk Life Center at the Library of Congress, co-author with Carl Fleischhauer of *The Hammons Family: The Traditions of a West Virginia Family and Their Friends*, looked very closely at my thinking about Dwight and the old time music community in Lexington, Virginia, in the early 1970s, and added much to my understanding of the 1970s revival of old time instrumental tunes played in ensemble in places such as Durham and Chapel Hill, North Carolina.

Dan Levenson, old time musician and teacher, offered me a professional musician's perspective on many key issues throughout this project including instructional approaches, musical creativity, banjo playing technique and style—in a fashion that added depth to my understanding of old time music, and helped me articulate important issues about Dwight Diller as an artist and teacher.

Carroll "Cas" Smith, a photographer and videographer and clawhammer banjo player from Florida, recorded some of Dwight's earliest public performances in West Virginia. Carroll, a friend from my earliest days as an avid attendee of the annual Appalachian String Band Festival in Clifftop, West Virginia, helped manage the audio and visual resources I called upon in doing this work, and dug into his own archive of photographs and audio recordings to provide indispensable material in support of this effort.

Aaron Smithers, Southern Folklife Collection, Research and Instructional Services Department, Louis Round Wilson Special Collections Library, the University of North Carolina at Chapel Hill, facilitated access to a recorded interview conducted in August 1983 with Dwight Diller in the Jack Bernhardt Papers.

Kilby Spencer, originally from Whitetop, Virginia, made available to me recordings of the banjo contest taped at the 4th Annual Old Time Fiddlers and Bluegrass Convention in Hillsville, Virginia, in June 1970. Kilby learned old-time music from his parents, Thornton and Emily, who have been in the Whitetop Mountain Band for over 40 years. He collects and digitizes rare local recordings, and serves on the board of the Field Recorders' Collective, whose mission is to preserve and release rare field and home recordings of old time music. Dwight was amazed that his first contest tunes from June 1970 had survived, and was deeply grateful for the chance to hear himself playing so soon after he had solidified what became his signature banjo sound.

William Talley, of West Chester, Pennsylvania, who began playing clawhammer in the mid–1960s, tapped his memory and his audio library to come up with absolutely essential recordings of Dwight playing at the vaunted "Alternative Galax" hosted by Armin Barnett in Charlottesville, Virginia, in 1972.

Stephen Wade, musician, recording artist, and writer, spent long hours above and beyond the call of duty and friendship sorting through the conceptual foundations of this project, and providing me with careful and expert guidance on the craft of building a book.

A long list of old time musicians, teachers, writers and researchers, West Virginian banjo and fiddle players, as well as some of Dwight's friends, and his sister, Nancy, made themselves available for interviews during my attempt to wade through various parts of Dwight's life. All were patient, cooperative, thoughtful, and profoundly devoted to old time music traditions in general and to Dwight Diller's musicianship in particular. I conducted these discussions in a variety of ways, via email exchanges, telephone conversations, and in some instances in face-to-face meetings. I think it was the intensity of commitment to traditional music on the part of these people that eliminated the difficulties that often emerge in pursuing such vigorous questioning. Many of those interviewed allowed themselves to be drawn into long, involved discussions, and ended up schooling me about folk music revivals, the preservation of traditional music, concepts of field recording and collection work, early banjo luthiery, old time music festival "cultures," and old time music communities. Many of those interviewed agreed to be questioned multiple times, responding articulately and patiently whenever I parachuted into their lives seeking information and looking for clues as to where else I might turn in hunting down eccentric facts and esoteric information. I owe a great debt to these people who helped me in innumerable ways during the course of this project. I have listed their names at the end of this book.

I would like to single out several people who allowed me to assail them with emails and phone calls throughout the course of this writing project. All of these interview subjects allowed me to belabor various points, to push and pull on ideas and poke various hypotheses, and to sustain conversation on some very specific issues. Carl Baron, Mark Campbell, Bob Carlin, Rock Garton, Bill Hicks, Diane Jones, Brad Leftwich, Bates and Jody Littlehales, Gerry Milnes, Tom Mylet, Len Reiss, Al Tharp, Bob Thren, and David Winston were especially generous with their time.

Throughout my efforts to shape the manuscript into a book, I relied on a handful of "trusted readers" who I knew would give me their unvarnished views of the various drafts I put before them, offer me constructive criticism regarding content, and good advice and guidance regarding the trajectory of my writing effort. I knew that I could count on them to do this because they were friends and acquaintances from the old time music world, and because they valued the contribution Dwight had made to preserving, performing, and teaching traditional music. Catherine Rowe offered helpful views regarding the content of an early draft of Chapter One ("Early Life"). Carl Fleischhauer, Bill Hicks, John Huerta, Janet and Kit Burton, and Alan Jabbour read and commented on multiple versions of Chapter Two ("Learning Music") and/or Chapter Three ("Playing Music"). Cece Conway provided valuable views on elements regarding the old time festivals and associated banjo contests that became part of Chapter Three. Allen Johnson offered important perspectives on the substance of an early draft of Chapter Four ("Studying Religion"). Cindy Harris commented on an early version of Chapter Five ("A Life of Teaching"). Doug Van Gundy commented on a section of this chapter regarding Dwight's approach to teaching fiddle. Andy Fults, Jeff Kramer, Chuck Lee, Ron Chacey, David Dagget and Len Reiss provided valuable information that went into composing the section of the Conclusion regarding Dwight's banjo preferences and set-up choices. I am deeply

Acknowledgments

grateful to all of them for their frank and pointed, and extremely thoughtful and informed comments that enabled me to strengthen this product. I alone am responsible for the manner in which I utilized their good advice.

Finally, I owe Dwight Diller a sincere, heartfelt thanks for enduring long, long discussions over many, many years, and all the while remaining a good friend in spite of the discomfort that dredging up details and unwrapping often tough memories sometimes entailed for him.

I alone am responsible for the manner in which I interpreted the information provided to me, the way I organized this biography, and the conclusions I drew in this writing.

The manuscript on which this book was based was completed in October 2015, and called on material, documents, interviews and other resources available to the author up to that date.

* * *

Dwight was always very sensitive about, and protective of, West Virginia. He abhorred the use of the term "hillbilly," and thought it was as demeaning as any racial slur. He could hold forth with an articulate, impassioned explanation of why this term was wrong, just wrong, and should not be part of the vocabulary any more than some of the worst racial and religious epithets that were freighted with frightening histories.

In 2003 Dwight was chosen as one of the representatives of the Appalachian region at the Smithsonian Folklife Festival in Washington, D.C.

In this first photo, Dwight has just holstered his banjo after a performance, and was walking away from the stage, hat pulled down over his eyes shading him from the notorious Washington, D.C., summer. I had just arrived on the mall, spotted him, and

Dwight Diller on the Mall in Washington, D.C., after finishing a set at the Smithsonian's 2003 Folklife Festival (author's photograph).

stepped in front of his path, my camera up in front of my face, as I said "Oh, my good fortune, a real hillbilly here in our capital. Please let me take some pictures." I saw the scowl appear on his face, and the smoke begin to pour out of his ears—just like in those Bugs Bunny cartoons of yesteryear. He slowed his gait, and lifted his head toward me.

I do not recall for what triggered his recognition of me, the first glance at my face or my voice, but the flicker of a smile that quickly broadened on his face, captured in this second photo was the Dwight I knew and loved.

I hope you enjoy reading this book as much as I enjoyed writing it, and I hope you enjoy Dwight as much as I have.

Introduction

Meeting Dwight

Dwight Diller pulled up to my home in northern Virginia in January 2002 in a big old American-made automobile, laden with the dust from West Virginia roads, filled with artifacts of past banjo workshops—videos, tune lists, compact disk recordings. He unfolded from the driver's seat, unpacked a kit bag from his car's trunk, reached for his banjo case, and turned to me as I came to greet him at the curb. "You're much bigger in your music," I said, looking him over as I extended my hand to clasp his. The photos on his numerous albums displayed a big bearded man perhaps the size of the mountains that I imagined encircled his home in Pocahontas County, with hands that appeared, to me, to be enormous. Now I held a hand that was, unarguably, strong, but was also gentle in its grip and almost ordinary in size.

I knew Dwight's music because his approach to southern Appalachian down-picking banjo had been pressed on me by my first banjo teacher, Bates Littlehales, himself a student, a friend, and a neighbor of Dwight. Bates would, in late years, become Dwight's videographer, producing his several instructional tapes as Thornapple Productions. Bates provided me with my first taste of this archaic regional music, and my introduction to Dwight. Bates brought him to my front door, urging Dwight to agree to a multi-day banjo workshop in my home in Arlington, Virginia. And Bates pushed me through my first drills aimed at teaching me this percussive, right hand driven clawhammer banjo.

I never grow tired of telling this story that I have wrapped and re-wrapped as my own legitimating narrative over the years I have been involved in this banjo music—as a vintage banjo collector with a decidedly modest assemblage of old instruments, a writer on various eccentric aspects of banjo music and banjo building, a banjo teacher in northern Virginia and later in Staunton, Virginia, gradually shifting my post-retirement life to focus on banjo, banjo, banjo.

I was lucky enough to get an old, beat up long neck banjo—a Bacon Belmont—as a gift from my parents upon my graduation from junior high school in the mid-1960s.

I later came under the spell of Earl Scruggs' compelling bluegrass sound, and eventually migrated toward the guitar. I hauled my first banjo with me to Southeast Asia in the mid-1980s and when I came back to northern Virginia, field stripped it with the goal of rebuilding it, but soon lost interest in this venture.

In the early 1990s I offered it to anyone who might want it via the online forum for banjo enthusiasts called BANJO-L, the predecessor to Banjo Hangout, an online community for banjo players. By then my banjo was in parts and pieces and resided in a grocery bag.

Bates Littlehales, who was then in his seventies and lived not far from me in northern Virginia, offered to take it and insisted on giving me "one clawhammer lesson" in return for the banjo. I agreed.

Bates came to my home every Saturday morning for about two years, and would spend a couple of hours or so each session drilling me in clawhammer, teaching me technique and tunes, and talking about the art form and the artists, especially West Virginia banjo players. When he got ready to "retire" back to his mountain in West Virginia, I reminded him that he had signed up to do one lesson. Bates replied that it was one lesson. It just took two years because I was a slow learner.

During our time together, Bates engendered an interest in banjo repair and building, and taught me the basics of cutting wood and caring for machines. After many years, perhaps sometime around 2005 or so, I visited him in West Virginia. He handed me a paper bag filled with a banjo, my Bacon Belmont, and told me to make it right again. I did, and pretty quickly after fixing it up I sold it. I don't really pine away for it because I have this great story in its place.

When I met Bates I had no preconceptions about clawhammer. I had never tried it, except for one brief attempt in the 1960s to figure out the right hand work from the Pete Seeger book, which left me believing that I simply did not have the capacity to flex my digits in the proper way in order to get the clawhammer sound.

In the end, though, clawhammer struck me as the right road to take. Clawhammer did not seem to have as many grammatical rules as bluegrass, and it also appeared to be less of an athletic challenge. While bluegrass style three finger rolling is a pleasure in its own right, it struck me that after a while there are real limits to the possibilities, unless one can figure out a way to roll with four fingers and thereby multiply the possible up-picking patterns geometrically. Clawhammer seemed to offer a greater range of possibilities in a manner that was less circumscribed by both physical realities and the parameters of "The Sound." To me, there is a definite bluegrass sound that comes from pattern picking. In clawhammer, there appeared to be fewer rigid prescriptions, and a much more relaxed learning curve.

Bates had a deep reverence for old time music, an inexhaustible knowledge of players, styles and methods, and a real love for the banjo. Our lessons quickly turned into an exercise in figuring out how to get a kid from Brooklyn to understand how to make the banjo work this special way. Bates underscored exactly how important it was for me to listen and listen and listen again to Dwight Diller's banjo. He lent me cassettes and videos, and I eventually accumulated a little audio library of my own featuring Dwight's CDs and various cassettes and videos from all manner of esoteric sources. And Bates planted the idea of enticing Dwight to head toward northern Virginia for a workshop that I would host in our home.

So, when Dwight pulled up to my front door in January 2002, I knew him, or his music, and it was truly a gigantic sound. To many of my newfound clawhammer banjo friends in northern Virginia, Dwight's playing sounded as though there were two people in the room deploying two separate banjos, or perhaps just one man with four or five arms capable of musical gymnastics. His sound was clean, lean, strong and sparse, and it permeated any space where it was played—to the point that my then teenage children, Ethan and Anna, felt compelled to post "No Plucking Zone" signs around their rooms, presumably because they were so devoted to doing their homework in utter peace and quiet.

Listening to Dwight

Going back over my notes from that 2002 banjo workshop experience, what struck me was that in those days Dwight was the dynamic center of this workshop experience, the center of gravity of the process.[1] He remained firmly in command throughout the process. I saw that as an impressive combination of the characteristics of a teacher, a minister, an organizer, and a tour guide, an expert, a sympathetic soul, and a good judge of human nature.

Dwight showed himself to be an intense man with a real interest in many, many things, a hunger for discussion, and a driving desire to acquire knowledge that prompted him to scour all manner of sources for ideas and information. He did not ask idle questions, but put probing, thoughtful propositions on the table and, in a most gentle fashion, asked for help to learn what others might know. Dwight had long been involved in a consuming attempt to understand himself. He would use any tool possible, entertain the validity of all manner of hypotheses, and integrate ideas into his arsenal that contributed to his effort to sort through pieces of his life. He asked anyone who would listen to help him figure out things about himself. That did not ever seem to diminish; he continued to scrutinize the twists and turns in the trajectory of his life, and looked closely at the emotional hardships, financial trials and physical discomfort life had brought him.

Some of this vigorous, continuous introspection had to do with his music. Some of it did not. At times, he looked at a troubled life history in a detached, analytical fashion, and at times with great emotion, seeing the music as a fulcrum for his development, a saving grace, a motivation to live, and a practical way of making a living—but also, at times, as an overwhelming burden. He attempted to describe to his students what drove him to pursue teaching this music, largely on the assumption that it might clarify his passion, offer an insight into the biological internal combustion engine that fueled his rhythm, or suggest the extent to which learning the language of West Virginian music energized his life in a manner he hardly expected.

For whatever reason, at a difficult point in his life—and Dwight was never very shy about spelling out these difficulties—he found himself embraced by the Hammonses, and clung to the community that they offered and the sense of belonging that he derived from these relationships. It fueled a passion for their music, and a habit of closely scrutinizing the tunes and the stories they told. It stiffened his spine about reorganizing his life, gave shape to his thinking about what was important, what it would take to live in the way of good men, and engrained in him a sense of responsibility to the music. I think Dwight sought to draw a distinction between the work of scholars and collectors of Appalachian music who systematically, and in accordance with standards and practices of established academic disciplines, recorded and preserved music, and what he found himself doing with the Hammons family beginning in the late 1960s. His enterprise was less an academic undertaking or a lofty commitment to preserving archaic tunes than it was an act of self-preservation. In his own explanation, he latched onto the music in a time of need, and grabbed onto the lifeline that this old West Virginian family threw to him.

I do not think Dwight set out on a mission to preserve this music in return for the kindness of the family, to reciprocate for the restorative powers their embrace offered. I do not think he said to himself, now that I have rejuvenated my will to live thanks to the goodness of these folk I will repay them by enshrining their music and protecting its meaning and cadence. I think instead that Dwight felt several things:

First, I think he felt an obligation to capture some of the tunes in as original a shape and form as possible. This, I believe, was his "native son" obligation at work, his sense that as a West Virginian he should care about seeing this stuff recorded and made available to others, including those looking to explain, if only to themselves, what being a West Virginian meant.

Second, I think he felt a need to protect the Hammons family from close and invasive scrutiny that would pry away at the context in which they lived and end up reshaping the simplicity of their lives by turning it into a showcase example of some American frontier caricature. That was why he has never trotted out the lives of the Hammons family in some sort of memoir or reminiscence, and why he was consistently careful about the slide show developed in the late 1980s that took a look at the lives of the Hammonses through a collection of photographs that Dwight took in 1970. He was reluctant to make a spectacle of them, probably because they did not volunteer to be the Hammonses. They ended up being who they were, and in Dwight's view should not have had to pay a price as a consequence of being splayed out in ethnographic studies that could bring embarrassment or unwanted attention to people who did not want things that complex. This was not necessarily the most sound of arguments Dwight made, and I found myself chiding him from time to time because he would have been precisely the one most capable of depicting the family in a careful and sensitive manner, in a way that protected their interests while offering insight into them. To be sure, over time, after much persuasion from a variety of friends, Dwight turned his attention to sorting through the massive collection of stark black and white portraits and family pictures he had taken of the Hammonses, systematically recording the old stories they told that constituted the stuff of local lore, and more analytically looking at what they represented in a fashion that generated the inspiration for his 2013 *Across the YewPines* project and gave rise to ideas about more work that could be done on the stories the Hammonses told and the tunes the Hammonses played.[2]

Third, I think he felt a "responsibility" to the music, a term Dwight often used to describe a key requirement for anyone delving into this archaic art form, and certainly for himself as he set about the task of teaching the music. This was the most interesting, and potentially most complex feeling that Dwight had about the music. The "responsibility" appeared to mean something distinct from the quid pro quo relationship assumed to exist between any type of music and its champion. That is, the "responsibility" appeared to have little to do with a struggle to keep the music pure, to protect its original, primordial sound, and to capture and repeat its authenticity in every act of playing the music in return for what the music did for Dwight personally.

This is clear from the way in which Dwight distinguished the music he played from the styles and renditions of the Hammonses. He played "his music." He changed tunes. He put pieces of tunes together because they sounded better and worked out more effectively than what he heard. He tied parts of tunes together because they sounded more pleasing that way to him, or because they solved a puzzle left by failed memories of what an original tune sounded like—though he almost certainly preferred the old and original tunes that came directly from the Hammonses.

The "responsibility" had more to do with recognizing the extent to which the music did not belong to the music maker. It was not a commodity that could be reshaped, recorded, and distributed. It was not an artifact of mountain life that could be embalmed and stored in a museum for selective viewing and historical appreciation. It was a living entity with shelf life that would transcend the time on earth of anyone who touched it. So, the responsibility entailed recognizing that the music sprung from an ancient creative moment and that anyone who played it had but the smallest role in the lifespan of this music. Dwight, after all, did not say he was responsible for the music. He said that he had a responsibility to the music, and that anyone who learned it would hopefully come to understand the responsibility they then had to the music. There was the sense in these words that it was not a "responsibility" in terms of a curatorial obligation, and it was not a "responsibility" to save and protect the music. He was "responsible" to the music. He "reported to" the music. The chain of command was clear: he was the subordinate agent of the music.

The use of the term "responsibility" was intended to telegraph the notion that one ought not to try and use this music for individual glorification or enrichment. He made that point emphatically. He generally followed this explanation by noting that should one try, "the music will turn on you." That was, in effect, a warning that went back to the argument that this was no ordinary commodity. It was not something that could be recorded, sold, and simply added to a discography. Of course, musicians do precisely that, so we need to discount the possibility that Dwight was saying that making living out of singing and playing these tunes was a transgression. Dwight was saying there was a need for humility before the force the music represented, the profundity of its creative core, the simple strength and durability of its attractiveness and seductiveness, and the ancient rhythms it enshrined. To Dwight, the Hammonses were not the font of all Pocahontas County creative originality and talent, the most perfect representatives of this style of music, or the best representatives of this old-time music. To Dwight, they were just the best listeners.

They listened to the music, repeated the old tunes, told the old tales, and shared them unassumingly. They played them quietly and without seeking to make themselves grand and bigger than the music. They welcomed the music into their lives, and integrated it into the way they organized their households. The black and white photos Dwight took with a simple camera in the early 1970s depicted simple folk seated on roughly hewn porches playing plain banjos, trading tunes. Besides their music, especially the dark and modal tunes, what Dwight admired most about the Hammons family was the way they went about their tough lives, with as little as they had, incorporating this music into it, deriving pleasure and pride from their capacity to offer the music a way of living on in their modest, native talent.

Learning from Dwight

Dwight's banjo workshops, his multi-day marathons, were the stuff of banjo world legend from the 1980s through the early 2000s. Dwight slowed down his teaching schedule after a 2005 car accident and a series of medical challenges that complicated his life from 2005 through 2007. He still taught, but preferred very small groups or one-on-one arrangements.

His workshops were living, evolving creatures that changed as he got a better idea, or as an insight catalyzed self-critical thought about how he had been doing things all along. Those who took his courses repeatedly, Diller Recidivists, could see the extent to which his teaching changed as he learned. He was a communicator, anxiously looking for the best way to put a thought. And, in the course of a three day class, he could find several alternative means of getting his thoughts across, try them all vigorously, and wake up the next morning with yet another thought on how to make himself clear. That, to me, was the core of what it meant to be a teacher.

In the end, he offered a portal into a difficult dialect of a musical language, a rarely taught linguistic form. He started with the grammar and the physicality of that dialect, the rhythm. It was elusive, hard to define, and not easily understood by merely listening to its sound or hearing and seeing it dissected and reassembled for others to imitate.

Learning a new language, though, was more than acquiring sufficient vocabulary, becoming competent with the logic of a system of grammar, and obeying rules of syntax. Sometimes, learning to speak a new language entailed figuring out what the silence meant, determining what lurked behind lips poised to speak, discerning the flexibility of words and the parameters of their power beyond obvious meaning. Sometimes learning to speak a new language meant understanding the cadence of sentences and how they varied in subtle ways that worked to communicate massive changes in intended messages.

That was the true challenge communicated by the experience of Dwight's workshops. I learned that though I figured out how to make the snapping, pumping rhythm with my limbs, posture, muscles and bones, I had not quite broken the code, though I had been captivated by its allure—in much the same way that reaching a significant plateau in mastering a foreign tongue rendered communication easier, and at the same time made conveying meaning that much more difficult.

Breaking through the barriers to fluency brought the responsibility to tread carefully so as not to confuse mastering the rules with achieving native familiarity with the texture, taste and the internal codes of conduct of a language. Learning to utter an idiomatic phrase, and sensing the perfect time to employ that wording, did not always mean that one had internalized the genetic material that made fluency possible beyond the masterful use of a list of vocabulary and development of a command over a formal set of rules governing sentence structure. So, sometimes learning a new music meant looking for complexities that were not communicated by rules, finding out when simplicities that were too elusive to be apparent were necessary to communicate meaning, and discerning when the cadence of the uttered word becomes the meaning of the word itself.

Dwight was the knowledgeable local guide immersed in this dialect, and willing to help explore the complex paths, capable of offering hints as to when the twists and turns have meaning, and when they are just such a permanent part of the landscape of the musical language that they have no separate, discreet meaning themselves. In that way, he was better than a dictionary, or a grammatical guidebook. All his CDs, and his wonderful videos, helped teach the music but somehow did not offer the best way to get at this language. Sitting knee to knee with him remained the best way to begin to absorb some of the essence of this music.

Dwight sought to explain this by describing his own gradual revelation that part of each human was explained by the stories they carried along with them and the stories their family or community told and retold. It could take years to decipher the codes and catch onto the signals, and more time still to catch onto the social and cultural nuances that explained more than words did. To Dwight, the way people spoke, the regional dialect plus the elements of language unique to families together constituted a separate and distinct life rhythm that in effect was the internal pulse of person, an identifying fingerprint as unique as any physical feature. This rhythmic core was essentially an internal music that underpinned a person's life. That was the music Dwight zeroed in on, a music that was, as he saw it, so close to the spirit as to be identical with a person's DNA.

To Dwight, there were limits to how much music one could "learn" using just the brain. Instincts, hunches, guesses, experiments all contributed to figuring out what sounded right, true, and pleasing. He talked about hearing the music with the heart. My first banjo teacher, Bates Littlehales, used to admonish me to listen to what he was doing instead of just watching what he was doing. Old timers talk of "catching" a tune, not necessarily learning it or studying it, as though it was something ephemeral and hard to grasp instead of an equation of melodic sound that could be summarized, notated, in a precise way.

There is a dimension to this music—to the physical skills necessary to get the sound, to the mental appreciation of the rhythmic component, to the soulful comprehension of its dynamism—that cannot come exclusively from hearing and seeing, but must come from touching and smelling, and the use of other antenna that videos and CDs do not arouse. All those many years ago, after he climbed out of that car and entered my home, and set up for his class, what I started to understand was that learning the tune was not learning the music, and that learning the rhythm was not the end, but the beginning.

Writing Dwight's Story

The idea for this book emerged from a discussion I had with Dwight during one of his visits to northern Virginia in the early 2000s. Dwight was sitting in my home. He was tired. He was scheduled to teach a multi-day course and had arrived a few days beforehand to catch up on some sleep, get over "car lag," and have some quiet time before the class. We talked about many things, including his recent musical projects, his teaching schedule, and his desire to continue to honor his West Virginian music and the founding fathers of this branch of Appalachian string band music. I blurted out that Dwight needed to face up to a reality: he, Dwight, was himself now one of the Old Timers, and he, Dwight, needed to take steps to capture his part in the history of this music.

We came back to that proposal several times over the next four or five years. Dwight was immersed in an undertaking that resulted in his multi-media project about the Hammons family, *Across the YewPines*.[3] I was committed to several of my own writing projects, and we agreed to allow the idea to drift—I presumed it would either gain some traction with Dwight at some point down the line, or simply and unceremoniously be abandoned.

During the summer of 2014, Dwight telephoned me and made clear his interest in getting back to business on a biographic project. He was about to turn 68 years of age; I thought this birthdate might have been a significant motivating factor for him. We worked to regenerate the discussions that he and I had first conducted, to capture basic chronology of his biography, and I developed a sense of what the writing effort should accomplish.

I made the case that Dwight had many dimensions, and that we should focus on these elements of his identity: the Musician, the Teacher, the Minister. This was my way of making the subject of Dwight manageable. It was probably as difficult for Dwight to think of himself as being composed of these various parts as it was for me to devise a way of thinking about Dwight, the Whole Dwight, as the subject for a book without dissecting the subject.

Dwight was a consummate musician. He preferred small concert halls and house concerts so he could converse with audience and guide them toward a better appreciation of the old tunes and the old tune makers; he called it "sharing" the music, not merely performing the tunes. He knew many of the old fiddlers in his area, worshipfully played the music he learned from them, and looked for ways of telegraphing his respect for the lives of the people who taught him about the music. He played steadily, strongly, and with humility. He told stories about his 40-year struggle to learn to play the fiddle; for a master banjo player this was a posture that he assumed with no concern for being thrust back to status as a rank amateur.

Dwight was also the eternal teacher. He was continuously interested in talking about what it took to learn this music, what it took to play this music, and what it took to teach this music. He closely scrutinized the way his own playing evolved over time, and fixed his attention on ways to make his teaching better. Dwight taught more than the physical motions, the left and right hand coordination, necessary to replicate this percussive style of banjo playing. He talked about how the rhythm of life was reflected in the pulse of the music, how the character of the local banjo players impacted on the tradition of tunes played locally. He sought to breathe life into the music so that his students had a sense of who played the tunes, the lives they led, the things they believed in, how music fit into those systems, and how those systems of belief fit into the music. To Dwight, learning these old, close-to-the-earth tunes meant finding a way to think about aspects of life. Being a teacher made it easier to talk about these enduring questions, and to find connections to larger matters of the heart and the mind.

Dwight was also a constant, consistent and convinced Minister. He was avidly, passionately, devotedly intent on talking about belief, faith, religion and what it meant to his life. Dwight was an ordained Mennonite minister for some years, though by the time I met him his troubled life had caught up with him and he was no longer able to manage a ministry. The church recognized his passion, acknowledged the difficulties he confronted, and relieved him of the obligation to head a parish church. Music became his ministry, and music has been the language he used to teach people about what God meant to him, what religion meant to his life, what Jesus Christ did for him, and why that prompted him to try his best to do good in the name of Christ, in his own words. Dwight told me that "music playing ... means nothing unless I am playing in front of someone" and that music "is a way to teach Jesus Christ's discipline without abusing people by beating them black and blue with a Bible." To some, this suggested that Dwight had made a strategic decision to use music as his stalking horse, as his means of climbing into other lives and spreading the word—his word, the church's word, or Jesus' word. However, it was not like that. Music was not the excuse for discussing matters of belief. Banjo playing was not the excuse for sidling up to unsuspecting people and preaching. Instead, music was the way to become familiar with the rhythm of life, the force or the pulse pushing things forward in dramatic, beautiful, personal ways that invited reflection and enabled hope.

I saw Dwight as a musician. And I saw him as a teacher. I saw Dwight as a devout soul, a committed minister. And I saw Dwight as a good native son of West Virginia, fixated on the history of his state, the hardscrabble life matching the rough terrain that combined to yield tough citizens who often lived hard lives.

This is my attempt to capture Dwight in these various facets, and to describe the integrating forces that brought this package together.

Documenting Dwight

In assembling this work, I have relied on years of correspondence with Dwight, long telephone conversations, and personal meetings—"visitations" either to my home in northern Virginia or to Dwight's abode in Pocahontas County, West Virginia. I have looked at family and personal documentation, tracked down the paper trail that resulted from his years in college, his employment history, his time in the United States Navy, and I have viewed some of Dwight's personal correspondence and the notes he kept on his own ancestry and the story of his family elders.

I also relied on Dwight's life narratives. Dwight organized his thinking about his own life into narratives that he carefully nurtured, rehearsed and developed as explanations of self throughout his life. There was a good deal of consistency in his telling his own story from the earliest points in time when Dwight was called upon by audiences, by journalists, or by fellow musicians, to explain himself. As a "public figure"–that is, as a performer and a "conveyor" of the archaic tunes, and a point of contact with the old people who played those tunes–Dwight was interviewed, sought out as a teacher, and questioned by students.[4] Dwight singled out the most powerful cultural and political ideas regarding his life, his corner of West Virginia, the music and the old people who played that music, and he configured a set of reliable ways of synthesizing his core thoughts on these subjects. He organized, in his mind, the key historical events that shaped his perceptions and he relied on the narratives that he erected around those events to the point that they formed the infrastructure of his biographic memory. Over time, Dwight's narratives about himself, and about the music and stories that were the center of his creative universe, were shaped by his own changing perceptions of things. Across time, as these perceptions evolved, Dwight was able to change his mind about some elements of his life, and adjust the narratives about the objects of his passion: the music, the stories, the "Old People," and West Virginia itself.

These narratives formed an intellectual infrastructure for Dwight's thinking about his life, his history, his family, and his accomplishments. I have attempted to use these narratives to discern the shape of Dwight's own understanding of what his life meant for him—and I have attempted to probe beyond them, to nudge Dwight away from the comfort these afforded him, and to get him to think beyond the formulas and established explanations of his life.

Editing Dwight

Dwight chose his words carefully, formulated his thoughts in a direct, straightforward way, organized his arguments coherently, and stated his mind clearly in a manner that made his message unmistakably accessible. He spoke slowly, deliberately, in a measured manner, and when he needed to punch home a thought, he would frequently alert his listener to "pay close attention," to "follow" what he was saying, in order that there be no mistaking his meaning and intention. What he said, and how he said it, could sometimes appear grave, and sometimes sound sermon-like—not preachy, but cast in well-rounded thoughts phrased to be memorable, laden with words selected for their maximum impact. He could also be very playful with his words and relaxed in his communication. Dwight could turn a phrase with a devilish side to it, and he could carry a joke in words that twinkled. He could also shift quickly to a dark way of saying things. All this was amply clear in our many years of face-to-face dialogue, and in many phone conversations focused on the stuff of this project. Dwight wrote the way he spoke, and his notes in our long email correspondence reflected both his serious thoughtfulness and his frolicsome side.[5]

As was the case with many of us who came to computer use late in life and perhaps reluctantly, Dwight adapted to word processing without evolving to the point of efficiency. His keyboard skills displayed lingering artifacts of manual typewriter use. He never really embraced wrap-around sentence formatting where the word processing program did the work. He persisted in hitting the "return" button to mark the end of a sentence, breaking his lines where he wanted, meaning that his paragraphs looked as though they were written by e. e. cummings to the point that they sometimes resembled blocks of sentences stacked eccentrically that did not really lend themselves to editing in a Microsoft Office-run world. He generally did not bother to engage spell check mechanisms so that his writings were littered with typing errors that did not reflect the care with which he selected his words—but did reflect his frustration with having to rely so extensively on a computer for basic contact with the rest of the world.

Dwight delighted in reshaping words and sounds, preferring to type "Minny Night" for "Mennonite" or "In Terry Gator" for "interrogator," "mir ak culs" for "miracles," "thot" for "thought," all of this being just another way in which he seized on a chance to play with language, to enjoy its elasticity or marvel at its limits and brittleness. He also seasoned his writing with the occasional West Virginian turn of a phrase, using them to punch home a meaning, or to transport the subject back to a broader reality suggesting that this was not just Dwight Diller speaking, that many West Virginians shared the particular sentiment he might be discussing at the moment and even had their own way of capturing the idea.

One of the "terms of art" that Dwight preferred was "the Old People" as a reference to elders who carried the local traditions, who embodied old social and cultural ways. It was a term that Dwight used for a long time; I have always thought it had a lot more of an affectionate ring to it than "old musicians" or "old masters," or "Appalachian masters," a term once used by the annual Appalachian String Band Festival organizers. It had the added advantage of not pigeonholing the oldsters as musicians when they were, as Dwight argued, far more than just banjo or fiddle players. I used the term "Old People" in this book, in quotations, when the remarks are attributed to Dwight.

I have relied on some editorial conventions intended to render his words accessible, and type-set-able. I have "adjusted" spelling when it was clear that quick typing left a word rendered incorrectly, but I have left his "unique" spelling intact when appeared that he decided to toy with conventions, such as when he types "dire reckshun" instead of "direction." I have captured some of his inventive spelling in quotation marks, or marked them with the Latin adverb "sic" as in "sic erat scriptum,"–"thus it was written"– when the previous word or phrase just before this editing convention appeared this way in the original. Where he digressed from a point and diverged from the trajectory of a discussion in pursuit of a tangent that I did not want to capture in a quotation, I have indicated a surgical excision using [...] in the middle and at the end of a sentence. I have also relied on this method to indicate an excised portion of the original text that mentioned a name or place irrelevant to the thought at hand, or unnecessarily distracting from Dwight's key point and intended meaning. Additionally, I have resorted to editing in this way when a thought of Dwight's took a direction that, in my view, required the exclusion of his words to "protect the innocent." I have compensated for his reliance on the return button by allowing modern word processing wrap-around technology to prevail, preserving the unique stacking of short sentences or artfully broken up lines only when it seemed to me that he intended this to reflect the cadence of his words, or when it struck me that he resorted to a layered structuring of paragraphs in order to capture some of the drama and poetry of what he was trying to say.

DWIGHT TYPED ALMOST EVERYTHING HE WROTE WITH THE CAPITAL LETTER LOCK ENGAGED. In some instances, this represented his "line in/line out" alternative to automated track changes or textual commentary. I have elected to rely on the broadly accepted conventions of sentence case, using both lower and upper case together, in concert, in a nod to the conventions of English.

No ideas were harmed in the development of these editorial devices.

Thinking "Biographically" About Dwight

I decided to use Dwight's first name in this book, to detour around the convention of biographic works and refrain from calling the subject Diller. Dwight referred to himself from time to time using his own last name, usually to enshrine a concept or an idea in an unmistakable and easily remembered fashion, as in "Diller says don't forget to bend that right hand thumb," or "Diller says listen, listen, listen to the Old People playing this music." In writing, he frequently called himself "dllr," in what was in fact a device he deployed to separate this failed, frail human self ("Diller") from the being he might become with guidance, divine intervention, and reflection ("dllr"). I elected to use "Dwight" because I thought that would make it far easier to understand the dramatic use of the "Diller says" formulation that Dwight called upon to emphasize his messages. Additionally, I did not want to run the risk of creating a proofreader's nightmare by toggling back and forth between "Dwight," "Diller," and "dllr." Moreover, I thought the use of the last name sounded too ponderous, official, and analytical. I suppose I wanted a gesture in the direction of the informality and openness that characterized much of the goings-on in the old time music community among musicians, between musicians and audiences, and within classes, between teachers and students. "Dwight" sounded right.

Though I call this a biography, and envisioned the project as that from the outset, I believe I very consciously took some liberties with the biographic art form. I have made no attempt to refrain from being passionate about the subject of old time music, and I have made no claims to having achieved journalistic, analytic or scholarly distance and perspective on the subject. I devised ways of managing sensitive, personal issues in Dwight's life that fit with my sense of propriety. For example, I made the choice to refrain from doing anything more than acknowledging Dwight's two marriages. I went so far as to mention the marriages, and to record their dissolution, and to acknowledge the birth of two children without delving into any of the details because I judged those details to be sufficiently personal and not germane to the part of Dwight's biography that I hoped to capture. I have written about the people Dwight has influenced, musicians who have influenced Dwight, and relationships that have been central to his ability to play specific roles in the old time music world, in the process of collecting and preserving "cultural artifacts" regarding West Virginia's history, and in the universe of teaching old time banjo playing. However, I have not delved into any of the rough patches with individuals or groups that have engaged with Dwight, except when it was immediately and unarguably relevant to the story I was attempting to tell about Dwight, old time music, West Virginia history and culture, and the teaching and preservation of central West Virginian old time music. To a certain extent, I have exerted editorial privilege—or taken tyrannical steps to influence the way an episode or story might play out in these pages—when it came to "third parties." Dwight was strongly opinionated about many things, and had his share of quirky ways of managing human relationships. I wrote about these issues as clearly as I could without characterizing people or describing relationships in a way that might be viewed as decidedly unfriendly or harsh or simply embarrassing for any of the principals in the story, or for me as the author.

I have directly addressed the issue of Dwight's abiding religious faith, his seminary education, and his pastoring but I have not gotten into the weeds on his religious philosophy, his beliefs, and the profundity of his Christian faith. I have sought to make connections between this religious dimension of his life and Dwight's view of his teaching obligations, and to explore Dwight's sense of the parallel between the creative life of the mind and the life of a believer who, armed with musical tools and cultural resources, looks closely at the ultimate source of man's creativity. As I ceaselessly reminded Dwight, I did not need to believe in this. I merely needed to be able to represent the connections articulately, reflect the nature of Dwight's belief, and connect that to the subject of music and the importance of family and other key life commitments that described Dwight's path.

I have confronted the tough, uncomfortable elements of Dwight's life story when they were relevant and basically widely known, when their absence from a text on Dwight's life would have demonstrated something less than due diligence—especially in the face of widely circulated conventional wisdoms, rumors, innuendos, community "folk lore" and speculation about these matters. I benefited from Dwight's open and aboveboard personality, his willingness to disclose details and discuss hard issues. We talked at length about what Dwight calls his "mental health," and I decided to engage on the issue in this story to demonstrate how this element of his circumstances impacted his life in the musical lane, his teaching, his ministry and his West Virginian citizenship.

Pursuing Dwight

Dwight ushered me gently, yet firmly, and with unwavering patience through elements of his life, talking to me about things that I insisted on knowing when to him those matters would not guide me toward grasping what his life had meant to him.

He nudged me through parts of his life that were hard to understand, escorted me toward things that were important to him, and allowed me to detour down "rabbit holes" that would snake around the edges of what his life meant to him without getting me closer to its core—until I re-emerged and re-oriented myself for another try at getting through the tangle of warrens and maze-like paths that crisscrossed his life without necessarily defining his trajectory. He guided me quietly, and from time to time issued forceful edicts aimed at shaping my thinking about his life, but when I'd fail to take those clues in hand and run with them, he calmly regrouped, remained understanding and helpful, and allowed me to run down the alleyways I decided to traipse through knowing I'd emerge at a dead end somewhere and look around for another set of clues. Dwight was pretty clear about how he looked at his life, though occasionally untangling some of the cues involved extravagant investments of time and energy, and sometimes, in respect to both benchmark moments in his life as well as more prosaic events, the gap between what was and what seemed to be took me on excursions that put me off course and did not necessarily get me closer to my quarry.

I pursued the "Minister" part of his identity by trying to immerse myself in Mennonite writ only to have Dwight say, calmly and repeatedly, that it was not about the religion and he was not about the teachings of one brand of thinking. I pursued the "Musician" part of the equation with equal vigor, tracking down field recordings, long missing private tapes and other archeological evidence of his early playing, only to hear Dwight suggest that there were reasons he sought to avoid allowing himself to be photographed banjo in hand, and there were perfectly good explanations of why he never reached for a banjo in the privacy of his home to either "practice" or find solace in the old tunes. The banjo was just a tool, he'd say, and if he could accomplish his goals with another tool he'd gladly throw over the banjo. I went after the "Teacher" dimension of Dwight's story with the same intensity of focus I attempted to bring to bear on the other components of this biography, looking for metrics on the number of students and the number of classes taught that would demonstrate the impact of his teaching. Dwight reminded me that he never really kept records of the sort that would enable this kind of quantification of his teaching impact, and if he had kept such files then he'd probably not recall where he put them—such was the artistic chaos that provided the underlying order for his life.

My goal throughout was to explicate Dwight's thinking about the music and the old practitioners, to explain his approach to teaching the old music, and to describe benchmark moments in his life in a manner that represented Dwight's reasoning and captured his way of thinking about these things. There were matters, issues and episodes that I interpreted through my own prism, using my own life references and lessons, bringing to bear ways I thought about things. Sometimes those diverged from Dwight's way of getting at such subjects. I alone remain responsible for the views expressed in this book.

* * *

That having been said, Dwight Hamilton Diller, a musician from West Virginia, was devoted to traditional fiddle and banjo music of his small slice of Appalachia. He was a seminary-trained minister steeped in local Christian traditions and devoted to finding his own faith. For the past 40 years Dwight navigated between several related interests: preserving the history and provenance of old banjo and fiddle tunes and local stories, learning the music from elders who were playing music in the 1920s and 1930s, playing music in old time bands, and teaching banjo and fiddle.

This book is an attempt to tell the story of how Dwight, who has wrestled long and hard with depression and other challenges, integrated these several paths, and how decades of teaching music became the way he sought to impart a sense of how music might guide us to what we should be. This became the a key notion informing Dwight's teaching work, especially during the late 1990s and early 2000s when he began thinking more systematically about what "teaching banjo" meant to him, and how it could have a positive impact on the lives of people who enrolled in his classes, because, as Dwight saw it, although he produced numerous commercial CDs, instructional videos, a popular tablature book, and a feature length film, the key "product" he "marketed" in his banjo and fiddle workshops was hope.

ONE

Early Life

Family Tree

Dwight Hamilton Diller, the first child of Faith Agnes Sue Woodell and Vernon Charles Diller, was born on 17 August 1946 in Charleston, West Virginia. Dwight's father, Vernon Diller, (1914–1993), traced his family's origins to Hess, Germany.[1] Dwight's mother Faith (1917–1974) was the seventh of ten children born to Geneva Sharp and Edgar Bowd Woodell.

Edgar Bowd Woodell (1881–1953) was a timber cutter, a woodhick, on Redlick Mountain, near Marlinton, West Virginia, from roughly 1900 to 1930.[2] He worked for Campbell Lumber Company that had established its base of operations on the Williams River in Pocahontas County in the early 1900s.[3] Dwight remembered stories about the tough, rough life of the woodhicks:

> In the early years of the timber boom, by maybe the late 1890s while still a teenager, he went to the log camp. Already hardened, the extremely hard work was easy to grab ahold of and keep going. But after six days of work for 10 to 12 hour days, he and the other hicks would get out and fist fight all day on Sunday. Many of the hicks would stay in the log camp for a few or several months at a time. But when they came to town, it was "Katy bar the door." In the larger boom towns, generally a hick would draw his pay for whatever months it was, purchase a new change of work clothes and often a pair of "AA Cutter" high tops. The soles were thick with some layers of sole leather. The bottoms of the soles could then have calks which are pointed and screwed into them that would give the needed traction when working on slick places. They could get a grip on the logs which had the bark removed. Or slick places in the woods.[4]

Edgar married Geneva Sharp in 1903. Dwight's mother Faith recalled a strict family. She told Dwight that her Dad "wouldn't even let us say the word 'durn' and he would make us sit down in the front room and read out of the Bible to us every night." Dwight remembered that people described his Grandmother Geneva Woodell as deeply devout woman, a kind, reassuring presence—the only one for whom he would stop crying as a baby.[5] Daughter Betty told Dwight that Geneva would talk to anyone, anywhere, about Jesus. The Belle Alkali Chemical Plant in Pocahontas County was owned and operated by D. W. Stubblefield. Dwight remembered:

> At that time, Stub was somewhere around a "millionaire" but he would visit my Grandmother and Grandfather Woodell's home on Jericho Road, Route 1, Box 163, Marlinton. Stub really liked my Grandmother Sharp's Woodell family from Frost and would often visit her brother, Melvin Sharp. Aunt Betty told me, "Mom would talk to anyone who came along about the Lord. It didn't make any difference who it was. Yes, when Stub would come up to the house, he seemed to always be wearing some worn out trousers. She would make him change into some old trousers and then patch whatever he was wearing. All the while she was working on his britches, she would be talking to him about the Lord. Oh, it didn't

matter who it was, she would be talking to them about the Lord. She'd even talk to Ed Mclaughlin about the Lord." Ed was the closest neighbor. He had a hilly but productive farm at the base of Giles Mountain. Ed, being relatively well off, was seen as more or less unapproachable. Except for Ed McLaughlin, everyone else on Jericho Road from Marlinton who went to "The Old Log Church"—Hamlin Chapel—were in hardscrabble living conditions. Poor, but not totally destitute poverty.[6]

When the Sunday service was over, Dwight recalled, Geneva always invited the preacher to Sunday dinner. "She prayed all their lives for members of her own family and saw them fall and die away from their home and the people that they knew during war." Dwight remembered the log house church in Edray, an unincorporated community in Pocahontas County, near U.S. Route 219 and West Virginia Route 55, about 3.5 miles north of Marlinton. Hamlin Chapel was built in 1839; the wooden plaque above the front door of Hamlin Chapel stated that the church was founded in 1835. In 1973 Dwight married his first wife, Molly Trimble, in the Hamlin Church. The Hamlin Chapel was Methodist in his grandparents' lifetime; many of the outlying churches in the rural areas of the central Appalachians were Methodist.[7]

The Stony Creek Church was built in 1929 by Dwight's grandparents and the other members of the community who at that point no longer felt welcome at the Hamlin Church. According to Dwight, Ed McLaughlin donated land for the church. They were allowed to use the land as long as they used Presbyterian literature in the Sunday school and kept up a connection with the Presbyterian Church. This was the year of the stock market crash. This was also the year that the timber ran out and the logging boom ended, and Edgar Woodell, with ten children to feed, lost his job. Dwight remembered that though his Grandfather was not a church going Christian, and tended to the "rough and tumble" side of life, after the logging industry bottomed out he made a significant change in his

Faith and Vernon Diller with newborn Dwight at their home in Rand, Kanawha County, West Virginia, around August 1946 (courtesy Dwight Diller).

The Woodell family in 1939 at "the home place" on Jericho Road, near Marlinton, in Pocahontas County, West Virginia. Dwight's Grandfather Edgar Woodell and his Grandmother Geneva Sharp Woodell, kneel in the foreground, and Dwight's mother, Faith, stands (dark coat) just behind Grandfather Edgar's right hand. Ten children made it to adulthood. Two daughters died in the diphtheria epidemic in 1917 (courtesy Dwight Diller).

life, hewed closer to church teachings, banned swearing in his home, and read the Bible every night to the children. Dwight's mother Faith used to complain about this. She also did not relish having the reverend for dinner each Sunday after services. Dwight recalled that his grandfather Edgar would get up early on Sunday morning and walk a mile to the church, light the fire over in the church, walk home to get the family and walk back to church with them, and then teach Sunday school. Geneva Woodell had a stroke around 1946. Sometime after the stroke she was at a revival service at the Stony Creek Church and started shouting. Dwight remembered being told that her daughter Alice, sitting beside her, tried to pull her down "because she was afraid that she would die while she was up shouting. What a glorious way to die!!"[8] She died in 1948.

In his 1901 *Historical Sketches of Pocahontas County, West Virginia,* William Thomas Price painted a picture of a rigid, conservative form of religion that dominated east central West Virginia in the late 1890s and early 1900s, noting: "the strict attention to religious concerns, the catechizing of children, the regular going to church, the reading of Bible, and keeping Sabbath from the beginning to the end of the day; the singing of hymns and sacred songs, all blended, presented a beautiful picture of enterprise; economy, and religion in laying the foundations of society."[9] Dwight's experience with religion during his growing up years reflected some of what Price saw of life in Pocahontas County. Dwight recalled the church that his grandparents built, and remembered the requirement imposed on family members to attend Sunday services. He was, at the time, staying with his Aunt Ada, Faith's sister. Ada, born in 1909, started teaching fourth grade in a public school in the area, and taught for almost fifty years. She made sure Dwight walked to the Stony Creek Church, attended the church service along with the approximately 15 other people who made up the congregation in the 1950s, and that he sat through Sunday school.[10] Dwight also remembered that neither of the two uncles he was closest to in his youth, after his father and mother divorced in 1952, were serious, committed and consistent church-goers. The West Virginian churches that Dwight knew, and especially the one he attended as a young boy, were organized around fundamental Protestant viewpoints informed by a rigorous sense of sin and punishment. God was a stern judge of unrepentant sinners in this context. Importantly, as a friend of Dwight's observed, if this approach to God did characterize the way he was brought up, then in his adult years he distanced himself from this dualistic view of God, and developed a much more complex sense of both his relationship with God and his understanding of the things he had to do to fulfill his obligations to his faith.[11]

Remembering Grandfather Woodall, Dwight said:

> Granddad Wooddell grew up in a tough situation. His father was cutting a tree on the side of a hill that is extremely steep. Lee Hammons and I stopped by Tolbert Waugh's house one day about 1970. Tolbert had a mill that ground the grain for folks like my grandparents. The state of West Virginia purchased Tolbert's mill and moved it piece by piece to Babcock State Park. [...] We had stopped by Tolbert's because he used to play the fiddle. In fact, my mother and her brothers and sisters would go to his house to square dance at night in the 1920s and 1930s. I was sitting on his porch steps and he pointed across the road and said "There's where your great granddad died. A log kicked back and landed on him and crushed him. He laid there for a long time but they couldn't get the log off him." Andrew was his name and he was killed in 1894. That was the same year my Granddad Diller's father, Henry Diller, died there in York County, Pennsylvania. There was several children left behind. Edgar, John Lester, Clark, Massy, Amos and two girls. Since there was no [social welfare] net, they had to be sent to different families in the community. Far too often, children like this were seen as servants/slaves. It was said that Granddad was mistreated where he stayed. After the timber boom was over in 1930 and he was out of work, even with a large family to feed, he still took in some children to help out.[12]

Vernon and Faith Diller

Vernon Diller's father Samuel purchased farmland on the York County side of Yellow Breeches Creek in Pennsylvania, across from Cumberland City, near the small town of Lisburn in the 1930s. The land was flat and fertile, and the Diller family was successful at farming. Samuel and his wife Edna sold their produce in Harrisburg, Pennsylvania, raised chickens and kept cattle, and made a decent living, enough to enable them to purchase pickup trucks and personal vehicles.

The family was able to send Vernon to Pennsylvania State University's two-year forestry school at Mount Alto during 1933 and 1934. Vernon studied hard and did well, completing the two-year degree that certified him to work as a forest ranger. He relocated to Pocahontas County, West Virginia, hoping to work in the newly established National Forest system, but with the creation of that system the educational requirements for employment in the forestry service were revised to mandate completion of a four-year course of study. In 1935, Vernon Diller took a job as a surveyor in the Civilian Conservation Corps for the newly established Monongahela National Forest, where he worked through at least 1939; some of that employment may have been shift work.[13] Faith was in her last year of high school; she graduated in 1936. In a chance encounter, Vernon was

All of Dwight's grandparents, from left: Samuel Diller and Edna Greenfield Diller of York County, Pennsylvania, and Geneva Sharp and Edgar Woodell. Edgar was born on Stoney Creek and Geneva was born and raised in Frost, West Virginia, 20 miles northeast of Marlinton. According to Dwight, this photo was probably taken in 1939 by his father, Vernon, near the Woodells' home near Marlinton, West Virginia (courtesy Dwight Diller).

driving down a road as Faith and her sister were walking to school. He stopped to offer the two young women a lift. Dwight recalled his dad as handsome, a real gentleman, and a really kind person; Faith would have found this man attractive for all those reasons. Faith and Vernon eloped to Red House, Maryland, in 1936. In 1939 or 1940, Vernon found a job as a safety inspector with the Dupont Chemical plant in Belle, West Virginia, near Charleston. Dwight remembered that his parents lived in a small trailer for some time before they could find a house to live in, and that Faith was able to get a job as a clerk typist at the Belle Alkali Chemical Plant.[14]

In 1943, Vernon enlisted in the U.S. Army. Dwight recollected that following basic training, Vernon was sent to Louisiana for special training and was deployed to England after D–Day where he was attached to a unit responsible for keeping the gas flowing and the pipelines operational in the European theatre; at the time, a number of different U.S. Army engineer units were involved in the distribution of petroleum oil and its byproducts in support of military operations in the field, including Engineer Maintenance Companies and Engineer Petroleum Distribution Companies. In Dwight's recollection, his father traveled across France, Belgium and Germany, and at some point was assigned security duties at a Prisoner of War camp in Germany. At the end of the war, Vernon returned to Charleston and took a position with the Dupont Company, once again in a job in which he was responsible for plant safety.

Dwight's recollection was that following basic training, Vernon Diller received specialized training in Louisiana in 1944 and was attached to a unit responsible for keeping the gas flowing and the pipelines operational in the European theatre. In this photo, which according to Dwight was taken during training, Vernon is second from right, kneeling and facing the camera (courtesy Dwight Diller).

Faith joined the WAVES (Women Accepted for Volunteer Emergency Service) during World War II and worked in a paymaster's office in Washington, D.C. She drew a salary, her food and shelter were provided by the Navy, and she found herself, a country girl from a small town, with significant independence and her own discretionary income.

When the war ended, Dwight observed, so many women in his mother's position found it hard to return to the status quo ante. Faith returned to Pocahontas County and took a position as an executive secretary at the Pocahontas County Memorial Hospital, in Marlinton, earning $75 a week for a six to six and a half day workweek.[15] Though their marriage would begin to unravel in 1943, Faith and Vernon would have one more child, Dwight's sister, Nancy Faith, born in 1948.

Dwight had vivid memories of the disruption and conflict that accompanied the decline of the relationship between his mother and father. He remembered arguments, screaming, and confrontation, and the escalation of conflict between Faith and Vernon to the point that each of them, in very different ways, attempted to take their own lives. He recalled his mother pledging her sisters to look after Dwight and keep him from his father.[16] Vernon and Faith parted in January 1952, following his father's hospitalization after he attempted to harm himself with a kitchen blade. In that episode, young Dwight ended up standing between his father and mother, and while she was hollering and trying to take the blade away from her husband, Dwight got blood from his father's self-inflicted wound on his clothing. Dwight was five years old at that point, but that incident would remain with him as a vivid memory throughout his life. Years later he would say that it seemed

Faith and Vernon: Dwight's father, Vernon, signed up for the U.S. Army in 1943. Dwight's mother, Faith, joined the U.S. Navy through the newly established Women Accepted for Volunteer Emergency Service program. According to Dwight, this photograph was taken in early winter 1944 before his father pulled out for England and his mother went to Washington (courtesy Dwight Diller).

to him he was "baptized in his Father's blood."[17] Dwight missed his father greatly, and suffered from what he remembered as his mother's efforts to get him to despise his father.[18] In his words:

> After about a year and a half from the time we moved and I was staying with my Ada. She had left me behind drawing on my black board while she had "gone down on the hill" [to] another piece of property which belonged to the Home Place and was located maybe an eighth of a mile down a wagon road and through the woods. She would not be long and I was too young and small to keep up with her pace. While on the black board, I saw someone walk up around by the window in the rock path between the "wash house" and the house. That person knocked at the door. When I opened it, there was a man there that seemed familar but I didn't really recognize. It was Dad. Trying to think back, I wasn't sure how to deal with it. He had been washed out of my life. My Daddy was long gone. This man, Vernon Diller, was not my Daddy. He was kind of like him, but then again, he was not the father that had read to me almost daily for those early five years.[19]

Dwight in Pocahontas County

Following the divorce, Faith took Dwight and his sister Nancy back to Pocahontas County, and Vernon moved to York County, Pennsylvania, where he took a variety of odd jobs for about two years before moving to Toledo, Ohio, where he went to work for Sinclair Oil as a pipeline manager. He was there for two years before taking a job on the loading docks for General Mills where he worked from about 1953 or 1954 until he retired in 1984. In 1991, Dwight brought his father back to Pocahontas County. Vernon died on 23 December 1993. Faith passed away in 1974, two years after she had become a committed Christian.[20]

In Pocahontas County, Dwight spent a lot of time living with Faith's sisters on a piece of family property, an isolated mountain homestead:

> The little piece of Home Place property had barn, chicken house, wood shed, grainery, cold cellar with one room on top, wash house, outhouse toilet, and small bedrooms here and there. It is still referred to as "the home place." I spent most of my early years, from January 1952 to 1957, living there with my Aunt Ada who was a fourth grade school teacher at Marlinton Grade School. It was those years until about the fifth grade that my time there at the Home Place were in total isolation. Since there was no other children nearby, I had to learn to live a life that would meet my needs. The time alone in the fields, forests, wagon road, small stream of water gave me something to build a special dream world. There were no adults who I would talk to to give me ideas of what to do.[21]

His memories of childhood suggested that his relatives preferred a tough and sharp-edged way of teaching him, though Dwight himself was very charitable in his recollections of these family members, and appeared to accept the argument that they were preparing him for what they anticipated would be a difficult, essentially solitary life.[22] Because Dwight's dad was from Pennsylvania, some relatives presumed that Dwight would always be an outsider in West Virginia. Dwight concluded that he spent much time after the divorce looking toward adults who might provide him with guidance, but without too much success:

> When my mother brought us here in January 1952 and left me with her sister Ada to take over much of my raising, Ada and [...] her sisters and their husbands realized that I would never make it in the mountains. Without malice aforethought, they began to treat me in some ways harshly. It was never to hurt; it was try to prepare me for the kind of life here which I was going to have to face. To get me acclimated. It was instinctive. My father, my world, had been stripped out of my life. I was nothing but pain inside. But there was never anything said to console me. No matter what happened, it was "You're gonna have to tough it out. You're got to tough it out." My one uncle, by marriage, would tease me until I wet

Beginning in 1955, after Faith and Vernon divorced, Dwight and his sister Nancy would spend the summers visiting Samuel and Edna Diller in Lisbon, Pennsylvania. This photo was taken during the summer of 1956 when Dwight was 10 and Nancy was 8 (courtesy Dwight Diller).

> my britches. I was desperately looking for a man who would help me along, give encouragement, but there was no one. By the time I was eight or nine, the teasing didn't have much effect any more. But my eyes and heart was always watching and searching every man that I met.[23]

Dwight's father would travel from Pennsylvania to West Virginia about four times a year to see his children, and several times took Dwight and his sister Nancy to stay with their grandparents in Lisburn, near Bowmansdale, in Cumberland County, Pennsylvania.[24] Dwight remembered Lisburn as a rural village with a population of about 75 people. He stayed at the home of his aunt, Mable Eppley, and recalled several boys born after World War II, basically his age, with who became close friends:

> Terry Lauver lived near Troutville, Virginia, and Tom Frew came from Boulder County. Chick Kline was one of the other boys. Roger Lectheller was another. We never won a baseball game. Terry lived beside old man Hartman. Glen Crone [smoked a] cigar [and was always] walking up and down the road [wearing] bib overalls. Huffman's Mill was in Yellow Britches Creek [in York County]. The firehouse was built when I was first there. Tom's younger brother [was] Ronnie [and his] older sister [was] Barb. Ray Hoffman married an Eppley girl. Junior Atticks was a distant cousin. Yoder had the store in mid-town. Terry had Venus fly traps. Terry and Tom knew me by Reb. [...] My sister stayed with Dad's brother in Mechanicsburg, Pennsylvania, ten miles away.[25]

Dwight remembered many of the "tests" he endured as a younger boy, the challenge of running with the "big dogs," and the way he learned to "stand up and stand out":

One good thing about a couple months in Pennsylvania with Frew and Lauver, I was tough enough and had more attitude than they did. So I could easily hold my own and actually stay ahead. [West Virginia] is much harsher than where Dad was from. He grew up a mile away and across the Yellow Britches Creek in York County, Pennsylvania, on a farm. But they were gentle people. [...] Those boys, friends, in Lisburn were really good friends. But I had "something" about me that was far harder inside. But I never used it at all against them. [...] The teenagers who were maybe around 16 or 17 years old—we were maybe 12 years old at the time—couldn't believe that I knew so much about sex. And they thought they "knew it all." It was an amazing thing that I would top anything they had. [...] I was on the low end of being tough because I was not strong at all here in Pocahontas County. Sure enough, in Pennsylvania, I was equal or ahead.[26]

Schooling

Dwight recalled his elementary school years Pocahontas County, West Virginia, especially the strict teachers and the inflexible rules:

When I began grade school, Eleanor McLaughlin was my first grade teacher. My aunt Ada taught fourth grade for 35 or 40 years in Marlinton Graded School. By the time she retired, she had taught 47 years. Eleanor probably taught 55 or more years. She was a rough and tumble mountain woman. Neither she nor my Aunt were married. When they began teaching in the 1920s and somewhat later, it was against the law for women teachers to get married.[27] There were other teachers who were not married when I began schooling there. That gave the classes a different slant somehow. The teachers never missed school days because there was no substitute for coverage, unless the teacher was to be out for a longer period. This also gave the classes a certain continuity which has long passed.[28]

Dwight was slight in stature and did not have much in the way of sports prowess. He remembered being on the receiving end of bullying because of his size, but he also remembered an alliance with a friend, a much bigger boy, who fended off kids looking to start trouble. He recalled the schooling in Marlinton as being focused on offering "smart girls" a way of learning; the boys confined themselves to decidedly non-academic adventures.[29] Dwight remembered in a very detailed way some school yard games, particularly marbles, and showed a level of fascination with the rules and a sense of the contours of the playing field:

There was a lot of marble shooting with large and small rings in the coarse dirt. And the sound of "anys, dubs and trips" was being heard with regular voices or shouts to see who [could] get it said quickest. And one of the main rolls was "no hunchin." That was the shooter could not let his clenched hand to go past the ring and into the inside. This technique would put the shooter closer to the marbles to knock out and would put more speed on the "shooter" when it hit one of the marbles inside the ring. And another object was to have developed the technique of putting a spin on your "shooter" so that when it hit the marble you were shooting at, your shooter would stop right at that spot after it hit the marble you were aiming at. Then if you called quick enough, you could call "tater humps" which would mean you could mound up a small mound [of soil] and put the next marble on top of it which meant when you hit the marble up on tater hump, there would be far less resistance when the "shooter" hit. And also keep the "shooter" from rolling out of the ring and not being able to keep on playing as long as you kept on knocking the marbles out of the ring. [...] If you happened to knock two marbles out at one shot, you had to holler "dubs" [doubles] instantly in order to keep both [of the marbles] you have knocked out. If someone hollered "no dubs" you had to put one back in the ring. I don't remember what happened when "trips" versus "no trips" would show up. I was never good at marbles. Nor was I any good at sports. When they would pick off teams, I would be either last or near the last [...] through junior high and high school.[30]

Though he said, repeatedly, that he was not good at games and sports and physical challenges, Dwight looked back on things like the schoolyard games of marbles, and on his ability to learn to split shift and double clutch on big trucks when he was just eleven years old, as signal achievements. Automobiles, engines, trucks—all that represented mobility and independence for him. Dwight began driving on the roads when he was about ten years old during visits from his father, who would seat him behind the wheel of his car. Not much later, his mother Faith's second husband, Eugene Dilley, who she married in 1963, began letting him drive his pickup truck. Dwight told a "coming of age" story about learning to drive two ton trucks on rough, mountainous country roads. He remembered being 11 years old when he got behind the wheel of a serious truck with a 292 cubic inch V-8 motor and a two speed rear axle that used electric power to shift. He mastered what he recalled as the "rhythmic precision" required to get double clutching and split shifting right, and by the time he was 12 or 13, he was hauling cattle "up, down and around really steep crooked roads from up Stompin Crick to the stockyards on Greenbrier Hill in Marlinton."[31] Dwight remembered these moments because they set him apart and marked his capacity to learn and to achieve.[32]

Dwight got his first car, a 1921 Chevrolet roadster, when he was 13 years old. He spent $15 for that car, but could not put together enough money to fix it up, so he purchased a 1936 Chevy coupe for $65 that needed body work. Dwight traded the Roadster to get the coupe painted what he called "Cadillac Lilac." In his words:

It was a really tough car to drive. No heater and the winters would get down to as far as twenty degrees below zero and the temperatures were such that the river would freeze ice two feet thick. That was a big deal to see the spring break up and watch the big blocks of ice slam into the bridge. The car's wheels were 5.25/5.50 × 17" tires. Impossible to find. Problem with pulling the floor board out for heat was that I ran it with a short exhaust pipe and no muffler. So the exhaust fumes would come up into the interior so I would have to run with the window down much of the time. At that time, they still used wood in the body that then would rot away after many years. The list went one and on. So I did all my own mechanic work. Tearing down the engine and putting it back together. The mess of a new clutch and pressure plate was really tough the way the car was built. And in order to keep it on the road when I was a junior and senior in high school the only job I could find was to work as a night clerk, on duty from 11:00 p.m. until 6:00 a.m. It was $1.00 a night seven days week. Wasn't much but since I had learned

Dwight's second car, a lilac 1936 Chevrolet Standard coupe, was purchased for $65 when he was about 14. He drove that vehicle through at least 1965 and recalled that there were none others like it on the road (courtesy Dwight Diller).

to be really close with money, I could keep it going even with buying parts, gasoline, and whatever else. [...] I would take my cars into this Ford garage and do all my own work. They would tell me what to do once then I would be able to keep on doing it.[33]

Firearms and hunting were, for Dwight, the basis for his sustained relationships with adults who meant something to him. He got a .22 single shot bolt action J.C. Higgins when he was six years old. He remembered getting his first serious weapons, an over and under .410 shotgun and a .22 rifle model 24 Savage gun, when he was about eight. His Uncle Bill took him out squirrel hunting, and though hunting trips were to figure prominently in his association with local elders and adult men in his family, there was a level of the hunting activity that eluded him, and reminded him of his shortcomings. Dwight was in third grade when his Uncle Bill took him out shooting. He knocked a fox squirrel out of a tree with his little shotgun, but did not manage to dispatch the animal. His Uncle Bill finished off the squirrel with his 12 gauge double barrel shotgun. Dwight was really proud of that accomplishment. However, in Dwight's words, "I was never able to sit still easily" and so Dwight never quite mastered treating the kill from a hunt. Thinking back on this time, Dwight stated that he did not "measure up" in school, but he proved himself hunting in the mountains with the adult men: "Those men were [...] the patrons at the beer joint. They treated me with great respect."[34] What they taught him gave him confidence, and he took great pleasure in their company. Dwight hunted with his elders, learned the rules, figured out how to function as part of a hunting group, and was particularly proud that he was able to handle a Marlin model 36 lever action 30–30 caliber rifle.[35]

Dwight dwelled on the war stories that older family members and friends would tell him. Dwight's interest in firearms, and his early experience with hunting, tied into this appetite for the company of elders and his intense interest in the stories these men told. Dwight emphasized that these were not tales. These were not exaggerated, comic, or fanciful accounts, embroidered upon as the basis for entertainment. These were stories, plain and simple. In Dwight's explanation:

> Like so many of the men here in the mountains, they did not feel a need to make up stupid "tall tales" to tell children. Things like the "Jack Tales" from farther south or Paul Bunyan. Their lives were so full that the truth could be used to guide children in certain kinds of ways. [...] Those were/are not the kind of stories we would ever use when playing. There was something in there which we did not understand, but there was something solemn that would bring me up short.[36]

Dwight lapped up wartime history:

> I was just a sponge in those days; sucking up every story that came along. For whatever reason, there was "something" which had been placed inside of me which compelled me seek out and absorb everything which might have something about the past embedded inside of it.[37]

He described his first motivation to absorb and cling to these old stories that, to him, provided the soundtrack that was part of the infrastructure of his life:

> Because my father had had to reluctantly leave when I was five, I have spent my life searching to fill this gap, [looking] for that *person imprinted on my soul and spirit*. Looking back now at the age of 67 years, the extremely desperate search for that *person* turned out to be [a] great blessing because it drove me already at age five to endlessly watch and listen. Without realizing, I began to absorb the stories that I was hearing around me. Those stories have given great meaning to me as well as to the lives of other people. This search has continued throughout my life up to this minute. Though we later spent time together and I loved him dearly, the *person imprinted in my being* was gone forever.[38]

Dwight "hungered" for the embrace of family, for the guiding hand of firm, loving adults:

> There were many blessings in my life during those years from those men who accepted me. My uncle [by marriage] was the first to take me into the mountains hunting with him. I was eight years old and had owned guns since I was six years of age. By the time I was twelve, he was taking me on the hunt in the high mountains with a group of a dozen or more men. Or sometimes it was just he and I who were fishing and hunting in the high mountains, deep valleys, and out in the briar patches with the dog. I was often hunting alone out in the hill country. All this was shortly after I was twelve years old. He and my aunt were without children, so he poured what he had into me. But there was strict unspoken discipline. And I tried desperately to never let him down.[39]

Dwight has said that he "can't remember when I wasn't interested in stories." The role as a "cultural receptor" seemed to Dwight to be intrinsic to the West Virginia character, very "native" and natural. Something in the "character" of the West Virginian provided a predisposition to soak up these stories and these tunes.

Dwight's Stories: A Sample

Dwight's recollections of his young days came to the surface with some urging, and then sprawled back and forth across decades, reeling from the 1940s to the 1950s, back to the 1920s, then returning to touch his young life—often focusing on his time living with his Uncle Bill, and frequently revolving around time spent in the beer joint. He remembered the bar as being exceptional: "It was a beer joint which was different from the norm. The room was clean, everything in it was clean, the language was clean, no one was allowed to get hog drunk, the toilets were clean." He remembered the rhythm, the music, the jukebox that was always cranked up with Johnny Cash or Little Richard. And he remembered great meandering stories that often culminated in the sudden recollection of a detail, a brief recall of an odd mountain fact that tied the story up neatly. For example:

> Uncle Bill, as a teenager, had a gang of boys on outskirts of boomtown of Cass. The name was "The Slabtown Training Camp." […] they would smoke and play match poker up on top of high hill. And they had some rifles and always kept a lookout for the "town boys" from next door in Cass. The boys from Cass only had bb guns. But finally Uncle Bill's father, who ran a store in Slab Town, got tired of all that was going on up at the fort. He had town cop Lincoln Cochran put up to stopping the whole thing. Linc Cochran was the one who cleaned up the moonshiners in the Smokehole Mountains. Those moonshiners were so brazen that they kept posted guards on the mountain roads and with plenty of firepower. But Linc alone went in and over a period of time was able to start shutting down the operation. Linc's son, Clyde, was the administration at the hospital where my mother worked in the office. Clyde came in to work late afternoon and would overlap with my mother before she went home around 4:30. But Clyde was my ride down to Hillsboro where the beer joint was. I would catch him late at night but the beer joint was still open till midnight.[40] Linc's son Clyde showed me the two pistols that his father had carried back in the Smokehole's. Ends of the barrels were worn down from crawling around and hiding in the mountains and there was a Huckleberry Finn boy that was part of the gang. He slept in a barrel and was tough "as a pine knot."
> One Halloween, the Slabtown Gang decided to push Linc's old car [in the late '20s] down over the 25 foot drop off in front of Linc's house and it would hit the railroad tracks at the bottom. They were all out there pushing and Linc came out. This Ken Totten was still pushing when the other boys ran. Finally he jumped over the almost straight down bank, across the tracks and jumped into the Greenbrier river. Linc had his .38 revolvers and was emptying them at Ken crossing the river and Ken was hollerin back, "Hoot, you sumbitch, Hoot." So Bill's father and Linc had it made up. Linc put his pistols on and climbed the hill. The lookout on guard duty spotted him but they all knew the jig was up. Linc had brought all his handcuffs along.

> Cass at that time was literally wild west. Before Linc came, the Smokehole bunch, and it was during prohibition, Bill said that they would come into town with cars with running board and men standing on them, holding on with one hand and holding a gun in the other hand. Bill said it was like Al Capone. Bill's brother took over the beer joint at the corner of the bridge in 1919 but the moonshine deliveries were going up "Dirty Street" where the whore houses and poker games were going. The liquor would be unloaded and the Smokeholers would get out. All within a few minutes delivery time.
>
> The woodhicks came off Cheat Mountain on a log train cars. There was a certain whistle that the engineers would blow to let the people know the woodhicks were on their way. The one side of the river is where the sawmill families lived. They knew what was coming and to prepare.
>
> The other side where the whorehouses were, they were also ready receptionists. The hicks might stay on the mountain working for 2–3 months before coming off or some might stay for six months or ever more. They would get their money, buy a new set of Richie wool clothes, pair of A.A. Cutter high top shoes (14 inches high approximately), a new hat. The old one would have notches in the brim to count the time on the mountain. Then, they would hit it across the Greenbrier River. Some to the whorehouses with the liquor and poker games. They would have a big "blowout" and by Monday, with their money all gone, they would hit it back to the mountain. But this was the reason Linc Cochran was hired. I think the special whistle may have been called North Carolina Whore's Dream?[41]

Often these stories wandered in and out of one another, overlapping, dividing into more stories, or circling back to the original narrative, like this one:

> The most populated whore house on Dirty Street was called the River View Hotel. It was run by guy named Breakiron. There was a young guy came off the mountain, picked up his wages and the put them in a satchel. I think left it where he picked up the wages. In the office of the "Company Store." He was planning on catching the local in the morning to White Sulphur.
>
> He got a room at the River View. They couldn't get him to buy liquor, get in a poker game or take up with a whore. When he went to bed that night, Breakiron had man and woman who worked for him by name of "Big Six" and "Butcher Knife Slim." They lived down [...] behind where my Uncle Bill's brother Fred's beer joint was.
>
> No one noticed that the guy was not around next day. Bill's father delivered goods with a horse and dray wagon. As he was going up along Dirty Street, there was some smoke and when it hit the old horse's nose, it went crazy. He had a time getting it quieted back down.
>
> But it was some time later that a dog came dragging an arm down on Dirty Street. Big Six and Slim had cut the man's throat and bled him like a stuck hog down into a wash tub. And were burning the sheets which caused the problem.
>
> They found his body up behind a log on the extremely steep hill behind the hotel. Breakiron [headed] for North Carolina and they couldn't get him back. But Bill's father testified at the trial for Big Six and Slim.[42]

These stories sometimes just came to a halt, like this one that Dwight unceremoniously punctuated:

> So there was Linc coming in on the Slabtown Training Camp with the tough guys. Since he had all those cuffs to put on the hicks when they began tearing the town up, he put one on each teenager who was tough of course. Bill, who was the leader of course, said "I was holdin it off good but all those others were crying behind me." Then I saw my mother, who didn't know dad had sent Linc up there, she was really crying. It was then I couldn't hold it any more. Cass had a small but solid jail at that time. My dad was sayin' when we walked by "Now, I told you! I told you boys what was gonna happen if you kept on!" and he was pointing his finger right at me when he was saying it. Linc marched us all down and put us in jail all night. Everyone was bawlin' and squallin.' You could'ah heard us all over town. Then the next morning, Linc let us out.... I can't remember anything more of what Bill told me.[43]

And often these stories just drop off right in the middle of time and space, where memory just loses the thread.

Life's Soundtrack

Music was not an important part of the first two decades of Dwight's life. In his memory, as early as the 1950s, life choices and financial hardships for some in his part of West Virginia, and for others the allure of commercially available recordings of popular music, gradually stripped the local music out of the lives of people in eastern central West Virginia.[44] The relatives he lived with from his early childhood through his late teens had grown remote from the mountain music:

> I grew up in the country—outside toilet, wood stoves to cook on—but my people never played the music. My aunt that I stayed with had been to college and had been a schoolteacher but she still lived with these modern inconveniences. But they'd gotten away from the music. Someone said my grandfather had a fiddle at one time but I didn't know anything about that.[45]

He does recall that by the late 1950s, when he was in his early teens, that the recordings of Elvis Presley, Johnny Cash, and Little Richard were the background soundtrack in the beer joint his Uncle Bill and Aunt Ada owned beginning in 1957, a local place in Pocahontas County where as a young man Dwight spent a lot of time. Through his teenage years he had little access to phonograph records of the popular commercial music to which youths in his circle were drawn, largely because they were expensive and beyond his means. He recalled that he had no consistent set of friends, no circle of schoolmates or neighbors who listened to the same music or shared recordings.[46] In hindsight, to Dwight, this was a "blessing." Left to his own devices, he gravitated to the beer joint music and this engendered an interest in this severe, tightly coiled percussive music that later, as Dwight told it, infused his banjo playing. To Dwight, that music resonated with the rhythmic core of the archaic traditional West Virginia fiddle and banjo music to which he was ultimately attracted. Dwight said of his uncle's collection of records:

> There were some records mixed in with what was known as "Country Music." These records had a different kind of rhythm to anything else that I was hearing and my spirit/heart was gobbling it up while excluding the rest. The rhythm came from the black people in the Deep South. Looking back, I have no way of knowing why internally I could not get enough of the heavy syncopation. I had no access to it anywhere in my whole life. These three men were at their peak: Johnny Cash, Little Richard, and Jerry Lee Lewis.

Dwight looked back on the music of those days and identified the "exact rhythm" that underpinned his banjo playing in the music of these three performers. He spoke of their "raging rhythm" and their strong voices.

Dwight also remembered the music his mother Faith listened to, probably from the mid- and late 1960s, including the singing of Doris Day, Patti Page, Jo Stafford, and Vera Lynn, but those tunes drove him to a melancholy spot, reminding him of his parents' difficult relationship; those tunes brought back "too much hurt from those days when confusion and rejection reigned." Dwight remembered that a song by Guy Mitchell from the 1950s, "The Roving Kind," written in collaboration with Mitch Miller and his orchestra, was "banned" on local radio. He also remembered the recorded singing of Teresa Brewer, Eileen Barton, and Phil Harris from the same time frame and recognized that after all that time, the lyrics and the music that provided the soundtrack for life in the 1950s—juke box music, radio music, records—were "burned deeply in my mind and more in my heart."[47]

Dwight was "greatly effected" by the organized sound of Glenn Miller and the big band singers who plunged right into their rhythm and brought out the core spirit of the tune.[48] He pointed to the orchestra playing "Chattanooga Choo Choo," in the 1941 movie *Sun Valley Serenade*, a tune along with several others that showed there was a lot more "in my heart and mind from high school days and on into early college days."[49] He also pointed to Ella Fitzgerald singing "Cry Me a River,"[50] and to Peggy Lee singing "Why

Don't You Do Right" (circa 1942) with the Benny Goodman Orchestra, as distinctive sound memories.[51] He paid very close attention to the singing of Peggy Lee:

> Her shoulders, her torso, move; she's dancing imperceptibly as she sings, reflecting the internal mechanism driving the song in a way that goes beyond the notes, beyond the lyrics. She is bouncing, slightly, in a way that identifies the rhythmic core that keeps the tune moving along.[52]

Dwight also underscored the importance of the tune "In the Mood" by the Glenn Miller Orchestra,[53] and listed several iconic love tunes, slow moving, even sultry in their tone—including "Sentimental Journey," sung by Doris Day with orchestration by Les Brown,[54] and Jo Stafford's 1952 recording of "You Belong to Me"[55] –as meaningful tunes to him. His reference to "I've Got a Heartful of Music," played by the Benny Goodman Quartet—Goodman, Gene Krupa, Harry James and Lionel Hampton—from the 1937 film *Hollywood Hotel*, was more clearly understandable as a piece that would have seized young Dwight and held his attention, with its percussion substructure.[56] Alongside that, Dwight singled out Glenn Miller and Tommy Dorsey's collaboration on "Boogie Woogie," a throbbing instrumental with a consistent, strongly played beat that would have insinuated itself into Dwight's musical imagination.[57]

Something about the trombone caught Dwight's attention during his high school years. Decades later he would draw a straight line from big band trombone to the banjo, and make the case that these two instruments were both played in very similar ways, and that very basic rhythmic character to the trombone made it easy for him to get the basics down to the point of being selected from among the members of the Marlinton High School Marching Band for separate duty with a ten person school dance band.[58] During his high school years, Dwight was drawn to swing music and, armed with a trombone, played musical events with some school friends. He recalled:

> During those same years that I was hearing those three men on the jukebox, we had a small "dance band" in high school. The dances we were playing for were for people who had grown up in the 1930s, 1940s, and part of 1950s. I was on trombone, which is arrogant like a banjo, and our music was "Swing Music" from that era. "TUXEDO JUNCTION"; "CRY ME A RIVER"; "SENTIMENTAL JOURNEY." I didn't have a clue, but even then my syncopation was already shining forth.[59]

By the late 1950s, Dwight was captivated by the juke box music of Richard Wayne Penniman, better known as Little Richard, whose music was far more assertive, tensely wound, and incendiary than the Big Band music that had grabbed Dwight's attention. Tunes such as "Keep a' Knockin" and "Lucille" had a vocal explosiveness for Dwight, a strong brass section, and an unrelenting role for the drum set.[60] Jerry Lee Lewis also caught his fancy, singing tunes such as "Whole Lotta Shakin' Goin' On," and "Great Balls of Fire,"[61] as did Johnny Horton, performing "Battle of New Orleans" in the late 1950s,[62] Tennessee Ernie Ford and his "Sixteen Tons,"[63] and Patsy Cline singing "Walking After Midnight."[64] Dwight remembered North Carolinian truck driver Lonnie Irving singing sang "Pinball Machine" in the early sixties; Irving died at the age of 28 from leukemia.[65] Bluegrass tunes, such as Flatt and Scruggs performing "Cabin on the Hill," were constantly on the juke box at his Uncle's place, too.[66] Around the same time Dwight was equally drawn to young Johnny Cash in his early 20s while he was performing on the Tex Ritter show, before Cash began writing and performing tunes that found their market in Nashville in the sixties and seventies.[67]

Sometime during the sixties Dwight's attention was drawn to the banjo playing of Dave "Stringbean" Akeman and Louis Marshall "Grandpa" Jones, especially the recordings that these two made during the fifties.[68] Grandpa Jones' banjo playing had an especially important impact on Dwight, and eventually would guide him toward understanding the old mountain music that was so central to his life.[69]

* * *

In his late sixties, Dwight mused that one can learn a good deal about a person by the music they select as their life's auditory furniture, as the musical backdrop for their memories. "I have a whole great big of range of music that has molded me," he said, as a prelude to the argument that people should have more than one kind of music in their lives, because having a narrow interest in music or confining oneself to a single kind of tune yields a sadder, more narrow life.[70] Dwight grounded himself in several different kinds of music. Rock and Roll. Delta blues. Hill country blues music. And bluegrass. Old bluegrass, vintage 1940s and 1950s bluegrass, inspired by Bill Monroe who, Dwight believed, latched onto the "fire and rage" of the bluesmen and the early rockabillies. Though he said, repeatedly, that bluegrass was something he just could not "catch," he was able to perform the duties of the bass player for six years with the Black Mountain Bluegrass Boys largely because of his rhythmic sense. He spoke about the old bluegrass with reverence for its roots.[71]

After his 68th birthday, Dwight confronted constraints on his mobility imposed by mounting physical ailments and other challenges, and one way he found some relief was through the musical resources the internet brought to his mountaintop door on Browns Creek. He gained some pleasure by searching online for old tunes that had meant a lot to him in his late teens and early twenties, and was glad, for example, to be able to track down some of the more esoteric songs that were important to him during his high school life, such as the truck driving songs of Lonnie Leon Irving from Stoneville, North Carolina.[72] "To me," he said, "it expands a person's world if that person has no way of traveling to many places and getting a glimpse."[73] And, as he approached his seventh decade he was guided by a knowledgeable, caring friend towards discovering the continued relevance and enduring musical strength of Beethoven.[74]

* * *

In College, in Uniform

Dwight finished high school in 1964. He attended West Virginia University from August 1964 to December 1965, registered for 18 classes, and accumulated a total of 47 semester hours and 100 grade points with a cumulative average of 1.96. In the first three semesters (including the 1965 summer session), he secured a 2.21 grade average, but the pressures he felt during the first semester of the 1965–1966 term tipped him over the edge. He earned a failing grade in Introductory Physics, a D in General Psychology, and a D in Elementary German. Across those three semesters, Dwight took three Military Science classes, pulling his first semester grade of C up to a B in the second and third classes in this arc of four that were billed as "leadership laboratories" focused on military theory, national security policy and the role of the U.S. Army, counterinsurgency basics, and weapons and small unit tactics.[75] Dwight earned C grades in introductory level algebra, geometry, trigonometry and biology classes, as well as in the second semester of Composition and Rhetoric and Growth of the American Nation to 1865, though he earned a B in the first semester of Composition and Rhetoric.

In spite of his memory of himself in youth as lacking in stamina and being generally poor at sports, Dwight earned A's in the Physical Education Department's General Program for Men, and in Fencing, a co-ed class taught during the first semester in the 1965–1966 cycle by Mary Jane Pearse, who began teaching at West Virginia University as an instructor in physical education in 1958.[76] The class engendered Dwight's interest in fencing. He recalled that the school offered an opportunity on Wednesday evenings for students to borrow a jacket, mask and foil, and start learning in one of the university's gyms. He took a liking to the sport, purchased his own equipment, and began learning the basics. While this was going on, Ms. Pearse, who was in charge of the school's fencing program, had become his friend, helping him, essentially counseling him, in what was a period of worsening depression. Sometime in 1972, in Dwight's recollection, Ms. Pearse became seriously ill and he took over her women's fencing classes for her, teaching the basics of the sport during the course of three semesters from the fall term of 1972 to the fall term of 1973.[77]

Dwight dropped out in January 1966 after three semesters (plus a summer school semester in 1965) of full time schooling, during which he existed on minimum financial support and a small income from a variety of brief employment opportunities. He felt burned out and stressed, a cycle that would repeat itself throughout his life.[78] It was clear to Dwight that he was about to be drafted, so he sought to join the Navy in February 1966 through the CACHE program, the title of an enlistment program designed to generate a "pool" (hence, "CACHE") of highly qualified personnel who agreed to enlist in the regular Navy but were allowed defer the start time of their assignment to extended active duty.[79] Dwight recalled: "Mom was in the U.S. Navy (USN) as a second class paymaster. Two uncles by marriage were in the USN. Two blood uncles were also in the USN. Vietnam was heating up. I dropped out of school in 1966."[80] Dwight was inducted in early February 1966; because of his college time, he went in as an E2 Seaman Recruit rather than Seaman Apprentice.

Dwight was sent to the Great Lakes in the spring, and completed boot camp in early July 1966. He was then dispatched to Little Creek, Virginia, for Assault Boat Training School where he received instruction on the operation of the LCVP, Landing Craft, Vehicle, Personnel—the infamous Higgins boats that were deployed in amphibious landings in World War II. Dwight remembered that though this was his first experience in a boat, he finished training with the distinction of being first in his class.[81] Following a 30-day leave he reported for duty during the first week of August 1966 aboard the APA 44 *Fremont*, an attack troop transport berthed at Norfolk, Virginia. He was assigned to the deck division and served alongside the assault boat coxswains as the ship was made ready for a Mediterranean cruise. A squadron of five ships consisting of three APAs, one LST, and one LSD were involved in the deployment. The officer in charge of the squadron was a Commodore, and Dwight's ship was itself under the command of a Commodore. In early September the squadron moved to the North Carolina coast to pick up about 3,000 Marines and load all the gear they had to take with them to the Mediterranean for seven to eight months of training before the Marines were deployed to Vietnam.

Very quickly, Dwight managed to get crosswise with his immediate superior and was assigned three months' worth of mess duty. He was on night shift for most of that duty. Dwight recalled suffering a good deal of personal harassment and enduring what he described as unwanted attention from the E5 Boatswain's mate. During first week of August 1967 he entered the U.S. Naval hospital in Philadelphia for hearing problems that resulted from not wearing ear protection while on gun mount firing duty: "My mother [...] contacted congressman Harley Staggers and he got me sent to Philly Hospital for hearing tests. When got there [I] had [...] hardly slept for couple weeks."[82]

Dwight had suffered some hearing loss as the direct result of his shipboard duties, but the Navy decided to reassign him back to the same squadron. The stress of sleep deprivation brought on by night duty and other strains prompted Dwight to request that he be allowed to see a psychiatrist. On 17 August 1967 Dwight was put into a "Legal Hold" status until his discharge from the Navy on 26 September 1967. He recalled the end result of his 1 year four months 25 days 2 hours and 10 minutes of active duty:

> [It] was/is one of the main "hinge pins" of my life. Walked through an open door and it slammed shut behind me. If you read about Jacob whose name changed to Israel by God back in book Genesis, there was the final deal when his brothers (the children of Israel) showed up down in Egypt. Joseph was sold to slavers by his brothers. His life was up and down and around. Finally, God saw to it that he was near the top rung in Pharaoh's Court. There was famine back at family home country. After he finally revealed to them that he was their "dead brother," he said "What you meant for evil, God meant for good."

Dwight came out of the navy in late December 1967.[83]

Return of the Prodigal Son

Dwight returned to Hillsboro where his Aunt Alice and her husband Woodrow "Bill" Hamrick were building a home; in July 1967 they had sold the beer joint in which, as a young man, Dwight had found sanctuary. They let Dwight work with the two carpenters who were building the new house. Dwight resumed his studies at West Virginia University in January 1968, using the $100 of his monthly GI Bill entitlement to pay for his tuition, room, board, food and necessities for his schooling, so he cast around for jobs to supplement his G.I. Bill.

He registered as a student in the Horticulture Department of the School of Agriculture. It was the smallest department in the school, he recalled. West Virginia University's enrollment had grown dramatically from the mid–1960s to the point at which Dwight decided to return to school after his stint in the navy. He knew there were fewer than twenty students in the Horticulture Department, and felt that this would guarantee

Faith and Dwight Diller, posed in front of the family home in Marlinton, West Virginia, in September 1966 during a short leave from the Navy before he embarked on a cruise as part of the crew of the USS *Freemont* (courtesy Dwight Diller).

him the quiet, the space, and the anonymity he very much wanted: "Being manic, I kept an up road going [in those days] until I got on meds." He looked for classes that did not require written term papers, and ended up enrolling in cooking, housing and design, counseling, psychology, and violin.[84] Dwight attended West Virginia University from the second semester of the 1967–1968 cycle to the second semester of the 1972–1973 cycle. He earned a bachelor of science in agriculture on 19 December 1970, and completed three semesters of graduate school level courses before leaving Morgantown. He earned a grade point average of 3.0 across seven semesters in classes offered by the College of Agriculture, Forestry and Home Economics, and a 3.56 grade point average for the three semesters of graduate level classes he completed.[85]

In March 1968 he learned that the Green Giant Company was sending staff to agricultural schools to recruit students who they would send to the Midwest to harvest crops for the company. He submitted an application, and waited. He still had not heard from that company by May, and so he submitted an application for a federally funded summer job program in the Monongahela National Forest near Marlinton. Dwight thought back on the way this issue resolved itself as yet one more example of heavenly intervention in his life. The National Forest Service and the Green Giant Company called to offer him employment on the same day. Dwight accepted the forest ranger job because the service was the first to call and because taking that job enabled him to stay in West Virginia.[86]

Two

Learning Music

Seeking out the Old People

Dwight's summer job with the forest service enabled him to stay close to home, and he took comfort in familiar places and the company of relatives and friends. Just a few days after landing that job, Dwight paid his first visit to Hamp Carpenter, a fiddler from nearby Poker Flats who, with his banjo playing musical partner Rob Scott from Droop Mountain, had for many years been playing for square dances on Friday and Saturday nights at Hoppy's beer joint, then Jack's beer joint, and earning $6 to $7 each for three or four hours of playing.[1] Dwight knew these two local people, and he knew a lot of the people they knew. Hamp Carpenter was about 60 years old when Dwight first started visiting him in 1968; Dwight was about 22 years old, roughly the same age as Hamp's two boys. Hamp's oldest son Harley would end up playing in the bluegrass band, the Black Mountain Bluegrass Boys, that enlisted Dwight as their bass player in the early 1970s.[2]

Dwight was very careful in his choice of words used to describe what he was doing, and what he was looking for, when he began visiting the Carpenter home. This was, simply put, a visitation, a neighborly act of the sort that was common and central to everyday life in Pocahontas County. His visits more often than not revolved around friendly discussion and swapping stories. These visits were, in Dwight's way of thinking, distinctly different from an attempt to learn banjoing or fiddling from an experienced elder, or to learn about the old tunes from people who had been around the old music for a long time.[3] Dwight was drawn to Hamp Carpenter's stories as much as to his music, and felt a level of familiarity with the man and the life he had led:

> Nobody had ever stopped by to talk to Hamp about the music, or what it was like when he was young. Hamp made whiskey a lot out in the mountains in the 1920s. Sold a lot of it to the woodhicks in the logging camps. My grandfather and Hamp worked in the same log camps. Hamp was not cutting timber like my grandfather. He was a Lobby Hog. The logging companies put up shanties for the woodhicks, where the woodhicks would sleep. These shanties had lobbies with a stove, and they'd sit in the lobby. Best I could tell there was no heat except for the stove, and these were temporary buildings. In those days, 20 to 25 degrees below zero [in the winter] was not uncommon. Lobby Hogs made sure there was plenty of wood to keep the fire going, they cleaned the ashes from the stove, and kept the lobby area clean.[4]

Dwight wanted to know more about those years, about the logging camp life, about whiskey making—he and Hamp Carpenter talked a good deal about building stills, fashioning barrels for mash, and the recipes used to make moonshine. Hamp Carpenter "just kept loading me up with stories," and "the stories were keeping my spirit alive." Carl Fleischhauer suggested that Carpenter's vision of the past and his own youth contrasted with

Dwight's sense of how his public school experience had neglected, even denigrated, regional culture.[5] As Dwight put it:

> After my first semester back at West Virginia University in June of 1968, I went combing the hills and mountains for any folk who still played the old music. There were only a couple of old musicians [living in] my old "stompin grounds" in all of Pocahontas County. Except for the two men, there was only silence. [...] Fifty years earlier Pocahontas County had been honeycombed with folks playing and singing the old music. [...] Sometimes local people would gather at a home in the neighborhood, move the furniture off to one corner or outside. They would then have a non-aerobic square dance. The music teachers in the public schools totally rejected all indigenous music as "ignorant." This part of the life of the old mountain culture had been silenced, basically to rise no more. This was a different angle that affected my music because now it had become personal.[6]

Dwight frequently remarked that the stories were always more important to him than the tunes. They called up memories of his young days listening to family and friends trading recollections. The tunes were also powerfully evocative. Sometimes the two mixed together in a manner that created stories out of tunes, and sometimes the tunes provided depth and meaning for the stories. Dwight remembered this moment in his relationship with Sherman Hammons:

> One night in January 1972 Sherman and I were taking a short cut through the high mountains where he had lived during his life. I was playing bass for a local band, the Black Mountain Bluegrass Boys and we were on the way over Black Mountain for me to practice. When we got near the top, my old '53 Ford suddenly broke an axle. I had recently ordered a '72 Ford pickup and it was due in on Ground Hog's Day. I always figgered [my old '53 Ford] was upset since I had had it for many years, and decided "I'll just show him." There was nothing to do but start walkin' the several miles out of there. There was no moon out that night so we just felt our way along the gravel road. Sherman started singing the old songs as only he could sing them. There was "The Little Babes," "A Rich and a Ramblin' Boy," song about a yankee soldier after the war being made unwelcome by southern soldiers, and on and on. Of course, in early times there was no reason to hurry the singing or the playing or the stories. The real art was the rhythm. So the music or story telling was an art form also in such a way to tell it so it stretches out the time while keeping it interesting [while] not [letting] boredom set in.

Hamp Carpenter, a fiddler from Poker Flats who Dwight started visiting in 1968. Carpenter was about 19 when the photo was taken in 1920 (courtesy Shanda Carpenter, with thanks to Jaynell Graham and Gibbs Kinderman).

> So as we walked, Sherman took his time singing. The slight echo as we walked down William's River plus [the river's] gurgling sometimes really added to [the] effect. When I sing the old songs, that is the time that most stands out in my mind.[7]

From 1968 until he completed his studies, Dwight was angry, confused, and frustrated, in his own description of his state of mind, and the only thing that rescued him was stumbling into the embrace of Hamp Carpenter and, later, Lee Hammons and Sherman, Burl and Maggie Hammons—two different branches of the Hammons family tree. Both lines traced their origins to Kentucky. He felt welcomed by these people at a point in his life when he was not, in his view, welcomed anywhere else and was looked down on because his state of mind prevented him from holding down a job. These old people showed him respect, as he put it, and would sit and talk with him for hours.[8]

Becoming a Banjo Player

Decades later, Dwight reminisced about how Hamp Carpenter, who in 1968 reconnected Dwight to his earlier fascination with the old West Virginian stories, encouraged Dwight's efforts to learn the old style banjo.[9] Of those days and that desire to learn, Dwight reflected: "As one old man who was working at the banjo in earlier years said "I wanted it so bad, that I'd rather pick at that banjar than eat when I was hungry." That was me.'"[10]

Hamp played an old open back Gretsch banjo. The first tune he played for Dwight was "Old Rattler," a tune that resonated with Dwight from the first time he heard Grandpa Jones sing and play a rendition of it sometime between 1967 and the summer of 1968, for a Trail Blazer Dog Food advertisement.[11] He remembered that Grandpa Jones played a robust down picking style, and described just how that little commercial had grabbed him:

> I didn't have access to any music. I had seen Grandpa Jones playing "Here, Rattler" for a dog food commercial.[12] I instantly knew that's what I wanted, even though I'd never heard any [of this banjo style] growing up. All I had heard was three-finger bluegrass style on the juke box in the beer joint. It was like my spirit, not my mind but my spirit, leapt inside of me the instant I heard Grandpa Jones. My spirit knew that that's who I was. It wouldn't have mattered what the tune was, it was the way he played it. If you listen close to my playing you'll hear that [way] that Grandpa Jones played. Grandpa Jones, his style, his approach, brought me to the point where I found life.[13]

Dwight had not asked Hamp to start off with that tune. It just happened that way, and it just happened to be a tune that earlier had such a strong impact on Dwight.

Throughout the summer of 1968 Dwight stopped by Carpenter's home on weekends. On Fridays, after class, Dwight would drive from Morgantown to Marlinton—he remembered this as a trip of about 150 miles. He would get some sleep, wake up early Saturday morning and spend as much time as he could visiting with Hamp before driving back to be in class Monday morning. Dwight believed that his system was drawn with a magnetic power to the stories of the sort he had listened to so avidly from the time he was five years old: "My system wanted the old stories. God was using the music to keep me alive, but underneath it was the stories." In his state of mind, and as the result of his untreated depression, the "music played out [...] after a while, but the stories didn't because it's always been the stories."[14]

Dwight worked through the summer of 1968, and probably accumulated five or six hundred dollars. Between that money and his monthly G.I. bill he had $1,400 available to get him through the school year. The next summer, he did another stint for the National Forest Service, and began seeking out other older banjo and fiddle players in the area. In June or July 1969 he met and started talking to members of the Hammons family; he had heard about old musicians such as Lee Hammons in the summer of 1968.

Paris Hammons was born on the Kentucky side of the border with West Virginia around 1856, one of seven children born to Jesse Hammons and Nancy Broughton Hicks. He was a child when his family moved to east central West Virginia just before the Civil War. Paris and his wife Charlotte had ten children, including Sherman, Burl and Maggie whose stories and old tunes captivated Dwight. Paris himself was a fiddler; his sons Sherman and Burl both had their first crack at the instrument as youngsters by sneaking turns on their father's fiddle. Among Paris' brothers were Edn Hammons and Pete Hammons, both celebrated fiddlers in their time, and Cornelius, the father of Currence whose banjo playing was recorded by Gerry Milnes.[15] Paris' daughter Emmy married John Roberts, the grandfather of Ralph Roberts, a fiddler and banjo player from southeastern West Virginia, a well know fixture at the Appalachian String Band Festival in Clifftop, West Virginia.[16] Lee Hammons, himself a fiddler and banjo player of note, was born in Kentucky. His date of birth is given variously as 1883 or 1886.[17] His father, like the family of Paris Hammons, migrated to West Virginia. Lee Hammons was not related to Sherman, Burl and Maggie. He knew their uncles, Edn and Pete, and he knew Edn's sons. He had worked in the logging camps in eastern central West Virginia, as had the other Hammonses.[18]

In Dwight's recollection, he first broached the subject of visiting Lee Hammons' home at a little music contest in his hometown of Marlinton around the 4th of July 1969.[19] Dwight knew about Lee Hammons from Loy Burgess.[20] During his grade school years, Dwight rode the same school bus in Marlinton as Loy who was seven years older than Dwight. Loy and Dwight both ended up working for the National Forest in later years. Sometime before July 1969, Loy, who lived near his father-in-law, Lee Hammons, told Dwight that Lee had just purchased a banjo and a fiddle.[21] Lee Hammons, who would have been about 86 years old then, stopped playing music in 1923 when the radio and record player had dislodged any inter-

Lee Hammons, circa 1970 (courtesy Dwight Diller).

est in old style local music, and people's fancies turned to store bought music. From 1923 to 1969, Lee did not own a banjo or a fiddle, but in 1969, as Dwight told the story, he just had "a notion" to buy a banjo and a fiddle, "and as an old man once said to Lee, 'Don't never spoil a good notion.'"[22]

Lee had purchased a Harmony banjo with a Bakelite rim and a hide head. The fiddle, Dwight remembered, was Japanese made. Dwight immediately struck up a relationship with Lee who knew Dwight as a local boy who had grown up not 300 yards from where Lee's son grew up. In Dwight's memory, the music instantly came back to Lee even though it was 46 years since he last played it: "He hadn't played any and he was immediately playing well."[23] A week or so later, Dwight gathered up enough money to buy a reel-to-reel Aiwa recording machine:

> I ordered a seven inch reel to reel stereo [...] with two microphones. Never done any recording in my life, never knew how to do it, never saw anyone else do it. I just jumped in trying to use my common sense and instinct. At that point I knew the music had to be recorded to keep it for the local mountain people. Sometime down the road, maybe fifteen, twenty or thirty years, I knew the music would be gone and I had to catch it before it was gone. [...] I got $140.00 and ordered that recorder but I didn't barely have any money to buy recording tapes so over the years I was recording I had to do all sorts of gyrations to capture as much as I could. I'd record on both tracks, erase one track so I'd have two different tracks going in opposite directions.[24]

Dwight experimented with the speeds to maximize space on the tapes. He recalled he had no clue what he was doing, and that it took him a while to figure out the impact on recording quality of decisions such as the placement of the microphones—leaving the mike on the floor while a banjo player was patting his foot resulted in with some undecipherable recorded sounds.

After taping Lee for a while, Dwight approached Sherman Hammons. As Dwight recounted: "Sherman was known locally by a lot of people, and there were a lot of stories about him that either weren't true, were partly true, or were true. I just one Sunday went to his house and started talking. He knew who my grandfather was."[25] Sherman worked in the woods on Redlick Mountain, the

Sherman Hammons, circa 1970 (courtesy Dwight Diller).

same mountain Dwight's grandfather had worked on as a woodhick at the turn of the century.

Sherman's sister Maggie also knew Dwight's grandfather, and that link became the basis for a friendship and the catalyst for long running visits to the homes of various Hammons family members.

By July 1969, Dwight began recording the music of the Hammonses and their stories.[26] The Hammonses were content to have Dwight around; they were not ill at ease about being recorded. They were, in Dwight's memory, an open people, honest and straightforward, and inclined to share. There was a level of simple, unencumbered trust in their relationships; everyone depended on everyone else, "and so it was for them to share and so they shared."[27] However, these were not necessarily easily managed relationships. The Hammonses were in their sixties at the point Dwight started visiting them, and had lived quietly, in an isolated way, partly from choice, partly because their residence stood a bit beyond the outskirts of the county seat of Marlinton, a town of about one thousand residents. The Hammonses were not deeply integrated into that community and, in Dwight's recollection, some in the town considered them eccentric and their lives uncommon and distinct from the norm in Marlinton. And they had a long history of living "off the grid," outside of the structures of the town, in their own orbit.[28] As Dwight suggested, there were many, many stories about them and their ways, partly because of their longevity in the area, partly because they had made life choices that separated them from the way most of the people in the area lived their lives. All of that had an impact on the way they comported themselves, the level of relationship they were capable of sustaining, and the extent to which they would invest themselves in friendships.

Lee Hammons was in his early or mid-eighties when Dwight met him, and as Dwight recalled "there really wasn't anything that he could do that would perk him up."

Maggie Hammons Parker, circa 1970 (courtesy Dwight Diller).

Two. Learning Music

During those months of fooling around with the banjo and fiddle, when I'd get there his mind would have just trailed off. It would take a little while to get him back to the moment.
[...] Old people [sometimes] just sit. That's where he was at. His mind wasn't working. We'd get to talking, he'd pull the banjo and fiddle out, and perk up. I'd be late at night talking, playing. [...] He wouldn't talk when I was recording. And he wanted to get it just right. [...] He was really conscious and didn't want anything recorded that wasn't a good reflection on him. He wanted to make sure it would put him in a good light. I never recorded him talking.[29]

Burl Hammons was 61 or 62 when Dwight first started spending time with him. Dwight remembered that Burl could hear a tune and play it immediately on the fiddle. He would "swallow it and it became his tune." Dwight felt that Burl had as much skill as anyone on the fiddle, and felt no need to copy anyone. Seven or eight years after Dwight first started "coming around" the Hammonses—again a very specific choice of terms, suggesting something more than just a visit–Burl told Dwight "Daddy said you can either work or play the fiddle but you can't do both." Dwight took this to mean that fiddle playing was an exalted skill, far preferable to banjo playing which itself was a notch or two below the ability to sing tunes the old way.

Fiddling was a calling more than anything else. Fiddlers embodied and sustained local traditions, preserving the old ways, breathing life into stories that captured local history. Fiddlers were "the keepers of what was important." However, in those days, Dwight was not enamored of fiddle music.[30] What seized him in those days was banjo. He recorded months and months of tunes and stories, but they were, as he later recalled, all jumbled up on his reels, not systematically sorted. Many of those field recordings captured fiddling, but what Dwight recalled wanting more than anything at that time was the banjo.

Burl Hammons and Dwight Diller, summer 1981 (courtesy Bosco Takaki).

Taking on the Banjo

Dwight told two stories about points at which the banjo entered his consciousness before he took up the instrument in earnest. The first story was a recollection from when he was just a child, about five years old, and was walking the streets of Charleston with his family. Dwight remembered seeing an old man sitting on the sidewalk. The man had pencils in a cup at his feet, and he was playing the banjo. Dwight was transfixed by the sound, though his parents paid no mind to the music. That first encounter with the banjo, sometime around 1951, stuck in his mind for many years.[31] The second story dated from just before Dwight went into the Navy in September 1967. He returned home to Hillsboro, and many years later recalled telling his cousin, as they were hauling water in buckets to make maple syrup, that he wanted to play the banjo:

> It was winter [...] I was helping my cousin Artie Barkley at Cass. [...] I was helping him gather sugar water, so that would have been in March when sugar waters are running. They were making maple syrup. So Artie and I were carrying buckets of sugar water and we were having to wade through snow almost up to our knees [while] carrying sugar water in those mountains near Cass. I remember saying to him that I wanted to learn the banjo.[32]

Dwight credited Hamp Carpenter with encouraging his efforts to pick up the old style of playing the five string banjo.[33] Sometime in 1968, about the time he started going to see Carpenter, Dwight borrowed an old banjo from his stepfather's sister-in-law, Mary Lou Dilley. Worthy Reed, who lived at the Dilley's home place when Dwight's stepfather, Eugene Dilley, was a boy in the late 1920's, was the original owner of the banjo. Dwight purchased his own banjo, a mail order Gretsch, for less than $150 in 1969; he recalled that this was not much of a banjo. In the summer of 1970 he found an old banjo, an "Improved George Washburn," in southern Virginia at an old time festival. He played that banjo until 1973.[34]

In the summer of 1968 Dwight put together enough money to purchase a simple Gretsch banjo, the instrument he is holding in this photograph. He played that banjo until the summer of 1970, when he purchased an "Improved George Washburn" (courtesy Dwight Diller).

Dwight looked back on his fascination with Carpenter's stories, and his growing connection to the old music, as a rebellion against rebellion. Beginning in the 1980's, he often referenced the Flower Power movement of the mid-1960s, and especially the San Francisco influence on the national fixation with a "hippie lifestyle," as his point of departure for thinking about what was important to him: "being the rebel I am, I rebelled against hippies and didn't want anything to do with all of that. So going and listening to the old time music and learning the old time ways [was what I did]."[35] In the summer of 1969, while still in Morgantown, Dwight began learning to play the instrument he borrowed from Mary Lou Dilley. In his memory, he had a terrible time of teaching himself banjo.

In 1969 Sherman Hammons had introduced Dwight to Burl Hammons, who Sherman described as an accomplished banjo player. Dwight's exposure to the Hammons family was important, but not sufficient in getting him to the point of being able to play old style down picking competently. Those first sessions with Sherman and Burl convinced Dwight to do what he could to collect their music, and their stories, and he learned a good deal from them, but he has never really felt that he learned banjo playing from the Hammonses. Dwight seemed to make the case that what the Hammons family gave him, beside the firm embrace of an enduring friendship, was a sense of the importance of the past they knew, the traditions they recalled, and the stories they told and retold. The tunes they allowed Dwight and others to tape provided a rock solid basis for thinking about the old music.[36]

Lee Hammons had the greatest impact on Dwight, especially because of the way he treated Dwight—"his way with me, toward me."[37] Dwight's affection for Lee focused in part on his welcoming way, and in part on his music, but Dwight was also captivated by his inventiveness, his native intelligence, and his capacity to solve problems cleverly and quickly[38]:

> Lee was different than Maggie and Burl and Sherman in some ways. He was always fooling with something mechanical. To me he was a mechanical wizard, a mechanical genius. He could take junk and make machinery of it that worked. I remember one time he decided he wanted a band saw. So he took pieces of plywood, cut them in circles, had four pieces, nailed two together, hooked them up, and took inner tubes off of a bicycle tires, nailed it around outside, and ran the band saw blade around the back and made himself a band saw. Another time he took a gasoline engine off of a power mower. He needed a jigsaw. He took a gasoline engine off of a power mower, he took the sparkplug out and welded a rod on top of the piston, and the rod came out of the sparkplug hole, and then he hooked an electric motor up to that then he had a frame built around and had the blade hooked to the rod so when the electric motor ran it turned the crankshaft and when it turned the crankshaft it moved the piston up and down which moved the rod up and down which was going out the sparkplug hole. He had a beautiful jigsaw. Well, all of these things were exciting to me because looking around me and seeing so much technology to do so little sometimes, and people throwing things away. Here's somebody who was doing the opposite of taking junk and making something useful.[39]

Lee quit playing music at about the time record companies were organizing efforts to record country musicians, and looking to expand rural markets for phonographs and recorded music. This, Dwight explained, essentially froze the music for Lee Hammons, and when he resumed playing his music came out with an accentuated archaic character[40]:

> Since Lee Hammons dropped out of the Music at the exact same time when there was the great invasion of commercialism by way of the radio and 78 rpm records. It was beginning of the disintegration of the traditional music because with it came the band music. The old traditional music born on the American Frontier Music, it was an individual's either playing or singing alone. So, 1923 was the beginning of the end of the mountain culture's heritage. Mr. Hammons was exactly 40 at the time. During the next 46 years, he would have heard commercial music but it would not have made any change in what was deeply embedded in his heart.[41]

Lee Hammons resumed playing the banjo and fiddle in 1969, shortly before Dwight started visiting him. Dwight and others identified the tinge of commercially popular music in some of the fiddling and banjoing choices that Burl Hammons made in playing the old tunes. However, in Dwight's view, Lee and Sherman Hammons never went down that path. Sherman, Dwight observed, was never attracted by the commercial music, and Sherman's fiddling style was even more archaic than the fiddle playing of Edn Hammons. Edn had to keep changing his style, modernizing his repertoire, and incorporating new and unique elements in order to win contests against the fiddlers who were playing music in the "new style from down in Kanawha." That is, Edn had to change or run the risk of losing prize money, the only income he had. Lee Hammons remembered that he was just a boy when Edn visited Lee's father's house on Spring Creek in Greenbrier County, the next county below Pocahontas County; Lee's father, Steven, came from Whitley County and settled in Greenbrier County. Dwight remembered Lee saying that eventually Edn started tuning his fiddle high and playing too fast in deference to the demands of contest fiddling. Sherman's brother Burl was also "taken by contests." As Dwight put it, Burl integrated commercial music so fully into his way of fiddling that "he could never go back across that line."[42]

Just before Dwight met him, Lee had put the new Bakelite banjo and the Japanese fiddle on "lay away" at Richardson's Hardware Store in Marlinton and was able to pay them off. By the time Dwight started visiting him, the old tunes "had begun coming back to him very quickly because he was a musician's musician." Dwight described the eccentric fiddle tunings that Lee preferred:

> His timing was impeccable. His touch on the strings with his right hand was perfect. Sometimes he might miss with the middle finger on his left hand. It had been damaged and I think lost its feeling. His tuning on the banjo was always what is now called "double C" tuning. BUT the pitch on his instruments was always one step to one and a half steps lower than C on the banjo and G on his fiddle. That is, his fiddle would have been somewhere between the pitch of F and E. After going to my first or second festival in southwest Virginia [in 1970], I remember coming back and retuning his "double C" tuning up to about "C." He didn't say anything, but when I returned, it was back down to A# or A.[43]

Five of Lee's tunes, played in clawhammer style, exerted a profound and enduring influence on Dwight's music and on his way of thinking about the old tunes. These five were tunes that Dwight felt absolutely compelled to learn, tunes that typified the archaic way of fiddling and banjo playing that Lee had learned before he set his music aside. The tunes, as Lee referred to them, were: "More Pretty Girls than One," "Kitty Snyder," "Walkin' in the Parlor," "Dead Man's Piece," and "Callaway."[44] Lee would sometimes play these in a two finger up picking style. Dwight commented:

> Black and Cranberry Mountains were where the Hammons and the Roberts were the first settlers in the 1800s. These mountains were deep woods, virgin timbered exactly, like the Frontier wilderness in the 1700s. [...] Both branches [of the Hammons family] carried the tune "Callaway" with them from there. Paris Hammons' children, Maggie, Burl, and Sherman, each had their versions on banjo. Lee had his on fiddle and banjo. I retained his on banjo and fiddle that were the best. I liked the other versions, but Lee's was far more intricate.[45]

Lee Hammons clearly exerted a lingering impact on Dwight's music, on his way of thinking about what the old tunes represented, and on Dwight's own approach to playing.[46] Dwight pursued the depth and grace that Lee brought to the music, but often averred that these qualities and the capabilities Lee brought to bear just remained so elusive.[47]

The late 1960s was a period of intense personal challenge for Dwight. Dwight looked at what he termed the trauma in his early life as having impacted his capacity to function in his mid-twenties. The depression that derived from the family conflict that led to his parents' divorce, his relocation back to Pocahontas County at about the age of five without his beloved father, and the constant movement from the household of one of his mom's sister's to another who provided care when his mother Faith was unable to—all that exerted a cumulative impact that caught up with him. The firm embrace of the extended Hammons family helped diminish his feeling of isolation and enabled him to cope with residual family matters and other difficult issues.[48] By 1969 Dwight had met and become friends with two old West Virginian fiddlers, Glen Smith and Lee Triplett. He learned enough banjo playing to be invited to play with them for audiences at local festivals. Glen Smith was an exacting, demanding fiddler who once said that Dwight played banjo like Smith's father did.[49] Dwight had strong respect for Smith.[50] Dwight thought back on such playing experiences, and reasoned—forty years down the road—that what he had to give a fiddler like Smith was the muscular, pronounced right-hand driven syncopation that he brought to his own banjo playing early on.[51] By that time Dwight had been taken in by the Hammons family as a virtual grandson, and had became immersed in their everyday lives.[52] Dwight said that spending time with the Hammonses and Hamp Carpenter had taught him far more about the music than just simple banjo playing. Dwight had learned the importance of a strong and driving rhythm propelled by an unerring right hand, and that recipe made what he managed to do relevant to the music of the Morris Brothers, with whom he played during the summers of 1972 and 1973.[53]

A convergence of variables shaped Dwight's interest in and commitment to music. He had gone looking for "something" after he had gotten out of the Navy in late 1968. He began searching for the stories that were so important to him growing up, the local narratives about life and people and events that were repeated often, and formed a bedrock

Dwight Diller, right, at Glen Smith's home in Elizabeth, West Virginia, circa 1993 (courtesy Gerry Milnes).

for him. He gravitated to the elders in the area who he had learned so much about in the stories people told about the remote living Hammons family. He craved the company of these older folks, and he wanted the sturdy friendship he knew they could offer, and the social and familial embrace he could expect from them just on the basis of the hospitality they would extend to visitors.[54] He heard the music that the Hammonses and other old people he called on had to offer, and "took a notion"—acted on a lark—to learn the banjo himself. For Dwight, the music was a part of a tapestry of things that shored up a shaken life. He was coping with the misery and depression that he had wrestled with into adulthood, and learning to deal with stress by limiting his interaction with people, and these select engagements with his elders who were familiar to him enabled him to manage a life that had grown complex in social and clinical terms by the time he reached his twenties. Though the music was a part of this package, it was not singularly important by itself, but by the early 1970s it began to offer Dwight a validation that he so dearly wanted. He found a harbor in the company of like-minded people craving older music, and saw some self-worth when he was able to place in banjo competitions. Though in the early 1980s Dwight suggested that his embrace of the music and the old musicians in Pocahontas County was his way of rejecting the materialism of Middle Class America, it seems more likely that he had reached out to the older local musicians and story tellers for the kind of anchor he needed to center himself.[55]

Dwight Diller, left, and Lee Triplett at a festival in Chloe, West Virginia, September 8, 1973. Performers seated in the background include Wilson Douglas (far left), Jenes Cottrell (with hat, between Diller and Triplett), and Sylvia O'Brien (Cottrell's sister, just to the right of Triplett) (photograph by Carl Fleischhauer).

"The Banjo Lesson"

Dwight was always frank about a key distinction that set him apart from other old time musicians from his generation: many of them grew up with the music all around them. He did not. The sound track of his life reflected the myriad of musical influences that filtered into his consciousness from a young age through wide range of sources. However, his cultural "background noise" did not include the traditional old time fiddle and banjo music that he uncovered in the late 1960s when he went looking for the company of people such as Hamp Carpenter and the Hammonses. West Virginian musicians such as Ron Mullennex, John Morris, Tim Bing, David O'Dell and Jimmy Costa grew up with that music. Ron Mullennex's family was musical. He heard the traditional music throughout his growing up years, and by the time he was a teenager Mullennex was invested in learning to play the old tunes. When he started to learn, he was "playing the music I grew up with and danced to at my high school prom."[56] Jimmy Costa grew up in a family where not much old time music was played, but in a community that was full of the old sounds. He first became attentive to old time music when he was ten or eleven years old, in a neighborhood at the foot of Bluestone Dam, where the Greenbrier and New Rivers converged. He recalled the fiddling of Marvin Lacy, and remembered first learning clawhammer from Wilson Ballard who was born in 1876. The harmonica was the first instrument Costa learned to play. He took up the banjo around age 15, and kept a scrapbook of newspaper and magazine articles about West Virginian players, including articles from a newspaper published in Richwood by Jim Comstock that was called *The West Virginia Hillbilly*. The music was an ever-present backdrop to his life; as Costa puts it: "I heard it, it made an impression, and I sought it out."[57] Dwight, on the other hand, did not know about the old time music until he established his relationship with the Hammons family in the late 1960s, by which time, in Dwight's account, many of the "old people" had stopped playing the old music and fewer and fewer people were listening to it.[58] Ron Mullennex observed that old time music did not seem to have survived in any significant way in and around Huntersville where Dwight lived in the late 1960s and early 1970s. Mullennex recalled Dwight telling him that when they wanted to have a square dance in Pocahontas County in the 1970s and 1980s, the people would have to "import" the fiddler Woody Simmons from Randolph County.

Dwight started trying to play banjo in June 1968, mostly by closely watching Hamp Carpenter and the Hammons family's banjo players, but he could not figure out the traditional down-picking clawhammer style of banjo playing. In October 1969, once he fixed on the idea of learning to play the old music, Dwight sought out Dick Kimmel who was working in a music store in Morgantown, West Virginia; later, in 1971, the two musicians, by then friends, joined the Black Mountain Bluegrass Boys, the band for which Dwight played standup bass.[59] As Dwight told the story, Dick Kimmel gave him one banjo lesson, showed him the basics, though as Dwight thought back on the experience what he learned from Kimmel was not quite clawhammer. Decades later, Dwight could not remember with any precision what Dick Kimmel showed him with the right had in that single lesson in Morgantown. He was fairly certain that it did not resemble anything at the time that was talked of as clawhammer, frailing, or rapping. It may be that what he observed being played by Kimmel was Pete Seeger's strum, as it became known, though Dwight did not necessarily recall it that way. Whatever it was that Kimmel showed him, it had a rhythmic core that seized Dwight, and it reminded him of Grandpa Jones' strong right hand attack.[60]

He pursued that rhythm until he grasped it. As Dwight recalled:

> I watched Dick Kimmel move his hand in a certain way. It was just so hard to teach me things. It all rubs together, but I could memorize. And the way Dick Kimmel said it, he said "I showed you one thing and then you went to the woodshed and came out sometime later, came out flying." That was the fall of 1969. All winter long I would hear something at the Hammons home, and pick it up.[61]

Though Dwight did not necessarily recall the specifics of that lesson, Kimmel did. Kimmel was born in Philadelphia, Pennsylvania, in 1947 and lived the first ten years of his life in Woodbury, New Jersey, the boyhood home of Mac Benford, and thus—in Kimmel's words—a hotbed for clawhammer banjo. In an interview with Dan Levenson in 2001 Kimmel stated that when he was in grade school he took his mother's Weymann tenor banjo and added a 5th string to it. In his early teens his parents gave him a Vega Folk Wonder; he was responsible for paying half of the $125 price tag. Kimmel was living near Chicago at the time and was aware that Pete Seeger and Fleming Brown played clawhammer but he did not really attempt to master the basics of clawhammer until 1969. Kimmel went on to become an award winning musician, playing both clawhammer and traditional bluegrass.[62] He gave Dwight credit for being both a student of his—for this single lesson—and at the same time for being his inspiration, his single most important teacher.[63] In a 2001 interview with Dan Levenson, Kimmel credited Dwight Diller for helping to give him a musical trajectory.

In his interview with Kimmel, Levenson returned several times to the idea of learning from one's student. Levenson pointed out that, as Kimmel explained in his book, *Fishin Creek Blues*, Kimmel gave Dwight his first lesson, yet in the first response to the interview question Kimmel implied that he discovered clawhammer banjo through or because of Dwight, listing him as a major influence. In his first attempt to explain this, Kimmel replied:

> In the fall of 1969, Dwight came into O.B. Fawley Music Store in Morgantown, West Virginias, for one banjo lesson. I was the banjo teacher there and gave him the basics of clawhammer. Six months later he was playing wonderful music and taught me to play clawhammer. Around 1972, he and I played with a bluegrass band. He was playing bass and a little clawhammer with them–I played mandolin, some guitar, and a little clawhammer when Dwight played fiddle. We toured throughout the east as part of the New York/Bitter End Coffeehouse Circuit. Dwight and I have stayed in touch over the years. I consider him a wonderful player—very solid and not afraid to keep his playing very basic and traditional. Dwight will undoubtedly become the next generation of old-man banjo players![64]

Kimmel took another run at the issue after Levenson rephrased the question:

> I gave Dwight some pointers on banjo before he played. Then he learned to play the music he had grown up with. Growing up with the music was his major influence—not me in any sense at all.

Kimmel elaborated further, noting that in 1969, after enrolling in graduate school at West Virginia University in Morgantown he decided earn some extra cash by teaching banjo and guitar in Morgantown:

> Early that year Dwight came in for a lesson. I didn't know Dwight, and knew little of old-time music other than seeing Fleming Brown when I was in Chicago and having some New Lost City Ramblers records. I wasn't playing clawhammer at the time—but knew the Seeger basic strum which is the same type of bump-ditty rhythm and I had read that clawhammer involved the two down strokes with the back of the finger. I showed Dwight that. He told me later that had I (someone) not told him the words "bump-ditty" he wouldn't have gotten the rhythm and thanked me for showing him that. Today he says just "thanks for the one banjo lesson." [...] Dwight's and my styles evolved quite differently—he is very big into heavy rhythm and using the entire forearm. I use more wrist action and like to vary what I do in style—although I love rhythm, especially the lilt—and the principle Dwight called KISS–keep it simple

stupid! The time with Dwight on the road [in the Black Mountain Bluegrass Boys] was important to my clawhammer playing. Thus, the story is (1) Dwight was my student for 1 lesson and (2) he is one of my major influences. I hope we can just leave it at that. Dwight was from Pocahontas County and knew the Hammons (family) and had no doubt heard real old-time music for years or all his life. I had very little old-time exposure at the time. Dwight and I got together some months later and he played me many West Virginia tunes in grand fashion. I was glad to have had an influence on him, because getting together with him after "the lesson" taught me the beauty of and how to play clawhammer.[65]

All of this, alongside of the manner in which the Kimmel Lesson was mentioned in prior interviews with Dwight,[66] made this moment in clawhammer history the single most scrutinized lesson since Henry Ossawa Tanner's 1893 painting "The Banjo Lesson."[67] Dick Kimmel recalled that Stu Cohen, owner of the Music Emporium in Cambridge, Massachusetts, was the first to use the term "sledgehammer" to describe Dwight's driving, forceful right hand work, though it appears that even earlier the term was used to describe Dwight's playing because his first credible banjo, the "Improved George Washburn," was so loud and had such projection that the folks in Lexington, Virginia's old time community christened it "Snotty" for its obnoxious and overbearing sound.[68] As Dwight put it:

I loved to go into one of the jams at a festival. There might be a dozen or more playing. I would step in with "Snotty" and what quickly came to be called "sledge hammer" banjo style and take over with my rhythm, my drive.[69]

Kimmel offered this recollection in October 2014:

Dwight did come into O.B. Fawley Music Store, in Morgantown, WV, where he was a college student, in the fall of 1969 for his banjo lesson. I had just graduated from college and started a Ph.D. degree in Biology at West Virginia University. Dwight, in his words, was struggling learning clawhammer. I already played Pete Seeger's "basic strum," knowing that clawhammer was the same basic rhythm except for the "first" picking stroke—basic strum uses an up-pick and clawhammer a down-stroke. Dwight later told me that "my showing him the hand movements and especially just telling him 'bump ditty, bump ditty' was the most important $1.80 he'd ever spent and that I had set the stage for his being able to learn clawhammer." I was extremely proud of what he told me; my influencing one of today's greatest clawhammer players in some small way.[70]

Kimmel was wrong about one thing. In the Levenson interview, Kimmel stated that:

Dwight and I have been great friends and I think it embarrasses him to have taken a formal banjo lesson.[71]

On the contrary, Dwight gave Kimmel credit for trying to show him some of the basics of banjo kinetics, while acknowledging that what he learned in this lesson was not so much the mechanics of the right hand work that he would come to rely on as he refined his playing, but the importance of a percussive, pulsating rhythm for any kind of banjo playing.

Importantly, the porch of Kimmel's small cabin in the woods near Morgantown became a site of a handful of informal retreats. In Kimmel's words:

Thinking back, it was a real West Virginia nature type experience and Dwight probably welcomed it as an opportunity to get out of Morgantown without having to drive all the way to Pocahontas County. It was during a period of time between when he first learned to play banjo and the time when he […] first [understood] that the artistic nature [of] his playing was something that people from all walks of life wanted to listen to. We'd often have a small crowd of folks, from musicians who were visiting me to the surgeon and family who lived up the hill. […] Although it wasn't "billed" as such, Dwight and his banjo became the center of focus at this gathering whenever he was there. I believe this may have occurred because of the seriousness in which Dwight took his playing and the beauty and basic nature of his playing. I remember him playing and singing "Hog-eyed Man" over and over for the people that were there. There were certainly a host of other tunes/songs that Dwight played, but that one stands out in my memory.[72]

These may have been the first instances of Dwight's public performances on the banjo; they could have been among the first experiences that signaled to Dwight that he could perform music in a manner that would become the central organizing dimension of his life.

Studying the Old Time Way

In the late spring of 1970, Dwight audited a class taught by West Virginia University professor Patrick W. Gainer, probably one of the senior level classes listed by the University's English department, possibly the Appalachian Folklore course. Wayne Howard recalled that Gainer encouraged his students to "seek out tradition bearers and collect their music, songs, stories, herbal cures, and techniques of craftsmanship," something Dwight had been doing since 1968 when he sought out the old musicians living in Pocahontas County—largely because it filled a void he felt, and connected him to the old people and their stories in a way that brought him back to the same kind of embrace he felt as a young man while sitting and listening to his elders.[73] The decision on Dwight's part to spend time hunting down old musicians in Pocahontas County coincided with his Morgantown college studies, and probably received a boost—and perhaps some structure—from the classwork urged on students by Professor Gainer. However, Dwight's primary motivation was far more personal, and predated his classroom experience with Professor Gainer. By the time Dwight registered for Professor Gainer's courses, he had begun to focus on the "Old People" and their music, but he had also absorbed two decade's worth of his slice of West Virginia—folk art, music, stories, rites and rituals. He came to the door of the classroom with an ingrained sense of that culture, and a very sharpened view of the extent to which the old music, and especially "Old People," were for him a life preserver.

Sometime during the spring semester of 1970, Dwight played some of his recordings of the Hammonses for Professor Gainer.[74] Gainer, the author of several noted publications on folklore and folk music in the region, taught at West Virginia University from 1946 to 1972.[75] He enrolled at West Virginia University in the 1920s at a time when the school was a major national-level center of gravity for folk music scholarship. Studying under John Harrington Cox and Louis Watson Chappell, Gainer earned both baccalaureate and master's degrees from West Virginia University, and joined Cox and Chappell in conducting studies of surviving musical tradition in the West Virginia countryside.[76] In 1928, Gainer took an instructor's position in the English Department at St. Louis University. Between 1928 and 1932 he pursued doctoral research under the tutelage of the folklorist Archer Taylor at the University of Chicago. Gainer received his doctorate from St. Louis University where he continued to teach until 1942. He directed United Service Organizations (USO) activities in the Caribbean and South Atlantic during World War II.[77] At the end of the war, Gainer returned to West Virginia and began teaching at the Morgantown campus of West Virginia University in the Department of English. In the early 1970s, Carl Fleischhauer worked as a cameraman for WWVU, the university's public television station, and accompanied Gainer on visits to several West Virginia sites to shoot footage for television programs.[78] Fleischhauer remembered Gainer as a friendly professorial figure who enjoyed performing the music he learned in his fieldwork, and was effective in his efforts to become acquainted with people he dealt with in the course of his own folklore-related research.[79]

Dwight and Professor Patrick Gainer of West Virginia University on the cover of the university's magazine, fall 1970 (courtesy *West Virginia University Magazine*, with special thanks to editor Diana Mazzella).

Gainer "drew a sharp distinction between authentic folk music and hillbilly music and rejected the pseudo-folk music that swept the country in the 1960s and 1970s," according to Otis K. Rice and Stephen W. Brown.[80] The professor focused on the Scottish origins of tunes that were sung or played in central West Virginia. The folk songs he collected and the lore he documented in West Virginia beginning in the mid–1920's led him to conclude that "many musical traditions of the mountain settlers derived from their British Isle forebears." Of the 299 ballads recorded by Francis Child in the British Isles during the latter years of the 19th century, Gainer was able to show that 55 were also played and passed on by Mountain State musicians."[81]

Dwight's perspective on the character of the old music in east central West Virginia was in effect shaped by his association with the old fiddlers and banjo players who he encountered and befriended, people with whom he played banjo and from whom he learned local tunes. Dwight had become acutely aware of the unique ways the old tunes were played and sung in east central West Virginia. By the early 1970s he was attentive to the differences between mountain music, hill country traditions, and other evolutions elsewhere in his home state where commercial country music, hillbilly rock and other forms achieved some traction among local audiences. Dwight thought that the old traditional tunes he heard in the late 1960s were derived from local influences, leavened perhaps by residual old country ways but primarily informed by very local variables.

The music in the hill country of central West Virginia, particularly the area around Gainer's place of birth and the county in which he grew up, developed at least somewhat differently than the mountainous east central region that was Dwight's home. Dwight saw different traditions and practices as being at the core of the music he knew best. Dwight's observations suggested that playing and singing was not the preferred way in Pocahontas County. Hammons family members, and Maggie Hammons in particular, would play a banjo tune and then stop, sing the words to a tune or tell a story, and then pick up playing again, but it was not common practice to sing and play an instrument, in Dwight's memory, and playing to accompany a singer was also not part of this tradition.[82] Dwight's experience suggested that dulcimer was a minor instrument where he came from compared to the five string banjo and the fiddle; Maggie Hammons called dulcimers "hog fiddles," a vaguely derisive term.[83] Gainer, known for his ballad singing and his dulcimer playing, had a very different view.[84]

Preserving the Old Time Music

Dwight's field recordings of the tunes and stories of the Hammons family, made during 1969–1970, became the inspiration for and part of the audio core of the Library of Congress Hammons Family project. In October 1970 he took anywhere from 600 to 700 black and white photographs of Sherman, Burl, Ruie and Maggie Hammons; some of those were incorporated into the 1973 booklet that accompanied the two LP record set entitled *The Hammons Family: A Study of a West Virginia Family's Traditions*, based on fieldwork by Dwight Diller, Alan Jabbour and Carl Fleischhauer.[85] Dwight also organized several notable "get togethers," local jams that featured the Hammonses, and he was in effect a central point of contact for musicians, folklorists and filmmakers others seeking access to the Hammons Family for social, musical, filming and research purposes.[86]

Dwight was integral to the work connected to the field recording portion of the

Hammons family project conducted in the early 1970s under the auspices of the Archive of Folk Song (later renamed Archive of Folk Culture). In 2015, Carl Fleischhauer stated that "Dwight was a real part of the fieldwork effort rather than separate from it." However, "as the collecting project morphed into a publication project—with the shift to analysis, library-based research, writing, and editing–Dwight played less of a central role." Fleischhauer noted that Dwight's July 1969 to July 1970 field recording collection ran about 32 to 36 hours. It included some odds and ends apart from the tunes and stories of the Hammons family, including a recording of several musical performances by Gainer. The core of the collection might have been 30 to 32 hours, consistent with the numbers derived from the duplication work undertaken by David Nemec who beginning in the late 1990s translated the reels into digital format and copied the original tapes over to 25 CDs that contained something on the order of 30 hours' worth of recordings. Additional tapes of the Hammons family were recorded in phase two of the operation, beginning in October 1970, when Dwight and Fleischhauer made recordings in Buckeye. Relying on round numbers, Fleischhauer calculated that phase two of the project, the "publication project," yielded about 40 hours of new recordings: 8 by Dwight and Fleischhauer, 10 by Alan Jabbour on his own, and about 22 by Jabbour and Fleischhauer, who concluded that, if correct, this analysis indicated that the cumulative hours of recordings created in phase one (Dwight on his own) was essentially similar to those created during phase two (the combined work of Dwight, Fleischhauer and Jabbour), although each set include "treasures not in the other."[87]

The Library of Congress work was informed and organized research, rigorous ethnographic field work and systematic observation that led to hypothetical conclusions supported by carefully culled evidence buttressed by corroborating scholarly resources, but it was also far more than that. It represented a window onto another way of life that in many ways reflected the simplicity, and complexity, of living in the rough environment of a frontier state. It offered a perspective on folks who organized their lives uniquely, simply, and essentially, people who preserved old ways of doing things and thinking that provided access to practices and lore that were increasingly important to a broad range of people—academics, artists, explorers—seeking to learn more about America. It compelled many of these people to seek out the Hammons family, and to search their own locales for others living in ways that harked back to older practices that defined the possibilities life offered.

The study prompted many musicians and academics to seek out Hammons family members as source musicians and storytellers. Musicians and folklorists who traveled to Pocahontas County to meet, listen to, learn from and record the Hammons family members were drawn to the sharing nature of these people; the open and honest, guileless way in which they conducted themselves; the extent to which their native abilities, experience, what they learned on their own and from their elders equipped them for the lives they led; and to the nature of their devotion to principles, to truths they held to be enduring and self-evident. As Carl Fleischhauer observed of those who visited the homes of the various Hammons family members:

> The consistency of their reports is striking, highlighting the profound if not electrifying way that the family captured each visitor's heart and mind. The Hammonses' music was compelling and their narratives powerfully evoked the past and life in the mountain wilderness. The ways in which this artistic and human force was integrated into the visitors' lives, however, varied considerably. [Some of these musicians have] continued to let that experience guide [their] musical performances, and [their] sense of its cultural meaning.[88]

Fleischhauer noted that both he and Alan Jabbour were strongly drawn to the family:

> [We] carried out the core portion of [our] fieldwork over a three or four year period, with important contributions from Dwight. This ethnographic project yielded the dozens of new recordings and hundreds of photographs that are now part of the collections of the Archive of Folk Culture at the Library of Congress. This corpus was distilled in 1973 to produce the two-disc album published by the Library, intended to reach an audience of folk music enthusiasts as well as scholars, and another album on the Rounder label. The booklet that accompanies the Library set features a family history and analyses of the musical and narrative selections, all supported by corroborating scholarly sources. Both [of us] continued to visit the family for years after the album had been published.[89]

Dwight's visits were more frequent and of longer duration; the relationship he formed with the Hammons family became part of his "quest for self-understanding and self-identity"; and his memories and impressions of the musicians became critically important elements in his own life, and a motivational force in his musical career.[90]

Sometime around April 1970, Dwight introduced Professor Gainer to the Hammons. That summer, on behalf of a television program being planned by WWVU, the university's public television station, Gainer organized a visit to the Hammonses. At the time, Carl Fleischhauer worked for the television station and joined the trip as cinematographer. As Dwight remembers it, Alan Jabbour, then a Library of Congress researcher, learned about the family from students who were playing old time music around the University of North Carolina at Chapel Hill. During the summer of 1970, Dwight met members of the Fuzzy Mountain String Band at an old time music festival and played a cassette he had made of the Hammonses' music.[91] Band members went to West Virginia not long after that and met Burl. Upon their return, they told Alan Jabbour what they knew about the Hammonses.

Dwight recalled that Professor Gainer was enthusiastic about Maggie's singing, and that he felt she had sung the tune "How Far It Is" that she had known for a long while, a tune Gainer and other folk song collectors thought had never come to the United States. In early 2015, Carl Fleishhauer confirmed that "Gainer glommed onto the fact that Maggie's repertory included a Child ballad not previously found in West Virginia," but remembered that the ballad that Gainer had found to be special was Child 17 ("Hind Horn"), a tune Maggie called "In Scotland Town," probably because those words appear in the first line of the tune.[92] Maggie Hammons Parker told Jabbour: "They claim that's a good one; I don't like it too well."[93] Fleischhauer explained that though Gainer's name was not mentioned it was clear from Dwight's accounts at the time that the professor was the antecedent of "they claim" in Maggie Hammons statement. It was also clear, as Jabbour's commentary on the ballad indicated, that this ballad was a genuine rarity in the U.S., as Gainer had discerned.[94] Gainer's intense interest in that song "was no doubt partly due to his work on a book that would present some of his discoveries." The book came out in 1975, five years after he collected Maggie's version.[95] In what he acknowledged was an oversimplification, intended to illustrate a point, Fleischhauer stated that in the 1930s, 1940s, and 1950s, "folklore in the U.S. was most often based in university departments of English and many who pursued it were scholars of ballads and tales." Gainer represented something of a respected anachronism, a ballad collector whose scholarly inquiry was "illustrative of the direction and thinking of the previous generation, and tended to be distinct from the approaches taken by folklore students in the 1970s and 1980s."[96] Fleischhauer continued:

> Many of those who worked in this field beginning in the 1960s and after tended to take an ethnographic approach. (Yet others went in other directions, e.g., sociolinguistics and more.) Those who moved in an ethnographic direction often looked at material culture as well as oral and musical traditions, hence the growing use of the term "folklife" in place of "folklore." And you start to see on-campus connections to departments of anthropology and the formation of distinct folklore/folklife programs or departments, like the one at Indiana University[....] The work that Alan and I did with the Hammonses represents this increasingly ethnographic approach, highlighting people and their ideas—describing the human context for folk expression.[97]

The key point, for Fleischhauer, was that both the rigorous academic method and the collection and assessment performed by field workers were often leavened by learned affection for the subject. There was, to Fleischhauer, a synergy between an ethnographic approach and Dwight's emphasis on seeing and understanding people "whole," not just isolating their art.[98]

In the late spring, in 1970, while visiting the farm, the WWVU-TV film crew and Pat Gainer shot some footage of the Hammons family, footage that they intended as material for a future broadcast. Before they could work that footage into a broadcast program, the station required signed releases from those who were filmed indicating that they consented to being shown on television. As Dwight remembered it, the chore of obtaining the releases fell to Gainer. He in turn sought help from Dwight. Although no longer clear at this distance in time, it may also be the case that Gainer sought a similar form of consent from Maggie for the use of her text for "In Scotland Town" ("Hind Horn") in his book.[99] Dwight recalled, Gainer sought releases for the TV show to be produced, but the Hammons weren't going to sign:

> I got in the middle of that. [...] Gainer and I split up over this. [...] Musicologists start getting really protective of what they discover. [...] [Gainer] jumped on me and said "I don't care what you say but I've talked to a lawyer and we don't have to get this thing signed." Carl [Fleischhauer] told him they weren't going to do it until a release was signed, and they didn't want to sign. Pressure on me to get them to sign. Really made me confused. Alan [Jabbour] showed up. Alan is very diplomatic sort of person, he kind of understood. Offered to help me out. [...] In an "unofficial capacity" he gave me some advice. I just remember things were so touchy.[100]

Dwight remembered the back and forth about obtaining the releases as painful, and recalled that exchanges over the issue drew Fleischhauer (then at the television station) and Jabbour (visiting from the Library of Congress) into the discussion. In the end, no releases were signed and the film footage was never broadcast. The pressure Dwight felt in being asked to get the Hammons family to sign the required release forms shaped his perception of how established organizations (such as the television station) with their formal, legal requirements, and academicians with their vested interests in research and publication could alter the tone and content of social encounters. In later years, Dwight would interpret this episode and similar incidents in his life from a premise that suggested such moments had the hallmarks of a kind of "colonialism" intent on extracting West Virginian cultural resources—sometimes with the cooperation of indigenous actors who were coopted or controlled by the forces bent on what amounted to strip mining of a metaphorical sort.[101] However, in the ten years that followed this quarrel with Gainer, Dwight remained confused and stunned that he could fall so quickly from grace over a difference of views after he took a position of respect for the wishes of the Hammonses, and made a good faith effort to explain Gainer's perspective on the requested release.[102]

It is entirely possible that as a result of encounters of this sort, Dwight in later life became far too uncharitable to scholars and that he was a bit too jaded in his attitude toward their scholarly products. Much of this was probably at the center of Dwight's argument that "local power brokers and the school system" had done a lot to relegate the archaic culture, the old tunes, and the mountain people to irrelevance by, in Dwight's estimation, rejecting all indigenous music as "ignorant." This, too, may be an especially harsh judgment regarding the views of outsiders and "power brokers" toward local cultures. However, the fact remains: Dwight's perspective, much later, was that the academic paraphernalia deployed to study the old music ended up being far too clinical to get at the moral core of the old musicians and their tunes. As he saw it, the "elitist" character of the universities and the professorial experts who sought to study the old ways interfered with the act of developing an intimate familiarity with their subjects.

Edn Hammons' Lost Recordings

In the early 1970s Dwight played a role in bringing attention to the "lost recordings" of Edn Hammons, which spurred efforts to resurrect those recordings.[103] Dwight learned about Edn Hammons' recorded material from his son Smith Hammons in 1973. Dwight knew of Smith at the time, and was friendly with Smith's brother James. Both brothers lived with their father Edn, not far from Dwight's home in Hillsboro.[104] Louis Watson Chappell was a West Virginia University Professor with an abiding interest in regional folksongs engendered by his colleague John Harrington Cox. Smith Hammons told Dwight that Chappell had met Edn in Richwood and recorded him during two days in the Yew Pine Hotel in Pocahontas County in mid–August 1947.[105] Dwight related that when the townspeople heard about Edn playing fiddle for the professor, they packed into the hotel, filling up the downstairs areas, lining up on the staircase, and crowding into the hotel floor outside the room where Edn was recording.[106]

According to Dwight, Smith was given an extra copy of the recording at the time; Dwight believed the recording may have been made on a wax cylinder although another source described them as aluminum disks.[107] In a 2014 discussion of this episode, Dwight stated that in 1973 he took this information to West Virginia University music department Professor Thomas S. Brown; Dwight had introduced many of the old music makers of Pocahontas County to Professor Brown from 1970 to 1973.[108] Brown began investigating this story, and learned that Chappell had taken the 1947 recordings of Edn Hammons and other materials he had collected in his field work with him when he retired from West Virginia University and relocated to North Carolina.

John Cuthbert, Director and Curator, West Virginia and Regional History Center, wrote that Chappell had learned about Edn Hammons from Patrick Gainer who had learned about Edn from a student in a class that Gainer was teaching in Richwood. Cuthbert related that Gainer brought Edn to Morgantown in the summer of 1947, and Edn spent the night at Chappell's home. Gainer recalled he had taken Edn to a folk festival in Arthurdale, where the fiddler played his music for a small assembled audience, though Cuthbert documented that the Arthurdale festival occurred two weeks before Chappell's recording session with Edn Hammons, and suggested that the original plan may have been for three days of taping.[109] Cuthbert stated that Chappell's notes indicated the recording sessions had taken place on 14 and 15 August 1947, and that a third session occurred on 23 August 1947 in Chappell's home in Morgantown, where Edn had stayed during the several days of recording.

Dwight recalled that Brown brought this information on Chappell's recordings of Edn to the attention of Alan Jabbour, who had by then completed the Hammons Family project.[110] Cuthbert stated in his essay on the recordings, included in the liner notes for volume one of *The Eddens Hammons Collection*, that "In the mid–1970s Chappell donated his archives to West Virginia University's West Virginia and Regional History Collection."[111]

* * *

Dwight came away from these three experiences in the early 1970s—his role in the Library of Congress project, the confused issue of the "releases," and his tangential role in assuring that Edn Hammons' music was preserved—with some definite ideas about the work of recording the music of the "Old People," compiling the stories these folks told, and closely observing the way they went about their lives. He came to believe that an exclusively analytical investigation of the Hammons family and what they represented missed an opportunity to understand elements of their lives by shunting aside their words, the way they tell their own story. Dwight himself sought out these people for the warm embrace they offered to a young man who was out of sorts, without any social, familial anchors, and in need of a place that would allow him to simply "be." He wanted to spend some time in the company of the Hammons Family, and his understanding of what they were and what they thought emerged from that link, not a more dispassionate, clinical way of framing what they represented and the platform they provided for understanding archaic, remote times, places and people.

Dwight played a direct, essential role in the original collection work conducted by Fleischhauer and Jabbour, contributed to the interviewing process, and offered his understanding of context. He recorded the old tunes sung and played by the Hammons family members, and he learned many of these old tunes from them. He formed his ideas of how the music was to be played from his interactions with the Hammons family members. But his relationship with them was passionate and involved a level of interaction in which they derived some intangible dividends such as a special friendship, and a link with younger people who thrived in their presence. Importantly, Fleischhauer noted that Dwight's regular visits, and his bringing "other enthusiasts of traditional music" to meet them, did much to rekindle Burl and Maggie's interest in music.[112]

Dwight had his own perspective on the Hammons family that was essentially organized as a counterpoint to emerging conventional wisdoms about the songs and stories of the Hammonses that developed in the context of old time music festival circuits and within old time music "communities." His perspective may have been influenced by the intellectual tools he absorbed in his studies, and his exposure to the thinking of the folk tune collectors in West Virginia University. However, he was not a trained field researcher, and if he did absorb elements of a musicologist's skill set in his studies, he did not necessarily bring those capabilities to bear in his own effort to create his special relationship with the Hammons family. He thrived more on the "shared memories" that emerged from his stay with the Hammonses, and he sought to "spend some time in the company of the Hammons Family." His goals were far more personal, and his attachment to the family was far more emotional, and consequently that frame of reference became the basis for his understanding of what these people represented; what they indicated about Appalachian life, local history, and archaic cultural forms; and what to do with, and how to play the play, the tunes the Hammonses shared.[113]

Three

Playing Music

In the Trenches at the Old Time Festivals

In 1970, Dwight went to work as a Nutritional Aide for the West Virginia 4-H Club, an organization focused on teaching farm children basic agricultural management skills and animal husbandry and undertaking such projects as teaching women to can groundhog meat in Cass, West Virginia. Sometime that year, he and his friend Paul Haggard went to an old time music festival near Hillsville, Virginia. Dwight had met Haggard, an assistant forest ranger, in the summer of 1969. Haggard was from the north, an "outsider" as Dwight put it. They met when Haggard, on behalf of the National Forest, was trying to get Sherman Hammons to agree to build a fence to keep his sheep from grazing on federal land. Sherman was adamant in his position: "If you want to build a fence, that's just fine," Dwight remembered Sherman telling Haggard, "But I'll not build a fence." Haggard got to know Sherman, they became friends, and that led to the link with Dwight. Haggard played guitar and on the basis of their common interest in old time music Haggard invited Dwight to accompany him to the 4th Annual Old Time Fiddlers and Bluegrass Convention in Hillsville, Virginia, in June 1970.

That festival was Dwight's first exposure to the burgeoning "old time scene." The festival opened up a new world for him, brought him into contact with peers his age, and introduced him to a concentration of old time music talent. Dwight met the Fuzzy Mountain String Band members and made the acquaintance of several banjo players with whom he became lifelong friends, and from whom he learned some banjo playing skills.[1] Three men in particular befriended Dwight: Bob Thren, an avid caver and banjo player who moved to Lexington, Virginia, in 1975; Len Reiss, an accomplished banjo builder and clawhammer player originally from New Jersey; and Alex Varela, a lawyer by training who showed Dwight how to play Henry Reed's version of "Frosty Morn" and "Angeline" in an impromptu ten or fifteen minute lesson at the Hillsville festival. That brief lesson helped Dwight consolidate what he had picked up from Dick Kimmel in Morgantown, and what he had absorbed from close observation of Hamp Carpenter, Lee Hammons, and Sherman and Burl Hammons and Maggie Hammons Parker.[2] Thren, Reiss and Varela had come to listen to the likes of Tommy Jarrell, who played fiddle at the festival.[3]

At Hillsville, Dwight also met Tommy Thompson, who was born in St. Albans near Charleston, West Virginia, and whose banjo playing caught Dwight's attention. Thompson was a graduate student in philosophy at the University of North Carolina in 1965; by 1970, he was teaching college philosophy courses. Thompson held a number of appointments over several years at the University of Alabama at Birmingham, where he taught from the fall of 1971 to 1972, and at North Carolina State in Raleigh, where he began teaching in 1972. Thompson was a founding member of the Hollow Rock String Band that recorded their first album in 1967, and The Red Clay Ramblers.[4] Dwight was drawn to Thompson's playing, and to his big personality.

Dwight did not remember exactly how, but he ended up registered as a participant in the festival's banjo contest. Someone might have entered his name, or he might have been cajoled into signing up himself; his memory is vague on this point. A fellow with the name of Mutt Worrell took first place. Worrell and his brother, old time banjo player Matokie Slaughter, were from Pulaski, Virginia.[5] Dwight remembered that Mutt played two tunes: "Long Tongued Woman," and "Monkey on a String," two tunes he was not familiar with then and has not encountered since that time.[6] However, a tape of the contest showed that one of Mutt's tunes was "John Henry," and that another contestant by the name of Russell Worrell (contestant number 4) played "Monkey on a String."[7]

Dwight and Tommy Jarrell at Union Grove Old Time Fiddler's Convention, North Carolina, probably 1971 (courtesy Bill Hicks).

Dwight took second place at the Hillsville competition. He played two tunes, and while he remembered playing "Arkansas Traveller" in that contest, the audio tape that identified him as contestant number nine from Sally Holler, West Virginia, showed that he played "Old Folks Comin' Down the Road" and "Soldier's Joy."[8] At a later point in the audio tape, Dwight—mistakenly identified as Dwight "Deley"—played "Sixteen Horses Was My Team," though the tune was identical to what he had played earlier on the tape, identified as "Old Folks Comin' Down the Road."[9] Tommy Thompson, identified by the announcer as contestant number eight from Chapel Hill, North Carolina, played "Devil on a Stump."[10] Dwight said of the Hillsville experience:

> Here were all these young people playing. Fuzzy Mountain String Band folks and Tommy Thompson. Here were people my age playing this music. I'd hit bottom several times in my life. I hit bottom spring of 1970 and just had no reason to live, felt terrible for months and months. And I went to that thing, [and it] was a rebirth for me. I couldn't play clawhammer. I tried to figure it out by ear and it came out sounding like that Pete Seeger stuff. [...] One of the things that really helped me—I went on stage competed with ten or 11 people, and I competed and I couldn't play anything hardly and I got second place. It was fast and it wasn't fancy. Fast and clean. Caught the judge's ears. Well, I don't know anything except that was a real gift for me.[11]

A few weeks after Hillsville, Dwight attended a 4th of July festival held at Independence, Virginia. He remembered that Wade Ward placed first in the banjo competition, and that Ward may have played "Chilly Winds" as one of his two contest numbers. Tommy Thompson took second place. Dwight did not recall who took the third place spot. Dwight ranked fourth in the field of contestants.[12] Dwight said:

> The thing about Independence—traditionally, people who win are the people in house. So, nobody knew me. They might have known I was from West Virginia but that would not have held any water. I still took fourth place. That really validated me and who I was or who I was becoming as a banjo player.[13]

Dwight entered other contests after these two first events in 1970, though four decades later he did not have a specific memory of any subsequent competitions.[14] Brad Leftwich recalled that Dwight asked him to fiddle "Sugar Hill," a classic Galax/Mount Airy tune, in the banjo contest at Independence, Virginia, in 1974, and that Dwight "either won or placed in the contest, and very generously shared his prize money with me."[15] Dwight competed in the banjo contest at the 1974 festival in Independence, Virginia. According to one festival attendee, Dwight played banjo with a fiddler, performing the tune "Johnson Gals," a tune of Mississippi origin, not the more widely known "Johnson Boys."[16]

The old time festivals that Dwight attended in the early 1970s, in Virginia and West Virginia, became an important crucible in which his musical skills were formed and tested, and also the incubator in which his basic views regarding musical orthodoxy and authenticity were shaped. Dwight was drawn to these events in the early 1970s and immersed himself in the old time scene in Lexington, Virginia. At the same time he

Dwight at the festival on Droop Mountain, near Marlinton, West Virginia, in July 1972 (photograph by Carl Fleischhauer).

became a galvanizing force for musical gatherings in Hillsboro, West Virginia, that showcased the Hammons family musicians (Sherman, Maggie and Burl) and offered a venue for younger musicians committed to learning the old tunes. These gatherings were important events both to Dwight and to the musicians and folklorists who were becoming immersed in local music, and focusing their attentions on the Hammons family and other source musicians.[17] Dwight was also instrumental in bringing some of the Hammons family musicians to Pioneer Days in Marlinton, West Virginia.

Wayne Howard remembered accompanying Burl and Lee Hammons, along with Paul Haggard, to the annual festival in Glenville, West Virginia, in 1971.[18] There were other such gatherings, and Dwight often played a role in facilitating the presence of Hammons family members at such events.[19] Fleischhauer recalled that Maggie Hammons preferred performing at the Droop Mountain Festival because it was "close to home and she could be taken back to her own house at the end of the day."[20]

Dwight and the Old Time World in Lexington, Virginia

Dwight and Paul Haggard drove back to West Virginia through Lexington, Virginia. That was Dwight's first exposure to the Lexington old time scene. James Leva recalled that Lexington was "the magnet in the center[...], like an atom with the electron cloud all around." It was a crossroads, a convenient stopping place for bands from Ithaca, New York, and from Asheville, North Carolina, that visited Lexington for the concentrated old time music experience that developed around Odell McGuire. Interstate 81 was the corridor that brought musicians heading to and from summer festivals to Lexington; Leva recalled "Ithacans" coming to Odell and Mata McGuire's for the "Breaking Up Christmas" parties.[21] In Leva's words:

> The Highwoods were the most influential band of that time and they lived in Ithaca but traveled I-81 regularly. Walt Koken was good friends with Odell and Mata. Odell even sent his son Forrest to Ithaca to live with Walt and his wife, Annie, for a couple of years. The Highwoods and the Correctones used to come visit us in Virginia and we used to go to the Highwoods party up there every summer. I still consider all those Highwoods folks good friends. The New Yorkers would come down for festivals and then stay and hang out. Joe Puryear used to come and spend months here and often brought his boys Ward and Jeb with him. I met Richie Stearns when he was about 15 years old and he'd come here for Breaking up Christmas. Those bonds were very strong back in those days. Some of the folks from farther away would come here and then we'd go visit older musicians like Tommy Jarrell together. It was a moveable feast, if you will. Everything revolved around music.[22]

Dwight had met Odell McGuire at one of the Morris Brothers' festivals in Ivydale, West Virginia, in 1970, and they formed a fast friendship. McGuire, a geology professor at Washington and Lee University in Lexington, Virginia, began attending regional festivals and soaking up the music, interacting with the musicians, and taught himself banjo.[23] He and his wife Mata opened their home to old time musicians, and their house—and Mata's restaurant, the White Column Inn—became two main centers for old time music and dance in Lexington. McGuire wrote in a brief "memoire" about the earliest days of the old time scene in Lexington, Virginia:

> I went over to the Morris Brothers festival in Ivydale, West Virginia, in September, 1970 with a friend and student, Coley (Cully) Blake, who'd served with Dave Morris in Viet Nam. I met Dwight Diller there. I had just learned the drop-thumb banjo lick from Steve Keith at Galax in August. Dwight was learning to play from Lee Hammons and was some months further along than me. We formed a friend-

Odell McGuire and his son Forrest at the Rockbridge County (Virginia) Old-Time Music and Dance Festival, circa 1976 (courtesy Dennis Slifer).

ship which has endured. Within a couple weeks, through Dwight, I met the Hammons family: Maggie, Ruie, Sherman, Burl and their older cousin, Lee. I also met their friend, Mose Coffman. He was the first fiddler I ever played with and he taught me much.[24]

Beginning in the summer of 1971, Dwight travelled frequently to Lexington in the company of his future wife, Molly Trimble, fiddler Andy Williams and others. Together they joined Lexington old time musicians in puddle hopping from one Virginia festival to the next, entering band contests, building the circle of players in the Lexington area that centered around Odell and Mata McGuire's household, establishing relationships, and planning visitations to learn from the likes of Tommy Jarrell.

Leftwich provided a picture of the way Lexington old time music folks organized themselves at these festivals:

> Dwight wasn't among the Lexington folks when I met them that year [1972] at Independence. I followed them home and stayed in Lexington for a week or so after the festival, and I may have met Dwight then, although I can't remember for sure. At the festival I met Odell and Mata [McGuire], Len Reiss, Chris Murray, maybe Bob Thren. They were mostly playing modal tunes from West Virginia, especially Henry Reed tunes. I remember "Hogeye Man," "Frosty Morning," "Texas." Their little enclave was very different from everything else going on at the festival. For one thing, there were no guitars, just banjos and I think one fiddle. At that time there was in Lexington a feeling that guitars didn't really belong. That changed gradually over the next five years, but there really weren't any guitar players in town for several years. Steve Gendron may have been the first. Scott Ainslie was a blues guitar player, but he mostly played fiddle in those days.[25]

Dwight strongly shared the view held by old time musicians in the Lexington old time community that the "Old People" were an invaluable musical resource, and that the culture and lifestyle that had been "the spawning ground for the music for so many years" was worthy of great respect.[26] He enthusiastically took Lexington friends to Pocahontas County to introduce them to the old musicians and their music. He may have played a role in helping to engender an interest in reviving the mountain community tradition of "Old Christmas" by working to set up a Breaking Up Christmas event in Lexington, in concert with Odell and Mata McGuire, that was in fact a schedule of interlocking parties running through the New Year celebration.[27] This week-long string of music parties that moved from house to house brought old time musicians from all over the United States, including the Highwoods String Band folks, Sheila Kay Adams and many others, to Lexington.[28] Dwight became integrated into a circle of active, creative musicians. He married his first wife, Molly Trimble, who was from Lexington, in the Hamlin Church in Pocahontas County, West Virginia, in 1973. That wedding service was presided over by a student friend from West Virginia University who had paid $15.00 to an outfit in California to get ordained in order, Dwight recalled, to avoid the Vietnam war.[29] Odell McGuire remembered:

> In an old log church at Edray, West Virginia, on Dec 29, '73, Dwight Diller married Molly Trimble. Many musicians from all over attended. All were invited to a reception and [an Old Time Music] bash at my house on faculty row in Lexington. The party lasted til New Years—many old as well as new faces. Among the latter I remember Lisa Ornstein and Mike Burns. To look ahead, Bruce Molsky, having moved to the County around '75, married Jan Lee Trimble, Molly's younger sister, in April, '77, and became Dwight's brother-in-law.[30]

During the summer of 1973 "the Mongrel Horde," as the musicians called themselves, rented three large farm houses in the Lexington area. McGuire recalled that he and likeminded old time musicians traveled to festivals almost every weekend and entered festival contests in various band configurations, and with various band names. Liz Shields and

Becky Williams called themselves "The Leather Bitches." Dave Winston and Brad Leftwich lived near Fairfield until Al Tharp invited them to move in with him. They formed a band that took its name from the street on which Tharp lived, Plank Road.[31] James Leva recalled that Mata McGuire's bar and restaurant, the White Column Inn, was a focal point for the music scene in Lexington throughout the 1970s.[32] This was less of an effort to create a durable institution than it was a coalescence of a cadre of leaders and organizers who galvanized a rank and file of committed musicians to come together in a series of cascading events throughout the year—festivals in the summer, jams and informal gatherings of like-minded old time musicians during the rest of the year.[33] The unique communities of this sort that emerged in the early 1970s throughout the United States were wedded to other such conglomerations through networks of friendships forged in college settings and relationships born and bred in the summer festival circuit. Bob Carlin pointed out that the Lexington, Virginia, old time scene from the mid-to late 1970s, and the Green Grass clogger parties in Greenville, North Carolina during the 1970s, along with the community in Ithaca, New York, inspired other communities such as the Philadelphia, Pennsylvania, old time music cooperative that ran a weekly square dance. These loosely organized communities sprawled across like-minded groupings of dancers, musicians, artists, and created synergies that were fueled when members met, jammed and bonded at the old time festivals in Virginia and West Virginia, and elsewhere.[34]

In Alan Jabbour's words, in the 1960s Durham/Chapel Hill was probably the first major old time music revival scene:

> The Durham/Chapel Hill flowering was probably the core original college-town revival of old time instrumental tunes played in ensemble—certainly the key revival in the Southeast, to be quickly echoed by revivals in other towns. The New Lost City Ramblers were more a blend of bluegrass and old time Southeastern folk music, and they did more performance of song repertory than instrumental repertory, much of it from 78-rpm records. They might have influenced Tommy Thompson later (the 1970s) in shaping the Red Clay Ramblers, but they didn't influence either the repertory or the ensemble style of the Hollow Rock String Band.

Jabbour made the case that what shaped the Hollow Rock repertory and style was personal encounters with older rural musicians and jamming at fiddlers' conventions. The Fuzzy Mountain String Band was a second outgrowth of the Hollow Rock String Band revival. That band, Jabbour noted, included Bobbie Thompson as their anchor and they were all part of the original music scene in Durham/Chapel Hill: "Then Tommy and others organized the Red Clay Ramblers. All those revival scenes like Lexington followed yet later and were significantly influenced by us—though of course they may have had their own distinctive qualities as well." To Jabbour, these various communities were not "parallel cultural phenomena." The communities emerged, coalesced, and developed in a pattern reflecting the ripple effect influence exerted by the "Durham/Chapel Hill flowering." The entire repertoire of the Hollow Rock String Band was drawn from old time fiddlers who Jabbour recorded in North Carolina, Virginia and West Virginia. In his words: "neither the New Lost City Ramblers nor the later college-town revivals did what we did, but the later college-town revivals like Lexington (and there are many others) were greatly influenced by us."[35]

Lexington was a complex music scene with a lot of moving parts in the period during which Dwight traveled to Odell McGuire's home.[36] Gary Ruley, a guitar flatpicker who was born and raised in Lexington, Virginia, grew up surrounded by old time and bluegrass musical talent. Ruley provided a sense of how the Lexington music community consisted of a multiplicity of organized musical interests, including active performance-focused musicians and social/jam focused musicians, and the points at which the bluegrass and old time scenes converged. A good deal of the music in Lexington during the early 1970s was made by bands playing in public venues, and a lot of music was made in private homes. Those two "scenes" did not necessarily converge, though friendships between musicians were not constrained by these distinctions and the mixing of the two types of musicians created the basis for some cross-pollenization. Olin Bare, an old time musician from Lexington, Virginia, was a neighbor of Odell McGuire's. Bare played music with McGuire in the late 1960s and early 1970s, and attended the musical gatherings at Mata McGuire's home in the early 1970s. Bare's grandfather, William Henry Fix, played fiddle and banjo at dances in the Lexington area during from the 1930s through the 1950s. Bare stated that old time music and bluegrass crossed paths in Lexington, especially in Mata's home at the regular musical gatherings there. Bluegrass and old time musicians would "intermix socially" but they did not necessarily play music together; the two groups tended to gravitate to like-minded stylists. Bluegrass musicians found their ways to different rooms than the old time enthusiasts in the McGuire home during these gatherings.[37]

Many of the musicians in these old time communities were intent on making pilgrimages to the homes of the Appalachian Masters such as Tommy Jarrell and Wade Ward. The Lexington old time scene had the particular advantage of an iron core of members with profound links to "the Old People" who played this music, and a willingness and ability to broker introductions to such masters. Dwight brought the music of the Hammonses to the attention of Lexington musicians, sharing his library of field recordings, and took musicians from the Lexington area into Pocahontas County to meet with this family and share their company and their traditions.[38]

In a 1997 interview with Ken Perlman, Dwight described the fiddler's role in a local community in the 1940s and 1950s: The fiddler was seen as "an important part of the community that passed along tunes and kept track of tunes." He explained the obligation to keep track of tunes as knowing, and retaining the memory of "the right way" to play a tune. In Pocahontas County, from the late 1800s to World War II, Dwight said, there were "a lot of fiddlers around like Jack MacElwayne, who won the fiddle contest at the 1892 World's Fair in Chicago. He and Edn Hammons competed and argued with each other. But you had people like that who were ahold of the music and were keepin' things in order. Because even though they played it different, they was still holdin' on to the right ways."[39] In Lexington, Virginia, the long-running friendly arguments that Dwight described as the main form of sport in which he and Odell McGuire engaged focused on questions such as from whom to learn the old tunes, what to study, and how to shape the old tunes into contemporary repertoires. These discussions, as Dwight remembered them, seemed to have replicated the fiddler-centered process of developing memory-fueled "archives" of tunes and authoritative judgments about how they were to be played.

Debates over precisely such issues resonated deeply in old time communities in places such as Lexington, Virginia and Durham and Chapel Hill, North Carolina. The manner in which such debates were resolved, and the "models" for playing, teaching and learning music that emerged in an authoritative way, influenced the character and direction such communities took.[40] Brad Leftwich recalled:

> No question that Odell was the heart of the scene. He was a deep thinker, and had strong opinions. He came across as kind of a bear, but he had a very good heart and was very encouraging and nurturing of younger musicians. He would talk to anyone who would listen about his ideas and theories. Some people [...] would argue and advance their own ideas, others really just wanted to play music and party. I think I was more in the latter group, although I'm sure all of us were influenced in some degree by Odell's ideas. Some of the ideas were more about what characterized "good" old-time music and were more technical in nature–I remember Odell was always talking about the qualities of "bounce" and "drive" that he valued highly. Then there were more philosophical discussions about the deeper ethos of the music, and what distinguished it from, say, bluegrass. I remember one late-night discussion about romanticism and fatalism. [...] I sometimes thought the intellectual hair-splitting reached the point of absurdity, but we loved Odell for it anyway.[41]

Mark Campbell remembered McGuire as "a hard driving man of great enthusiasm." In mid–January 2015, Campbell said that McGuire was "a great shot in the arm and a great counterpoint to the academical approach." However, he recalled that McGuire had some very definite, inflexible views about what constituted old time Appalachian music. In Campbell's words:

> I recall vividly that he would jump all over us if we tried to play any "Irish" music. Sure, Armin [Barnett] was also a great Irish fiddler too, he and David Molk had won the Chicago fiddle and flute duet competition and won a trip to Ireland for the Traditional Championships. Odell's strict view to the south and [his tendency to downplay] Irish music shifted the music away from one of its base components, the Irish stylistic influences. Sure, there is more Irish influence on the northwest side of the Appalachians but it can be seen in some ways through the rest of the south also.[42]

Olin Bare recalled that McGuire being adamant about playing the old tunes the way they were intended to be, and remembered that McGuire would stop the music if someone was playing the banjo too hard and taking away from the fiddle. Bare reiterated what others had said: McGuire had very definite views about how the old time music should sound, and those views fit with the ideas of others in Lexington who were determined to see the local fiddle styles and dance music played the way they sounded in earlier times. Bare also recollected discussions between McGuire and Dwight on the distinctions between West Virginian tunes and the sound of old time music in Lexington from earlier decades. He remembered a sense shared by many of the musicians who showed up at the McGuire's home that both Virginia and West Virginia were bound in some ways by the way people who traveled regional rivers such as the Greenbrier and came to depend on them for commerce. The idea was that this manner in which such populations intersected might have established the basis for similar old tradition, commonalities in musical repertoire and tune preferences. He also remembered that there was another shared conventional wisdom in the Lexington old time community to the effect that different musical idioms emerged in these distinct areas. Bare stated that these distinctions between Lexington's old musical traditions and the archaic tunes of eastern central West Virginia were often at the center of the animated discussions that Dwight recalled.[43]

These discussions often revolved around the idea of "authenticity," and the question of whether one could play the old music without being a part of the culture. The notion of "insider" and outsider" was critical to these discussions, as was the idea of threshold levels of authenticity—how much time did a musician spend at the feet of an old practitioner of the archaic music, how many visits to the fertile crescent of old time music were required before a young musician established credibility as a student of the old way of playing the old tunes. There were fervent discussions of whether musical talent from outside the communities of Appalachia could learn the music and play the tunes in a fashion that did justice to the archaic traditions.[44] Bob Carlin stated that discussions in

Lexington and other such old time communities posed this question: could one play the music if one was not part of the culture, and at what point does one become part of the culture by playing the music? Who was authentic and who could pass judgment on authenticity?[45] Bluegrass musician Gary Ruley, a long time Lexington resident, stated that the Old time scene did sometimes blend with bluegrass in Lexington at least in part as the result of long-lived friendships. At the same time, Ruley averred, there were many old time musicians in Lexington who were serious about their music and wanted to keep it separate and distinct from bluegrass, and on a "separate track" aimed at establishing the "authenticity" of their old music. Ruley also described the emergence of an "insider/outsider" split, and abiding disagreements regarding the nature and character of local music versus music that emerged from external influences:

> I know there was a misconception of the roots of this music. My Dad gave me a good background as to just that—at least here [in Lexington] and in his lifetime, being born here in 1915 and living and performing his whole life with a musical family of seven brothers and five sisters; his mother and dad both played here his entire life. We often talked about a lot of outside influences that infiltrated our town as well as the whole region with their ideas and what they wanted to put forth—which in our opinion wasn't a true reflection of roots music here so much as [it was a reflection of what ...] they had studied and brought here [to Lexington] claiming that was the authentic way to play certain tunes.

Olin Bare made the case that in Lexington the music was influenced by older players. Locals tended to be protective of the elders and tried to learn their sound. Some musicians drawn to the area by, for example, the friendships formed at festivals brought different influences with them, played different styles, and often emulated the music of other locations, a fact that brought old time music from North Carolina and other places to Lexington. Lexington fiddlers tended to play straight out of standard tuning. The cross tunings that were favored by Tommy Jarrell and some West Virginia players were not learned as avidly as the locally preferred approach to fiddle music, but were clearly introduced by people who gravitated to Lexington's growing and active old time jam opportunities and social gatherings.[46]

Authenticity was clearly one of the salient issues in the ongoing discussions within the Lexington Old Time music community in the early 1970s.[47] There were subtleties observed in framing these discussions in the Lexington Old Time community, and much of this took place in a good natured way; people remembered these dialogues taking place in a party atmosphere, and people recalled that the community had several "sages" who occupied themselves with arm wrestling about these intellectual constructs—while most of the musicians simply preferred to play music animatedly. Bob Carlin remembered a certain amount of boisterous and sometimes inebriated though basically friendly arguments on behalf of one approach or another. Brad Leftwich stated:

> I don't think anyone in Lexington at the time was using words like "revivalist" or "tradition bearer" or "carrier"—and personally I think too many people have used those highly charged, judgmental words carelessly, as a way to bludgeon others and advance themselves, without ever bothering to carefully define them[....] According to strict usage in the field of anthropology or folklore where those terms come from, pretty nearly everyone playing music today, including Dwight, would be revivalists. Honestly, I don't remember that dichotomy ever entering the discussion until some years after I moved away from Lexington. The dichotomies I remember being discussed had more to do with [...] the approach to the music epitomized by two of the noted bands of the time, Highwoods Stringband and the Fuzzy Mountain Stringband[...], the "good time music" and "tune museum" approaches. Kind of a "spirit of the law"/"letter of the law" dichotomy[...]. The Lexington scene was definitely more aligned with the former than the latter, although I think people like Odell and Dwight felt like there were deeper issues.[48]

These discussions had a considerable influence on Dwight's thinking about playing the old tunes, and his own views shaped discussion within the community about these musical issues. Dwight remembered the long-running discussion with McGuire about the character of the archaic music and its practitioners, and the forceful way he propounded his views as to how to best preserve and learn and teach this musical tradition, as a central element in the gatherings that took place in McGuire's home. Brad Leftwich recalled that both McGuire and Dwight looked more towards West Virginian music and thought of that tradition as being somehow more pure than other local and regional old time musical traditions, though they may not have used that term to describe what it was they were thinking at the time. McGuire was dismissive of North Carolina fiddler and banjo picker Tommy Jarrell; Leftwich recalled McGuire professing respect and admiration for Jarrell, but harboring the feeling that Jarrell never had much to teach about music.[49] While Dwight developed a deep respect for Jarrell's fiddle playing, and in later years spoke of his music with an almost reverent touch, he did not think much of Jarrell's banjo playing.[50] Leftwich stated that Dwight was, "as one would expect someone from West Virginia to be, especially interested in West Virginia music as well. His personal experience with the Hammonses was especially powerful for him, and he wanted to share it with anyone he could get to listen." The sense of exclusivity about West Virginian music took on "an almost moral dimension" to the point of precluding continued discussion.[51] James Leva made clear that throughout their relationship, from the early 1970s until just before McGuire passed away in 2008, Dwight and McGuire were closely attentive to questions about how the "Old People's" music could be kept alive in the modern world. They discussed, heatedly and amicably, the impact of the fact that people no longer grew up the way Hammonses did, and wondered about how that re-shaped traditions such as music. They looked closely at the question of whether the old music was still the same music if people from outside the area of the music's origin began learning and playing it.[52]

By the mid–1970's, however, Dwight became increasingly uncomfortable with the way things were going in Lexington and began distancing himself from that old time scene. Dwight explained that he had come to feel ill at ease with some of the musicians who were less inclined to look at the old music as he did, and more inclined to play music that was popular instead of the old music that tugged at Dwight's heart.[53] Also, Dwight had begun to see a change in behavior within the old time community that involved more alcohol and other distractions, all of which contributed to his disillusionment with the old time music community.[54] Finally, the archaic musical forms to which Dwight was intensely committed began to be sidelined in favor of newer ways of playing the old music. Bill Hicks made the case that Dwight, Alan Jabbour, the Fuzzy Mountain String Band, the Highwoods Band, and his own Red Clay Ramblers, and other players interested in the mountain traditional music in the late 1960s and early 1970s "helped to 'create' the larger 'old time scene' exhibited at festivals like Clifftop today."[55] However, Hicks noted that as "more and more folks learned the tunes and created bands and such, the question of playing them in a 'sourced' way receded." This was probably the point in time–1975 or 1976–that Dwight had in mind when he told Ken Perlman, in 1997, that the "Lexington scene had changed so much and I realized they were playing music that wasn't my heart music. It was (just) music that was popular around."[56] To Dwight, probably around 1974 and 1975, the original musical intent and focus of the old time community in Lexington, Virginia, was diverted to a broader focus that took attention away from the commitment to the archaic mountain music. Reflecting back on the point in the mid–1970's, Dwight stated: "Once you go across a line with this music [...] there is no way back. That place has broken, snapped like a glass rod. Shattered like the finest crystal." Dwight believed that once the community of musicians in Lexington widened somewhat, once bands from outside the area began spending more time in Lexington at the invitation of Odell McGuire, and after McGuire himself turned more to alcohol, the tone, character and focus of the old time scene changed in a drastic manner.[57]

Black Mountain Bluegrass Years

In 1971 Dwight joined with the local Black Mountain Bluegrass Boys as their bass player and made music with them until 1977. They became known as "one of the greatest of the unknown bluegrass bands." Dwight played bass, fiddle and some clawhammer banjo with them, and apparently exerted important influence on the tunes they played and the band's configuration, and had an authoritative role in shaping the band's tune list.[58] He asked Dick Kimmel to join the band. Kimmel played the mandolin for the Black Mountain Bluegrass Boys, filling the slot left when Dude Irvine left the band.[59] The addition of Kimmel, Dwight said, strengthened the band's old time credentials by adding another banjo player to the mix.

Dwight played with the band during their tours of coffee houses and colleges in the northeast in the mid- 1970s, hitting venues in Pennsylvania, New Jersey and New York. As Richard Hefner explained:

> We went to New York City and auditioned and there was all kinds of people there. There were magicians and acrobats and country music and everything else. One of the agents picked us up so they put us on the coffee house circuit. So, we got to playing colleges up there on the northeast and we'd leave and stay gone for two or three weeks at a time. We'd go up and maybe played in Pennsylvania, and New Jersey, up through New York and back around and stay home for maybe three days. We'd load up and play different places. So, we did that for–I don't know how long—maybe a year and a half. It finally got to be pretty hard. [...] It was fun. I wouldn't do it again at all, but I wouldn't trade it for nothin'.[60]

Dwight believed that he never quite had what it would take to play good bluegrass, and never felt very comfortable or accepted in bluegrass festival circles. "Bluegrassers are born, not made," he maintained. Dwight recalled his alliance with these musicians, emphatically stating that these men were "real 'bluegrassers' which is separate breed unto themselves." Dwight was allowed to separate from the band in 1977; as Dwight put it: "So they did me a great old big favor [by] firing me in 1977 even though they still have not told me."[61]

Dick Kimmel recalled that Dwight visited Kimmel's Morgantown, West Virginia, home often in the 1970s, during his years with the Black Mountain Bluegrass Boys. He would sit on the porch of Kimmel's log cabin in the woods and talk about old time music. "He had people in awe, listening to how he played," Kimmel recalled. Dwight had a "spark, in terms of his enthusiasm, and how he approached [old time music], like a scholar," learning multiple versions of tunes, studying provenance, knowing the history. He also had a lot of "rules" about how old time music should be played, and he was careful about playing in the lane defined by these rules. Kimmel stated that Dwight was very much aware of the way his old time touch sounded in the context of the music of the Black Mountain Bluegrass Boys, and was very deliberate in making strategic choices about his role in that band. During the band's first gig in New York City, at the Bitter End, Dwight played the fiddle, and Kimmel the banjo, but Dwight "did not like the way it came across, and he went back to the banjo." Dwight was also very aware of the tensions between what bluegrass musicians did and the old time music way, the differences between ensemble playing and the bluegrass approach—giving each instrument a turn at the tune. Kimmel recalled that Dwight stuck to these rules, and imposed them on his playing, and deployed them during his time with the Black Mountain Bluegrass Boys. Kimmel added, "After a number of years I've come to the conclusion that he's right." Kimmel also remembered

Dwight played bass for the Black Mountain Bluegrass Boys from 1971 to 1977. This photograph was taken by Laurie Cameron of Hillsboro, West Virginia, in the early 1970s on the stairs of the old schoolhouse in Cass, West Virginia. From left, Richard Hefner, Bill Hefner, "Dude" Irvine, Harley Carpenter, and Dwight Diller. Of Dwight's bass, Hefner said: "That bass was in rough shape, but it worked. It was a flat back German bass. I can't remember where Dwight got it or where it is now. It had a flat piece of metal from the heel to the back of the peg head to keep the neck on. It was called a 'rollbar.' The hole in front made it easy to set the soundpost. We would often try to coax the dog out of the hole, since it was a doghouse bass" (courtesy of Richard Hefner).

Dwight as an excellent bass player, and an actually nice bluegrass tenor singer—recalling that while he did not sing much on stage with the band, he certainly did sing in the car. "His genetic code had him liking Old Time better than bluegrass," Kimmel reflected, "but he loved that bluegrass sound."[62]

Two Years Before the Mast: Playing with the Morris Brothers

During the summers of 1972 and 1973, Dwight played with the Morris Brothers Band. From Dwight's perspective, the band, spearheaded by Dave and John Morris, made crossover music. They did not necessarily play bluegrass, but they played bluegrass songs. They were billed as an old time band, but they had musicians who could carry the tunes in either direction, toward bluegrass in the old and early style, or toward old time.[63] The Morris Brothers organized old time music festivals at their home in Ivydale, West Virginia during 1969–1973.[64] In 1972 and 1973, the two brothers organized old time music festivals—twice in Virginia, North Carolina and West Virginia and once in Kentucky—with support from a Rockefeller Foundation grant; Dwight took primary responsibility for setting up the event in Kentucky. Wayne Howard recalled attending Ivydale in 1970 and 1971:

Ivydale was small, as these festivals go, but I think there were as many as 2,000 people there. It featured contests, [...] and three days or so of camping, and one year there had been a hard rain during the night and the place was a mess. [...] The Morris Brothers had hired several musicians to perform apart from the contests. Jenes Cottrell was one. [...] I remember him performing a great version of "The Three Nights' Experience," in which he had an extra night that concluded with "a John B. Stetson chamber pot I never did see before." He had a homemade, foot-treadle powered lathe set up in the vendor area, on which we could watch him turn heads and handles for little wooden mallets [that] he was trying to sell. Nimrod Workman came there from Eastern Kentucky, but at the time I thought he was a West Virginian. He was strictly a singer—no instruments. He worked as a coal miner and performed mining songs, union songs, and the like. John Jackson was a black singer and guitarist from Rockingham County, Va.—not exactly a blues singer, but more what they call a songster, with a varied repertory. He was fairly young then—in his thirties, I guess—and I remember noticing how powerful his arms were when he sang "John Henry." He really looked the part. I don't remember anything else he did at Ivydale, but I met him, about ten years ago, a couple of years before he died. He performed a benefit concert at Warrenton, Virginia. [...] I asked him if he was the man I had heard at Ivydale, and the way he put it was, "Yes, I used to work for the Morris Brothers," so he must have been at other festivals they promoted. He had gained considerable fame by that time, and I later learned that he had worked for years as a gravedigger, which explains the muscles. In Warrenton, he played not only guitar but a beautiful Whyte Laydie [banjo], and the songs he did were mostly Hank Williams and other country western numbers.[65]

Dwight's time with the Morris Brothers was a most important part of his musical life: "With them I found my music." In his words:

You can go anywhere in the world and any time in the world to find any group that say they are an "Old Time Music Band" and I will put them up against what the Morris Brothers were doing back in those days. They all pale in comparison. When I went with them in June 1972 I could hardly play much of anything. Listen to where I was in September of 1973. I have never ever played any better in my life and had only been with them a total of about seven months.[66]

With Dave and John Morris running the band, organizing a showcase musical festival in West Virginia at their Clay County home place, and helping to found the Vandalia Gathering, what emerged was a musical powerhouse, an influential old time force—and a concentration of considerable musical talent.[67] Over five decades later, Dwight still summoned the enthusiasm to describe the richness of the experience, the personal bond he formed with the two brothers, and the special context they filled in his life:

> John and Dave Morris [...] were powerhouses. Incredible.
>
> [...] We were all in our late 20s. John and I are two weeks apart in age. We are still brothers. I am right sure that the main thing we had in common was a Central West Virginia "Way." The Hammons welcomed me in in 1969 and because of my background locally, I fit in as family so much they basically adopted me as grandson. But the Morris Brothers, Glen Smith, Lee Triplett fed coal to my boiler and turned the heat up. It's still there. I just have to try to do it at a far different pace [now, after] these many years.[68]

David Morris (guitar) and John Morris (fiddle) with Dwight, during a visit to a banjo retreat conducted in Cass, West Virginia, in 2002 (courtesy Dwight Diller).

However, whatever it might have been musically, the band was an agglomeration of troubled people, and Dwight ventured into their embrace with his own baggage, his own cocktail of ailments:

> There were four of us in the Morris Brothers Band. All four were in your face with the music and off stage also. There are three now. [...] One [had a] really harsh time with bipolar disease, and he killed himself by jumping off [an] interstate bridge in front of a tractor trailer. He never drew a happy breath. Neither did the rest of us. Not a happy breath. Lot of laughter but it was not really happy.[69]

They played in some tough places, for rough audiences. In Dwight's words:

> 9 September 1973 was approximately the date when the Morris Brothers 45 rpm [record featuring the tunes] "Hog Eyed Man" and "Angeline" [...] was recorded in Charleston, West Virginia, [and] when put on a juke box in a beer joint, "Hog Eyed Man" would be played over and over. However, it would have to

be removed before long because fights would break out. We thought that would only happen in West Virginia. About ten years ago, a man stopped in restaurant at nearby snowshoe ski resort. Friends of mine were playing banjo and fiddle there. The man shouted "Can you play 'Hog Eyed Man'?" Of course no one can play the Morris Brothers version. But they made an attempt. The man said "I'm from Jacksonville and that song was on the juke box down there. I remember it because they finally had to take it off. It kept starting fights all the time."[70]

Probably during this period, Dwight began to develop a bunch of eccentric musical habits and practices that were part of his increasingly erratic, dark and depressed dimension. Dwight put it this way:

> I can play in front of 500 who are there to hear people present this old music. The numbers do not bother me. But I have always resisted playing the music as background but had to do it to provide for my family. Have managed to almost never play for a square dance. My music is too important to me [...] to let a square dance round the edges off. [...] I do not like applause. Applause breaks up what is going on and keeps the people from having to face things that can give them relief inside. But it is too scary for most people, especially in an audience of much over 30 if they are there to let music do anything more than surface entertainment. That is OK if that is what they want.[71]

He did all he could to avoid being photographed with a banjo in hand.[72] Over time, he became increasingly uncomfortable playing music to an audience, and struggled to find ways to compel himself to take the stage.[73]

Shaping a Banjo Style

Some examples of Dwight's banjo playing during this early period have survived in personal libraries of old time music enthusiasts who attended the festivals at places such as Independence and Hillsville, Virginia, in the early 1970s, and captured some of the contests and jams on personal recording devices.

- The fiddler Kilby Spencer had in his own audio library recordings of the contests staged at the 4th Annual Old Time Fiddlers and Bluegrass Convention in Hillsville, Virginia, in June 1970.[74] Dwight competed in the banjo contest, and played two tunes, "Old Folks Comin' Down the Road" and "Soldier's Joy."[75] At a later point in the audio tape, Dwight plays "Sixteen Horses Was My Team" though the tune that comes out of his banjo is identical to what he had, earlier on the tape, identified as "Old Folks Comin' Down the Road."[76]
- William Talley of West Chester, Pennsylvania, tapped his memory and his audio library to come up with absolutely essential recordings of Dwight playing at the event dubbed the "Alternative Galax," hosted by the fiddler Armin Barnett in Charlottesville, Virginia, in 1972. The event took place at a farm that Barnett was renting, and was attended by Dwight, Barnett, Carl Baron, Len Reiss, Bob Thren, Odell McGuire, and possibly Mark Campbell, according to Talley. Members of the Fuzzy Mountain String Band were there, too, but they mostly stayed at the house while a clutch of other musicians including Dwight and Barnett played up on a hill.[77] A total of 26 of the tunes played by Barnett and Dwight were recorded.[78]
- On 11 July 1975, Dwight joined Mike Seeger on the steps of the Pocahontas County Courthouse in Marlinton for a workshop that featured the music of Lee, Burl, Sherman and Maggie Hammons. Wayne Howard recorded all the Hammons musi-

cians playing or singing—at times solo, at times joined by either Seeger or Dwight, the music interspersed with discussion of the tunes and stories. On at least one tune ("Jimmy Sutton") Seeger fiddled and Dwight played banjo.[79]

According to musicians who knew him during the 1970s, Dwight's banjo playing was loud, brash, and favored a "frailing" type Grandpa Jones inspired style in the start-up period. As one West Virginian musician put it, he was "crashy" during "The Early Playing Days." He dominated jams, but he was progressing, evolving, and experimenting with his banjo sound. His solo playing at contests in the early 1970s, for example, tended to be rather fast, far faster than his banjo playing from the mid–1980s through the early 2000s. As Dwight later said of his own playing during his "start up" period of learning, the basics of clawhammer remained too hard for him to learn alone and by ear. Attempting to figure it out by ear yielded an approach that resembled Pete Seeger's sound. By the end of 1969, Dwight had untangled the clawhammer equation, and by mid–1970 he had managed to figure out the rhythm necessary to drive and sustain this particular old time music. After traveling to his first festival in Hillsville, Virginia, the summer of 1970, and "catching the judge's ears" with his fast paced, percussive playing, speed and volume appear to have become the essential characteristics of his banjo playing, perhaps for this first year.[80] Interestingly, as Dan Levenson recalled, many old time musicians during the 1970s tended to play fast.[81] By the time his musical career was well under way, certainly by the early 1980s, Dwight had come to believe that much of the music played at festivals was far too fast.[82] He thought the same way about square dances: "I don't want anything to do with square dances because the music is too important to take to a square dance and have it destroyed. Square dances make you cut the edges off the music." Square dances, Dwight argued, put a primacy on speed, and the music played there required technical proficiency and fast paced playing. He would frequently tell a story of about Lee Hammons' square dance playing days to underscore what prompted him to take the view that slowing down the music represented the way it was played much earlier, by the older practitioners:

> Lee Hammons would have been playing [fiddle at square dances] around 1900; that's about the only time I've heard it told that Hammonses—in this case, Lee and his sister—played at a dance. These would have been dances staged out of cabins, [modest] homes where they'd clear the room of furniture [to make dancing space.] Lee would say, [years later], that the music was all about the pace of the tune "Walking in the Parlor," [meaning that] it wasn't about aerobics. It was about social relations, [with a music that was played so] people could dance quietly. It wasn't "barn dancing." That came later. And it was people traveling miles by foot at the end of the work day, arriving tired, setting up for the dance. Lee would walk from Greenbrier to Nicholas County, through mountain woods, play all night, go back home and go to work the next day.[83]

These were small social circles that developed such dancing events in socially intimate ways to the point that one generation would imitate the dance steps of their elders, and name these steps after the originator, such as the "Lizzy Wohl Back Step," a geographically specific small town reference that remained a very local way of remembering elders who attended such dances. Those relationships set the pace, though later moonshine and store bought liquor would lubricate things, alter the pace of the music and change the nature of the social interaction in a manner that prompted Lee Hammons, in the early years of the 20th century, to quit playing at such square dances.[84]

What was most notable about Dwight's playing in this early period was the extent to which the central features of his banjo work emerged and became the bedrock on which he developed playing in the later periods. Beyond a growing sense of the need to modulate the speed that began to emerge in the latter part of this first developmental period, Dwight began to think more systematically about the mechanics necessary to produce the sound he wanted. Dwight's playing style in later years, especially the 1990s and 2000s, has been characterized as sparse, cleanly paced, a combination of rhythm and melody that captures tunes simply and accurately, without sacrificing the intricacies that make the old music interesting. Those same characterizations applied to the style and technique that was emerging in the first development stage, in the 1970s. His playing technique came to be centered on a rhythmic right hand approach to striking the strings and the head, achieving a consistent syncopated percussiveness.[85] That is, Dwight's playing came to be driven by an efficient right hand that snapped onto the strings in the downward arc, and a thumb that drove behind the fifth string on every downstroke in a fashion that was often described as double thumbing; though constant, the thumb string was not always audible—meaning that his playing did not produce an often dissonant fifth string ring. Dwight occasionally deployed a brushstroke that became a "chuck" on the first and second strings. The rhythmic pattern, the clawhammer cycle so to speak, sometimes omitted repeated notes or played them almost inaudibly, and achieved the pronounced syncopation by the "slight prolongation of the first and third beats of a four beat measure."[86] His recipe for this rhythmic clawhammer playing remained essentially stable, though he has not been inflexible about accommodating to aging limbs and finding new ways of articulating how to get at the rhythmic character of his playing style.[87]

Wrestling with the Fiddle

Dwight's forty year-long attempt to master the fiddle began in 1970. During the summer of that year, Edn Hammons' son James, who was born about 1904, took Dwight to his sister's house on Stamping Creek, at the junction of Route 39 West and Route 55 West, and for about twenty dollars Dwight purchased a fiddle, a bow and case.[88] During late 2014 and mid–2015, Dwight frequently said that though he chose the banjo in 1969 or 1970, and was not at all taken with old time fiddle music at that time, what he came to understand was that he really wanted to play the fiddle.[89] However, as Dwight told the story, he engaged in a long wrestling match with the fiddle before he was able to get his playing where he wanted it to be, how he wanted it to sound:

> I could never learn to get the rhythm right. [...] People would often say "Don't play the fiddle; I wish you wouldn't play the fiddle; you are never going to learn to play the fiddle; please play the banjo, please don't play the fiddle." Whatever the words were, that was the message that I got all those years. Sherman Hammons, around the time he was on his death bed in 1988, someone said "Sherman, do you think Dwight will ever learn to play the fiddle?" [Sherman answered] "Well, sir, I don't think he ever will." Even yet, I will not get my fiddle out around my peers in West Virginia. [...] Over the years, have not attempted the fiddle out and about except if there was a concert, I will pull it out for a tune or two. And so it has gone on and on and on and on and on for four decades and a half.[90]

That is how Dwight told the story. Others told a far different story. Dave Bing, for example, a fine fiddler himself, said that after a decent interval of playing hard on the fiddle, Dwight was able to take his playing to a place that sounded remarkably like the old style playing of the central West Virginian fiddlers whose fiddling Dwight held as his measure. Sherman Hammons' distant cousin, Ralph Roberts, born in 1929, the last fiddler in the Hammons family line, told Dwight in several instances in 2014 that Dwight had

Ralph Roberts, a cousin to Sherman, Burl, and Maggie Hammons, in his home in Frametown, West Virginia, in July 2015. Roberts, a well-known fiddle player and a longtime friend of Dwight's, plays an old style of two finger banjo picking and has been learning clawhammer style banjo for the last few years (courtesy Andrew Fults).

"the old sound."[91] He described Dwight's fiddling as consisting of a good amount of "up bowing," the style in which the Sherman and Burl Hammons played.[92] While that might have given Dwight a boost, it did not diminish his tendency to be very hard on his own fiddling.

In early November 2014, Dwight went to an old fiddlers reunion in Elkins, West Virginia, about 75 miles from his home in Pocahontas County. He was, as he put it, actually able to take his fiddle on stage and play really well. That gathering was "the first time I have ever been a fiddler." After four decades, Dwight was prepared to acknowledge that he had gotten closer to the old time fiddle sound:

> So it was Ralph who broke the curse by his words to me. And they were from someone who does not say such stuff and someone who grew up in these mountains that when the Great Depression hit[....] Ralph said the family would gather up and go over to his grandfather's house every Sunday and play the fiddle all day. Consequently, if Ralph said it that way, then it took me to the edge. Then with a couple hours of help here and there, I found that I was already close to what I needed. Just needed some pointers in a few places.[93]

For all those years, Dwight looked hard at his fiddling, casting around for explanations of why he just could not, in his view, bring it to a point where it was recognizably musical to him. Periodically, he would opine that it was essentially just too hard to play two stringed instruments well, or that learning to do two different things on a stringed instrument—bowing on the fiddle, up picking or down picking on the banjo—was just too difficult. Though it may have been true that fiddle and banjo were "apples and oranges," radically different instruments, there were probably a sufficient number of commonalities between banjo and fiddle music in the context of eastern central West Virginian old time music. The rhythmic core of the music on both fiddle and banjo, or the percussive character of bowing and the power necessary to capture the propulsive way of playing fiddle were probably close enough to make elements of banjoing accessible to fiddlers and fiddling possible for banjo players. Certainly by the first years of the 1990s, after a 20-year long apprenticeship, Dwight was making very credible fiddle music, in spite of his protestations to the contrary.

The fiddle, more than anything else, captured the archaic character of the old time music for Dwight who felt that real old traditional mountain fiddling was a holdover from the 18th and early 19th century frontier. The fiddle music of central and southern West Virginia, parts of Kentucky and southwest Virginia seemed to leave a wake of emotion and a residue of the hardships that captured the essence of life in the mountains. As Dwight told it, the fiddle, more than the banjo, injected the realities of life, and especially of death, into the mix. That is, the music reflected the edge to which people were pushed by circumstances, by physical challenges and emotional turmoil. Some of this derived from the precariousness of life in the unsettled mountain range wilderness of the area. Some of it derived from the way hardship weighed on and shaped individual lives, with some doing better than others to bear up.[94] Phyllis, Nimrod Workman's daughter, was from the same West Virginia coal fields as Hazel Dickens. The Hammonses from Kentucky played and sang much the same way. Kenny Baker's father, Thaddeus Baker, was also from Kentucky. Ward Jarvis was a woodhick in the mountains of Pocahontas county. The music that came from all of these people "reached into the depths," in Dwight's words. It had a common core, a rhythmic dynamic that was passed down as much as any genetic material from one generation to the next. Dwight could fit his banjo playing to any of the old West Virginian fiddle music because it was the exact same rhythm that he played on the banjo.

The old music brought him in contact with the physical, mental and spiritual stress the mountain environment imposed on the settlers, and continued to impose on those who elected to live in his part of the country—and probably, more widely, the entire state of West Virginia—though in more recent times the stress and strain were as much political and economic as it was personal, physical and emotional.[95] Dwight delighted in saying that the "Old People" from whom he learned this West Virginia and Kentucky music had a great deal in common with house cats: "They were/are never totally domesticated. And the music from them is semi-domesticated which still retains much of the mid–18th century American Frontier. It still carries a quality that is so alien as to be only picked up in teensy-tiny crannies." He saw learning this archaic music to which he was devoted as a lifelong process, a heritage that was bequeathed along with the rhythmic realities of all aspects of mountain life.

Dwight, however, saw a long, slow process of diminishing interest in the old music as it was edged out by commercial alternatives. He saw the impact of natural selection on the music as the old fiddlers died out, before they had a chance to teach a cadre of younger fiddle players. And he saw the simple, rock bottom rhythmic form being replaced by a music cluttered with notes, melody, and distractions. The music was in a receding phase, Dwight believed. It was dying out, being replaced by a music that overpowered the rhythm with tricky notes, fancy phrases, licks and embellishments. That was not to say it was "bad" because it was new. It was to say it was not a true and real reflection of the character of antique West Virginian music. It neglected the part of the music that had resonated for so long in the spirit of the central West Virginians who passed the music down to people like Dwight.[96]

Dwight recalled that Burl Hammons could hear a fiddle tune one time and within moments it was "his tune" but, according to Dwight, Burl was not careful with that gift. He did not "protect" it. He was born in the first years of the 20th century in wilderness, "pure wilderness" as Dwight described it, and 20 or 25 years later, he "could hear a tune one time on the Grand Ole Opry and know it. But what was happening? He was losing the Frontier." Dwight's point was that Burl "crossed that border" from the Frontier state into the world of commercial music, and commercialized music "castrated" the old music. Lee Hammons said essentially the same thing about Edn Hammons.[97] Dwight "finally realized Edn had to compete with that bunch from Kanawha valley," including the blind fiddler Ed Haley, and that in order to win contests, and win the money that was essentially his only source of income, he had to move further and further away from central West Virginian fiddling.[98]

Dwight's point was that there was no real guardianship for this music, and that the institutions that had sprung up beginning in the 1950s with the presumed responsibility for fostering and preserving the old tunes ended up "festivalizing" the music, finding the least common denominator and, by making it popular, stripping the character and key elements of its archaic form from the music. Dwight felt musicians were losing touch with the "cultural message" that this music transmitted, perhaps not through the most obvious and flagrant ways this might happen—by casually profiting from the music—but by collecting, freeze framing the music, using all manner of innovative recording devices, they were to Dwight sapping the music of its connection to its context. By playing it on performance stages, or capturing it in published collections, the music was being "pasturized" and losing its connection to its distant past. His key point was that any effort to capture and pin these tunes down could ultimately round off the corners, make presumptions about what the music should sound like, and thus have a deleterious impact on this fragile art form. Just by virtue of the commitment to making these tunes widely available, and easily replicated—through the composition of tablature and notational collections of these tunes—the process ended up altering the old music, especially fiddling, its most brittle form.

The challenge Dwight confronted was finding young people who had the "stuff" that could bring this music out—the spirit, the capability, the drive, and the commitment to learn the old music.[99]

Becoming a Musician

To some extent, old time music communities in the early 1970s and through at least the early 1980s seemed to select their repertoires based on the inspiration drawn from old time musicians who were held out as examples of what the old time music sounded like, and/or effective and talented contemporary interpreters of old music who played versions of tunes that were taken from recordings or learned directly from old people who played in what was presumed to be the old way.

In considering local repertoire choices, Dwight thought about the manner in which various, sometimes competing traditions of music emerged in local communities, and became the predominant music that people, especially younger people, wanted to learn. He appeared to look at his own experience as a clearer, simpler example of how people come to embrace a music, and saw his own experience far more useful as a way of looking at this than taking the festivals themselves as the basis for how old time music and old time musicians emerged, developed and evolved. Dwight heard several different kinds of music growing up, including commercially recorded music and local traditional music. Young people in his area, born in or around the mid–1940s, would have begun to witness what Dwight viewed as the withering away of old musical traditions that were giving way to what radio and phonograph records were making popular.[100] Old musicians, such as Burl Hammons, would have begun integrating new and popular recorded tunes into their playing repertoire. Rather than attempting to discern the origins of old time music, Dwight appeared to have concluded that focusing on untangling the strands of influence, the manner in which traditions converged, was a more effective course of action. He talked about this in 1983:

> We didn't come out of this tradition. In the old time music tradition the sons came out and went into bluegrass. Tommy Jarrell and Ben. Sherman Hammons' son Roy will listen to country but sure won't listen to old time. Took college kids, pseudo intellectuals, to pick the tradition back up. Since it wasn't our native tongue we didn't understand it because we didn't grow up with it. We were searching with it. The New Lost City Ramblers were imitating it. Alan Jabbour and the Hollow Rock String Band played it hard and fast but it still had that something that wasn't in there. [Local bands] played good music but to me the early stuff wasn't old music. They were imitating older people but they were afraid to go ahead and let loose and really put it out.[101]

Dwight saw communities of musicians with which he was familiar in West Virginia, the community he came to know closely in Lexington, Virginia, and those he became familiar with at old time festivals in the early 1970s as being divided into three groups:

- Those that embraced *imitated* old music taken from recorded sources (such as the tunes studied and played by the New Lost City Ramblers),
- Those that closely studied the field recordings of old time music makers and the recordings and live playing of contemporary bands (such as the Hollow Rock String Band) that produced music based on a variety of sources. This group would laboriously study the old tunes played by such groups at festivals and concerts and by this method they *replicated* old sounds, and
- Those that were *inclined to push the envelope* beyond the inspiration, based on their own sense of what old musicians offered up and based also on what it took to capture the intensity, the creativeness, and the internal energy of old music in a way that got at the essence of the music without sacrificing the creative urge to notions of authenticity.

Jack Bernhardt, a music critic and commentator, made the case in his 1983 interview with Dwight that so much of this music, at least in the form it took on the East Coast, derived from single source inspirations. He dated a lot of this from the mid–1960s and pointed to local old time music parties in places like Chapel Hill, North Carolina, as the birthing place for contemporary old time music. In Bernhardt's words:

> Alan Jabbour provided the model. Alan provided the tapes, and Alan introduced these people to old time music in a wide variety of settings because he was doing these field recordings for his master's thesis. He'd come back with tapes and Hollow Rock String Band people would sit down and listen to them and work on them and they were all very dedicated to try to get the music proper. Alan was the trained musician and he had the ear and he may not have understood entirely what was going on in the music but he had the ear and could provide guidance. He may not have understood the language completely but he knew enough of what was going on to provide guidance. Everybody involved moved through Alan's influence. So it's not surprising when the Fuzzy Mountain [String] band got together. Bobbie Thompson [...] and Bill Hicks [...] would sit down [...] and would go over and over tunes until Bill got it right according to what Bobbie thought to be correct which came out of her experience of Alan and Hollow Rock in terms of his experience and standard of correctness and authenticity.[102]

Dwight remained concerned with what he felt was sacrificed by exclusively imitative approaches to the music. He felt that the old time music played in Chapel Hill was "very, very studied and very precise," and that it lacked the "guts" displayed in the fiddle music of Tommy Jarrell and the banjo playing of Fred Cockerham. He thought the exclusively "studied" way of getting at the old tunes, which he felt was the way preferred by Mike Seeger and the New Lost City Ramblers, was improved upon by the way the Hollow Rock String Band went about getting at the old tunes, but he still felt this was "learning the tunes in a studied way."[103] Dwight was clearly a strong proponent of learning the old music from the Old People, and at times spoke ardently in favor of this approach over others, essentially dismissing more scholastic approaches to the archaic music that emerged as the favored way of thinking about and studying old tunes in old time communities across the country. He did not allow for the possibility that a close and analytical approach to recreating the music was relevant in circumstances such as those that characterized the work that Alan Jabbour did on Henry Reed's music. As Bill Hicks explained, when Dwight found the Hammonses, their music did not need to be rescued from oblivion. They were still able players when Dwight met them. As Hicks explained, Jabbour studied Henry Reed when the fiddler was already advanced in age:

> Henry Reed was quite weak and infirm for some of that time, and certainly was not the player he had been when he was legendary in his locale, back in the '40s and further back even. Alan attended closely to Henry Reed's playing, applied his own musical ear and abilities to what he was hearing, and reconstructed Henry Reed's tunes. This is a feat of some proportion. In some cases [such as the tune] "Mony Musk," Alan put the tune back together from various parts heard at various different sessions. [...] He's said, many times, that he felt he was rescuing specific tunes[...], that with Reed's repertoire he'd found the last grain in the hour glass and captured it as best he could, and revived that body of music, turned the glass back over.[104]

At the same time, Dwight was thinking a great deal about his own development as a musician, his own relationship with his native West Virginian music, and the trajectory it might describe for him. Dwight spent an intensive two to three years with the Hammons family, but it was not all about the music. He was living with them, immersed in their lives, and thinking intensively about what they believed, what they thought, what they remembered of their pasts and how they managed issues and problems. He was playing music in this context, and thinking about all of this in a focused way:

> So even though I wasn't a very good musician I had spent a lot of time thinking about it, I had spent a lot of time with those people. And I was getting the big picture according to the Hammons. Whether I knew it or not or they knew it or not it's a whole different thing than it is to live in Chapel Hill and run up to see Tommy Jarrell once a month. It's out there. It's a whole different thing. I was broke. They were broke. I was getting saturated [with their philosophy as well as the music].[105]

Dwight labored their farms with them, undertook work on their tractors, in the forests, on their cultivated land. There are films of the Hammonses dating from the 1970s that capture them working teams of horses, managing tackle, hauling cut lumber. Dwight showed up in these frames, in the midst of the rhythm of the work, clearly a part of the family, closely involved in the everyday tasks of managing their lives in the forested mountain areas the Hammons family carved out as their homesteads. Dwight was being "saturated" in their lives, and while the musical was integral to this, there were also a lot of other things going on in the relationship.[106] The notion of "saturated knowledge" remained a key conceptual point that motivated Dwight's playing, and that informed his approach to teaching through the early years of the 2000s.

To Dwight, there was a distinction between growing up with a music and parachuting into a locale to study up on the local culture, learn the music, and return to one's perch to think enduring thoughts about that music from a distance. It is hard to avoid seeing this as an invidious comparison, an implication that a person cannot play music that is not part of their genetic code in some way, part of their familial heritage or local lifetime experience. And at some points his lifetime, Dwight may have come close to making this case in a manner intended to suggest that "outsiders" studying the music will always be outsiders, but for the most part he retained the teacher's perspective: it is possible, but by no means easy, to teach this music, to convey aspects of this element of cultural language, to people with an avid interest in learning it and a commitment to working hard to get at it. However, in the years after his experiences with the Lexington old time scene, in the years following his turn to Christianity, and at the outset of his efforts to shape himself as a teacher in the early 1980s, Dwight looked somewhat more clinically at the act of acquiring music through total immersion, and thought about this and its impact on his music making capabilities in an essentially analytical fashion. Much of his thinking about the music delved into the character of West Virginian culture, critically important itself to the mix of influences Dwight brought to music. Apart from that, though, Dwight dwelled the way he learned the old time music, and about how this impacted his music.

Dwight learned music in a more plodding manner, in a labor-intensive way that could not rely on innate talent or learned capacity, but instead fixed on slowing and painstakingly integrating elements of the tunes into his playing. He did not "learn" the Hammonses' tunes in a "studied" way. As he saw it, he lived them, heard them, plopped down with the others and listened to a story, heard a tune, took a crack at playing along or pairing up with a Hammons fiddler.[107] Later, in the context of the festivals and the intensive "Old Time Music Scene" context in Lexington, Virginia, he saw young musicians avidly seeking out the old sounds. Dwight remembered that these musicians would replicate the immersion experience by spending concentrated time around the old musicians such as Tommy Jarrell, and by engaging in focused attempts to get at recorded tunes through intensive listening, repeated efforts to replicate those sounds, and continuous efforts to dissect tunes and decide which banjo (and fiddle) technique was the best way to get a tune down the way it was originally played and recorded. Dwight's "saturated" experience, and his own learning capabilities, suggested an alternative way to get at the music, and left him with a sense that what was distinguished about the Lexington, Virginia, old time community was the extent to which much of what was taking place in jam parties was a reaction to the approach typified by the Fuzzy Mountain String band.[108]

Not that Dwight discouraged a close analysis of the music, or that he refrained from paying focused attention to the granular level details of playing tunes. He did this himself at certain stages. He engaged in long and laborious arguments over how to play esoteric tunes, especially during his years of close association with the Lexington, Virginia, old time community. This close analysis of tunes made sense to Dwight, and was probably an important part of the process, as long as the process itself involved teaching the tunes, communicating what was learned, and expanding community in that way. And, in his view, this kind of intensive parsing of tunes did not necessarily result in a "studied" or stilted, stiff and unnatural music. The music became stiff and lifeless when it was separated from the context of community.

This is important because when he talked about the old time scene in those days in Lexington, Virginia, Dwight described long-term visits to Odell McGuire's home that was the center of gravity of this scene, in a sense replicating the kind of "saturation" he experienced in the years from 1968 to 1970 when he was taken into the embrace of the Hammonses, the Carpenter family, Lee Triplett and others. He described intensive dialogue between earnestly interested, committed players in Lexington, and he talked about wide recognition of the fact that a connection to the mountain communities that were the source of this music was essential to any effort to figure out how to play the music, what it meant, and why it was worth investing this much in trying to sort through all these things to get at the music this way, to get at what he would later call the "cultural message."[109] This was critical to Dwight, and this represented what he saw as his contribution to the process of studying the music—at least through the early 1980s. The recognition of what saturated knowledge brought to the table, coupled with collegial and creative small group dialogue on musical ideas, and a fanatically intensive focus on playing—and teaching—seemed to be, to Dwight, the hallmark of the Lexington, Virginia, old time community at least during the first five or six years of the seventies.[110]

Interestingly, the aspect of a larger context—the emergence and development of a community of interests beyond small regional groups—did not appear relevant or important to Dwight, though it may have attracted the attention of some of the Plank Road musicians. What distinguished this community for Dwight was the commitment of a core group to conveying the importance and character of the music through thoughtful, disciplined, focused teaching:

> Me and Odell were compulsive teachers and so because we were compulsive teachers we'd take a whole different tact than what I understand the Chapel Hill kind of thing was going on. We kept to teaching people. At that time you had to be pretty tough, there was a lot of power play going on or something I don't know; it was strange. [...] We were still taking a lot of people and teaching them[....] We studied about the music and how it was supposed to be played and what resulted [...] Dick Kimmel said they played "rude banjo" ... Rude music, sledgehammer banjo instead of clawhammer banjo. Lexington took the music and instead of studying the music turned loose with the music. Walt Koken said [You could] pick out the Lexington sound, hearing it across a field.[111]

Dwight and Odell McGuire, and music critic Jack Bernhardt, conveyed the sense that there was a significant distinction between the old time community that sprung up in the Durham and Chapel Hill area in North Carolina, around the concentration of talent represented by Alan Jabbour, Tommy Thompson, the Hollow Rock String Band and the Fuzzy Mountain String Band. Bernhardt suggested, in his 1983 interview with Dwight, that the Hollow Rock String Band "took it in a very different direction" from the New Lost City Ramblers, but opined that without the New Lost City Ramblers it is not clear whether Hollow Rock would have pursued the old music the way they did. Bernhardt noted that both Tommy Thompson and Alan Jabbour stated that they were not very influenced by New Lost City Ramblers. They were aware of their music and had met them before 1968 when the first Hollow Rock album was recorded. However, Bernhardt argued, it would be difficult to factor out the influence of the New Lost City Ramblers.[112]

Bernhardt appeared to go further, suggesting that the Lexington, Virginia, musicians, the Plank Road people, would not have been doing what they were doing in the early and mid–1970s had those old time musicians not reacted to what was going on in Chapel Hill. The distinction in approach is not necessarily captured by the terms "revivalist" versus "tradition bearer." To a certain extent, at least a part of what emerged from Durham/Chapel Hill, and what was encouraged by the Hollow Rock String Band approach, focused on the tunes versus the tune players, "rescuing tunes" that musicians passed from one player to the next. In that thinking, players served the tune.

Dwight, though, appeared to believe that the Lexington old time scene was not simply reacting to the music emerging from Durham and Chapel Hill and other old time communities. The Lexington old time musicians, from Dwight's perspective, were seeking to transcend that sound, to go beyond what had been replicated in Durham and Chapel Hill by those musicians who recorded old practitioners in Appalachia and brought those field recordings back to old time communities for close study. Dwight observed in the 1983 interview with Bernhardt:

> We were reacting to that but if you go back and listen to the very first time that I played on Hillsboro, it was hard driving banjo. It was really simple[....] You won't find much variation from that and what I'm doing now. There's more notes. The approach to it is the same. [...] I think that Odell and I together set the tone for the Lexington sound. I'm not saying that to make me special or anything like that. I think [...] we discussed it and we were the beginning of that thing and we set the tone for it and we kept saying in reaction to the Fuzzy Mountain sound we kept saying "there's more in it, there's more in it, there's more in it.[113]

Later, in the early 2000s, Dwight would suggest, in a thoughtful and private moment, that though he had been credited with being the "Guardian" of the old time music of at least his corner of West Virginia, and that he had enshrined much or this music in his commercial recordings, in point of fact what he was learning to play during his time spent with the Hammonses and other old masters of the archaic music was his music, Dwight's music, not merely the old music played the old way but tunes filtered through Dwight's capabilities and sensibilities, capturing the personality coiled tightly inside himself at that point in his life. That appeared to capture what Dwight meant when he suggested that what was taking place in Lexington, Virginia, was—at least to Dwight, to McGuire, and to others like Len Reiss—unconnected to a larger music revival. That formula captured what being a musician, an old time music player, meant to Dwight at the time and continued to mean during the years he played in organized bands, during the time he spent showcasing old music, and during the time he spent focused on teaching. To Dwight, the music was about learning, and growing, going beyond conventional wisdoms and predictable sounds, thinking beyond the question of how tunes were played to the point of contemplating how they should be played to reflect the individual musician's energy and the coil of tension and personality that lurked inside and could thus become a creative force. Dwight told Jack Bernhardt in 1983 that he and Odell McGuire had talked about this in the spring of that year after the Mount Airy old time music festival:

> We were looking back on this and as we were leaving here's all these kids playing and he said these kids are playing stuff we'd never even thought of. We were a small segment we took the music and gave it a kick in the ass. And it went on and became something more.[114]

Importantly, at the same time that Dwight was sensing that the music was in what he felt was a receding phase, and at the same time he began casting around for ways that he could to preserve and protect the old music, he was beginning to look for something else to fill a void in his personal life.

Four

Studying Religion

The Foundation of Belief

Dwight had his first thoughts about entering the seminary and becoming a man of the cloth in the mid-1970s. Two experiences drove him in that direction. The first experience, as Dwight explained, occurred after he had moved from Cass, West Virginia, to Frost in the summer of 1975. One day, he saw a man sweeping the streets, and talked to him enough to learn that he had a wife and two children and was, as Dwight put it, "another lost ball in the high weeds," down on his luck and scraping by in life. Dwight invited this man, a preacher, to dinner. As Dwight recalled:

> I invited him in. He sat down and just quietly rocked the rocking chair and listened. I got to going on and on and on about how I could believe in "God," [saying] I do not know why I have to believe in Jesus. "I am not interested in believing in Jesus." It was just at dark. I was sitting there quiet for maybe sixty seconds, and all at once "something" hit me in the chest with a heavy thump. And there was a burning sensation around my chest and belt buckle. And then it was gone.

Dwight dated his desire to know Jesus, to learn "who Jesus was and is," from that point:

> Never from that instant was there any really strong wanting to turn back. I burnt all my bridges. […] I could never find [that preacher] again. Never got a lead. However, in recent years I have finally realized for sure and certain that "he" was an angel.[1]

The second experience, in Dwight's words, took place just about a year later:

> The Lord called me that day [approximately] 17 August 1976 when I turned 30, [and] was baptized. [A] few hours before when I was speaking to an old friend out in the hills and saying how my life, which he knew had gotten worse and worse […] and I was saying "…what am I going to do with my life!! What am I going [to do…] ??"! And God was approximately 5 or 6 inches from my left ear more around near the corner of my left eye and glasses … [and in a] tiny whisper [that could not be] mistaken [said]: "You are going to be a minister, otherwise nothing that has ever happened in your life doesn't make any sense." So when there has been a question, and there [have] been hundreds, I go back to that place, as Elijah did and it helps me to remember that I am called to be a minister, to minister.

This moment sent Dwight reeling:

> [The day] Jesus rolled into my life unannounced and uninvited [I was] in a little Church of the Brethren meeting house here in the mountains and hills of Pocahontas County. My family and I were living at Frost at the time. Approximately 100 yards from where my grandmother grew up. No date sticks in my memory, but I know that the only plant, except for ramps in the high mountains, to be "out" in the woods was the tiny Spring Beauty. At that time of the year, there is nothing but the "dead of winter." Death with its greys and browns and decay all around. I remember nothing was said from the pulpit or anywhere else. Nothing like some sort of "altar call." No one had said anything; it was just a normal

quiet Sunday morning like it always was. I was sharing a hymn book and there was about 60–90 seconds until the end of the singing. Suddenly, when the "call" came, there was two choices. Since I am so often an extreme person, the Lord has to deal with me in an extreme way. There was only a powerful sense deep inside and the sense carried some words with it. Not words that you would hear, but powerful ones. I could go forward, there was no one standing up there, and if I did go forward, there would be something, to me, which would be terrible for me. But if I did not go forward and did not go when called that morning, I had to get out and never look back. Forget the walk with the Lord forever. The reason I know the Spring Beauties were in bloom was [that afterwards] I drove back into the hills in the deep forest. Got out of my pickup and sat down totally confused about what I had done. And there were the tiny flowers with pink petals with red veins. Otherwise, I was totally alone.[2]

As Dwight put it, almost four decades later:

I was literally "called to the Ministry" in mid-August 1976 out in the hills near Lexington, Virginia, while really up against life. Absolutely broken. No place to turn. [...] I gave my life to the Lord that day in spring [...] I gave my life totally over. Years later I was reminded [by that same Voice]: "When I was standing there and we were sharing that hymnal, there was so much power around you that I could hardly stand beside you."[3]

Many West Virginians believe deeply in God, and shape their lives around fundamental religious precepts, often taking as their motivation a benchmark moment, perhaps in the form of a dream, a reverie, or a sign. The Morris family was very important to Dwight. John was an especially close friend. John and David Morris' grandmother, Lula Hill, was a deeply religious woman. David Morris recalled that she lived that every day: "Her testimony was, 'I want to live every day right at the foot of the cross.' She said, 'I love everybody. I love the sinners, but I don't love sin.'" Morris related his grandmother's experience:

She was 16 years old when she married Willis Hill. There's a photograph of her in her wedding dress. It was not a white dress, but oh my goodness, she was a beautiful girl. She was living out there on Mountain Home. She told me that she had been praying for a sign for her faith. She was out there in the garden. She said, "I was hoeing in the peas, and I got to the end of a row and stopped for a minute to lean on the hoe and straighten up my back." She said, "David, I heard the angels sing. The music was all around me, behind the clouds, and all around. And they sang all the parts. And it was beautiful." That was her sign. She lived that. She taught us "Jesus Is a Rock in a Weary Land." It was one of her favorite songs.[4]

Dwight's recollections of his own vivid moments of inspiration, lessons he derived from a dream or a moment of extremely sharp reflection, run parallel with a common thread in many West Virginian stories about the decision to take devotion to God seriously.[5] Dwight recalled these events in his life shortly after his 68th birthday, in August 2014, and acknowledged what they meant to him those many years ago. He accepted that nothing surrounding these two moments in his life could be easily explained in rational, dispassionate ways. To make sense of them, and to make sense of his life, he had to embrace the possibility that these instances meant what he took them to mean. He had to accept the idea that one does not have to believe to understand, and one does not have to understand to believe.[6]

Dwight lived in Buena Vista, Virginia, from 1979 to 1981. During those years he worked as a house painter, a blacksmith's helper, and as an officer for the Department of Juvenile Corrections in Natural Bridge, Virginia, where he had responsibilities for young men in their middle to upper teens enrolled in a wilderness program. He moved back to Pocahontas County in 1981, the year his first marriage ended in divorce.[7] Dwight went to work on a friend's cattle farm in Hillsboro, earning about $135 a month. He remarried in 1982, and he and his wife Elaine had a son, Caleb, born in 1984. Their daughter Susanna was born in 1986. The marriage ended in divorce in 2006. In Hillsboro, they lived in an unheated home with a partially functional electric stove, no refrigerator, and water pipes that were frozen throughout the winter. Between Easter of 1981 and December 1983 the family relocated 17 times. He was not earning enough money to cover his rent, and was increasingly troubled by the kinds of problems that drove him into psychiatric care facilities after his stint in the Navy. At that point, he decided to abandon his objections to returning to school, and made preparations to enter the seminary.

Dwight believed that he did not elect to attend the seminary, and did not have a hand in the selection of the school. After his college experience in Morgantown, he had no personal intention or desire to return to school. But, he explained decades later, the choice was not his. He determined to do what the one power he believed in told him to do, and so he entered Eastern Mennonite University, attended the seminary, and came out at the other end as a man of the cloth.[8] Dwight looked at the decision to attend Eastern Mennonite seminary as one that was never really in his hands, but provided a way out of his severely broken life—he had endured a divorce, lost his home, fell in and out of minimum wage employment and found himself shifting from one address to the next:

> Jesus drove me into seminary. I vowed I would never go back to college again after six and a half years at West Virginia University. Jesus [was] bound and determined I would go to seminary or totally get out. [...] I staggered into Eastern Mennonite Seminary in January 1984. I was still in the Church of the Brethren (COB) at the time, but was warned against going to the COB seminary in Elgin, Illinois. [...] God sent me to Eastern Mennonite Seminary knowing that they [were a] "Peace Denomination." [...] They tolerated me.[9]

In the context of these tumultuous times, the Mennonites and their seminary in Harrisonburg, Virginia, provided an opportunity for Dwight to regain stability and purpose.

The Seminary Years

Dwight enrolled in Eastern Mennonite University's (EMU) seminary in Harrisonburg, Virginia, in January 1984 and completed six semesters of seminary study in December 1986.

At EMU, a private liberal arts university in the Shenandoah Valley affiliated with one of the historic peace churches, Dwight pursued a Masters of Arts degree with a double major. Professor Don Augsburger was his advisor for Christian counseling and Professor Lawrence Yoder was his advisor for evangelism and church planting. Dwight registered for and completed a total of 23 classes between the spring of 1983 and the fall of 1987, accumulating 180 course credits (including four credits transferred toward his master's degree that he earned at West Virginia University). On 23 May 1987 he earned a Master of Arts in Church Ministry, with a concentration in Evangelism and Church Planting, and Christian Counseling, and achieved a GPA of 3.39. Dwight garnered eight A's, eleven B's, one C (in a "general" course on the New Testament) and 4 "Pass" grades during the seven semesters in the seminary. About 17 percent of his classes were taken on a Pass/Fail basis. Setting aside those courses, he earned a grade of A in 37 percent of classes and a grade of B in 58 percent of his coursework, a substantial achievement.[10]

Professor George Brunk taught New Testament at Eastern Mennonite Seminary from 1974 to 2011, served as acting dean from 1977 to 1979 and as dean from 1979 to 1999.[11] He taught three of the classes Dwight took at EMU and awarded Dwight two A's in Church History and Introduction to Theology and a B grade for his work in the Inter-

Eastern Mennonite Seminary in the 1980s, from the 1986 yearbook (courtesy Eastern Mennonite University Archives).

preting the Bible Text class.[12] Professor Brunk remembered Dwight as a very down to earth person who did not take easily to the more academic studies:

> He had a very practical bent. I wouldn't call him a poor student. He was above average in intelligence as I recall. He was just not a book person. He was an outgoing person who made his presence known and with whom one could easily relate. He had clear opinions and he did not hesitate to share them.[13]

Dwight took several courses taught by Professor Augsburger, including four classes in the school's Congregational Life and Work series: Foundations of Preaching and Industrial and Commercial Ministry, for which Dwight earned two of the B grades he was awarded, and Pastoral Care and Counseling and Marriage and Family Counseling, classes in which Dwight earned A grades.[14] Professor Augsburger was one of five brothers and a single sister from a family that served the Mennonite Church for many years. He served as EMU's pastor of students from 1958 to 1964. From 1970 to 1989 he was a professor in EMU's Seminary program, and pastored in the college community church from 1975 to 1980.[15] Dwight had strong, fond memories of studying Christian counseling under Professor Augsburger, to whom he attributed the words: "Never forget that everyone you meet is standing in a pool of tears." That was a singularly important quote to Dwight, one that stuck with him as a critical life lesson, perhaps the most important thing he learned in Seminary. Dwight connected to this "pool of tears" as the place "where […] the big dogs exploit the old mountain folks," and he tried in his life to never assume that he could

Professor George Brunk, from the seminary's 1986 yearbook (courtesy Eastern Mennonite University Archives).

discern the pain of others. Instead, he started from the premise that if what he felt was close to what had driven others into despair, then he knew that they were "being crushed from all sides."[16]

Professor Augsburger recalled that Dwight was a serious student and that he did a "fine job" in his classes. Dwight had an "open personality" and was easy to talk to. The professor remembered that Dwight came from a "rougher background" than most of his fellow students and that he became involved in the Mennonite church later in life than his classmates. The professor also remembered Dwight's banjo playing, and knew that he used this music in his ministries. Professor Augsburger learned over time that Dwight had burned out at some point after Seminary, and surmised that it was the result of the challenges of being a minister. "Being a minister is not an easy task," he said. One has to both "please people" and "tell them about growth," two distinctively different kinds of responsibilities that often required delivering hard edged messages. "The pastorate can get heavy," Professor Augsburger said, "especially if you are trying to do too much too fast." Dwight was, the professor stressed, a good Christian with a strong faith, a "dedicated Christian." He reminisced about a well-behaved student who had a "sensitive personality," and concluded that some of the obligations of the ministry were probably not easy to bear for someone so inclined.

Professor Yoder graduated from college in 1966 and seminary in 1969, and earned Th.M. and Ph.D. degrees from Fuller Theological Seminary School of Intercultural Studies where he studied Islam, Indonesian language, Asian Historiography and Asian and

Professor A. Don Augsburger, Dwight Diller's seminary advisor for Christian counseling (courtesy of A. Donald Augsburger).

Indonesian church history in preparation for a nine-year assignment teaching church history and Anabaptist studies in Indonesia. He also served four and a half years in Indonesia as country administrator for the Mennonite Central Committee and two years as researcher and writer working on the histories of the Muria Javanese Mennonite Church (GITJ) and the Muria Mennonite Church (GKMI). He began teaching mission studies at Eastern Mennonite Seminary in 1983.[17] Professor Yoder taught three of the classes Dwight took in the school's Missions and Evangelism series: The Practice of Evangelism, in which Dwight earned a B, and Modern Religious Movements and Dynamics of Church Growth, in which he earned A grades.[18] Professor Yoder was Dwight's main source of guidance during his years at Eastern Mennonite. When Dwight entered the seminary, the professor had just returned from Indonesia, and was thoroughly experienced in church planting work. His interests paralleled Dwight's focus on evangelism. Dwight recalled the care with which Yoder discussed the process of immersing oneself in a different culture.

However, in Dwight's own mind and memory he was not a very good student. A master of arts degree required an investment of sixty hours of classwork. A master of divinity called for ninety hours of class work. Generally, students completed this degree in three years, carrying thirty hours of classwork per year. It took Dwight six semesters to complete his master of arts degree. Some years later, Dwight noted

Professor Lawrence Yoder, from the seminary's 1986 yearbook (courtesy Eastern Mennonite University Archives).

that he was compelled in seminary to read massive amounts of religious or biblical literature:

> I remember my first class in seminary. It was the break between semesters in January 1984. [I was in the] upper division. I did not have a clue what I was doing taking a class in "Pauline theology" [but] the instructor [had] us read 1,200 pages during that three week class. So after class, I ran down to the library and got out some of the books he said were easiest to read. Quickly took them to our home up in the hills. That night I gathered up those books and began reading. I read for between 2 and 3 hours. It was hard going but I "knew" I was making progress. Then I noticed the page number: 36. I had three weeks to do the assignment. Finally, my only recourse was to "read fast and loose with the truth." I was really gaining on it when I could finish cover approximately 20 or 30 pages in about ten or twelve minutes.[19]

After three years at EMU, Dwight was sure that he would find an opportunity to secure a respectable job and earn a regular paycheck, and achieve a reasonable amount of success. However, he would find managing a church, building links with congregations, and sustaining effective relations with church executive committees to be daunting challenges.[20]

Two Ministries

Following his first semester at Eastern Mennonite Seminary, Dwight was licensed to work as a preacher. In June 1984 Dwight took a position as pastor for a small congregation of about 20 people who constituted the Fairview-Endless Caverns Church of the Brethren. He made his home about five miles south of New Market, Virginia, on the west side of the old Valley Pike (Route 11) near the Bethlehem Stone Church, in the small community of Tenth Legion.[21] Dwight recalled that the whole church community, which consisted of 12 to 15 parishioners, was asked one Sunday morning to express their views about this transition in church leadership, and agreed to it as a group. He was offered a salary of $9,000 a year for the part-time post, but an acting deacon overruled this decision, reducing the wages to $6,000 per year. That salary essentially covered his rent, necessities for his family, and the expense of commuting between New Market and Harrisonburg, Virginia.

The transition to the job at New Market was seamless. Dwight was already attending services there. The presiding pastor was scheduled to finish his seminary course in June. Since Dwight was just beginning his schooling in Harrisonburg, it seemed like a good fit. The congregants were mostly Virginians who lived lives that were typical Shenandoah Valley success stories. Dwight remembered that Wesley Buell was a church leader with long social and historical links to the church, and that his wife, Lena May, played the organ every Sunday morning. He also remembered that there was no job description for the role he was to play, no list of duties, and no support from the seminary, no guidance regarding pastoral dilemmas and difficulties. For Dwight, the first pastoral position represented a challenge on several levels. He was, in his recollection, "fighting to keep family together" and living close to the edge financially, in addition to taking on a new job in a new church. Nevertheless, he recalled it as a basically positive experience; he said of his first position of responsibility for a congregation: "I was learning and growing."[22]

In 1986, a position opened up in Mathias, West Virginia. Dwight recalled paying a visit to that church to see whether the congregants were predominantly Virginians or West Virginians, something he remembered as being very important to him at the time.

"West Virginians have a certain kind of strength," he explained, a strength that made them capable of living independently, under harsh circumstances, a resource that made them resilient, but, he added, that strength could become a weakness because the flip side of the coin was a tendency to relish the isolation, which ended up making them less than effective at sustaining community. Three months before his December 1986 graduation from seminary, Dwight accepted the position as pastor for the Church of the Brethren congregation in Mathias. He was licensed as a Church of the Brethren minister in March 1987, and was in that position about nine months before he confronted another personal crisis.

In Mathias, Dwight was a full time minister for an older, established congregation of about 100 members. His sense was that the church had its established practices, recognized leadership, a small group of key decision-makers and a core of influential members. Dwight had just completed three years of study at Eastern Mennonite, and felt the need and understood the importance of "establishing himself" in this church. He remembered the unique character of the congregation:

> This little West Virginian congregation was only six miles across the border with Virginia. Most of the congregation worked in Virginia, took their newspapers from Virginia, went shopping in stores on the Virginia side of the border, yet the people in the village of Mathias were real West Virginians. [...] The people in the pews were West Virginians. I understood the people in the pews who were not part of the power structure [of the church]. I wouldn't treat the people in the pews and the "power brokers" differently.[23]

West Virginian congregants, he recalled, felt this polarization, and made clear to Dwight that it could work to undermine him. Townspeople, born and bred West Virginians, told Dwight that they felt unwelcomed in the church and that inviting them to join Sunday services would be destructive to Dwight's ministry.

He had barely recovered from what he recalled as the extreme pressures of completing his seminary work. His increasing predisposition to spiral downward under the weight of earlier life stresses, in a manner that unleashed a tsunami of emotion and distress, caught up with him. He was emotionally spent, physically exhausted, mentally drained. Dwight was unable to manage the interior pressures, the responsibilities, the personal turmoil, and nine months into the Mathias job he experienced a breakdown that was similar to the crises that he endured in 1967 and 1969. He ended up admitting himself to a psychiatric care center. Dwight explained:

> We were living in the parsonage right beside the church house. And the pressure had been so bad I just felt fearful all the time. Underneath I always felt fearful just because I was burned out. A breaker box, when the circuit is overloaded, trips. Each time it trips it takes less of an overload to trip the circuit. So, each time you have a breakdown, the "circuit" trips, and in each subsequent incident it becomes easier and easier to overload the circuit. This is not about feeling bad. When this happens you don't just get out of it. System shuts down. [...] I got up one morning and cried, and couldn't stop. I got along great with the congregation, because 90 percent of them were West Virginians. I could not please [the church leadership] so I finally just crumbled. [...] The day I woke up crying I knew what had happened but when you reach that point you can't control it.[24]

He stayed in the care center for about three days, returned to Mathias, gathered up his family and returned to Pocahontas County "for some time to heal." But this was, for Dwight, a "highly adrenalized moment," and it became clear in his mind that he would not be able to restore balance and continue to fulfill his obligations to the congregation. Dwight likened it to a "fight or flight" moment, when he knew survival depended on standing and struggling at a point when all that was available to him were severely diminished resources, and the only other option was fleeing in the face of the reality that there had been no time in which to recover sufficiently. Dwight lasted at the church until December, and then left.

Dwight relocated his family to Clearwater, Florida, in December 1987 and went to work in Pinellas County with the help of a student he knew who was a land developer. There he experienced a breakdown and was treated in a Christian psychiatric hospital for about 17 days. He and his wife knew this was the wrong place for them from the start, but at the time he felt that he had few choices. They returned to Pocahontas County in March 1988.[25] Dwight found a small house in Hillsboro, out in the countryside, but could not find work; the stress and strain of life, his own personal health challenges and state of mind, contributed to making it impossible for him to perform effectively and consistently enough to keep steady employment. He picked up odd jobs that brought him the occasional thirty-five to forty dollars a week, but between his physical state and his mental exhaustion—and the generally depressed job market in the area—there was little chance of finding a way to stabilize his situation. The "kindness of strangers" gave him some breathing space but for the most part the family had it hard. To Dwight, that was "the beginning of really having to live by faith. Day after day there was no money. And living like that, God supplies, and we don't know how."[26] He could bring in about $500.00 from teaching week-long banjo classes conducted during the summer months, a sum that would not stretch through the winter but was often all he had to count on. To make some money, Dwight started teaching five day-long banjo "retreats" while he was still working in Mathias in 1982. He derived a consistent though modest income from teaching the five-day banjo class at Augusta Heritage Center in Elkins, West Virginia, from 1981 to 2001; he had conducted one week-long class for them in 1975. Dwight started his own week-long "banjo retreats" in 1987 in Hillsboro. In 1988 and 1989 he taught week-long summer classes at Cass, West Virginia. In effect, Dwight turned to teaching banjo so he could cover family financial requirements. Sometime between the late fall of 1988 or the spring of 1989, out of desperation, he reached out to the church. "I didn't know where else to go," he stated. "I had no place to go. I knew God called me to minister, but there was nothing out there."[27]

In response to his request for assistance, Dwight's former Overseer, Glendon Blosser and his wife, Dorothy, paid a visit to Dwight in Hillsboro. Dwight knew, from the moment they got out of their automobile, that "there was no way there would be a path open for me with the Mennonites." Dwight remembered being as direct, honest and straightforward as he could be about himself, about what he could offer the church, and about what he could not offer. Dwight was certain Blosser had done enough digging before the visit to know what kind of person he was, what kind of student and pastor he had been. Reflecting on all this two and a half decades later, Dwight was grateful to the Mennonites for all they had done for him, for putting up with an argumentative young soul who was searching for his path and trying to sort out the trajectory that he felt had been determined for him. He acknowledged that he did not "buy into the party line" during his seminary years, and that he probably was very combative throughout his schooling, but, he added, the Mennonites were "gracious enough to permit that."

Dwight knew that this visit would mark a friendly and polite parting of the ways between the Mennonites and himself, though not a complete and irrevocable break in communication or an end to old friendships. He continued to talk to Blosser, and he maintained a cordial relationship with Richard Bowman, even after he turned in his ordination papers to Bowman in the summer of 2005 knowing that he was headed once more to another divorce; he did not want to put the Mennonites in a complex position yet once again. From that point forward, though, Dwight pursued a course that was distinctively his own, claiming no formal affiliation with any church or fealty to any particular doctrine.

The Banjo Ministry

Sometime following his second pastoral job, Dwight, on his own, and the Mennonite leadership arrived at the decision that he was probably not equipped to manage a conventional congregation. Dwight recalled coming to a point of desperation sometime between the late fall of 1988 and the spring of 1989. At that time, he reached out to the Mennonites who had provided a home, a level of comfort, and some basic support and resources that helped him navigate life during his seminary years. However, by that time Dwight had simply diverged too much from the ways of the Mennonites to allow them to accommodate him again. Dwight understood this, and knew he could not ask the Mennonites to grant him some way of continuing his pastoral work.

As he recalled the episode, Dwight came to the view that he was still capable enough to manage an unconventional ministry, and so he began to think of the banjo and old time music as the focal point of his devotional activities, and he started to look at the old time community as the population he would serve. That is, Dwight made the decision focus his attention and ministerial capabilities on the "old time music communities" where the music was played, the festivals and gatherings where the music was performed, and the workshops and classes where the music was taught. By that time, he was a recognized fixture at some of these events and gatherings, and had begun to make his own recordings of his playing of old time fiddle and banjo tunes from east central West Virginia. No formal convocation of a decision-making entity of the Mennonite Church was involved in arriving at a decision regarding Dwight's thinking about this kind of ministry. The church leadership did not discuss the issues and arrive at a formal decision that was communicated authoritatively through church channels. In the face of Dwight's personal challenges that made conventional church work prohibitively difficult for him, he shifted his attention to the one activity he felt he was capable of managing, the one area in which he believed he had been successful: teaching old time fiddle and banjo, and conveying the value of the old music and the importance of the "Old People" who played it, and the life lessons entailed in all of that.

To Dwight, this course of action would allow him to continue to serve people looking for the kind of teaching, the kind of comfort, and the kind of guidance that a leader might deliver albeit in a very unique context, among a rather distinctive population, in a narrow and even esoteric musical community. As Dwight put it:

> The only success I am allowed to have is to teach Christianity using the banjo in a certain way within the confines of what is called old time music at present. And have a steady stream of bad mouthing because of the way I teach and what I see as most important. But again, I teach everything I "know" about the walk with the Trinity using my skill in teaching the banjo and context of the old tradition's music from here in these mountains handed down by my ancestors in a mental/emotional/spiritual sense.[28]

The reference to "bad mouthing" spoke to the issue of banjo students who were taken aback at Dwight's practice of making clear his primary interest, his commitment to a life of service to God, in Dwight's classes and workshops. To some extent, insofar as Dwight was concerned, this was merely an act of "full disclosure," information that helped center Dwight and his life work in the realities of contemporary West Virginia where a significant proportion of people were prepared to act on their devotion to their religious beliefs in everyday life. This was the way Dwight showed what was on his sleeve, the way he attempted to make that information more available and understandable to his students. It was, to some—perhaps to many, or at least to increasing numbers of students—unexpected and at the very least slightly off-putting. To some it was out of place in a banjo workshop, but to Dwight it was another way of nudging people beyond their comfort zones, rocking them back on their heels and requiring a "reset" of their basic knowledge load because, hold onto your brains, here comes something entirely different—whether it be the banjo rhythm he sought to teach, or the cultural context (the "cultural messages") he was trying to communicate and interpret for newcomers to the area, or his region's history and its music that he tried to explain to students.

In Dwight's view, he tried to avoid preaching and taking a posture or using words that suggested he was proselytizing, though not always with complete success. In his understanding, discussing religion, confessing weakness and ignorance in the face of the unknown, confronting mortality and asking Big Questions about God and belief produced serious discomfort levels. He remained convinced that this was an important course of action for him to pursue, and that it was similarly important for others, not because it could induce a commitment to God or a conversion to a religious life, but because from this discomfort emerged self-questioning, and from that came discovery. In some very important ways, he was less concerned with scoring a success in venturing into turbulent discussions of such fundamental matters of faith than he was with nudging people toward moments of reflection, whatever those moments might bring, even if they did not necessarily lead to "recruitment." Admittedly, he did not always hit a home run, and there was plenty of evidence that some students took his words as paid political announcements on behalf of conservative forces, or bald attempts to preach. In short, sometimes students connected to this, put it in context, and came away with a new perspective on a range of things—beyond religion, beyond banjo.[29] And sometimes they did not.[30]

To Dwight, the banjo had always been very secondary to what he sought to do in his classes: "The ministry is to use the banjo to give people hope. That's the reason I taught banjo all those years. To minister is to give people hope." In Dwight's view, he generally only had his students for a week, and they were often people who could take a tough schedule and a relentless regimen:

> Many of the people who show up in my classes are people who have achieved the American Dream and found it to be a nightmare. They are near retirement or retired, often in their fifties. These people [...] understand discipline because they've lived discipline all their careers. Doctors, lawyers, CEOs, schoolteachers, engineers. So many of them come from that world.[31]

Dwight's starting point was that if he could stiffen the spines of people who came to his classes, prod them to reflect on what it was they wanted, and encourage people by showing them they could learn something new—whether it was the banjo, or a new way of appreciating the importance of the enduring questions whose contemplation might help people live mindfully—then he would have served needs larger than those satisfied by simply showing someone how to tune up and play a song on the banjo.

This was unabashedly spiritual, though it was not necessarily imbued with specific religious content. Dwight's point was that people, all people, were operating in a complex, confusing world where they often did not know what was going on, and they were constantly taking risks. Reflecting on that was, in Dwight's thinking, one way of coming to grips with such challenges, one way of centering oneself in the midst of a life where everyday encounters had become more abrasive, invasive and threatening. People came to old time music festivals seeking at least momentary community, the fellowship of a jam or the embrace of a like-minded crowd. Why not equip them to find the basis of the strength that those brief events afforded deep inside themselves? So much of what Dwight was doing in his classes could be taken as an attempt to instill mindfulness. Viewing Dwight's banjo retreats as an exercise designed to bring students to Christ's doorstep misconstrued his simple commitment to helping students "find hope." He had carved out his own trajectory as clearly as his life allowed, and decided to work to nudge students toward a diligent awareness. What came next was up to the student.

"The Pool of Tears"

Dwight developed an approach to teaching banjo that focused closely on the context of old West Virginian traditional music, and he spent a good deal of time shaping a way of getting at the character of the people who played the old music, and what they brought to fiddling and banjo playing. He began by calling up the image of the men who initially came into the mountains of eastern central West Virginia, the "long hunters" who ventured into the mountains, and stayed for months at a time. They faced extreme challenges, and confronted the isolation of the dense mountain forests. They were born of tough, clannish European stock that, in Dwight's explanation, had the old world ways bred out of them. The early music expressed how those people lived and had to live. It was, Dwight said, a grinding, screeching music that conveyed the harshness of their lives, the threatening solitude of the inhospitable highlands, and it reflected the character these people had to develop "in order to fight on through."

The Iota-Chi Cross is formed by superimposing a letter I (Greek: Iota) on a letter X (Greek: Chi). Iota is the first letter of Ιησους (Iesous: "Jesus") and Chi is the first letter of Χριστος (Christos: "Christ"). This I-X combination then becomes a cipher for Jesus Christ. Dwight had the I-X combination inlaid on several banjo fingerboards, at the ninth fret (courtesy Bates Littlehales).

This archaic music from the frontier, Dwight argued, was a world apart from the music that was brought out into the open by commercial forces in the 1920s, by the fledgling recording industry that sensed market opportunities, and manufactured pressed disks that squeezed the life out of the music: enter money, enter commerce, exit the life and meaning of the early movement. And, with the discovery of this music by urban interests, college populations, the newly affluent in the 1950s and 1960s, and the burgeoning interest in bluegrass in the 1960s, the original primeval character of the music was sloughed off in favor of smoother, more palatable music that fit in with modern living. The old music, Dwight averred, had the roughness sucked out and replaced by attractive, marketable commodity music. This was what Dwight referred to as the "Doppler effect," the diminishing sound as the music becomes increasingly remote and inaccessible, a receding sound. In his view, when money entered the equation, when market forces began to drive the recording industry, and when all this began to have a hand in shaping the motivation of musicians, then arrogance entered the equation, music began to stratify populations, professionals played an increasing role in managing the art and the industry, and finally, "by the late 1960s and early 1970s [...] nothing was left of the Old People."

Dwight, in his teaching, attempted to convey the visual and aural image of this process. He attempted to speak to his understanding of the music, so that this consequential evolution became something that could be understood by the student—in mind and heart, as Dwight put it. The way he did this is to push people to look at the harshness in their own lives, to connect with elements of life that might have drifted far away in memory, or been consigned to the part of the memory that harbored recollections of times and places far off, gone and done with. Every life was touched by this kind of hardship, Dwight argued. Every life contained some element of rough times, challenges, and torment overcome; as Dwight's seminary teacher used to say, "Every person is standing in a pool of tears." Dwight tried to get students "to catch this stuff" in their own personal histories because they had each been in such places, but many pushed back, were reluctant to acknowledge that this was where they had to go to find the hard edge of their lives, and from there find the music, the rhythm, that would become their release from these terrifying moments. It was not an easy journey, not a simple, unencumbered exploration, as Dwight understood it:

> I try to find place where the person has been, the things in their life that will drive them to learn from hard, crushing terror. [...] To have rhythm, you got to go to those places. [...] You will never learn anything on the banjo until you go back to those days. [Without facing these memories, these moments in life, there is] nothing there to drive up against. Either you drive hard against those harsh places, [or you] have to forget playing this old music.[32]

Dwight's point was that for many people, the old music conjured up images of "soft green rolling pastures," a pastoral quiet and front porch intimacy of families gathered after a hard day of work. The tunes created pictures of imagined country folk traveling a rutted road in a horse drawn farm wagon, sitting quietly, playing with calloused and well worked hands, perhaps alone after a day of back-breaking work. The music that resulted from this produced a short, slight bit of happiness. Maybe a dancing rhythm that made the foot tap. The old modal sounds drove in another direction, building on sensations of sadness, mourning, bitterness derived from hardscrabble ways of living, describing how cold the farm got, and how working before and after school made you so very, very tired. And how a bit of cream skimmed off the top of a bucket of cow milk, laced with sugar, spread on homemade bread brought some happiness.

To Dwight, however, the archaic music went further than that: "Forget all that about the nice sweet, pastoral quiet on the porch. This music is not that at all." Dwight observed:

> Think of *these* pastoral images: your best cow laying there in the mud trying to have a calf and [the baby] is stuck. You have been with her all night trying to pull the calf. And she lays there dying. Your children have diphtheria, you have diphtheria, your wife worn to nothing because there are ten children in your family, and your household is totally quarantined.

Drifting into memories of his grandfather's life, Dwight continued:

> Your two daughters, the roof falls out of both of their mouths and they die half hour from each other and you cannot move because you are almost dead yourself. The job as a woodhick suddenly came to an end. You have been working at that for thirty years, from the turn of the century to 1930, and now you have the drought of 1929-31 and [the challenge of] trying to raise just enough to eat. Mother only has her lifelong connection with the Lord, the spirit of the Lord. It is a constant to have nothing hardly. You have one daughter who bitches and complains and causes constant trouble and nothing is ever good enough and causes problems with the rest of the children. [...] the oldest son is always raging, is mean to the animals, bad mean and out of control of his temper. And the father who was hell raiser as a young man working a dangerous job in the woods, he dies and his several children have to be farmed out to others in the community where they live mistreated, [outcasts, marginalized in their own extended families.] Hard scrabble kept taking its toll. He had a fiddle, but had to trade it for a stack of hay for the winter to keep his stock alive.

This music, Dwight argued, was about people who were under a constant tension in their lives, whose path was not going to improve, whose choices were constrained, and whose pain was unremitting. A lot of people refused to let that "pool of tears" drive their music. As Dwight put it, they stay "nice" and "light" and "self satisfied and there is nothing but melody." Dwight's point was that "the pool of tears" could give direction, structure, content to the effort to play music. In his most extreme formulation of the idea, Dwight averred: "no person will ever learn until there is desperation." The real tension that Dwight sought to communicate was the life of the hard working farmer who traded off the fiddle for a stack of hay to stay alive, to keep his family fed, and who knew he would never get his hands on another instrument, would never sit on the porch "and make some little sound that might break the pain and agony from frustration and confusion that permeates every day." Dwight's own response to such desperation was to "look to the Lord to find real eternal meaning." He did not preclude the possibility that some might find solace elsewhere, in other ways, but he believed life described a trajectory that tested people. He believed that people could be driven to play music by the "pool of tears" in which they stood, and he believed the music that resulted would be honest, sometimes harsh and melancholy, and sometimes wrapped in the moments of joy, the lightheartedness that life permitted. His own tests had been hard to bear. In his words:

> Everything meaningless except when there is someone I can minister to by teaching them stuff about the banjo and they get a light in their lives. I have hated my life. Hated everyday. For me inwardly, it has been constantly meaningless. It is that a certain part of the "self" was stripped out and so can only enjoy life through others. This perhaps [is] the real drive in my ministry. To see people get hope. To enjoy something that is real that they are looking for.

Dwight described a harsh life, hard in the way poverty and hunger could make a life hard, and painful in the way that internal suffering and tortured thinking impoverished the mind and made simple acts of living unbearable. This, as Dwight saw it, was how the music fit in: playing music that came out of these depths, playing "from your place of pain," could yield music that springs from these deep recesses of life:

> Let that pain come out. Music is the best way to get it out.
> [...] [Some] people have so much comfort. They don't have to put themselves in it. [For those in pain], letting who you are come to the surface, that is what music can do, if you play from your depths.[33]

People who are comfortable "don't need the release" and their music could then become a plaything, an assemblage of techniques, melodies, notes and songs—and to Dwight this is what ended up "insulting" the old music.

> Music is about reaching to that place where it is inside [of you], reaching to that place where the pain was really deep. When you are locked in, and can't conceive of getting anywhere else, getting away from the pain, when there's no comfort inside—that's where music comes from.[34]

The hard part is understanding how music from these depths could come to the point of provoking a smile, pushing a toe to tap and a foot to stamp, yielding dance, and a respite from the harshness.

On "Becoming"

Dwight looked at what he learned from the Hammons family, what he acquired that helped him to be a musician, as being distinctly separate and apart from things that had to do with capabilities, technique, repertoire. Community, upbringing, the echoes of the surrounding world, the sounds of life and the rhythm of the everyday—all that was distilled in each individual, and it either mixed up into an equation that enabled good music, or sometimes fine writing, sometimes eloquent speaking, or poignant poetry, meaningful acting, good cooking, responsible leadership, effective teaching, capable business mindedness, and so on.

Dwight's point was that a person cannot play just any music. A person cannot replicate or duplicate or imitate any music. The internal equation that derived from the sum total of upbringing, the cultural package that was entwined in physical makeup and the content of soul, all that went into making music. Dwight made the case that a person could learn a certain amount of technique that would make a difference. That person could master physical skills and learn elements of the music, or the contours and practices of writing poetry, teaching, running a business or being a good dentist, but the personal, chemical, genetic, cultural makeup that combined to define an individual's capacity was what pushed a person toward creativity, imagination, and inventiveness, and fueled the ability to perform, to do, to be.

Dwight personally saw this as something that was God given. "God will teach you how to play music," Dwight said:

> He will take all of that community and drive it into you, and whenever you play, "IT" will come out, God will come out, "IT" will come out. "IT" will chose you, put all of these variables together and "IT" will work through you so you can become a conduit. "IT" has to teach you. You can't play "IT." When you try to play another people's music, another person's style, [and] you don't have those combinations [of culture, nurture, genetics, upbringing] so "IT" can train you, then you can never be the conduit.[35]

Dwight used the word "IT," often capitalized and in quotation marks, when he referred to the innate genetic chemistry that signaled a special understanding of language and culture, music and stories.[36] His central point was this: "When you try to play [like] that, you don't have those combinations [of dialect, community, family, geography]. That chemistry is what is necessary so that "IT" can train you, so that you can be the conduit for this particular kind of creativity."[37] He tried to explain this further in explicit religious terms:

Christianity is based on faith. Nothing else. But you as a human, when you try to cook up faith, no human can have faith, just human faith, and be acceptable to God. Jesus said, when the son of God returns will he find Faith on this earth? The only way you can have Faith is God has to give it to you. [...] God has given Faith. What he looks for is his faith coming through you. [...] Works the same for music. [...] Dialect, community, family, geography. All this comes together, so you play a music that is [the product of] your dialect, community, family, and geography, and that's why it is so specific and that's why nobody can play it—because it's not them.[38]

For Dwight there was an arresting religious truth to this, an inspiration derived from what he knew, what he understood and learned from studying Jesus, and living his life in accordance with what the Bible told him. However, there were very basic elements of this argument that made sense just in terms of the manner in which we all become people, the way we wrap "dialect, community, family, and geography" together to give expression to the talent and capabilities that derive from who we are. That is, elements of Dwight's argument could clarify pieces of the puzzle of how to make music without requiring subscription to belief and dogma. And this was where he defined what being a musician meant to him by speaking to the issue of what he believed anyone playing music needed to know about themselves and their music in order to be good at what they intended to do. In Dwight's words: "as long as you don't make a claim to doing this or that, to playing this style or that style, [then] you are playing yourself," you are drawing on what you are, who you are, and the music that derives from the sum total of that equation.

It sounded as though there was a hint of mysticism, magic, divinity to all this, but looking at Dwight's own explanation of how he found himself capable of making music suggested that he was saying something entirely rational, practical, and derived from experience—though he personally saw this as thoroughly invested with the significance of his religious beliefs. Looking at the story that he told of his own development as a person made it clear that he was driving toward this point: playing music, or committing any act of creativity, depended on who you are, so playing who you are was the most effective recipe for achieving creativity. Speaking or writing "who you are" was the most sure means of getting to the point of being an effective, creative poet or story writer, leader or teacher. In the end, this was Dwight's message:

> I'm insisting you can become a musician if you just do whatever you can do honestly. Whatever you are doing, whatever you can do–[just] be an honest conduit, then anything you're doing is just as valid as what I play.[39]

The Linkages

Dwight's music amalgamated a lifetime of influences. As Dwight saw it, the music he ended up making fused sounds from his family life and his school years, including the commercial recordings of popular rock and the lounge acts of the 1950's that he recalled as his mother's favorites; the throbbing jazz and dance music that his aunt and uncle played in their beer joint; the boisterous and robust sounds that high school kids discovered in early rock and roll; the mountain music that was the sonic background noise even when it went unnoticed by Dwight until his college years. The common denominator that Dwight saw in those diverse sound tracks that were the background noise for various stages of his life was the strenuous, muscular rhythm that cut through in all of these forms, and prodded Dwight to think of music as a pulsing pattern rather than a melody line of strung together notes.

Dwight's teaching was a unique equation that combined didactic elements with a penchant for focused demonstration of skills, added in a homespun brand of Socratic "give and take" that pushed dialogue as an essential form of inquiry and education, while placing a primacy on individual introspection and self-discovery through quiet internal contemplation. He reached for every resource available and built an arsenal of teaching tools that were not hinged to any single way of thinking, valued flexibility and adaptability, and sought personalized and tailored way of driving students to be inquisitive.

Dwight's religion was similarly a union of disparate ways of thinking about enduring questions. His way of thinking about God, and the manner in which he sought to comprehend what his obligations were to higher forces, could hardly be looked at as an organized system of belief; he eschewed organized religion, in spite of his seminary education and his long list of enduring relationships with Mennonites and Brethren. Dwight saw churches as large bureaucracies that magnified the flaws of people, politicized human relationships, monetized adherence by charging admission fees or membership tithes. The end result was a system that neglected those who needed spiritual guidance most—the "underclass." His understanding was that his banjo and fiddle classes provided at least a momentary community, a sanctuary, and a place where some of these enduring matters could be carefully contemplated.

Dwight's view was that he tried to teach more than banjo in his banjo class. Maybe, as some seemed to believe, he was wrong to do that because people showed up to such classes just wanting to have fun, learn a tune or two, revel in the fellowship. However, Dwight had decided that if he was to serve, to help people by teaching music, then the focus had to be on the way he could help people. Not everyone took to it, but he believed the music could accomplish this goal, and he resolved to focus on these priorities in his classes. And even if students entered a banjo class just to learn more banjoing, in the end Dwight's hope was that the experience would prod students toward thinking more mindfully about what all this meant, what their focused interest in playing old tunes said about the old musicians and their music, and what any of this might teach them about themselves.

Five

A Life of Teaching

Early Teaching Experiences

Dwight started teaching banjo almost as soon as he himself learned clawhammer in the early 1970s. He taught old time banjo in the early and mid–1980s to supplement his paycheck as a Mennonite minister. He started his own home-based banjo retreats in Pocahontas County in 1988, and travelled to numerous cities conducting weekend workshops and longer retreats; from the late 1980s those retreats were his primary source of income.[1]

There are numerous examples of Dwight eagerly sharing his newfound ability to play clawhammer, embracing the role of a teacher. He showed Sheila Kay Adams some banjoing in the early 1970s, probably at Ivydale.[2] In the early 1970s, after he had acquired his first banjo, Dwight gave Wayne Howard "the only lesson I ever had, showing me the proper clawhammer sequence of finger and thumb, which I practiced for weeks without ever starting a tune."[3] In the fall of 1972, while he was still living in Morgantown, Dwight began teaching old time music, especially banjo, in his rented apartment in Morgantown. West Virginian fiddler Rock Garton joined this informal class:

> It must [have] been fate or God that connected me to Dwight Diller. I was a junior in college in 1972 and trying to learn to play a tune on the fiddle with little success. Being a recreation major I enjoyed fun classes, so I took a fencing class taught by Mrs. Pearse. Dwight Diller was a grad student instructor helping Mrs. Pearse. At the end of the first class Dwight made an announcement that he was starting a string band, was going to teach banjo and fiddle and knowing how to play was not a requirement. Sounded like fun so I grabbed my fiddle and went to Dwight's apartment one night per week for the rest of that year.[4]

Several other musicians joined these sessions at Dwight's apartment including Jack Ramsey, Jackie Horvath, Andy and Becky Williams from Virginia, and Ron Mullennex from West Virginia.[5] Garton recalled:

> Andy and I played fiddle, Becky, Ron and Jack played banjo. There were no guitars nor other instruments, just fiddle and banjo. Dwight taught us by ear with no written music, one tune at a time. He would start with one instrument, get them started on a phrase of a tune, and while they were working on that he would go to the other group with their instrument and get them started on the same phrase that the first was working on. Normally each two-part tune could be taught in four phrases or less. We must have learned a dozen tunes that first year.[6]

Jackie Horvath remembered studying old time banjo with Dwight in 1972 in Morgantown. She met him at Ivydale in 1971, but did not get started with banjo lessons until a year later. Dwight taught at the Mountain Lair, the student union building at West Virginia University's Morgantown campus. He would meet students for an hour with members of the band the A.A. Cutters.

Five. A Life of Teaching 103

The A.A. Cutters band in a jam or practice session in a church basement in Morgantown, West Virginia, April 1973. Dwight is at right center, wearing a vest and armed with a fiddle. The standing musicians include Andy Williams (second from left) and Ron Mullennex (playing banjo), at right. Seated musicians—the students—include Becky Williams, playing banjo, on the left, and Elizabeth Weil, seated at closest foreground. The names of the other three students are shrouded in the mist of time (photograph by Carl Fleischhauer).

Band members Jack Ramsey and Ron Mullennex would pair with a student. Horvath recalled focusing exclusively on two tunes, "Liza Jane" and "Jimmy Johnson," for the better part of a year: "I was only allowed to play these tunes for a year, and I was not allowed to drop thumb."[7] The second hour of the banjo lessons at the Mountain Lair were devoted to listening to Dwight's band. Dwight occasionally taught banjo at Horvath's home. They would sit outside on the porch. He would play a tune and then hand the banjo to her. Horvath recalled that Dwight stressed the importance of listening closely to the old music.[8]

In the early 1970s, when he first started attending old time festivals, and during the time he spent with musicians in Lexington, Virginia, Dwight was intent on teaching anyone interested in learning the intricacies of clawhammer.[9] David Winston remembered sitting down with Dwight at a gathering at Charlie Trimble's home in June 1973, and carefully going over the basic right hand clawhammer mechanics.[10] Old time musician Carl Baron recalled a similar lesson:

Dwight teaching banjo at the Augusta Heritage Center's summer 1975 session. The class contained banjo and fiddle students (courtesy Dwight Diller).

> During 1973, I was just starting to learn clawhammer banjo. I had been a guitar finger picker who had turned to using a flat pick to back up the old time band I was in. At one party I sought the advice of both Odell [McGuire] and Dwight (who at that time preferred to be called "De-white"). In the space of about 5 minutes, I got three lessons that I took to heart and which were extremely important in my playing development. I can't say which one gave which technique lesson but here they are: (1) "Stop waving your thumb around like a flag in the breeze." The thumb needs to be in a fixed position; (2) The thumb needs to land on the 5th string before the forefinger (strongly advised forefinger use rather then the middle finger) strikes down on a string; and (3) for the left hand, one finger—one fret, i.e. use all four fingers.[11]

In Dick Kimmel's words, Dwight was a teacher by disposition and personality. He was patient, and inclined to share freely. "He always shared his music. He had this stuff in his soul," and he gave freely to anyone interested. Kimmel recalled an evening after the Black Mountain Bluegrass Boys had played in Rochester, New York. They were in an attic with mattresses set out on the floor in the home of a kindly soul who put them up after the concert—whose name is long forgotten. Dwight was showing someone "Elzick's Farewell" on the fiddle, "playing each phrase slowly," guiding the other fiddler through every step of the tune. "That tune surfaces now and again," Kimmel said, and it always nudges him back to that memory of Dwight playing carefully, slowly, consistently for that single impromptu lesson. To Kimmel, Dwight was an exacting teacher who focused on all elements of playing. Kimmel remembered another impromptu lesson, this time a quick banjo lesson that Dwight gave Kimmel's banjo playing brother during a visit in November 1975 to Dwight's home in Frost, West Virginia. "Don't bunch up," Kimmel recalled Dwight telling his student, focusing on what posture does to playing.[12]

Retreats and Workshops

In 1973, Dwight taught at the Augusta Heritage Center in Elkins, West Virginia, when the Center was first established. Dwight taught a weeklong class during the summer sessions of the Augusta Heritage Center from 1981 through at least 2001. Beginning in 1987 to 1989, in various locations such as Hardy County, West Virginia, and later on his own property in Hillsboro and on a plot of land in Huntersville, Pocahontas County, he taught groups or individuals who made the trek up his mountain for a week of intensive banjo study. In the late 1980s, Dwight taught workshops in Cass, West Virginia; he co-taught one summer workshop at Cass with Ken Perlman in July 1998.[13] Dwight conducted banjo camps in the Portland, Michigan area from 1997 to 2002.[14] In the late 1990s he began traveling to England to teach banjo retreats and play at a variety of folk venues in the company of fellow West Virginian Dave Bing, with whom he produced the CD "In England" in 1999.[15] At around the same time, he began traveling to Pittsburgh, Pennsylvania, where he would hold weekend "banjo retreats" and house concerts, a practice that continued through 2014 and a venue to which he was personally devoted.

The years of annual travel to England provided opportunities to concertize in small pub settings that were uniquely English experiences. The workshop venues provided Dwight with distinctive teaching opportunities and the chance to exert influence and shape a completely different old time music community. Nick Pilley recalled:

> Dwight met with Keith Johnson who founded our organization, Friends of American Old Time Music and Dance, FOAOTMAD, and came over both to give workshops (with Dave Bing) and also to appear at the organization's annual old time festival in Gainsborough, Lincolnshire, Keith Johnson's hometown.

Dwight and his second wife, Elaine, in the summer of 1987 at his first week-long banjo class, held in Hardy County, West Virginia. Dwight's son, Caleb, born in 1984, holds the "Banjo Camp" sign, and daughter Susanna, born in 1986, is behind him, firmly in her father's embrace (courtesy Dwight Diller).

The workshops were held from 1999 to 2004. The one in 1999 was in December but others were November. He was unable to make 2005 when he was recovering from a car accident. With the exception of the first one that ran from 4 to 7 December, these were two weekends apart, the first for beginners and the second for intermediate. For example, in 2000 that would have been 18th-20th and 24th-26th November. In December 1999 Dwight performed at the Trinity Arts Centre in Gainsborough and he was a guest at the Gainsborough Old Time Music and Dance Festival in February 1998, 1999, and 2004.[16]

The first two years' worth of travel and workshop events underscore the uniqueness of Dwight's schedule in the United Kingdom. For example, during 20–22 February 1998, Dwight attended the Gainsborough Old Time Festival, where he concertized and did some teaching. He performed at numerous poetically named venues including the Junction in Ripponden, Yorks; Anchor Folk Club, Leigh on Sea, Essex; Black Swan Folk Club, Dog and Partridge, Bollington, south of Manchester; Robin Hood Folk Club, The Beech Tree, Nottingham. During the first eight days of March, he performed at the Grimsby Folk Club, Lincoln Castle, Grimsby; the White Horse Folk Club, Beverley; Dartford Folk Club, Kent; the Hale End Folk Club, County Arms, Hale End, London. Dwight did an interview on 7 March at the CMR Radio Session in London, and performed at the Whepstead Village Hall, Suffolk, and then finished up with a concert at The Horns, Gnosall, Stafford.

In February and March 1999 Dwight returned to England in the company of Dave Bing and attended the Gainsborough Old Time Festival from 19 to 21 February, where the two performed concerts and taught workshops. On 22 February, they were interviewed by BBC Radio Derby, and then, through the end of February, they performed at the Griffin, Plumtree, Nottingham; the Lewes Folk Club, Sussex; Dog and Partridge, Bollington, south of Manchester; the Davy Lamp Folk Club, Washington, Tyne and Wear; and the Horsham Folk Club, in Sussex. In March, the two performed at the White Horse Folk Club, Beverley; sat for an interview with BBC Radio Scotland, Edinburgh; and recorded the CD "In England" in a home studio in Gainsborough, after which they resumed their concertizing at the Islington Folk Club; The Empress of Russia, London; the Heart of England Bluegrass Club, Kenilworth; Angel Inn, Llandeilo, South Wales— where they also conducted some workshop teaching.

Phil Tyler, who was introduced to Dwight by the band Cordelia's Dad, functioned as the tour manager and driver for the tours in 1998 and 1999. Tyler noted that most of these shows were in folk clubs and were "very grass-roots" kinds of events where the first part of each half of the evening would be taken up by "floor singers," performers from the audience who took turns singing a song, playing a tune.[17] FOAOTMAD organizer Keith Johnson appeared to have sought the advice and guidance of several American musicians in 1995 at the Galax Fiddlers Convention regarding old time musicians in the United States who would be willing to commit to an annual banjo retreat in the United Kingdom. Old time fiddler Betty Vornbrock and her guitar playing husband, Billy Cornette, who themselves were performing in England as early as 1996, recalled the difference Dwight made: in the mid-1990s, they heard a handful of banjo players capable of "good, clean melody lines and timing, who knew their way around the neck." Just several years later, after a year or two of Dwight's annual lessons, they began to hear more rhythm, push and drive in the music of old time banjo players in England. Vornbrock stated, sixteen years later, that after a couple of Dwight's annual teaching gigs in the England: "We could hear a vast improvement. [...] It had become obvious that Dwight's insistence on embodying the beat and bringing it into the right hand had transformed the players—they were now striving for that elusive thing about old time music: how to make it move."[18] Dwight thought the teaching experience in England was vastly different than the retreats he conducted in the United States: highly collegial, much more relaxed, more homogeneous student populations perhaps because of the unifying influence of FOAOTMAD.

The annual banjo and fiddle workshops in Pittsburgh, Pennsylvania, began in the mid-1990s as part of an effort to broaden the audience to which Dwight was appealing by building on his multiple capabilities—musician, balladeer, storyteller, preserver of ancient cultural ways and traditions. Dwight was encouraged to travel more widely, to agree to bigger musical events in larger venues, and to call on his musicianship as well as his capacity as a storyteller and balladeer in order to attract more diverse audiences. Colleagues helped develop promotional literature, articles were placed in prominent old time music publications, and—at least briefly—Dwight consulted a publicist. From the mid-1990s through at least 2003, the annual December event in Pittsburgh involved a workshop hosted by a local music store, and a concert held at a local church—instead of the more familiar home-hosted workshops where the accompanying concert was limited to students involved in the multi-day instructional event.[19] In the early 2000s, Dwight probed the possibility of other annual workshop events; for example, in the first quarter of 2002 and 2003 he travelled to northern Virginia where he conducted three-day work-

Dwight's first banjo class in England. The students arrived for the class Thursday, ate and "camped" on the premises, and worked intensively from Friday morning until noon on Sunday on rhythm, "just rhythm" (courtesy Dwight Diller).

shops and a Saturday evening concert for students, an arrangement initially envisioned as a replication of the long-running annual Pittsburgh event.[20]

In 2003, at the urging of friends and colleagues, including one of the co-hosts of the annual Pittsburgh banjo and fiddle workshops, the Yew Pine Cultural Traditions, Incorporated, was established as a non-profit 501(c)(3) organization with the goal of facilitating projects aimed at identifying and preserving the cultural heritage of the Appalachian Region. That non-profit worked in association with the Pocahontas County Free Libraries on Dwight's *Across the YewPines* project, begun in earnest in 2005, that focused on the Hammonses; the Pocahontas County Free Libraries' Board of Trustees was involved as a sponsor and financial supporter of that effort.[21] The Yew Pine non-profit was meant to accommodate a range of specific projects driven by friends and associates, in which Dwight would be involved but in a fashion that would not detract from the smaller, more intimate home-based workshops and house concerts that he favored as his preferred venue for teaching. The years 2004 and 2005 were in effect a transitional point in this process. Dwight felt more comfortable with the smaller events run out of a home, with the house concerts staged expressly for his students. The co-hosting arrangement that had been at the core of the annual Pittsburgh workshop shifted; the model involving the music store that had hosted the annual workshop and the church that had been the venue for the concert gave way to a home-based package of events limited to subscribed students that continued from 2005 through 2014.

Dwight conducted banjo retreats on his Browns Creek property in Marlinton during the mid–2000s through at least early 2015, and engaged friends such as Bob Sattler from Charleston, West Virginia, to help him with the teaching work.[22] By late 2014, Dwight was scheduling fewer week-long workshops on his property, and by mid–2015 he began informing friends that he would probably not be teaching any organized retreats, though he remained amenable to conducting two or three day workshops with one or two students.

Additionally, in the early 2000s, in the midst of all this banjo-focused activity, Dwight was working on the feature length film *The Fifth String*, written and directed by Jack Gordon Phelan, in which Dwight and John Morris were the two main actors.

* * *

Phelan described the movie, released in 2004, as the story of Daniel Greenfield, an Ivy League music professor who returned to his West Virginia home after achieving success in the academic world in order to attend the funeral of the man who raised him. Greenfield, the character played by Dwight, abandoned his West Virginia birthplace and all it represented, turning his back on the poverty and humiliation that characterized his young life, leaving before he had to grow old with the burden of being a "hillbilly." Greenfield returned to the Yew Pine Mountains and ultimately confronted the shame he had long held for the mountain culture and the "old-timey music" of his youth.[23]

Phelan remembered that the project was first conceived in 1998. Phelan's wife's father, Joseph D. Rizzi, a banjo player, had attended one of Dwight's banjo camps, and encouraged his film making son-in-law to meet the musician. At that time, Phelan was working with the Discovery channel in Pennsylvania. He and Rizzi, the film's executive producer, spent a weekend with Dwight in Cass, attended one of Dwight's slide show presentations about the Hammons family, and were captivated by what Phelan recalled was, in his view, an "epic story." Phelan, Rizzi and Dwight talked about the idea of a film concerning West Virginia's traditional music and musicians, and discussed all manner of conceptual starting points. Before the plan for the movie became a fictional story, the idea was to make a documentary that, as Phelan described it, was modeled on Robert M. Pirsig's 1974 book *Zen and the Art of Motorcycle Maintenance* in the sense that the project's aim was to depict an "artistic journey." Rizzi envisioned a project that was intensely focused on the old music of West Virginia, a film that dwelled on the origins of the music, and showcased the contemporary musicians such as Dwight and John Morris who were steeped in the tunes and stories of the area.

Phelan met West Virginia fiddler John Morris in 1999 at an old time festival, possibly Clifftop, and engaging him in a long discussion on the planned film. In roughly that same time frame, Phelan travelled to Washington, D.C., and met with Alan Jabbour at the Library of Congress, poured over the Hammons family holdings in the American Folklife Center, and listened to the recordings made in the early 1970s by Fleischhauer and Jabbour. Phelan and Rizzi returned to Pocahontas County numerous times, and in the course of meeting and talking to local musicians and others who would help tell this documentary story they drew the conclusion, in Phelan's account, that these were a shy, reticent people who were protective of one another and not entirely garrulous in discussion. Gradually, the plan shifted to a fictionalized approach to the story largely because, as Phelan saw it, that would allow the development of the key ideas that had motivated him when he first immersed himself in the subject. Moreover, Phelan remembered, the archival video resources and the still photographs—including what Phelan recalled as Dwight's own stirring still pictures of the Hammons family—were simply "not enough." Those "visuals" did not come together in a manner that would tell the story Phelan wanted to put on film, so he opted to pursue his own images, developing a dramatic film story that would encompass the visuals that came to his mind when he first encountered Dwight and discussed these issues during his first trip to Cass.

Phelan wrote the script, and approached the development of the structure of the story in an actively collaborative manner. He and Dwight and John Morris had lengthy discussions on matters concerning "authenticity," and Phelan became acutely aware of the need to guard against any sense that the story was shaped by "outsiders." He worked hard to make certain the narrative that was the basis for the project emerged from continuous dialogue with Dwight and John Morris and others encountered in the course of making of the film.

The first cut of the film was about three and a half hours long, according to Rizzi. The final version emerged as an 83-minute film. A graveyard scene where John Morris spoke a eulogy for 15 minutes in the first cut of that scene was gradually trimmed to a manageable length that worked to grab and hold audience interest. Phelan recalled a first take in the film when Dwight, acting in the role of Professor Daniel Greenfield, awakens to John Morris' character fiddling "Little Cat." The first filming captured a full ten minutes of that tune, but that, too, was gradually trimmed. The first version of the film, Phelan recalled, was slow, and the "journey" approach required a lot of voice over work. The editing process brought that into more of a balance with the acting and dialogue.

Phelan recalled that he often referred back to Dwight's slide show about the Hammons family and the narrative that evolved alongside of those slides. Phelan saw the slides as the educational core for the film, a major motivating force that shaped the script and screenplay he developed, and informed the collaborative discussions that took place between Phelan, John Morris and Dwight over the dialogue and scene staging during the course of the movie's production. In that slide show, Phelan averred, Dwight was "educating, on a different level," and that didactic motivation suffused the entire project.[24]

In 2007, in a rare posting to *Banjo Hangout*, an online banjo community, Dwight replied to comments about the feature film:

> The theme and the issues [...] addressed were for West Virginians. We here in this state have been pushed, pulled, humiliated, shamed, exploited and have been treated the same as a "third world country" since George Washington, Lord Fairfax and that crew of henchmen came in around the mid-1700s. We here in this state are childlike and childish, and have done a really poor job of protecting ourselves. [West Virginia has] always [been] a state owned and operated by outsiders and continues to be moving into the future the same way, probably "forever." Plus, as far as the "politically correct police" are concerned, it is always open season on "hillbillies." [...] So, when John and I were writing the script along with Jack who was from the outside, John and I were wanting to reach West Virginians in general and the young West Virginians in particular. In most parts of my home state, different levels of shame, despair and depression permeate the culture. From a secular point of view, we wanted something, for once, that could possibly help offset the constant barrage. Hopefully, the young just might possibly find something to be proud of [and] to connect with.[25]

The pervasive influence and insidious power of outsiders had always been a component of Dwight's understanding of the political dynamics and economic realities of contemporary West Virginia. That coexisted with a historical sense, derived from numerous scholarly and popular sources, and fed into a view suggesting that West Virginians were different: they were hard and harsh, tough and resilient. They were survivors, but they were also singularly vulnerable because they tended to be open, honest, gullible, sharing and transparent in their intentions, simple and straightforward in their beliefs. As Dwight told the story, his own film ended up being an exercise demonstrating this, with "outsiders" seeking to superimpose on the enterprise the kinds of broadly accepted conventional wisdoms and stereotypes about Appalachians that always angered Dwight:

> It was folks in Hollywood hooked up with one of the three main networks who were advertising in newspapers going into the coalfields of southern West Virginia wanting—without saying [so]–poor, dumb, ignorant hillbillies and "snakehandlers" preferred. Those who don't have the brains of a downhill sled track. [They were aiming to develop] one of those "reality" shows [or] to revive "The Beverly Hillbillies"—that was the target.[26]

Dwight argued that some very critical seconds were stripped out of the film, a real loss from his perspective because those slim pieces of celluloid would have contributed to making this a film about West Virginia, and by West Virginians, a distinctive piece of work distinguished by its positive and uplifting approach to the state and its inhabitants. Instead, to Dwight, it ended up being by and large more of the same. Dwight dwelled on the way those in "control" sought to introduce the symbols of poverty, ignorance, isolation that had characterized the way Appalachia was thought of in the arts. This was a critical point to Dwight: the musical heritage that was at the core of the film was a precise reflection of the chemistry of West Virginians, and depicting it in the manner he urged would have captured the resilience of West Virginians, the crack of their step, their simple optimism and abiding faith, and their capacity to solve problems and live resourcefully. He bemoaned what he considered the lost opportunity to capture that power in the film.

However, devoted students of Dwight's were very positive about the film and, over a decade after its release, *The Fifth String* continued to be viewed with enthusiasm and interest by this audience—if only because it telegraphed Dwight's points about the need to respect the traditions, recognize their vulnerability, and exercise great care and personal responsibility in the act of attempting to learn about the culture and practices that were elements of West Virginian tradition, including the old music.

On Teaching

Teaching, to Dwight, was the mission to which he was most committed. From at least the early 1980s, he saw himself primarily as a teacher, not a musician.[27] He saw teaching as less of a skill than a "gift," an intuitive capacity to perceive needs, requirements and strengths in students; quickly assess the best way to draw out the student, to stimulate the appetite for learning; and keep the challenge intriguing enough that the student's desire to study becomes self-sustaining. Dwight described his approach:

> I just wade right in. I make instant decisions after trying to sense where the person or class is at. There are times I realize a certain tune I was going to use just won't work for a particular class—is too hard technically or too hard to understand its meaning. No matter how interested students are [...] the teacher can't overwhelm them. I don't mind giving students stuff that's really hard but I don't want to overwhelm them to the point that they can't do it. That'll break their spirit.[28]

The notion of "accepting authority" was a critical organizing concept for Dwight's teaching approach. He appeared to have meant that broadly, but he also used that point as a means of identifying what was important to him as a teacher, and critical to any intellectual exchange that might originate in a classroom experience:

> Somewhere along the line we as a nation have to start accepting authority so that we can start speaking with authority again whether it's the parents in the home or the teachers in the school or whatever and it also comes into the music world.
>
> [...] People who have had an opportunity and have spent a lot of years with it, have lived it, you better listen to what they're saying just like I've tried to listen to what the Hammonses have said about the music and accept their authority about things. And try to take my time. At times I didn't take my time, at times I did
>
> [...] Well if you're interested in the music there's something to be said for people who have spent time, whether it's in the trade or whatever it is.... As you're trying to learn things in the music, try to learn things from them. I need to put a lot of stock into what Sherman says about the music. It's one thing if people tell you lies, but I've never had Sherman tell me a lie. Whatever he says I accept that that's his word on things or Maggie or Burl. I'm saying we don't need to make these people into gods but we need on the other hand to accept their authority as they speak about the music.[29]

At least in part as a result of this, Dwight developed a reputation as a tough, unrelenting, occasionally unreasonable taskmaster, perhaps largely because he brought a level of seriousness to the task of teaching, and organized his workshops and retreats in a manner that challenged conventional wisdoms about teaching banjo.[30]

In Dwight's view, teaching was the challenge of balancing the needs of a small group with the requirements of each individual. The degree of difficulty in teaching banjo derived from the differences between people. As Dwight put it, each student was different in terms of where they were in their walk with the musical instrument. Groups were manageable; all that took was the capacity to demonstrate leadership and exert the authority necessary to keep a class on track. Managing the teaching responsibilities when it came to individuals was tougher because that involved pressing individuals who might be reluctant, shy, ill-at-ease, or lacking confidence to go beyond their comfort level. For Dwight, the music was the leveler, the variable in the mix that bridged the gap between income disparities, levels of literacy, distinctions between native abilities and talent. As Dwight told Patrick Costello in an interview in the early 2000s:

> It's important to know, yes, the music is hard but it's like anything else, if you want it and you are willing to accept the discipline then you can do it.[31]

Dwight consistently made the case that music was not about tunes. He was not a repertoire builder.[32] A student might come away from a class with just one or two tunes. Dwight discouraged building a repertoire in the way one might seek to amass a war chest, and urged that students put their eyes on a very restricted set of tunes as their long term learning goal:

> What I have been trying to get my students to do in recent years is to pick out 25 tunes to do for the remainder of life. And then work, work, work to intuit, intuit, intuit so they can be used to produce one's own "personal cultural messages" [that spring] forth from EACH person's internal pulse. If that is not there, then there can never ever be Music; as I said, melody without massive rhythm, which leads to powerful explosively violent silences leading to one's own personal cultural message, [without that] THEN it is only dull dreary drivel. Cece Conway pointed out that the most well-known old time fiddler in the world, Tommy Jarrell of Mount Airy, North Carolina, "never learned any tunes after 1920." [...] Pick out no more than 25 tunes and begin to really pay attention to them. Pick out those you are compelled to play. Think you might die if you had to give them up musically speaking. Then start in holding the number to 15. And if you were able to discipline yourself, keep the 15 in mind and let them go in and out. However, then only work on 4 or at most 5 at one time probably for a year. If you were to do that, then you would be able to start to begin to really learn the music.[33]

He focused relentlessly on the right hand work that sustained the rhythmic core of the central West Virginian music that he taught, but to Dwight it was equally important that the student understand the meaning behind the music, the "cultural messages" that the tunes conveyed. The notion of "cultural messages" transmitted by the old tunes and stories figured prominently in Dwight's classes. He described what this meant and how it was regionally and historically relevant to groups that had made home grown music in the United States, and indeed throughout the world. He integrated what he read, what he learned from observation, what he recalled from experience, and what he imbibed from wide ranging conversations with students and others, mixing all that together, assembling it as a package intended to communicate how this fabric of messages conveyed social and cultural values. He spoke about how these messages coexisted with historic and geographic realities, and how these were conveyed within cultural groupings by teachers, inside of families, and as the result of relationships that developed within specific and coherent populations that experienced life, challenges, and critical benchmark moments together. As Dwight put it:

> The music is not about tunes. It's ultimately about transferring cultural messages. What's the cultural message in the West Virginia music as opposed to Kentucky or southwest Virginia or wherever? Once you catch on to the fact that there is a message, then you can start working on how to understand that message and what your part is in transferring that message.[34]

Dwight deliberately refrained from characterizing or articulating the cultural messages themselves, leaving that part of the learning to students. He recognized, in an unstated way, that as the "conduit" of this music, he would have overstepped his bounds and taken on another role had he attempted to articulate the messages themselves or translate them for the student.

"Be careful with the music"

Dwight taught his students that the old music was brittle, breakable, and required care in playing it, listening to it, and learning it:

> As I keep saying in my music classes—be careful, be careful, be careful, be careful with the music. [...] What are you doing with the music, why are you here, why are you learning banjo from me. The older I get the more I listen to Lee Hammons play the banjo, hear Wade Ward play the banjo [... these are] people who touch the music very lightly. They've got a lot of snap, a lot of drive, but in their music they touch very lightly. When Lee Hammons played the banjo in the *Shaking Down the Acorns* album he was 86, 87 years old. You think about his age, his banjo playing was letter perfect without being stilted and studied. That was all those years' worth of living distilled down to about four or five notes. You talk about economy [...] well, he knew how to leave the empty spaces in there. [...] When you're young, immature, [...] you'll just run headlong into the music you won't know your mistreating the music and when you take the music for your own personal gain you're milking it. It won't really work for you. It will seem to work but it will turn against you, it will turn sour. Lee Hammons' music doesn't reflect that, and Wade Ward's doesn't reflect that to me. I guess that's what I've learned over the years: you'd better be careful with that music. It's just like knowledge; you'd better be careful with that stuff. It will eat you up you won't even know what's happened.[35]

He believed contemporary cultural tastes and commercial trends had combined with a lot of other forces and crowded out much of the fragile cultural structures that sustained this West Virginian music, to the point that it was seriously diminished and no longer a sustainable form. Dwight seemed to have fluctuated between a sense of pessimism regarding the staying power of traditional music, and optimism about the survivability of the music. The attention drawn to the old, traditional tunes, the commercialization of some aspects of the music, the growing number of "stars" in the late 1970s and early 1980s gave him reason to fret, but in the end he suggested the music could withstand the increasing attention. In his interview with Jack Bernhardt in 1983, Dwight stated:

> The question is can the music stand it. Can the music stand it. [...] I think, yeah, Madison Avenue, they're always looking for something new. I think the music is probably tough enough, just pure gut tough that it can stand it and come through on the other side and yeah it's going to be prostituted and manipulated—a few years ago I would have said no, it couldn't stand it, keep all these people out of it. I think possibly it can stand it and [for] the people that are really in a tight bind, that don't even know that such thing really exists except for the Beverly Hillbillies, it might even do some of them some good just to catch a little bit of it.[36]

In 1996 Dwight told Bates Littlehales: "As far as transferring it within its own mountain culture, the message in the old music is pretty much dead. The mountain people just aren't taking it up for the most part."[37]

In Dwight's thinking, the character of the old music itself was a democratizing force. It did not permit one person to be extraordinary, to be so far more capable than others pursuing the old music. As he told Patrick Costello in a 2012 interview:

> There aren't supposed to be any stars in old time music. I'm not a star. I'm a conduit. I'm supposed to pass it along to people. I'm supposed to give like the old people gave to me.

This old music was an accessible dialect that everyone could learn to speak, he continued, and it was valuable only insofar as it was played in the way it was intended:

> It's spoken. Forget about dots on a page. Listen, listen, listen ... listen to the Old People because that is the source. [This is] homemade music built for the parlor or the front porch out under a shade tree. It's not performance music. You put it on a stage and it loses its beauty and it's for everybody, it's not for a select few. The music is homemade music. If you set your mind to it you can learn it. Don't let anyone take that away from you.[38]

Teaching Banjo

Dwight described the process of learning the banjo as involving a series of phases, a gradual recognition of the combination of skill, capability and spirit required to make the transition to the new level of knowledge, using terms that resonated with the way philosophers have spoken of the process of "becoming." Students often came to the venture of learning the banjo after many years of working on the instrument and acquiring repertoire and facility. As Dwight stated:

> The problem that arises is often the student is familiar with "many tunes," but habits have been "learned" which are detrimental to playing the music as it needs to be played.

The student needed to "unlearn" habits and acquire a sense of the importance of "rhythm and pulse." In Dwight's words:

> The "tunes" themselves are of minor importance in this realm. Too much emphasis is placed on the number of tunes that a person can "play," when often they have no rhythm to play any properly.[39]

A "beginner" is a blank slate, and therefore did not have the burden of undoing habits.[40]

The next step involved integrating the practices of "deep listening" and "learning rhythm techniques," the first being a "mental" adjustment and the second being a technical capability. Successfully learning this meant that the student had mastered the techniques for strong rhythm and could achieve syncopation. It also meant that the student had become steeped in the archaic music of the "Old People" to the point that the idiomatic qualities and uniqueness of Appalachian traditional music had become at least intellectually accessible and familiar. The student then moved to integrating the physical skills and the levels of awareness of the music, especially its distinctive throbbing pulse, meaning that the physicality of the skill and the intuitive sense of the music began to become one whole rather than separate capabilities. At that point, the student could understand the environment necessary to preserve these archaic art forms and, at that point, the student was becoming attuned to the manner in which altering the context of the music acted on the music itself.[41] The student had begun to break the code, and was capable of a certain fluency in this idiomatic musical language.[42]

The final phase, in Dwight's linear representation of progress, was the point at which the student had understood (1) why they actively became invested in learning this art form, and (2) why they had become prepared to contribute to its protection and preservation—and perhaps become a conduit for communicating knowledge about this music. Dwight's goal was to "transform" the student by the process, so that the student could intuitively understand the value of this exercise and the extent to which the process became one of learning about more than the music—shedding light on motivation, desire, capability and life goals. The workshop should teach the student to hear and sense more dimensions to the music, and grasp the resonance of the past in these old, surviving tunes in a fashion that telegraphed "cultural messages." At that point, the student exercised care in moving forward with learning, taking "time to learn what was down inside the tune." The student had "now become able to shape the sound of every note and start to control the silences between the notes," a sort of transcendent sense of what all this represented musically, and personally.

This was, as Dwight averred, a costly journey in terms of time invested and energy expended. Quoting the old Clay County fiddler, Wilson Douglas, Dwight emphasized that "It gets awful expensive just to play a little bit of fiddle," a reference meant to signal the investment, the time, the energy necessary to produce a bond with the music, and an appreciation of what it means.[43] To Dwight this journey involved coming out of the process knowing a lot more than just the kinetics of clawhammer. There was a certain amount of self-awareness necessary to achieve the goal, and a great deal of processing. His classes involved a group dynamic, but also left enough room for an individual to stumble around and figure out what they wanted, and what they needed to do in order to learn this music.

Dwight struggled for a long time to find increasingly apt metaphors, examples of physical and mental exertions that in some fashion paralleled the task of learning banjo, expressions describing similar learning puzzles that could convey what he was attempting to argue about banjo basics. In the 2000s, he likened the degree of difficulty involved in trying to get the old style banjo right hand rhythm to attempting to learn crucial survival skills in an adrenalized state. He did not equate banjo playing with a life preserving skill, but he saw the mind/body coordination necessary to grasp and integrate the movements as being similar to learning target shooting, small arms or rifle shooting, and hunting skills.[44] He worked assiduously to back students off the analytical way of internalizing the locomotion he was trying to teach. He adapted elements of the teaching approach used by John Yeager, a weapons instructor, to in effect make the case that skills "not learned in an adrenalized state cannot be replicated in an adrenalized state."[45] Yeager argued that learning survival the way the "caveman" integrated this kind of knowledge into their way of living meant that knowledge became part of a life lesson that stuck more effectively than book learning, so to speak. Dwight commented:

> This is why I am working as hard as I can to move to the place that he [Yeager] is talking about. It is easy [in one way] to stay in data and analyze and so on but this is why I keep saying that people who [bring] their thinking brain to the table in this music, they will never ever in their whole life get it. People in task cultures, can they move to that place? School systems have trained them from beginning to think and think and think.

Diller appropriated these notions this way:

> So when you get to [the] "caveman" [stage], you are just beginning. A really good beginning ... but from that point you can learn to play rhythm. [...] Move into the caveman's [space], develop a strong rhythm. Art only comes from the human spirit. That is where "IT" resides; where the "way" resides. Where there is a void that God's spirit can reside in you. But it is also the place where demonic spirits will come in without invitation. God's spirit only enters by invitation. [...] To play the old music [you] must go to the spirit by way of the caveman.[46]

Dwight relied on references to all manner of activities that depended on an internalized, finely timed physical movement—archery, Olympic target shooting, martial arts—to drive home the point that this was a difficult skill set to learn in an entirely cerebral way. He argued that this particular use of bone and muscle mass required a sense of timing, a bit of instinct, and a level of relaxation paired to an internal music, a personal

Dwight teaching banjo at a 1991 banjo retreat conducted at Seneca Park, in the state forest that borders the Greenbrier River in Pocahontas County, West Virginia. In keeping with his practice of playfully bestowing nicknames on his students, these two serious women were called "Trials" and "Tribulations" (courtesy Bob Thornburg).

"pulse" that linked the dynamics of what the body needed to do with where the mind must go to let the "spirit" work its magic. So, it was a bit of alchemy, some spiritualism, a specialized calisthenics hooked together. Dwight stressed the importance of intuition in learning and playing old tunes. He felt strongly about the dangers of stretching beyond the boundaries, the natural elasticity, of the old tunes, and he was concerned with the likelihood that this would distort the cultural context or message. Dwight also stressed sticking close to one's "personal pulse," and after teaching the mechanics of the right hand movement that was the propulsive system for his percussive banjoing, he would pause and tell his students to feel their heart pumping away. This, he said, was the cadence behind so much of this music, the "personal pulse" that bound people to old tunes.[47]

There was a level of consistency in Dwight's teaching beginning with his first lessons in the early and mid–1970s and continuing throughout his active teaching career. From the earliest point, he taught with a level of seriousness about the music, and focused on the extent to which the rhythmic action on the banjo derived from the player's body itself—posture counted, the shoulders and back muscles and skeleton ("bone on bone") were an important part of the equation, and the right hand work was critical to the syncopated sound. Beginning in the mid–1970s Dwight taught a sparse and highly syncopated banjo style that was light on melody and emphasized rhythm. He taught students to work the thumb, cocked and primed to catch the fifth string hard, so that it aggressively produced a pop that played with every beat rather than every other beat. And from the beginning of his teaching efforts, he counseled students to keep a relaxed right hand, taught a snapping arm delivery that drove the clawhammer cadence, and coached students to stay ahead of the beat so as to drive the music forward.[48]

Dwight's recipe started off with teaching the importance of listening, and then impressing on students the importance of getting the rhythmic core of the music before going on to the ornamental use of notes. In Dwight's words:

> First, then, is the listening and listening and listening to music with good rhythm to try to get it internalized. The local powerful fiddler, Mose Coffman, said: "If you cannot whistle it, hum it, or sing it, you can never play it" meaning *never play "IT."*

The second step was getting at the rhythm, and this was a lifelong exercise of continuous learning, not something that, to Dwight, was easily acquired in an intellectual fashion. As Dwight put it:

> When I have students here, there is only a few hours that week to help folks when they leave, to go back home with some idea of how to begin to produce their own rhythm which is their own personal pulse. […] My goal has always been to help the student to get a grasp of the fact that rhythm is first, then to inject that melody notes inside of that rhythm.[49]

Dwight made the case that any effort to get at the rhythm needed to stretch the student's capabilities. The student must push beyond the speed at which they can play the tune, playing at least fifteen to twenty five percent faster than the slow beat they are used to. "There also has to be a strong downbeat which comes from the bull whip snap of the totally relaxed hand and wrist. As well as forearm, upper arm, shoulder, back, seat, legs." The tune needed to be "fast enough that you cannot use your mind for one second." The music cannot spring from the analytical side of the brain, it cannot be the result of reasoning and analysis, and that is why the element of speed played a role in learning the rhythm, internalizing the beat.[50] Dwight nudged the student to playing in a syncopated manner:

Play the rhythm hard up against the first drum beat. This means that everything inside of you must be relaxed. No muscles. No muscles. No voluntary muscles. You do all kinds of stuff daily with very little use of those muscles. Then get your *one tune*, not tunes, and start taking this syncopated rhythm and begin using it to drive your playing in order to get some good rhythm going and get some drive in your music. When you take the above route, you got to learn to drive the drum beat. You have to be hitting the drum beat so it is like you are getting ahead of it.[51]

If you play this "straight" it will be end up with a dull beat:

This has max syncopated rhythm. You must play your tune you been working on with this exactly. Exactly. This will take some doing. Your headphones are the secret. They will help get the rhythm internalized and help drive the banjo rhythm up against the beat. Initially, you got to let the drummer carry you until you start getting the rhythm. Then you start driving the drummer. That is hard to do. It takes your whole being to do that. Body has to be relaxed in order to do that. Will probably take months to accomplish but you will begin to see some improvement. Start with only one tune. You are not allowed to go to the second drumbeat until you can really hit the rhythm of the first one. That is how you must play all the time. Always hitting the rhythm hard NOT LOUD OR FAST but using the punch that Muhammad Ali used. Violent quick jabs. Strike and strike again. Plan on months for this to take place.

Dwight argued that this percussive, throbbing beat was at the center of the old time tunes and that it could be teased out by focusing initially on the rhythmic center of gravity of these tunes:

This what you got to finally master. THEN you can go ahead and play old time tunes but got to have this kind of rhythm underneath no matter how fast you play. What you will find when you got "IT" [is that] it will feel like you are lifting OR pulling the "Music" out of the banjo or, more important, "the banjo is playing you." When it happens, your system will know.[52]

Teaching Fiddle

From the 1980s through at least the early 2000s Dwight believed that even after decades of work he still had not captured the intensity of the old sound on the fiddle; he only began feeling comfortable with his fiddle playing between 2000 and 2010, and confident with his fiddle playing between 2011 and 2015.[53] His fiddling remained very straightforward and simple through the first decade of the 2000s; Dwight tended to play in cross-tuning, stayed away from patterns or shuffles, and built a strong rhythmic element into his fiddle playing. However, beginning in the early 1970s as he himself was learning the instrument, he was prepared to teach what he had learned and what he had come to know about old style fiddling in the traditions he was exposed to from the late 1960s in central West Virginia. As early as 1973, Dwight took on fiddle students, including Andy Williams and Rock Garton, in Morgantown, West Virginia; each of those students went on to become capable, unique fiddle players with their own special touch.[54]

Dwight appeared to prefer to work with young fiddlers on a one-to-one basis. Fiddling was, to Dwight, an intensive teaching experience. In the mid–1990s, he described a typical fiddle mentoring approach, and recalled his experience with one particular young fiddler:

In 1992 [the student] had a bunch of different instruments, and he was monkeying with this and that. He really didn't know that much but he wanted to learn old time music. I said to him, well ok, I'll help you, but if you really want to learn you'll let me know. [In October 1995] he called and said he really wanted to learn. I asked do you really want to learn, and he said yeah. But then you're not allowed to touch that fiddle for six months, you're not allowed listen to anything except what I tell you, you're not allowed to talk to anyone except me. You're not allowed to discuss what you're listening to. When I said you can't touch the fiddle for six months, he's real hyper anyway, so the phone got quiet when I said that, but he said "yeah" and what he did was I gave him Edn Hammons, French Carpenter and Burl Hammons ... on tape. So he listened and listened for month in and month out. And finally after five months he was slowing down some. He was starting to pick out what was the good stuff. He was deciding he liked this one, or that one. He is now coming a long like nobody I've ever seen. Why? Because he accepted the discipline of internalizing, keeping his hands off when he didn't know what he was doing.[55]

That story may very well have been a reference to the fiddle lessons Dwight offered to West Virginian musician Doug Van Gundy in the summer of 1992. Van Gundy was living in Dunmore, West Virginia, in the summer of 1992, and working for the radio station WVMR. He met Dwight during that summer when both of them became involved in a theatrical performance at Cass about the history of that town. Van Gundy played some guitar in the show and he and Dwight, who provided the old time banjo music for the play, spent a good deal of time during rehearsals talking about music. By the end of the summer, Dwight's two recordings, "Red Rooster," and Oh, Death!" had been completed, and Dwight gave Van Gundy copies of those two cassettes. Van Gundy had grown up in Elkins with the old music around him, and had gotten to know the "first wave" of people who were playing the old music again. Currence Hammonds and Woody Simmons and other old practitioners of the traditional music were fixtures in the area, well known to Van Gundy.[56] As a youth Van Gundy had turned to rock music and other musical genres, and never thought he would be attracted back to old time music, but by the summer of 1992 he had drifted back to traditional guitar styles, was listening to Norman Blake, and learning flat picking guitar. After hearing Dwight's recordings, he decided that he really wanted to learn to play fiddle. His wife's grandmother had given him an old and respectable fiddle, so Van Gundy called Dwight to ask whether he might recommend any fiddle teachers.

Dwight told Van Gundy that though he did not play the fiddle, he knew what it was supposed to sound like and had given a lot of thought to how to teach fiddle playing. Dwight suggested that he would be happy to try and help him learn fiddling, and at the same time put his ideas on how to teach the fiddle to the test. Between August or September 1992 and March 1993, while Dwight was working on his own fiddling, Van Gundy visited Dwight's Hillsboro home at least once a week, but because they lived in such close proximity, and because their families worshipped in the same church and carried on their daily lives in the same county, they actually spent a lot more time together, enabling Van Gundy to learn precisely what it was the drove Dwight to think so intensely about playing fiddle, listening to fiddle music, talking to fiddle players, and teaching the instrument.

Dwight played tapes of the Hammons family musicians, Hamp Carpenter, and Mose Coffman for Van Gundy, and in effect taught him to listen, quizzed him on what he liked in the music, and zeroed in on elements of the fiddling so that he might begin to know what he was hearing. Van Gundy recalled being bowled over by the source players. During that time, Dwight required that Van Gundy leave the fiddle alone. "Don't touch the fiddle," Van Gundy remembered Dwight saying, and the two of them just listened to and talked about tapes of fiddlers that Dwight would play, and discussed the style of various old time fiddlers. Later, Dwight introduced Van Gundy to the fiddle playing of John Morris, Bobby Taylor, and Melvin Wine. Dwight had Van Gundy listen closely to the fiddling of Lee Triplett and French Carpenter, and Van Gundy began to bemoan the fact that he had begun too late to hear some of the great source musicians. Lee and Sherman and other old fiddlers had passed on by that time, so when the West Virginia musician Jimmy Costa told van Gundy that Mose Coffman was alive and living in the Greenbrier Manor in Fairlea, south of Lewisburg, Van Gundy decided to call on Coffman, who welcomed the visit and offered to show Van Gundy his fiddling style. Van Gundy recorded two hours' worth of Coffman's playing on that first visit in 1993, and shared the music with Dwight. In keeping with his long standing view that a good teacher works himself out of a job by imparting all he can to his student, Dwight told Van Gundy: "You've found your teacher."

Thinking back, Van Gundy suggested that Dwight taught fiddle the way Coffman taught fiddle. The old fiddler would play a tune and then hand his student the fiddle to play the tune back. Coffman repeatedly told Van Gundy that there was never any reason to learn a tune that did not resonate with you: "Why would you learn a tune you didn't love," was the way Coffman put it. That, Van Gundy suggested, was a variant of Dwight's notion that good fiddling—and good banjoing—came from intensive, committed listening, "internalizing" the old sounds, and learning to hear more and more in the old tunes. Coffman also reiterated the view that if a student could whistle a tune, they could play that tune, which to Van Gundy represented another form of Dwight's argument that one had to internalize the music by repeated and close listening, dwelling on the variety and unique textures of the old sounds. The seven or eight months of intensive listening with Dwight, time spent refining Van Gundy's sense of who was playing styles worth studying and learning, taught the student to discern tone differences and to notice unique bowing styles, and showed him that "if you could get the tune in your head, you could access it on your instrument." Van Gundy remembered an intensive process with Dwight who had, by the early 1990's, already spent nearly thirty years listening to the traditional music, thinking about the old music and its musicians, and applying his way of getting at the music to his own fiddling. "When it came time to learn fiddle," Van Gundy stated, Dwight "knew what sounds he wanted."[57]

To Dwight, listening was probably the most essential capability necessary for learning any music, and perhaps especially for learning traditional fiddle music. For the most part, Dwight assumed that the idiom of old West Virginia music was new and unfamiliar to his students. He insisted that this was the part of learning music that was most challenging and that required time, intellectual and emotional energy, and patience:

> If you're from a totally different culture, different social bracket, different economic bracket, then it's going to take harder work and a lot of time, but you don't come at it with some sort of arrogance that you think you know. You come at it with the idea that here's a mountain people and they were transferring something just as black people in the Mississippi delta were transferring something to each other that they understand. You have to approach it with some humility and you have to approach it with the fact that it's going to take you a long time.[58]

He encouraged students to listen closely, repeatedly, and thoughtfully to recordings of the old music played by old banjo players and fiddlers who were born to the music. These people, Dwight said, had the music imprinted on them from birth, a sort of genetic coding that reflected the culture.[59] Early on in his teaching career, and certainly by the mid-1990s, in order to acclimate newcomers to the particular kind of old time music he was teaching, Dwight introduced the playing of fiddlers such as Harvey Sampson, who was—as Dwight delighted in describing him—a truly eccentric man with a very distinct, uniquely characteristic way of moving through life. Sampson's fiddling was, as Dwight put it, "rough." It was rudimentary music played on a homemade instrument, shrill in some ways, certainly not pleasing to the ear.[60] Sampson's fiddling typified the old music of the 1920s and 1930s, as Dwight saw it. In Dwight's words:

> Listen to Lee Hammons. His fiddling wasn't that easy to listen to. It wasn't as rough as Harvey's but it was hard to listen to. Sherman's fiddling was far better technically. Melvin Wine, even though he lived there, he has a different thing going on. Fiddlers from Clay County and Pocahontas County, those fiddlers have a different thing going on. Ernie Carpenter had it but not as much as the bunch from Clay County.[61]

Dwight factored several variables into the equation that described Sampson's fiddling, including the quality of his fiddle, the impact and influence of geographic traditions, the contexts in which local music was played—dances, for example—but these variables did not necessarily fit together in a formulaic way. There was still wide local variation in local musical traditions, preferred sound, social practices regarding music, and dance. As Dwight stated:

> Harvey, he made that fiddle. If he had played on this one it would have sounded somewhat better but not a whole lot better. I think part of it had to do with the kind of life, the way of life in the mountains. Melvin lived right there but his music was smoother, [and he played] a lot different tunes. It still sounds real old. [Melvin played a lot of dances.] Pocahontas County fiddlers did a lot less playing for dances. Sherman did not play dances. Old Lee did but he was playing that stuff before the turn of the century. That was my connection with the music.[62]

This was an "aged" music that was not easy to listen to. It fit in closely with the local mountain music of Pocahontas County, but was even more crude and homemade than some of the old time practitioners of the local style of fiddling who were Sampson's contemporaries. Listening and understanding required an experienced guide to walk the newcomer through the complexities of those archaic sounds.

Dwight taught mixed classes of banjo and fiddle players, especially from the mid-1990s to the early 2000s.[63] For example, he conducted two such retreats in Brevard, North Carolina, in January 1996 and January 1997. He taught both fiddle and banjo students during his annual retreats in Pittsburgh, Pennsylvania, beginning in December 1996, and he had both banjo and fiddle players in a September 2000 retreat in Red Lodge, Montana.[64] He also paired with instructors such as Doug Van Gundy, John Morris, Dave Bing, Jake Krack, and Pam Lund who shouldered most of the fiddle instruction work at the retreats conducted in Cass, West Virginia, from 1999 to 2002. Dave Bing traveled with Dwight to England in 1998 and 1999, and took responsibility for the fiddle instruction during those instructional sessions.[65]

Dwight started fiddlers who were new to the instrument on a basic shuffle, avoiding anything fancy. He stressed the importance of developing a good, solid rhythm to the bowing. He tended to start both novice banjo players and new fiddlers on the tune "Liza Jane," with the banjos tuned in standard G (gDGBD) and the fiddles tuned in GDGD.[66] In the mid-1990s, when both banjo players and fiddlers would show up to a workshop, he would have the students start off by singing the lyrics, imprinting the tune that way, developing a common denominator for both banjo players and fiddlers, before fine tuning the basic rhythm on the banjo and the fundamental bow approach for the fiddler.[67] He moved quickly to the point of drilling fiddlers in playing in cross tunings.[68] He taught "Cluck Old Hen, "John Brown's March, and "Sandy Boys," in progression, nudging students to explore the music that could emerge from modal tunings. And he taught "Pretty Little Dog," "Elzick's Farewell," "Rainbow Sign," "Texas," and "Santa Ana's Retreat," to push that even further—with the fiddle in either GDGD or AEAE. Then he would circle back around, pick up "Liza Jane" again, and play it on the fiddle in two distinctive versions, two different rhythmic approaches that paralleled what he called the "basic rhythm" on

Dwight teaching fiddle in a mixed banjo/fiddle workshop in Virginia Lakes, California, in 1998 (courtesy Bob Thornburg).

the banjo, and the "Boom a Lacka" banjo rhythm, a more complex, syncopated right hand approach on the banjo.

Dwight used the older term "high bass, high counter" to refer to the cross tunings for these modal tunes. In these tunings, in which the G and D strings would be tuned up to A and E respectively, G is the bass string and D the counter.[69] Dwight recognized that the relevance of precision in these tunings was "relative."[70] What he appeared to mean was that the older fiddlers tended to adjust the strings to achieve the most effective way of playing the tune at hand with little regard to such starting points as standard pitch.[71] A and D tunes were common in the Appalachian repertoire. Banjo players would know a tune as an A tune, or a D tune, and adjust their instruments accordingly, as would fiddlers. G tunes tended to work better in standard fiddle tuning such as GDAE, bottom to top. However, in some instances tunings that involved changing the pitch of the two upper strings would be the best way to get at a tune, especially in a fiddle-banjo pairing. In some instances, older fiddlers would associate certain tunes with specific tunings. What Dwight may have intended to teach by making reference to this was that a certain amount of flexibility, a solid familiarity with the local uses of standard or natural tunings, as well as knowledge of the traditions involving "discord tunings," would come with time for both banjo and fiddle students.[72]

Dwight stressed the importance of playing fiddle rhythmically in the same way that he emphasized the rhythmic character of the banjo, and called on some of the same metaphors in teaching fiddle that he used to impress banjo novices with the need to drive the music. He stressed the importance of finding the right way to deliver the punch by moving the bow forcefully, energetically, over the fiddle's strings. In the same way that he labored over the most effective combination of posture, flexibility, dependence on bone versus muscle mass to propel the right hand work on the banjo, Dwight dwelled on ways of giving expression to what the fiddle student should be doing to get a propulsive snap to the bowing arm:

> If you've ever done labor work, particularly driving nails over a period of time. You watch a carpenter. They don't use their muscles. Say you're putting roofing on. You bring the hammer up and you snap it and you let the weight of the hammer come down and drive those nails in. Well, that's what I want to see from you all, is that snap happening with a motion that starts from here and all those muscles here do, just like you're holding a hammer and driving those nails, all you do is hold on to that hammer enough so that it doesn't fly out of your hands. You don't sit there and do this with a hammer to drive nails because in a short time your muscles will give out. Just not strong enough. So you get it up here and snap it and then you let the weight of that.... And it's the same thing for the fiddles. Your motion needs to be coming out of here. You can't play dance music from here. It has to be out of here. And it rolls down through here and all this does is control what started up here. These images that I've figured out over the years, another one is a nurse shaking down a thermometer. You watch a nurse shaking down a thermometer. That's the same kind of motion. And it's the same thing for the fiddles. You get that arm floating. That's the way you can get that rhythm going, and if you don't have rhythm then you don't have anything. The rhythm is done by taking the notes and moving them this way or that way just a tiny bit. That's all it takes. And if you don't have good rhythm then you can't tell a story and if you're not using this music to tell a story then what are you doing with it? That's the big question. That's the stuff the books never mention to you. They give you all this tablature, and that's just fine, but they don't say, well, what story are you going to tell?[73]

Dwight taught fiddler players to get to the snapping rhythmic playing by pushing and pulling the bow, adding a little snap at the top of the bow's ascent. In the mid–1990s, Dwight tended to have a relaxed approach to how to hold the bow, and a much more stringent measure of what a fiddler had to do to get the music to drive. In his words:

> What I want you doing on fiddle is concentrating on that right hand and just let that bow be as sloppy as it can possibly be. Even if it ends up flying around like that. Make sure that you don't let your fiddle drop down. Keep it up parallel to the ground. Because the more you do this the more you have to hold onto your bow to keep gravity from moving it. I don't care, I want the hand loose. The classical way to hold onto the bow and it may be because they have developed it over a long time is getting that thumb on the frog and then holding on with the little finger and that may allow you to keep it as loose and still not lose it. I don't care how you play, the important thing is keeping it loose and whatever makes it easier, do that. What holds you back from keeping that arm loose then get rid of that and try something else.[74]

Dwight likened the formula for fiddle playing to what banjo students had to go through to get a good right hand working to drive the tune forward. John Morris told Dwight, probably in the 2004–2005 period, that the hand holding the bow needed to wave "bye bye" the way a little kid would, meaning it needed to be relaxed and flexible to produce that motion that babies make when they hold up their right hand to wave at someone.[75]

In classes with both banjo and fiddle students, he would have the banjos play the "high part" of a tune alongside of the fiddlers, and when the fiddler players got to the low part of the tune he'd have the banjo students mute their strings with the left hand, and focus on the right hand work. Then he would alternate that lineup, making sure that the banjo players muted the strings first on the tune's high part and then on its low part because that prompted both the fiddlers and the banjoers to think back to the basic rhythmic core of the tune.[76] He tended to teach a "joint" fiddle/banjo class the same tunes, moving from "Liza Jane" to "West Fork Girls," "Diamond Jim," and then "Lost Indian." He would also teach "Jimmy Johnson" and "Old Mother Flannigan" to both banjo and fiddle students, grouping these tunes together because of some common aspects of left and right hand work. He would toggle back and forth between several different tunes, "Reuben's Train," "Liza Jane," and "Lost Indian." By the early 2000s, this became a hallmark of his approach to a "mixed" banjo/fiddle class: Dwight would teach a tune, and then move beyond it by showing the students a rather different tune, and then switch back and forth between the tunes, drilling the basics first with Dwight playing the fiddle and students working through the various tunes, and then with Dwight playing the banjo while students vamped behind him—and then switching it up to keep moving between sounds, back and forth between tunes.[77] Diane Jones, both a former student of Dwight's and a former teaching colleague at various banjo retreats, observed that Dwight's fiddling was not fancy, and he was not a "fancy fiddle teacher." He did not teach lots of notes, and he did not teach lots of variations within the tune or different versions of one tune.[78] Interestingly, Jones pointed out that Dwight tended to encourage banjo students to learn tunes from fiddlers, to "catch" the essence of the tunes from the fiddle. In effect, that encouraged banjo students to devise their own interpretation of what the banjo needed to be doing to back up the fiddler.[79]

Dwight would very deliberately draw distinctions between what he was teaching and how he learned the fiddle:

> What I'd like to see when I look over there is your bow bouncing, dancing around on those strings instead of [… passing carefully over the strings…] I did it like this for many years. [Evenly, carefully.] And Sherman Hammons, someone asked him not long before he died in the late 1980s if he though I'd ever learn to play the fiddle and he said "Well, sir, I don't believe he has it in him. Doesn't have any life in his notes. And what helped me with that was there was one time back about 1971 where I was at his house, he was playing Liza Jane on banjo and I was holding the fiddle, and I was just bowing, letting go, just bouncing along. When I finished, he said "That Boy sounds pretty good." But I was never able to repeat that. Why? Because I was locked in. Just locked in. You all are getting locked in and you're not going to get any better, I guarantee it. I've been fooling with thing so long and you're doing what I did, we're on the same track and there's absolutely no reason for you to have to spend 20 years of messing with that fiddle and not having any life in it like I did. Turn loose. And just let it go, let it go, I don't care what it takes. I want to see it dancing.[80]

The internet, and particularly YouTube, enabled Dwight to construct a "library" of fiddle tunes for reference. In 2014–2015, he offered a video of the New Ballard's Branch Bogtrotters, featuring Greg Hooven, playing "Sugar Hill."[81] He also pointed to a video of the band Fox Hunt playing live at the Brazen Head Inn, Mingo, West Virginia, in May 2008, focusing on their medley of "Cherokee Shuffle," "Lost Indian," and "Dixieland."[82] Dwight also asked students to listen to a clip of Edn Hammons playing "Queen of the Earth and Child of the Skies," a version of a Jacobite tune from the British Isles called "The Blackbird."[83] Finally, he pointed to the Bing Brothers playing "Big Scioty," noting that the Bing Brothers were "All West Virginia boys who spent so much time around the Hammonses."[84]

In the same way that he told banjo students that sometimes music took place in the distances between notes, he told fiddle students in his retreats that fiddling was about putting spaces between the notes. Music can be linear, but it can also have intricate ups and downs. Fiddling, Dwight told new students, can find those ups and downs.[85]

For the banjo, the right arm/hand movement was the crucial component of his playing approach. The best way to get this down was to mute the strings with the left hand, laying fingers gently across the fingerboard so they only slightly touch the strings. Dwight encouraged the same approach with the fiddle, suggesting that the student deploy a mute or find some way to block out the sound so as to focus intensively on bowing:

Five. A Life of Teaching

> Take that one fiddle tune that you are working with. If you got head phones use them. If you need to, put a mute or a clothespin on it to kill what you can hear. Then play your tune for the four minutes or so. Put the fiddle down [for] five minutes. Pick it back up, and work hard to totally relax and not one voluntary muscle [is] to be used. Then you are not allowed to pay any attention to what you are doing with bow or fiddle. First let that rhythm begin to teach you some syncopation. After a bit, you will be ready to drive your music. Please do not listen to what you are doing. And never stop whatever happens. Do this five times each day. This will help you get a hold. [...] If you follow this suggestion of study it will end up with total of five practice sessions. [That would be] a grand total of 20 minutes of practice. But for now, please do not play any other tune. Other tunes are going to kill any progress in learning to play the fiddle. [...] Push yourself up against the wall of the music. If you do not do that every time you pick up the fiddle, it may cause you to never get "IT."

Dwight frequently sought to drive a student who was ever so close to catching the rhythm by pressing things harder and harder, by emphasizing the extent to which this rare capability must be pursued relentlessly. He tended to be particularly emphatic with students pursuing the fiddle, perhaps because fiddling had been for him, by his own account, so difficult and elusive a skill:

> [A student must] have enough lilt built in [to bowing] to put the violent hardness in there. [At the outset] it is not near strong enough. [At first the bowing will not have the character of an] attack. And the attack must finally be so strong and violent that no one can catch it unless they catch it with their spirit. But you must learn to do it first, thus the [recommendation that a starting fiddle student pick] one tune [and stick with it] for a year or so.[86]

Dwight's point was that the bowing motion, and the right hand/arm movement powering clawhammer banjoing forward, needed to become second nature. Until there was a level of intellectual recognition that a student needed to "dig deep," Dwight emphasized, there would be no recognition of the energy and force required to take these physical movements from a level of simple skeletal and muscle movements to a much more interior, emotional level of recognition of this "internal pulse." Once that level of recognition took place, a certain amount of this would become "second nature." There was a Zen quality implicit in much of this, and a kinship with some of the mental resources necessary for such physical spectacles as effective, efficient martial arts as well as the practice of *tai chi chuan*, archery, and precision marksmanship.[87] Dwight said:

> [It] will only work if you do not pay any attention to what your fiddle is doing. You have to only pay attention to the rhythm, concentrate on it with every bit of your mind and bury your whole mind down in the syncopated drumbeat. And relax in order to let your body alone in order to let it follow along.

To Dwight, such a capacity was not inherently available to "city folk," a phrase he uttered with not the slightest intention of invidiousness. Dwight presumed, on the basis of his experience in teaching banjo and fiddle, and in playing music, that "city folk" were likely to be a longer distance from their interior emotions than those who had lived in "people cultures," where the mode of exchange was not monetary, and the goals of culture were not acquisitiveness and accumulation of wealth. He found it harder to push "city folk" to focus on aspects of that interior self, to get them to call forth the energy and focus necessary to begin thinking about the "internal pulse" in a fashion that differentiated that from external things that drove their lives—the throbbing of traffic, the constancy of commuter trains, the background noise and distractions of crowds, fast food and ubiquitous, noisy entertainment. Dwight explained:

> This is like the way I try to teach rhythm and it almost never works with city based folks. It is to let your system, whole system, stop thinking. You are not allowed to think and analyze what is going on. It cannot work for city people virtually 100% of the time. This is a given. It will not work if you do not, as you are walking up a steep hill/mountain, push hard against [...] gravity.[88]

This resonated with a tradition that looked at learning, the acquisition knowledge and development of insight, as being premised on "letting your system [...] stop thinking," a tradition that harked back to the importance of forgetting, of shedding preconceptions, and giving oneself over to a new way of thinking.[89] Dwight's point was that whatever might be known about making music should be put aside so re-learning could take place, but he also nudged students toward the notion that the conceptual starting points, cultural rules, and conventional wisdoms about much more than just rhythm needed to be put aside in order to get to what was governing the old tunes, such as the old ways of organizing life, communicating, conducting one's personal journey, and establishing relationships.

Dwight as Teacher

Audio recordings of banjo retreats conducted by Dwight in the 1980s and 1990s, accounts of experiences in such classes by former students from the 1980s to the 2000s, and Dwight's own descriptions of his teaching ventures show a marked consistency of purpose over time.[90] His teaching focused on communicating the responsibility that comes with a commitment to study music, any music, but especially brittle, delicate, archaic regional "dialects" of old time music. Dwight's key points: anyone undertaking the task of becoming immersed in local traditional music needed to listen closely to that music, treat it respectfully, learn to hear the internal logic of its construction, and discern the character of the messages those old tunes sought to convey.[91]

Dwight also sought to telegraph the message that doing art of any sort required a profound level of investment in self-expression, a confidence beyond technique and technical capability that went to the central question of what it took to speak to what one wanted to get from immersion in music, or poetry, or painting, about what kind of certainty was needed regarding one's life and purpose before art could be integrated into one's life and identity in more than a merely decorative way.[92]

He had an uncanny ability to speak across levels of capability, and to integrate classes consisting of people coming to the old music with various degrees of experience and musical capacity. Part of that was his preferred starting point for his classes: a level playing field based on the assumption that few banjo players had any prior experience with the rhythmic character of the music he played, and fewer still had the ability to produce the percussive right hand work necessary to propel these old tunes forward. Another part of that was the extent to which he understood the importance of committing an act of leadership in organizing a mess of old time music students. Teaching was, to Dwight, exercising authority, and he muscled his classes into groups organized to focus on his instruction, keep up with the pace of teaching, and absorb the lessons quickly, efficiently, and completely.

He also had a stunningly effective way of grouping fiddlers and banjo players in one class, working with the entire population of old time acolytes from disparate levels and diverse backgrounds, in a fashion that left no one out, created a class identity, and at the same time paid close attention to individual requirements. He was able to do this while working with the group of banjo players and fiddlers in a fashion that created an integral whole, teaching the music rather than fiddle techniques or banjo tunes. Dwight could switch from showing a tune on the fiddle to playing on the banjo in a way that was organized to be instructive for both fiddlers and banjo players. He could pick out the sounds from a crowd of students on either instrument, banjo or fiddle, that signaled he needed to get someone to put more energy into bowing or into working the banjo with the right hand, or more finesse into left hand work on either instrument's fingerboard.

Dwight was dogmatic about his music, his particular style, insisting that students get at the rhythmic core of that style in very deliberate ways—using particular right hand techniques to achieve the percussiveness, and calling on specific left hand approaches to get the music's sparseness, economy of notes, and overall rhythmic infrastructure. The dogma that he elected to follow as his way of capturing the old tunes translated for some into a rigid, compulsively didactic approach that resembled "boot camp" to some, "basic training" to others.

Dwight's teaching paralleled stringent, disciplined military training in one crucial aspect: the relentless focus on mission. He provided the leadership necessary to achieve the stated goals, and the students signed up to accept the discipline necessary to produce the hoped for results. The singularity of purpose in that kind of instruction ensured that one could rely on the training to solve problems and produce results. The strict character of this approach might strike some, or even many, as fundamentally incompatible with "banjo"—it might seem that this regiment strips the fun out of music. In Dwight's view, his approach placed a primacy on a shared goal—playing and preserving the old music. He taught in a fashion that made clear to students what they had to do to learn these old tunes, how they had to practice, what they needed to accomplish to effectively deconstruct tunes and reassemble them in an accessible manner. He told stories, shared his views freely, and encouraged students to jump in with their views.

For a teacher committed to a disciplined way of teaching, he was remarkably relaxed, capable of making mistakes and recovering without losing ground as the instructor.[93] He was given to telling "West Virginia stories"–characterized by varying degrees of ribaldry—and was willing to try all manner of approaches aimed at putting people at ease, some of which worked and some of which did not. He liked to hand out nicknames, a particularly eastern central West Virginia practice as Dwight described it.[94] And he liked to chide, kid, and josh with his students, a practice which had varying effects depending on the mix of personalities. Some embraced it. Some found it abrasive. Dwight was never above backing off, standing down, in the face of student sensitivity. In later years, he himself developed a sensitivity to descriptions of his banjo retreats as, in effect, martial gatherings organized with military, and militant, attentiveness to discipline—and to descriptions of himself as a martinet, rigid in his demeanor and demanding as a teacher.[95]

Dwight made music accessible. He enabled people to break the code, and to do so in a way that was possible in the face of widely varied personal constraints and individual capabilities. He made it so that students could listen to a tune, find the center of gravity of the music, and figure out a way to get to it on their banjos and fiddles.[96] "Playing music" to Dwight did not entail having a massive arsenal of individual songs or tune versions. Quantity was not important. Quality was. What Dwight tried to teach his students was the importance of a carefully played tune, a version mastered and integrated into one's life so that it insinuated its way into one's quiet moments and became available whenever one needed music.

Conclusion

Introduction

In his book, *North American Fiddle Music*, Drew Beisswenger noted that just a few "string bands from West Virginia recorded in the 1920s, and the WWVA Jamboree was popular in the 1930s, but by and large the fiddle music of West Virginia has tended to be less commercial than some of the other Appalachian states."[1] Beisswenger pointed out that the Hammons Family project of 1973, and Miles Krassen's 1973 book, *Appalachian Fiddle,* featuring fiddler Frank George, brought attention to West Virginian music. So did the launching of the publication *Goldenseal* in the mid–1970s, and the 1973 establishment of the Augusta Heritage Center in Elkins, West Virginia, which began conducting workshops and research projects on West Virginian traditions including music. The Appalachian String Band Music Festival at Clifftop, West Virginia, was inaugurated in 1980, and quickly became a nationally known contest that featured old-time styles, and a great gathering of old time musicians. The emergence of a concentration of West Virginia old time music talent—including the Bing Brothers and the Morris Brothers—and the development of a cadre of academic authorities focused on West Virginia's traditions helped garner attention for West Virginian old time music, dance, folklore and crafts.[2]

Dwight's work on the preservation, popularization, interpretation, and recording of traditional West Virginian tunes and stories did much to focus interest on West Virginia's unique, antique tunes. Dwight's contribution to the Hammons Family project and his efforts to rescue the "lost" recordings of Edn Hammons; the large number of his commercial recordings, coupled with his substantial and still highly sought after instructional videos; as well as the feature length film, *The Fifth String*; his *Across the YewPines* project the early 2000s; his 40 or more years of teaching in various private settings as well as large, established venues made him the center of gravity for much of this effort to honor the old music and its practitioners.

In the late 1960s and the first years of the 1970s, Dwight began recording traditional old time music played by musicians in Pocahontas County, focusing on fiddlers and banjo players, and compiling audio recordings of stories and lore of the sort he heard growing up. During 1969–1970, he undertook field recording work that focused on the music and stories of recording Burl, Maggie and Sherman Hammons, and Lee Hammons. That work became the basis for a project organized by the West Virginia Collections of the Archive of Folk Culture, Library of Congress. He also took over 600 black and white photographs during two weekends in October 1970 as part of the effort to document the lives and traditions of the Hammons family. The visual resources were intended to supplement the field recordings of Lee Hammons and members of the Hammons family. Some of his recording work and his photographs were incorporated into the 1973 boxed two LP record set with a 40 page booklet entitled *The Hammons Family: A Study of a West Virginia Family's Traditions*, based on fieldwork by Dwight Diller, Alan Jabbour and Carl Fleischhauer. In 1973 Rounder Records released *Shaking Down the Acorns: Traditional Music and Stories from Pocahontas and Greenbrier Counties, West Virginia* (Rounder Records 0018), recorded by Dwight in two autumn gatherings near his home in 1970 and again in 1971. Those recordings were combined with *The Hammons Family: A Study of a West Virginia Family's Traditions* (AFS L65–66), produced by the Library of Congress and Rounder Records, and released in 1998 as a two CD set.[3] In 1988 Dwight developed an audio-visual presentation titled "Yew Pine Mountain" with a small grant awarded from the West Virginia Humanities Council, and for the next twelve years showed this presentation widely to many audiences in West Virginia.[4] In 1989 he worked on the CD *Banjo Legacy* produced by the Augusta Heritage Center, and in 1996 and 1997, the Center produced two CDs, one featuring the fiddle tunes of Burl Hammons recorded by Dwight in the 1970s (The Diller Collection, Volume 1) and a second containing banjo tunes played by five Hammons family members and Hamp Carpenter, recorded by Dwight in the 1970s (The Diller Collection, Volume 2).

In the 1970s, Dwight performed in two bands. Between 1971 and 1977 he manned the stand-up bass for the Black Mountain Bluegrass Boys; from time to time played some clawhammer banjo for that band. He performed with the Morris Brothers Band playing clawhammer banjo at their summer festivals in 1972 and 1973, events supported by a Rockefeller Foundation grant. Dwight also played banjo at numerous public venues including festivals, concerts as well as more informal gatherings, often appearing with well know old time fiddlers such as Glen Smith and Lee Triplett. Festivals and other public gatherings were an important component of Dwight's musical career, especially in the years from 1970 through the early 2000s, though his attendance of such events leveled off in the 1990s and diminished steadily thereafter as he began to focus more closely on teaching workshops and retreats, and as these larger venues became increasingly uncomfortable for him in terms of his state of mind and ability to manage the rush of events and activities. Dwight participated in the Stonewall Jackson Jubilee for about thirty consecutive years beginning in 1975. This was truly his favorite festival. He relished attending the annual four-day festival held on Labor Day weekend at Jackson's Mill, near Weston. The festival, started in 1974 as a gathering of craftspeople and musicians, was one of those events that Dwight felt brought out the best in West Virginian traditional crafts and music, and was—as he put it—truly an effort by West Virginians for West Virginians. Additionally, he made occasional appearances at the Appalachian Stringband Festival at Clifftop, West Virginia, in the late 1990s and early 2000s. He attended a host of events from time to time, especially West Virginia festivals such as the Vandalia Gathering and West Virginia State Folk Festival.[5]

Dwight organized the First Annual Hammons Music Gathering, "A Festival of Central West Virginia and Hammons Family Music," on 23 and 24 August 1996, at Stillwell Park, in Marlinton, one mile down Everette Tibbs Road.[6] The second gathering in 1997 and the third gathering in 1998 were held up on the Williams River on Edray Road in the Monongahela National Forest, on Black Mountain. The 1998 event was billed as a gathering in honor of the West Virginia fiddler Wilson Douglas; commemorative t-shirts bore his image. These Gatherings were in effect a "celebration" of the Hammons family music,

A rare pose: Dwight with a guitar. The bass player is unidentified (courtesy Denis Slifer).

organized for people who had learned from them and enjoyed their company, their tunes and their stories.[7] Dwight began teaching clawhammer banjo, conducting banjo and fiddle retreats, in the early 1970s. He had a sprawling teaching career that included several decades of work for the Augusta Heritage Center, a long list of multi-day banjo retreats taught over time at his various homes in West Virginia, workshops and retreats taught across the United States from the 1980s to the early 2000s, and retreats and concerts conducted in England beginning in the late 1990s through the early 2000s.[8]

In June 2003 Dwight performed at the Smithsonian Folklife Festival in Washington, D.C., as one of the representatives of the Appalachian region. The Yew Pine Cultural Traditions, Incorporated, established in 2003 to preserve the cultural heritage of the Appalachian Region, facilitated Dwight's *Across the YewPines* DVD project,[9] and beginning around 2010 or 2011 assisted three recording projects: "Lee Hammons: Complete Banjo Recordings," "Maggie Hammons Parker: Complete Banjo Recordings, and "A Sampler from the Hammons Legacy."[10] After *Across the YewPines* was released, in 2013, Dwight gave some thought to possible new projects, including ideas about utilizing the field recordings and still photographs of the Hammonses for further multi-media work. He continued teaching through at least 2015, though with a much-reduced schedule, primarily conducting small group or individual lessons at his Browns Creek home. In his late sixties, Dwight attended a few local festivals, performed on stage, and received some honors for his life's work at old time gatherings such as the July 2015 Fourth Annual Old Time Fiddlers Convention in Highland County, Virginia. Dwight entered the senior old time banjo competition at the 39th Annual Vandalia Gathering held at West Virginia State Capitol in Charleston on Memorial Day weekend in 2015. Dwight won that competition, and gave the ribbon to Trevor Hammons, who was in the audience, in memory of his great-grandfather Lee Hammons. Dwight fiddled regularly with his friend Ralph Roberts, and enjoyed visits from old friends who would come and stay with him at his home in Marlinton, Pocahontas County. In late 2015, Dwight began work on recording several new CDs, began thinking about a video project featuring his music, and entertained plans for a modest house concert in Port Republic, Virginia, for the last quarter of the year, the first such performance in a long stretch of time. Additionally, he contemplated a variety of other projects including a collection of his own stories, stories that spoke of old friends and events and local history in his part of eastern central West Virginia, the sort of stories that he would tell at his banjo retreats to telegraph home a point about the Old People, the tunes, and the character and culture of West Virginians. He started looking into producing digitized versions of recordings of his earliest music captured at jams and contests and in other venues in the early 1970s, and began gathering some of his previously recorded but unreleased music for inclusion in a multi-CD collection of gospel tunes, instrumentals, and some of the songs he liked to sing.

The Hard Part

In his later life, especially as he neared his 68th birthday in August 2014, Dwight struggled to find ways to undertake another burst of focused ministry work in his community of Pocahontas County; one idea he turned over in his mind, and in discussion with close friends, was to afford some of the poor people in Marlinton a place to gather in warmth, some words of encouragement and a sense that others did care about them.

His own diminishing strength and mounting infirmities crowded out the possibility of caring effectively for others and he never quite summoned the energy and resources necessary to support such an undertaking. In his late sixties, Dwight seemed to exist in a perpetual state of sleeplessness especially during the darker winter months in Marlinton, West Virginia, atop his isolated mountain homestead, when deep snows confined him to his Browns Creek compound. His manic tendencies left him incapable of grabbing more than catnaps, and this set the stage for more seizures. All this wore him out to the point that he could only function once he got enough adrenalin going—that, of course, guaranteed a cyclical process in which he crashed, found himself unable to get the required sleep, and then forced his body to push through another round before caving in once more.

Dwight looked at what he referred to as his early trauma as being part of the cocktail of ailments that dogged him all his life, beginning with the family conflict that led to his parents' divorce, his relocation back to Pocahontas County at about the age of five without his beloved father, and the constant movement from the household of one of his mom's sister's to another who provided care when his mother Faith was unable to. He saw this as the reason that "body and mind [had] constantly been unable to function with any strength." The West Virginia winter's "short day syndrome" made this even more consequential for him. He dated the manic cycling to roughly 2012, though he described lifelong wrestling matches to "keep suicide at bay."

Dwight described all this as a constant and lifelong circumstance, one that crippled his ability to function normally as a student, impacted on his time in uniform, and circumscribed work options for him. To manage any level of productivity he had to tax his system to the point of triggering the destructive, depressive cycle. In his adult years, during his most productive period, he would be crushed by the physical rigor of just keeping up, and then—once the cycle of banjo retreats finished for the year—he would be confronted with the reality that there was little work to be had, that he was not in good enough shape to pursue conventional job opportunities, and that other than occasional odd jobs there was little in the way of any concrete and realistic alternatives that he might pursue to stay afloat financially.

Dwight managed some of this with prescription drugs, under medical guidance, for 18 years, though friends who knew him from the 1990s suggested that he might have periodically shelved the medicines in the face of physical reactions to the drugs. In his mid- and late sixties, he managed to secure access to some counseling through the resources of one of West Virginia's veterans hospitals, but the care required him to drive long distances, and to get in line with a large group of people seeking assistance in a time of diminishing resources for such programs. The medicine provided some relief, but it deprived him of sleep and rendered normal functioning difficult. All this was complicated by Transient Ischemic Attacks that came with increasing frequency during the early 2000s. He dreaded going from Browns Creek to Marlinton, where he did his food shopping and picked up the mail. He avoided chance meetings with friends, and increasingly found routine interactions—in grocery stores, on line at banks—to be torturous.[11]

One way he coped with some of what he referred to it as his "mental illness" was through blunt and public statements about this challenge. Early in our acquaintance, perhaps in the late 1990s, during a performance in Washington, D.C., Dwight stopped the show with a comment about his mental illness. I asked him about it later, wondering why he would do that to an unsuspecting audience, in a fashion that rocked so many people back on their heels. His answer then was that if his statement about his ailments helped just one person suffering from anything remotely like what had impacted his life, then he had discharged the responsibilities of his ministry.

Dwight believed that this was one way he could help others suffering the way he had suffered. He had ample evidence from people in his audiences, in his retreats, over the years who had thanked him for his candor and poured out to him their own anguish and suffering that they lived with, alone, until occasionally someone like Dwight trained a spotlight on this mental prison that held many in isolation. Dwight felt this very precisely fulfilled what he had assumed as his responsibility to "the underclass," and often drove this point home by describing why the banjo and old time music were not at all important to him compared to this obligation that he had assumed. This seemed to be how he managed the conflict in himself between his identity as a musician and the deeper goals he harbored, the belief that compelled him to think about far more important things. This was how, especially in his later years, he retained enough of a balance in the moments he had to be out in front of an audience.

* * *

For a long time, I was not convinced by Dwight's explanation that if his message could reach the ears of one person similarly affected by such concerns, he had achieved his goal. I looked at this practice of his as an inexplicable eccentricity—until sometime in late 2014 when Dwight forwarded me an email sent to him by someone who met him at an old time festival and later took the time to write, saying of Dwight's musical performance at that event:

> I especially appreciated that you were willing and empowered to speak out about your challenges with mental health. It's these kinds of moments that help all of us—both those of us who struggle with such issues as well as those who have loved ones that do, too. So thanks so much for that.

Until that point, Dwight's approach to putting out messages of hope was essentially theory, a good idea and a noble mission, but one that was infused with a touch of wishful thinking and an impractical sense of how to accomplish such things. However, the truth of the matter was that Dwight got his message across, and made a difference in a concrete manner that helped people who struggled, whether it was as a result of his personal example or his firm and confident way of projecting the forceful message: hope was possible. Either way, after reading this note, I had every reason to believe that his words and the example of his own life helped people searching for some glimmer of the positive.

* * *

After long years of coping with multiple streams of adversity, he was finally diagnosed as suffering from Bipolarity Disorder II, manic depression, laced with Post Traumatic Stress—a reference to unresolved lifelong challenges, dysfunctional family dynamics, and his own personal brand of cycling doubt, crippling distrust, dependence, and isolation which kept him "in the cellar most of the time."[12]

Bi-Polar II Disorder is a medical condition of the brain that affects an individual irrespective of any traumatic events or personal life experiences. Dwight's strokes may have been a side effect of the long-term use of psychotropic medications as well as the lack of exercise and an inadequate diet. It is a vicious cycle for people with this type of chronic illness. The stressors in his life may have contributed to the biological expression of this condition, but Bi-Polar Disorder is fundamentally a medical condition, not a personal problem. The environmental limitations he has faced, such as precarious financial resources and the inability to secure health insurance, created barriers to his receiving quality care and an accurate diagnosis earlier in his life. Given the nature of most of his work, he may not have been eligible for federal Social Security disability with Medicare before age 65, and his state disability benefits for someone in his situation were almost negligible. As one experienced medical social worker remarked, ignorance about his condition and a dearth of available resources is the real devil here, sadly. What Dwight accomplished in the face of all this adversity was truly heroic.

Musical Influences

Dwight identified several kinds of influences on his music.

First, active and direct influence derived from close, personal relationships with musicians who taught him how to learn music, how to respect the traditions, and encouraged his curiosity about local lore.

Second, influence derived from a less direct level of personal engagement: from musicians Dwight saw perform at festivals, whose music he absorbed intensively, and perhaps jammed with on a much more informal, episodic basis.

Third, influence founded on support, intellectual sustenance, and friendship from a circle of friends and acquaintances, like-minded musicians and West Virginians intent on preserving traditions.

Regarding active and direct influence: The source of much of Dwight's knowledge of West Virginia tradition, lore and music was the Hammons family. Dwight also acknowledged the active influence of the fiddler Lee Triplett from Clay County, West Virginia, who invited Dwight to play banjo with him in public and in smaller, more personal venues. Dwight named Wilson Douglas and Glen Smith from Woods County who helped him focus more intensively on his music, or, as Dwight put it, helped him to become "extra thoughtful" about the music (Douglas) and prodded him to invest the energy and time necessary to play the music (Smith).[13] Dwight remembered Wilson Douglas fondly, and tried to put his finger on the difference between Pocahontas and Clay County old time music:

> Wilson became a good friend of mine as soon as we met in early June 1972. It was at Carter Caves, Kentucky, when I met him. The Morris Brothers of Ivydale, Clay County, had just hired me on as fledgling banjo player. [I] hardly knew any of the their tunes or songs and they were a powerhouse when playing their music. Wilson was there at Carter Caves also. He was playing the old tunes. [...] When I heard him play "Elzick's Farewell," I knew I had to some day learn it. I had already been around the old folks in Pocahontas County who were the best in the world at certain kinds of old mountain music. Clay County music was different from Pocahontas County music. I don't know how to say it. Clay County musicians were really good, but their music, for the most part did not have the old late 1700s/1800s "feel" like the Hammonses did. But that didn't make any difference. [...] Generally, except for Wilson, the other Clay County musicians played much faster than the Pocahontas County musicians. Especially Glen Smith who was originally from near Galax, Virginia. He was powerhouse and about the same age as Wilson and Frank George. Lee Triplett from Clay County was older [and was also a powerful fiddler.][14]

At Carter Caves, Dwight asked Wilson to show him how do the fingering on the fiddle for the version of the tune that Harvey Elswick was said to have played for his mother in the 1890s on her death bed. Wilson, Dwight recalled, "kindly and gently" showed him the fingering:

I knew it was far too hard for me, but I sure was grateful. I think at that time, he might not have had half his vocal cords, cut out from cancer. But shortly after that, he was hoarse, for sure. After Wilson died around 2000, I found out that he had been a tail gunner in a B17 bomber over Germany. Their life expectancy was just a few flights. And he made it through. Wilson was top-notch grader operator on a road crew building the I-79 Interstate from Charleston, West Virginia, up through Pittsburgh, Pennsylvania.[15]

Dwight credited the Morris Brothers with giving him a sense of the responsibilities of a professional musician, and for tutoring him about the obligations of a musician to local traditions. The Morris Brothers band hired him as their banjo player, and their approach impressed Dwight with the importance of remaining "steeped in the local musical traditions." He derived a similar kind of education regarding old time bluegrass music, concertizing, and commercial recording from his relationship with the Black Mountain Bluegrass Boys, for whom he played bass from 1971 to 1977.[16] Dwight recalled that his first stage appearance, banjo in hand, was with the Morris Brothers.[17] Dwight also remembered the David Morris band repertoire as including "John Prine," and "John Henry," and that all the versions were hard, loud and "in your face."[18]

Regarding the less direct level of influence: Chief among these, to Dwight, was Wade Ward who he first met at a festival at Hillsboro, Virginia, in 1970.[19] Additionally, Dwight learned about musicians such as Tommy Thompson on the festival circuit in the 1970s, and respected the music from these "young 'big names.'"[20] Finally, regarding the influence of a circle of friends: These relationships did not necessarily have an impact on his style of playing, but often contributed to strengthening his resolve, reaffirming his commitment, and helping him develop a network of artists committed to the same work on behalf of the old time ways, the old time music, and the old time stories. He credited Bob Thren, Len Reiss, Alex Varela and Odell McGuire with providing him this kind of support, good company, and friendship. He respected them because of their continuing interest in the well-being of "the Old People's music."[21]

Dwight came away from his first experiences at the music festivals in Virginia and West Virginia in the early 1970s feeling that the music represented a community for him, a refuge, a safe landing zone after a long and tough period in his life. By perhaps the mid–1970s, he had seen enough to conclude that festivals were experiencing deterioration, moving in a trajectory that, in his view, took them from being environments conducive to relaxed fellowship and focused creativity, toward much more of a disorderly, disorganized and even threatening experience involving alcohol and bad behavior of attendees, acts against personal property, and an increasing need for policing by law enforcement authorities.[22] The sanctuary these experiences offered to him at a tempestuous point in his life provided only a brief chance to recoup his emotional and mental losses. For decades afterward, he remained very committed to the handful of friends he met at Ivydale and Hillsville in the early 1970s. He continued to be reflective, wistful, about the few experiences he had at those festivals and the encounters with musicians that offered guidance and assistance to an aspiring banjo player.[23]

During the early 1970s, Dwight saw what he understood as the polarization of bluegrass and old time communities reflected in the evolution of festivals in Appalachia. Festivals such as Galax began with a decidedly old time orientation and a bluegrass component, but spun into a big bluegrass event that squeezed out the old time music and the old time folks. Dwight worked with the Morris Brothers on the three old time music festivals in Kentucky, West Virginia, and North Carolina in 1972 and 1973 and those experiences left him with a sense that many of these "experiments" had taken a turn toward intolerance, a trend line that would not be altered until the crowd behavior had been policed sufficiently, and rules of behavior regarding, for example, the use of alcohol, were applied and enforced. Dwight was decidedly less patient with or charitable toward more contemporary bluegrass music. Perhaps because of his earliest organized band experience (and possibly his longest continuous musical employment) with the Black Mountain Bluegrass Boys, he was favorably predisposed to some of the older bluegrass bands, and the older bluegrass tunes.[24] In the summer of 1970 Dwight went to Bean Blossom, and though he was not inclined to remember the bluegrass greats of that period as having played a music that would reach out and grab him, he was taken with Doc Watson precisely because he was a genuinely nice person on stage and off, a gentleman, a "pleasant person to watch" who played "pleasant music." The notion that a musician should behave on stage in a measured, appropriate, friendly manner that encouraged a positive view of the performer was seated in Dwight's mind from that point in time. In that period, he began thinking through the means of measuring his own musicianship—his behavior onstage as a performer, as distinct from an entertainer; his responsibility to project himself in a well-mannered way; and a responsibility for making the music positive, hopeful, and accessible.[25]

His first systematic thinking about the nature of old time music in general, and more importantly about old time music in eastern central West Virginia in particular, emerged in this period. Dwight met Odell McGuire at Ivydale in 1970, and their relationship went on to involve a long running dialogue about the character of the archaic music, how to play the old tunes, and how to teach the old music.[26] Dwight and Odell McGuire spent long hours discussing the quality that distinguished musicians who were "carriers" of the Frontier Mountain Music Tradition. According to Dwight's later memories, they dwelled on the innate, natural, instinctual, inborn qualities of the old people who played West Virginia—and focused a good deal of their attention on the question of what it took for younger people to learn the music, and master the music's rhythmic core. Dwight and McGuire may very well have spent time determining what it took for "outsiders" or people from other traditions to learn the old music, repertoires such as those of the Hammons family. Dwight reflected on his discussions with McGuire, over four decades later, as an attempt to identify what it was that the "revivalists" were missing about the soul of the old music in what Dwight characterized as their hasty attempts to learn old tunes. Such musicians failed, in his view, by not taking the time to look closely at "something which was totally alien to them." Dwight embroidered on this notion that the music the people in Lexington, Virginia, were looking at and trying to learn from represented a "foreign" culture, something extremely different from their own experience that required special care and unique sensitivity to understand and appreciate. Decades after his experiences in Lexington, Virginia, Dwight's view of things became attenuated, and in these later years he described the revivalists as an occupying army, predisposed to "arrogantly grabbing and interpreting what they knew nothing about." At least some of the discussions in Lexington in the early 1970s focused on the question of why these cultures, and this old music, were vulnerable in this way.[27]

Throughout his musical career, Dwight mused about the common core of Appalachian, or southern, living experience that enabled Kentuckians to understand West Virginian music, and North Carolinians to capture the internal percussive spirit of mountain tunes from other states. Dwight tended to refer to this musical genetic code as the

"IT," or the "WAY," and he capitalized these words when he wrote about the qualities that enabled musicians to be "carriers" of musical traditions. Interestingly, Dwight appeared to draw a distinction between his banjo playing and his fiddling, making the argument that what he did on the five string might have had the content and rhythmic character of the old music, but it was a learned capability that sounded true to the old tunes, though it was not "The Old Mountain Way." He believed that his fiddling more than his banjo playing came from a depth and reflected what it meant to "have" the "old way."[28]

Some of the thinking that fueled these discussions became the basis for Dwight's commitment to the practice of playing the music as close as possible to the way the "Old People" played the music. And some of it became the basis for the articles of faith that he brought to bear in his own home schooled way of "collecting" the old tunes, recording the "Old People," capturing their music and their stories, and thinking about the history and meaning of old time music. Dwight believed strongly that the tradition in his home county paired the banjo and the fiddle, and that no other instruments—guitar, dulcimer—entered into the equation during the years the musicians in the Hammons family, as well as the likes of Lee Triplett and Hamp Carpenter, played music. At the same time that he began to articulate the elements that characterized this old music, he also began to develop a sense of how these old tunes and the old way of playing them might be learned by contemporary musicians using modern banjos and fiddles, in a fashion that would both honor the archaic forms and at the same time allow the personalities of contemporary musicians to emerge in the music.[29]

Dwight's Own Sound

Though influences weighed heavily on him, shaped his thinking about what the music should be and how it should sound, in the end Dwight contoured his banjo playing in a manner of his own making. He devised his own techniques for getting at the rhythms he sought to incorporate in his sound, in a way that reflected the music he heard and the elements of mountain culture that were crucially important to him, but in a fashion that allowed him to structure a unique sound that belonged to him.[30]

Dwight emphasized that his banjoing did not sound like the play-

Dwight's portrait for his *Just Rhythm: West Virginia Clawhammer Banjo* DVD (courtesy Bates Littlehales).

ing he heard at the homes of Hammonses.[31] Since he had not heard any contemporary old time banjo players when he started trying to learn to play clawhammer in late 1968 and early 1969, Dwight reasoned that he was not influenced in his playing approach by anyone from the old time scene—at least at that early point. He heard the banjo and fiddle playing of Hamp Carpenter, but his visits to that household were spent more in conversation than in playing music. Later, in the early 1970s, he would meet Tommy Thompson and be significantly impressed with the banjo work of this West Virginian-born musician who was then firmly ensconced in the Durham/Chapel Hill old time scene, and more than surprised at how close his own banjo playing sounded to Thompson's spirited banjo style. Dwight recalled those intensive early efforts to get clawhammer playing down, from November 1968 to May 1969. He remembered the point at which things jelled for him and he began to have the sense that he had grasped the fundamentals and had something on which he could build. He associated that point, that May 1969 date, with a jarring moment when, after a football game at Morgantown during his turbulent college years he had managed to become rowdily drunk on whiskey, and been hauled off to jail by the police after a Saturday game. He was released on Sunday, and recalled that jailing as a critical moment, a most important event "because that kind of thing will stop your world."

He stopped drinking. That May 1969 episode coincided with the point at which he was able to bring together the old music, find the right way of banging the banjo, and locate for himself the rhythmic equation that became his signature sound. The next benchmark moment for Dwight was the first encounters with old time music festivals in 1970, and his first meetings with three men who became lifelong friends—Len Reiss, Bob Thren, and Alex Varela who showed Dwight "Frosty Morn" from Henry Reed, and "Angeline." Maggie Hammons called that second tune "Sixteen Horses Were My Team," and Dwight remembered mixing "Angeline" with "Sixteen Horses," and producing the tune that brought him second place at the June 1970 banjo competition at Hillsville, Virginia.[32]

Almost 45 years after he placed in this banjo contest at Hillsville, I played a recording of three tunes of Dwight doing "Soldier's Joy" and "Angeline" at that 1970 festival contest, recordings that Kilby Spencer, a fiddler from Whitetop, Virginia, generously made available to me.[33] Dwight was amazed that his contest tunes had survived, and greeted them as though they were a singular archeological find. He was deeply grateful to hear himself playing back then, so soon after he had solidified what became his signature banjo sound. He heard in those tapes the core rhythmic pattern that became the defining character of his banjo playing, and thought back to those early musical steps. Nobody in his area of central West Virginia played that rhythmic clawhammer style, he said, and so it could not have come from what little he had heard visiting Hamp Carpenter. And it probably did not derive from the banjo tunes he heard during his visits to the Hammons—because by May 1969 he had only been calling on them for about three months and had not been studying the music so much as just enjoying their company, absorbing the stories they told, and listening gratefully to any music they would make. His rhythmic core did not spring from the single lesson he had from Dick Kimmel all those years ago, though that gave him a starting point. And his energetically percussive banjoing did not derive from, though it was clearly inspired by, the likes of Grandpa Jones, whose playing stimulated Dwight and fed his hunger for the old music but did not inform his own clawhammering.

Dwight's idea was that the sound he came to play on the banjo derived from who he was, not what he learned. It sprang from the sum total of the sounds that had penetrated his life from his youth, and the background music and its cultural context that infused his everyday life. There was a mystical element to this explanation. It was not as though he was minimizing the impact of individual musicians on his thinking and playing—he gave pounds and pounds of credit to the Morris Brothers, and he clearly cherished and respected the creaky old music that Burl, Sherman and Maggie coaxed from their instruments for him, and allowed him to record to make sure those sounds survived.

However, Dwight remembered that he learned banjoing in isolation, in a very solitary time: "Nobody showed me, nobody taught me, I didn't have anyone else to play music with," he recalled, thinking of the point when things came together for him in mid-1969. What emerged was what he referred to as "Diller's Rhythm," using his family name in a way that, for him, distanced it from a claim to authorship and made it more an inheritance, a natural biological evolution that essentially—in Dwight's terms—made him the "carrier" of this music. That was a term he reached for, preferring it to the mantle of "Guardian" of the old music, or any of the other of the term chosen to credit him with the role of militant protector of the archaic sound.[34] He "carried" this music, and his special playing touch was the result of his own chemistry and the unique central West Virginian clay that went into the familial emulsion from which he sprang—a mixture that was part Pennsylvania, part Kentucky, and so many other parts unknown that coalesced in Pocahontas County.

Dwight's Own Banjos

Over the years, Dwight has used a good many banjos, and developed his own particular sense of what combination of wood and metal yielded the sound he wanted in a five string.

Dwight's first banjo was one that he borrowed from Worthy Reed who lived with the Dilley family in the Hill Country of Pocahontas County. He remembered it as a higher quality banjo that displayed some workmanship and well-made inlays. It was probably acquired by mail order from Sears and Roebuck or Montgomery Ward in the early 1900s. In early 2015 he became reacquainted with that instrument:

I had that banjo in my hands recently. It was almost unplayable for me. [...] The neck on this banjo is so skinny that there is no working the strings with the left hand. The scale was 28 inches [...] and the strings are down almost on the head so thumb cannot get behind/under the fifth string. Though a high dollar, for the time, the sound was similar to what comes out of the present day banjos that have snare drum slices for rims. Of course, that was 1968 and anything that was a "banjo" was certainly good enough. Though I treated it gently, the peghead broke off.

Confronted with the need for a replacement instrument, by late 1968 Dwight managed to put his hands on a few other banjos that were, in his memory, cheap mail order instruments. He remembered their hallmarks, and was motivated to find a playable instrument of his own:

Rotted pear wood fingerboard. Toilet seat plastic for fingerboard and peg head, and red paint. A fingerboard that was about as thick as ten layers of cigarette paper. So I bit the bullet: I found a new one in a wholesale mail order catalogue. When I got it, the name on it was Gretsch. At least everything was intact. And it was certainly a step up in playability. However, it wasn't much better.

When Dwight started attending old time festivals in the summer of 1970, he was armed with that Gretsch, and it was at his first festival, the 4th Annual Old Time Fiddlers and Bluegrass Convention in Hillsville, Virginia, in June 1970, that he found himself in the midst of a population armed much higher end banjos than he had ever seen.

Dwight traveled to the festival at Hillsville with Paul Haggard, a guitar playing forest ranger whom he had met in 1968. Haggard was a caving enthusiast, and introduced Dwight to Bob Thren, also a caver, and to his friend Len Reiss. Both Thren and Reiss played clawhammer and Reiss built open back banjos. Before the festival at Hillsville came to an end, Paul, Len, Bob and Alex Varela managed to locate a worthy banjo for Dwight:

> Somehow those four were able to snag a banjo for me at $110. It was an "Improved George Washburn." I think the banjo was a cobbled up neck from here and rim from there. But it did sound out. And played far better than my junker. Perhaps it was a year later that Len Reiss built me a neck for the Improved George Washburn. I somehow got a thin Five Star head and put it on the 11 inch rim. Suddenly it became a killer. Odell McGuire from Lexington, Virginia, began referring to that banjo as "Snotty" and it was Dick Kimmel who gave me a half hour banjo lesson in September 1969, a few years later, who said that I played "sledgehammer banjo." With that banjo, I could walk into a large bunch who were playing at a festival and totally take over. Snotty sledgehammer.[35]

Reiss does not remember finding the pot, but he does remember the neck:

> It was made from maple with an ebony neck. To the best of my recollection the inlay was simple, probably dots or diamonds. Because of the raucous sound of the banjo he named it "Old Snotty." If playing in a group, you could always hear Dwight. [...] That neck was the first one that I built for someone.[36]

Sometime in 1971, Lee Hammons' son James sold Dwight an 11.5 inch Lange tenor banjo dating from the 1920s that James had rescued from a dump in Long Island, New York. Dwight needed to have a five string neck made to fit this tenor rim. In the fall of 1970, Carl Fleischhauer, who was working at the WWVU television station in Morgantown, West Virginia, took Dwight to Athens, Ohio. Fleischhauer had attended Ohio University. His friends, Kix Stewart and Bill McDonald, had just started their luthier supplies business, and Dan Dagget, a skilled luthier, was working for Stewart and McDonald at the time. Sometime after meeting him, Dwight asked Dagget to build a neck to go with the Lange banjo rim. Dwight recalled that he sent Dagget the rim in 1971. Dagget and Ron Chacey, who did the inlay work on the neck, took about two years to finish the job. In the meantime, Dwight was still playing the banjo that had been christened "Snotty" when John and David Morris from Ivydale, West Virginia, asked him to join their band, the Morris Brothers.

> They were playing their powerful central West Virginia kind of Old Time Music. [...] The Morris boys were my age and, though I didn't know their tunes/songs and my skill level was lacking, I immediately jumped in like ducks in water.
> [...] This is also where Snotty found his home. All I had to do was keep driving the music, which demanded a extreme thump, and then fake the notes. In all the time I played that banjo, it never gave out no matter how violently I struck down on it. In fact, I had the strings close to a half-inch over the fingerboard where the neck and rim meet.[37]

Dwight played that banjo until 1994 when he sold it for a badly needed $325.00.

In 1973, Dwight received the neck built for the Lange banjo pot by Dan Dagget bearing Ron Chacey's exceptional inlay and engraving work.

The neck Dagget built was exactly matched to the pot, and fit like a glove. Even in

Dwight and the "Improved George Washburn" banjo. Dwight and friends found the rim at one of the Morris Brothers' old time music festivals in 1970. He coupled that rim with an old neck he purchased in June 1970. In 1971, as Dwight tells the story, Len Reiss built a new neck for the Washburn rim and the resulting instrument was branded "Snotty" by Dwight's friends in honor of its "obnoxiously loud" sound (courtesy Dwight Diller).

the old black and white photos from Dagget's personal files, the careful wood choice and exceptional finish work are clearly visible. The two parallel ebony center strips sandwiching a line of maple that ran down the back of the neck, repeated in the dowel stick, added a stately touch to the instrument's architecture. The banjo fingerboard and the one-of-a kind peghead were decorated with unique inlay work by Ron Chacey. Forty-two years later, Ron Chacey remembered:

> The pattern and engraving are somewhat traditional in style. The flowers on the peghead are much like what is on the back of a lot of old Vega banjo peg heads, but with different engraving. The engraving that makes the ends of petals look turned up, and the engraving on the dots are also old style engraving. I do not remember how the engraving in the leaves came about, but it is not typical of my engraving.[38]

Dagget recalled picking the curly maple wood for the neck and following Dwight's instructions about neck construction and his preferences regarding the lamination. Dwight remembered: "Dan did not stain the curly maple neck. The rim was old and darkened gold. Finally, after all those years, the neck caught up with the rim in color."[39]

Dwight and friends found a rim from an "Improved George Washburn" banjo at one of the Morris Brothers' old time music festivals in 1970. He coupled that rim with an old neck he purchased in June 1970, and the result was the banjo in this photograph. In 1971, as Dwight tells the story, Len Reiss built a new neck for the Washburn rim and the resulting instrument was branded "Snotty" by Dwight's friends in honor of its "obnoxiously loud" sound (courtesy Dwight Diller).

Conclusion 143

Ron Chacey's inlay work on the peghead and fingerboard of the banjo neck built by Dan Dagget for Dwight Diller (courtesy Dan Dagget).

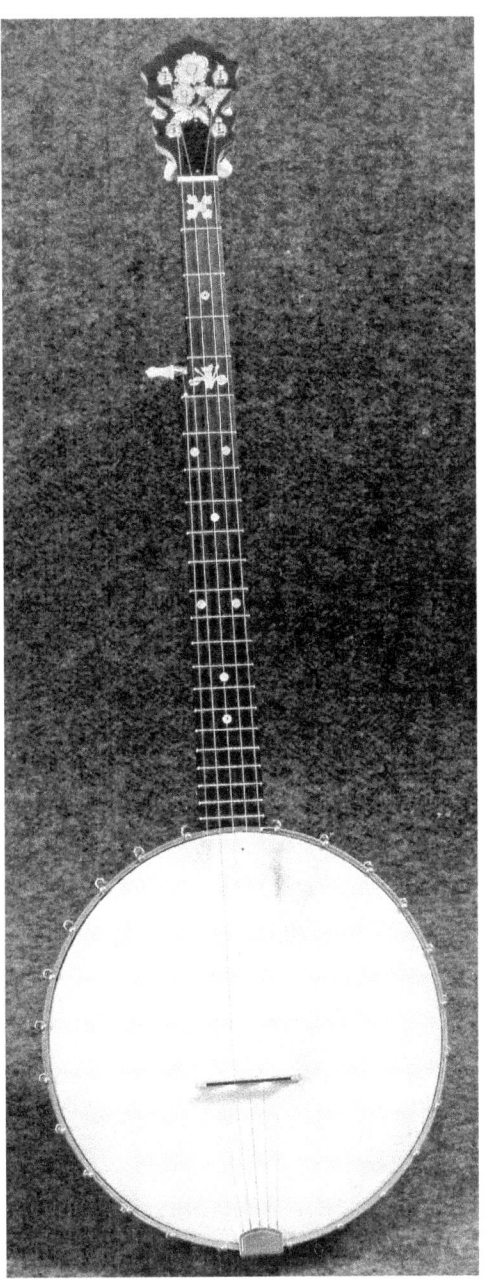

The banjo neck built by Dan Dagget, joined to the Lange tenor banjo rim (courtesy Dan Dagget).

Dagget made the neck thicker than usual to "fill Dwight's hand" and let him "try it on for size" before it was finished. In Dagget's words:

> I remember being committed to making the peghead of this banjo unique—my own, a signature, a statement. I also remember that I really liked the peghead of the banjo a friend of mine was playing, a banjo

with an RB4 Gibson style peg head on a neck made by Ron Chacey. So, I wanted to combine the soft curves of this sort of peghead with the sharp points of the old SS Stewart and Vega Whyte Lady banjos. What you see is what I came up with. I made the banjo in the Stewart MacDonald factory, where I was working at the time, with wood I bought from them. […] I remember being very proud of the banjo. I still am. […] I was also proud to have helped make a banjo for such an exceptional musician. I still play "Sally Ann" and "Pretty Little Miss" the way I learned to play them from Dwight (or I should say Dee-white, as we called him then.)[40]

Dwight had his heart set on a Fairbanks/Vega copy. He recalled that Dagget put on a scalloped brass rim on top of the old tone ring, recreating the Fairbanks Electric set up:

Because the brass ring had [been on the pot a while and had] aged, plus the thick rim of approximately 11/16th × 11½ rim, it was a really strong banjo[….] Later, I realized that the inlay was so good it was a scandal. The tiny short lines on the petals of the flower were perfect. And there had to be near a hundred of them. And there were two different kinds of pearl used. One was for the petals which [were] light red and green depending how the light hit it. The leaves were maybe an abalone that had ripples like leaves. […] it's only shortcoming was it was a copy of a 26 plus inch scale Gibson [style] neck. Too long and too skinny. Lee Hammons had put a thicker than usual hide head on that banjo. I tightened it down tight and never adjusted it in the 20 years it was on there. It would have held up except I play with such a force down in under and back up on the fifth string that it finally gave out in that area.[41]

In 1998 early, at a point when he was developing a business focused on building banjos in Brevard, North Carolina, Lo Gordon proposed that Dwight agree to put his name on one of Gordon's Cedar Mountain banjos. They discussed the aesthetics and construction of the banjo. Dwight chose the old "wasp shape" peghead design that had been popular over a hundred years earlier, and preferred walnut for a neck and pots colored to match the rim. Dwight remembered:

We went along for a few years. He developed his own style banjos with more of a standard peg head shape that of course suited people much better. In those years, I was doing a lot of traveling and teaching. Students would see my banjo and would often order one.[42]

That relationship lasted for about four years.

Around 2002, Bates Littlehales, who lived in Cherryville, West Virginia, right over the mountain from Dwight in a wonderful log cabin equipped with a basement full of woodworking tools, built Dwight a walnut fretless that made an appearance on one of Dwight's instructional videos—filmed and produced by Bates and his wife Jody. That fretless banjo was in Dwight's arsenal of instruments through at least 2005.

Dwight Diller, holding the banjo necked by Dan Dagget, inlay by Ron Chacy, circa 1996. The photograph, by Bates Littlehales, was the front cover for the June 1996 issue of *Banjo Newsletter*, containing Littlehales' interview with Dwight (courtesy Bates Littlehales).

Dwight once said that Sherman never played a fretless, and that there was not much in the way of fretless banjoing in his part of the mountains. As Dwight put it:

> It is impossible for me to play a fretless banjo and get the sound I want because the left hand can only be used to add a small amount of rhythm. [...] I was certainly happy with the little fretless banjo Bates [...] built for me. It was a fine little banjo. This might be the only fretless banjo I have owned for any length at all. Jeff Kramer built me one approximately 2002, but it wasn't long before I had him switch it over to frets. Tommy Jarrell, having been raised with a fretless banjo, may be the only person that I have ever seen/heard who can truly handle that style.[43]

Littlehales also build a traveling banjo that could be broken down into two parts—rim and neck—placed in luggage, and reassembled quickly and cleanly, a very inventive building approach that went through several prototypes. The one that Littlehales developed for Dwight used a Little Wonder 12-inch shell obtained from Bob Thornburg, a California builder of gourd banjos. Finally, Littlehales constructed a constructed a maple neck for a Whyte Laydie rim that eventually made its way to Jeff Kramer's hands. This was the "unique old Lange banjo" that Jeff Kramer was shown by Dwight in 2001.[44]

Chuck Lee, a banjo maker in Texas, built three banjos for Dwight between 2002 and 2003, when he was first getting his banjo workshop organized for business. Dwight remembered:

> Chuck Lee was beginning building banjos down in Texas around that time. We had become friends and were corresponding over the internet. He and his young children were playing music out in public at that time. We talked back and forth about building banjos at some length. He sent me perhaps one of his early or maybe first banjo.[45]

Dwight, Lee stated, was very helpful to him in the early process of deciding what kind of banjos he was going to build. They exchanged emails, talked often on the phone, and processed Dwight's feedback regarding his banjo preferences in the course of figuring out how to construct these three banjos to Dwight's specifications.[46] Lee recalled that the first banjo was fitted with a neck that was 1.5 inches wide, but after Dwight played it for a while both he and Lee agreed that it was probably a bit too wide.[47] That banjo was branded with the serial number "006," a later number than the second and third banjos Lee constructed for Dwight because Lee did not do the final lacquer finish work until after Dwight had played that banjo for a while, by which time Dwight had changed his mind about his preferred specifications.[48]

The second banjo that Chuck Lee built for Dwight, serial number "003," used a Tony Pass rim fitted with a Huber tone ring.[49] Lee remembered that Dwight was, at that time, looking for sustain, and "that's where the Huber [tonering] came in." Lee used Dwight's specifications for a distinctive peghead shape, a design that Lee utilized only four times in his building career: for the three banjos he built for Dwight plus one more banjo.[50] Dwight used the banjo in one of his instructional videos, and later sent the banjo back to Lee for some setup adjustments and hardware changes. The banjo was damaged in shipment to Lee. After the shipping mishap the damaged instrument took up permanent residence on a shelf in Lee's shop.[51]

The third banjo built by Lee for Dwight, bearing the serial number "004," was a traveling model with screw lugs in the heel, bolts through the rim, that could be disassembled so the neck and the pot could be stored in luggage and reassembled relatively quickly. The banjo was shipped from Lee's shop in April 2003.[52] Dwight played this banjo for a year or so before it was returned to Lee's shop. As Lee recalled, this was about the time that Dwight became acquainted with Jeff Kramer and his Cloverlick banjos.[53]

CONCLUSION

After attending a few of Dwight's banjo retreats in West Virginia in the 1990's, Jeff Kramer of Wisconsin decided to try his hand at banjo building in 2000. At a 2001 banjo retreat, Dwight pulled out his old Lange banjo with an 11.5 inch rim and asked Kramer to build a banjo that would duplicate the sound of this banjo. Kramer agreed to take a stab at it. As Dwight told the story:

> Around 2000, Jeff Kramer who had been a student for a few years, retired from his job and decided to build banjos. There were some ideas which I had carried with me for some years, and I mentioned them to him. Jeff had also had banjos for many years. Unlike so many of banjo builders, growing up he gained a lot of knowledge in metals. His father had several different businesses. One was a metal salvage yard. Any day he could, even during his early years, he was there with the metal. Plus he developed his great skill with wood working during those years and later years.[54]

Jeff Kramer's first banjo building job for Dwight was re-necking this banjo. This was the first time Dwight had the fifth string peg installed at the sixth fret, a notion that did not entirely spring from Dwight's own design ideas; Dwight recalled that he had seen vintage banjos in the Smithsonian's collection built in this configuration with the drone string dug in at the 6th or 7th fret. Dwight found Kramer inclined to listen closely to Dwight's banjo design preferences, such placing the 5th string peg at the 6th fret. Kramer was attentive to Dwight's views on tone ring composition that were an artifact of Dwight's blacksmithing experience in the 1970s that left him with some definite ideas about using brass and steel in tone ring design.[55]

Dwight put it this way:

Dwight's blacksmith workshop at his home in Frost, West Virginia, in 1976 (photograph by Carl Fleischhauer).

There was a constant experimentation with large improvements initially but then the tiny improvements began coming in some times in rapid secession. There are many tiny improvements which nobody else can catch. I know banjos relatively well. But there were experiments that improved how the weight was balanced as well as the balance in sound. But keep in mind, the sound was to be for the banjos that are for the old Appalachian traditional music. It had to fit between the normal flat sharp tinny sound of the so called "bluegrass banjo" and the banjos that are in vogue and sound like they are built from a wash tub. The dull/dead sound coming from a banjo that has a head that makes very little sound. A full, strong, round sound which will roll on up the road with a strong down beat because the sound has been driving ahead of the down beat. [...] The larger peg head is far better for the sound than the little things.[56]

Kramer recalled building five Piney Woods models for Dwight, including one with a four-inch rim.[57] From 2001 to 2007, the Piney Woods banjos were made with Tony Pass rims. Kramer started building two models—Knaves Run and Foxville—in 2007 and produced those models through 2015 using his own rims. Dwight preferred $11/16$th inch thick rims, 12 inches in diameter, with an overall depth (including the tone ring) of 2.75 inches. Kramer began calling the Banjos by nicknames, largely as a result of Dwight's habit of bestowing nicknames on people, and things.[58] Dwight offered many suggestions and ideas to improve playability and tone, including trying white oak and hickory. The EKBolt style tone ring system was Dwight's design. The EKLectric tone ring system was from the Lange. The EKWood, EKLyte, EKTNT, and EKTube tone rings were hybrids derived from ideas contributed by Dwight and John Morris, and combined with Kramer's ingenuity. As Kramer explained:

[Dwight's] banjos have had 10.5, 11, 11.5 and 12 inch rims. Thickness of rims has varied between ⅜ to ⅞ inches. Scale lengths were 22, 23.5, 24.5, 25.25, 26 3/16 inches. Woods have been maple, mahogany, walnut, maple, hickory, oak, Indian rosewood. Fingerboards and headstocks have been ebony, cocobolo, rosewood, bloodwood. Many combinations were tried and all were good banjos. What we found out was that eliminating steel parts, using permanent neck truss rods, good rim mass, and good tailpieces made for better sounding banjos. Overall, Dwight's style of playing changed over the years. The banjo that best suited his preferences and the one he likes the best was a hickory banjo, 12 inch rim, EKTNT tone rings, hickory neck and rim, cocobolo facewoods, brass hardware, brass "Fults 1934" tailpiece. This banjo was delivered in 2012.[59]

Dwight developed a particular formula for his preferred banjo in the context of this collaboration with Kramer:

- Dwight thought in terms of rims that were ¾ of an inch thick and 12 inches in diameter because they produced the sound of the old Lange rim that Dwight felt best served his musical purposes, and this was the sound that Kramer was looking for.
- Early on in his work with Kramer, Dwight opted for a 23.5 inch scale banjo neck that was extra wide at the nut "so the fingers did not hit the other strings while doing some heavy manipulating of the strings on the fingerboard."
- He opted for Kramer's brass or bronze eclectic tone ring or TNT tone ring set up on a brass scallop, explaining: "I want Jeff's all heavy duty brass hardware. He is one of the few who uses all heavy duty hardware for all his banjos unless the banjo is a custom model."
- Dwight preferred that the same wood be used for neck and rim, and he was strongly predisposed to either white oak or hickory: "I have had white oak and it is outstanding for a banjo. The present one is hickory and I prefer it. Both of these are really dense wood. [...] I do not like mahogany, maple, or some other woods that

might be called exotic. Black walnut is good. But nothing I have never had in my hands or owned will touch the white oak or hickory."
- He liked Kramer's slightly radiused fingerboard, and was partial to stainless steel frets. Dwight said that standard black ebony or rosewood fingerboards "are fine." He liked the bloodwood that Kramer used for peg head covers, heel caps, fingerboards, and rim caps.
- Dwight had a very specific way of thinking about neck angle and the neck/rim joint: "I want my banjos built with either zero degrees or -0.5 degrees and the fingerboard to be approximately ¼" above the level of the banjo head. When Dagget first built the neck on the Lange rim, he installed the fingerboard above the banjo head. That is why that banjo was so playable. My banjo necks will never ever have that foolish hacked out place on the neck where it connects with the rim. To play up there will only give one kind of sound. And it is almost impossible to control the rhythm up on the neck like that."
- Kramer's configuration situated his bridges 45 percent of the way from rim toward the fingerboard, a formula Dwight appreciated for the sound it produced.

Dwight's view was that Kramer's design permitted the banjo "to be played […] loud or soft, fast or slow, as long as it has the powerful snap, his banjos permit the right hand to quietly explode, and then the left hand to be a adjective modifying the noun."[60]

Sometime around 2010 or 2011, Andrew Fults of Tennessee attended one of Dwight's banjo retreats, hauling along a five string he had built for himself, and that led to a long-running discussion with Dwight about building banjos. Dwight sized up his capabilities this way:

Dwight and his two Cloverlick banjos, Marlington, West Virginia, May 2015 (author's photograph).

Andy Fults, from Tennessee, who has been a student of mine for the past few years. Some years back while taking banjo lessons at a local music school he saw some discarded parts from old banjos. Realizing there were folks who had little money but needed a banjo, he began gathering up old banjos and making improvements that made them playable. Having a steady day job, he finally built a couple banjos in spare time. He grew up helping his father build muzzle-loading rifles modeled after those pre–1850 rifles. It was very precise woodworking and the same with his metal working [such as] making a spring for a hammer for a rifle. First is the metal selection, shaping, and the hard part is the proper tempering. It was lots of time spent learning this delicate task. Present days he is working on building maybe three or four banjos a year.[61]

Sometime in 2011, Dwight decided that he wanted a short scale banjo (22½" scale). Fults recalled that when Dwight could not find anyone to make one like he wanted, "he ended up asking me to build one on a rim he had. He liked the work I did on that one, so I ended up making another short scale for him the next year with a tone ring setting on ¼" brass posts that were sunk into the rim." That led to a discussion about old "Snotty," and got Dwight interested in having Fults build an instrument "with the tone ring jacked up high enough to 'vent' the pot to the outside, similar to the old Washburn." Fults described the project:

> To speed up production Dwight sent me a big box full of banjo parts, including a real good walnut neck. The walnut pot that came off the same banjo had just about been ruined by someone else he got to tinker with it. I fixed that rim, but he wanted me to use that neck on the Washburn experiment, so I put a short scale neck on that pot and took it back to him last Summer. I had some 12" maple rim blanks from Cooperman, and we decided I would build the Washburn Improved style tone ring on one of them to use with the neck he sent me. I turned the rim to ¾" thick, and cut it to a 2¼" depth. I drilled it to accept ¼" brass posts, one between each bracket, and cut those posts to allow ⅞" above the rim. The tone ring was rolled from ⅜" brass rod and has two alignment posts that hold the ring centered on the support posts. There is about a ½" of ventilation between the rim and flesh hoop of the head. The banjo is the loudest open back banjo I ever played, and would be dangerous in the wrong hands. It sounded harsh when I played it, but Dwight can handle it and in his hands it sounded really good, especially when he tuned it down a step or two."[62]

Dwight played a custom built Cloverlick banjo with a 12 inch block style pot built by Jeff Kramer through at least 2015, but his sonic tastes wandered from time to time, and sometime in 2014 or 2015 he began to hark back to the louder, more brash banjo that he played during the his time with the Morris Brothers, perhaps wistfully, but also as part of an overall playful evolution in his interests in sound. He took an interest in another banjo project that Fults had devised that involved an old Ludwig Ambassador pot. The pot was a two-piece construction made of bronze:

> The bottom piece has a megaphone-like bell that goes up toward but does not contact the head. The top piece is a cast tone ring that is about 2 inches tall with scallops cut into the bottom edge, and the "legs" between the scallops sit on the bracket flange. This design also provides ventilation to the outside of the pot below the tension hoop and head. These were old jazz era tenor banjos, and have a reputation for being loud. Dwight wants one of these if they turn out good.[63]

Andrew Fults spent a lot time seeking out old Improved George Washburn rims that had the tone ring in them. Dwight explained:

> Andy had heard a tenor Washburn down in Alabama in recent years and remarked on its volume. That was what Snotty was, so Andy launched in on one with a 12 inch rim and a brass ring that is three eighths of an inch thick up on stilts. It has a warm sound to it. It is not a wildcat banjo. I don't need a wildcat banjo. I can put to good use this new "UnSnotty." I dropped it down in key of "F" rather than the standard "G." That key fits my voice and the more mellow tone fits with the voice better than the stronger aggressive Kramer Panther [model].[64]

There was another part to this tale. Fults related that Dwight told a story about the Old Langstyle II tenor Lee Hammons son rescued from a dump in New York:

> Some friend of Dwight's took the pot from that old banjo, made a Whyte Laydie style tone ring for it, and a real nice neck, and built the banjo Dwight played for 27 years. When I went up there to a camp I had not heard that story, and the banjo I had with me was one I had built from a box of old banjo parts

the Chattanooga Folk School had given me. It too was built on an old Langstyle II rim, with a Whyte Laydie style tone ring I built, and a new 5 string neck. So, it was similar to that banjo of Dwight's.[65]

In late 2014 Dwight asked Fults to recreate one of those for him, underscoring the extent to which Dwight's interest in experimenting with sound represented both a willingness to push the envelop and a lingering affection for the way things were.[66]

Dwight's Message

Dwight's musical interests overlapped with and at the same time derived from the obligation he assumed to listen to and preserve the tunes and stories of the "Old People." And this co-existed with his eager interest in teaching these stories and this music to students committed enough to take the immersive plunge that Dwight believed this material required. His earnest desire to impart the lessons he learned about the music converged with his penchant for talking about what the "Old People" and their old ways taught him about himself.

In the old time music world, Dwight navigated between several related interests: learning the Old People's music from the old people, playing music actively in bands and festivals, teaching banjo and fiddle, and preserving local banjo and fiddle traditions and stories. If anything integrated these various dimensions of Dwight's path, especially in his later decades of musical teaching, it was this idea of how music can guide us to what we should be. This became the a key notion informing Dwight's teaching work, especially during the late 1990s and early 2000s when he began thinking more systematically about what "teaching banjo" meant to him, and how it could have a positive impact on the lives of people who enrolled in his classes.

Dwight thought about his life in a distinctive manner. He thought about the music and the "Old People" who played the local tunes and told the stories that conveyed the area's unique "cultural messages" in a way that reflected his profound intimacy with the subject, and his enduring affection for the Hammonses, Hamp Carpenter, Lee Triplett, Glen Smith and others who touched his life. He shaped his approach to the responsibilities entailed in teaching this music, and conveying the dignity, special character, and the depth of meaning of the old music, in a way that relied on the Pocahontas County stories he imbibed growing up, and on popular histories and scholarship that provide a comfortable mooring for his perspectives. What emerged from this emulsion of ideas, notions, information, and memories was a narrative that has long provided a sturdy basis for explaining his motivation, describing his personal goals, characterizing the nature of what Dwight referred to as his ministry. It was not always consistent and seamless, and upon occasion it relied on a multiplicity of sources and a mix of methods of sorting through complex views that raised more questions than it answered, prompting more vigorous probing—challenges that Dwight relished, and appreciated as signs that what he was talking about was causing people to think and to learn. At times, the narrative relied on views that were not necessarily state of the art thinking. For example, Dwight spoke often of the unremitting isolation that characterized life in West Virginia. The abysmal, frightening isolation to which Dwight alluded was a very personal experience, an amalgamation of the physical realities of highland life that he endured—especially in the dead of winter when Marlinton turned into a sheet of rock cold tundra under significant, impassable snow—and his own insurmountable internal chemistry that captured him in a spiral of depression and unremitting sadness, aggravated by the realities of living alone in a state of diminishing physical health. But it was also, for Dwight, a historical fact, and a reality derived from the political economy, social realities and community ways. The idea of an overwhelming "isolation" that was a political, social and economic variable that shaped the situation in which West Virginia had long found itself, as Dwight understood it, was challenged by a close, discriminating look at West Virginia's extensive contacts dating from the mid–18th century with East Coast cities. Such studies showed that commerce had made manufactured goods from Richmond, Baltimore, Washington and other cities far more widely available in West Virginia. Studies documenting social change from the 1750s went far toward demonstrating that "subsistence cultures" immersed in and committed to preserving traditional values, organizing principles and social practices were not entirely resistant to change.[67] Further, attempts to deploy vaguely Marxist concepts to suggest that a form of "cultural colonialism" described the manner in which outsiders had come to dominate West Virginian cultural institutions in effect discarded a perfectly good argument that power—political, economic and social—was the critical variable determining the nature of relationships in the West Virginian; the habit and practice of cementing political alliances between state elites and outside sources of influence and largess were at the core of the political, economic and cultural weakness in West Virginia.[68]

Nevertheless, Dwight's thoughts were relentlessly focused on exploring the way the archaic music delivered messages, the way those messages were tied to one's sense of identity, and the manner in which identity enabled personal growth.

Dwight's preferred epitaph for his life was simply this: "He was obedient to Jesus and shared all he had."[69] That tied in closely with his sense that his teaching, his ministry, had less to do with teaching the banjo and more to do with ushering students to the point of knowing what they wanted of their lives. From time to time, Dwight gave voice to the notion that people who were not born and raised in West Virginia, or at least close by in Appalachia, would simply not be able to play that region's music, though his most thoughtful expression of the idea was simply that most people would never be able to play the "Old People's" music because most people did not have the life experiences that these elders brought to their fiddling or banjo playing or any other kind of expression.[70] He articulated this point in various ways throughout his life, but the central message he sought to communicate was this: a person will only be able to play music than emerged from and resonated with their own character and life experiences, and that ought to be sufficient.

Discography and Filmography

Several resources documenting Dwight Diller's recorded music are available. *Banjo Newsletter* contains a good number of tabs of Dwight's banjo playing undertaken by Dick Kimmell and Ken Perlman, among others, accessible via the online indexes of tabs. Dwight's own website has over the years provided a good source of information on his cassettes, CDs and instructional videos and other projects. *Banjo Hangout*, an online platform about all things related to all types of banjos and banjo music, is a good source of information—in forum threads, in the classified listings—of available CDs and DVDs. Gordon Banks' *Tablature for Dwight's Tunes*, as well as the CD that accompanies a tablature book produced in cooperation with Dwight, are also good sources of information regarding Dwight's recorded work, cassette tapes, CDs and videos. (Andrew Diamond, et al., *Yew Pine Mountain: Obscure Underground Clawhammer Banjo from Mysterious Central West Virginia*, revised, produced and printed in Pocahontas County, WV, 2006; http://dwightdiller.com/wp-content/uploads/2013/12/C.-DLLR-TabBook-2006_07_31-page-numbers-correct.pdf). Additionally, John Huerta of Elkins, West Virginia, developed a listing of Dwight's tunes, compiled alphabetically with the banjo tunings used, in the early 2000s. I owe a debt to each of these resources and the people involved in compiling these lists.

During the research and writing work for this book, two parallel projects began to crystallize: a cassette conversion project, and a slightly related effort to capture some of Dwight's earliest playing—from field recordings done with hand-held devices at banjo contests, jams, concerts, and banjo retreats and workshops. At some point, a systematic inventory of selected recorded material that represents Dwight's performances at festivals, concerts, workshops and retreats might emerge from this ongoing work. This discography/videography does not attempt to include any of these field recordings in the list of Dwight's recorded music.

Albums

On CD unless noted otherwise

Hold On! 1989. Yew Pine Music (YP-001), cassette, later released as a CD. *Musicians:* Dwight Diller, banjo; Tom King, guitar; Bowling Hughes, fiddle; Johnny Burks, bass. Tunes: Diamond Joe, Lizard in the Spring, Cindy, Put Your Hand to the Plow, Sally Ann, Pretty Little Dog, Yew Pine Mountain, Blue-Eyed Girl, Cluck Old Hen, Stay All Night, Otto Wood, Old Mother Flannigan, Banjo Medley (Walkin' in the Parlor, John Lover's Gone, Callaway), Sail Away Ladies. Availability: https://dwightdiller.bandcamp.com/album/hold-on-3.

Say Old Man. By Glen Smith with Dwight Diller. 1990. Marimac Recordings (AHS # 3), Augusta Heritage Series. Cassette. *Musicians:* Glen Smith, fiddle; Dwight Diller, banjo; Gerry Milnes, guitar. Recorded November 1989 in Elizabeth, WV. Tunes: Cattle in the Cane, Molly Put the Kettle On, Old Tin Pan, June Apple, Grandma Take a Look at Uncle Sam, Old Mother

Flannigan, Dance Around Molly, Leather Britches, Lost Indian, Pretty Little Widow, Say Old Man, Tennessee Wagner, Jimmy Johnson, Patty on the Turnpike, Sally Ann, A Rose for Polly, Lead Out, Blackberry Blossom, Wagon Tire Tightener, Pretty Little Indian, Hell Among the Indians, The Cat Come Back.

O Death! 1992. Yew Pine Music (YP-005), cassette, later released as a CD. Musicians: Dwight Diller, David Nemec, Dirck Westervelt, Mary Maxim, Ruby T. Maide. Produced and recorded by David Nemec. Tunes: Elzick's Farewell, Frosty Morn, Yew Pine Mountain, Jay Legg, Wild Bill Jones, John Brown's March, Wild Hog (Bangum), Old Christmas Morning, Tom Dula, O Death, Reuben, Texas, Greasy Coat, Pretty Polly, S.A.D., Angeline, Jimmy Johnson, The Dead Man's Piece, Heard the Thunder Roaring. Availability: https://dwightdiller.bandcamp.com/album/o-death.

Just Banjo. 1996. Yew Pine Music (YP-002), cassette, later released on CD. Recorded by David Nemec at the Mennonite Church of the Mountains, U.S. 219 North, Hillsboro, WV. Tunes: Fall of Richmond, Mississippi Sawyer, Chilly Winds, Arkansas Traveler, Greasy String, Cripple Creek, Sweet Sunny South, Yew Pine Mountain, West Fork Girls, Blackberry Blossom, Cluck Old Hen, Waynesboro, Shootin' Creek, Sally Ann, Jake Gilley, Old Bill Cheatum, Black-Eyed Susie, Three Forks of Reedy, Turkey in the Straw, Boatman, Shaking Down the Acorns, Big Scioto, New Caledonia, Abe's Retreat, Piney Woods. Note: On one side of the cassette, Dwight is playing "Greasy String," and the other side he is playing "Greasy String" but that cut is labelled "Three Forks of Reedy" on the liner notes. Availability: http://www.tagtuner.com/music/albums/Dwight-Diller/Just-Banjo-96/album-v26b3e2.

One More Time. By Jake Krack. 1998. Wise Recordings, (SKU-WISE-1221-CD). Musicians: Jake Krack, fiddle; Dwight Diller, banjo; Danny Arthur, guitar; Dara Krack, guitar (on Stack 'Em Up in Piles only). Tunes: Jimmy Johnson, Waiting for the Federals, The Route, Temperance Reel, Cold Frosty Morning, Say Old Man, Charleston Gals, Old Joe Clark, Muskrat Sally Ann, Yew Piney Mountain, Lost Indian, Elsick's Farewell, Jack of Diamonds, Waiting for the Boatsman, Lock Leven Castle, Old Sledge, Ryland Spencer, Rocky Road to Dublin, Cluck Old Hen, Rainy Day, Keys to the Kingdom, Lost Girl, Stack 'Em Up In Piles, Tippy Get Your Hair Cut, Grigsby's Hornpipe, Paddy on the Turnpike, One More Time.

Just Banjo '99. Yew Pine Mountain (YP-99), CD. Tunes: Boatsman, Cluck Old Hen, Turkey in the Straw, Black-Eyed Suzie, Shootin' Creek, Texas, Cripple Creek, Kitchen Girl, John Lover's Gone, Fall of Richmond, West Fork Girls, Arkansas Traveler, Abe's Retreat, Cumberland Gap, 3 Forks of Reedy, Caladonia March, Sally Ann, Santa Ana's Retreat, Reuben's Train, Rocky Mountain Goat, God Gave Noah, Piney Woods.

Papa! Undated, 1990s. Yew Pine Music (YP-1X), cassette, later released on CD. Musicians: Dwight Diller, banjo, vocal; Dan Gardella, fiddle; Frances Hammeye, flute; Ernestine Hannah, vocal lead; Larry Combs, guitar; Ginger Music, vocal; David Nemec, vocal. Recorded by David Nemec and Doug Van Gundy. Tunes: Canaan's Land, There Is a Fountain, Oh Those Tombs, Satan Your Kingdom Must Come Down, The Darkest Hour, Down in the Valley to Pray, Jerusalem Moan, The Old Crossroads, When the Roll Is Called, River of Jordan Cryin,' Holy, Dark and Stormy, Sinner Get Ready, 90 + 9, Heard the Thunder Roaring, Be Thou My Vision, Wayfaring Pilgrim, I Wanna Die Easy, Standing on the Promises, Come Thou Fount, The Way of the Cross.

Piney Woods. Undated, 1990s release. Yew Pine Music (YP-007), cassette, later released as a CD. Musicians: Dwight Diller, banjo; John Gallagher, fiddle; Tom King, guitar. Tunes: Jimmy Johnson, Muddy Roads, Shaking Down the Acorns, Fine Times at Our House, Sandy Boys, John Henry Blues, Washington's March, Walkin' in the Parlor, Big Scioto, Sugar Babe, Fall of Richmond, Mole in the Ground, Greasy Coat, Shelvin Rock, Piney Woods, Calloway, Hogs and Sheep A-Goin to the Pasture, Waynesboro. Availability: https://dwightdiller.bandcamp.com/album/piney-woods.

Red Rooster. Undated, 1990s. Yew Pine Music (YP-003), cassette, later released as a CD. Musicians: Dwight Diller, banjo, vocals; David Nemec, acoustic bass; John Gallagher, fiddle; David Nemec, guitar; Tom King, guitar, mandolin; Middle Mountain Boys, vocals. Recorded by David Nemec. Tunes: Old Joe Clark, Ground Hog, John Henry, Fire Next Time, Sourwood

Mountain, Red Rooster (Comin' Around the Mountain), Kitchen Girl, Jerusalem to Jericho, Grey Mule, Sweet Bye and Bye, The Yellow Rose of Texas, Barlow Knife, Courtship and Marriage of Mr. Frogge and Miss Maus, Quince Dillon's High D, Old Dan Tucker, Cumberland Gap, Carry Me Home (Note: labeled "Swing Low" on CD), Jimmy Johnson, We'll Work Till Jesus Comes. Availability: https://dwightdiller.bandcamp.com/album/red-rooster.

Harvest. 1997. CD compilation of Dwight's favorites from original cassettes and CDs plus 16 new selections. Tunes: Greasy String; John Henry; Waynesboro; Satan Your Kingdom Must Come Down; Dead Man's Piece; Angeline; The Old Drake; Shelvin' Rock; Crying Holy Unto the Lord; Greasy String (actually, John Brown's March); Put Your Hand to the Plow; Jake Gilley; Yew Pine Mountain; Big Scioto; Die Easy; Walkin' in the Parlor; Sinner Get Ready; Abe's Retreat; Come Thou Fount; Come Back, Boys, Let's Feed the Horses; Bob Porter; Standing on the Promises; Pretty Little Cat; Callaway; Wayfaring Pilgrim; The John Henry Blues, Jimmy Johnson; Sail Away, Ladies; The Way of the Cross. Notes: According to the liner notes, these tunes were recorded or re-recorded for the CD: Greasy String; Dead Man's Piece; The Old Drake; Shelvin' Rock; Put Your Hand on the Plow; Jake Gilley; Yew Piney Mountain; Die Easy; Walkin in the Parlor; Come Back, Boys, and Let's Feed the Horses; Bob Porter; Pretty Little Cat; The John Henry Blues; Sail Away Ladies. Also, the following tunes were previously released on six of Dwight Diller's cassettes: *Hold On!, Red Rooster, Piney Woods, Papa!, O Death!,* and *Just Banjo*: John Henry, Waynesboro, Satan Your Kingdom Must Come Down, Angeline, Crying Holy Unto the Lord, Big Scioto, Sinner Get Ready, Abe's Retreat, Come Thou Fount, Standing on the Promises, Wayfaring Pilgrim, Jimmy Johnson, The Way of the Cross. Availability: https://dwightdiller.bandcamp.com/album/harvest.

New Plowed Ground. Recorded in 1998. (Yew Pine YP-IX-4.) Musicians: Dwight Diller, Northampton Harmony/Cordelia's Dad. Tunes: Bright Morning Star, Betsey Lichens, They Obeyed, Brushy Run, Hiram Herbert, Old Mother Flannagan, Shady Grove, Would Not Be Denied, Lone Pilgrim, West Fork Girls, Lisbon, Abe's Retreat, Jordan's Stormy Banks, Ducks on the Pond, Sweet Hour of Prayer, Muskrat, Liza Jane, John Hardy, Sandy Boys, Shelter in a Storm.

In England. Recorded 1999. Musicians: Dave Bing, fiddle; Dwight Diller, banjo. Tunes: Muskrat Sally Ann, Groundhog, Lost Girl, Wild Bill Jones, Big Scioto, Otto Wood, Waynesboro, Old Christmas Morning, Jerusalem Moan, Cranberry Rock, Angeline the Baker, Jimmy Johnson, West Fork Girls, Picked Up a Hammer, Greasy Coat, Old Mother Flannagan, Shelvin' Rock, John Henry, Camp Chase, Gospel Plow.

Black Mountain Bluegrass Boys, 1968–1973. 2000. Issued by Black Mountain Bluegrass Boys/Pocahontas Communications Cooperative Corporation. Musicians: Harley Carpenter, guitar, lead vocal; Bill Hefner, mandolin, baritone vocal; Richard Hefner, banjo, tenor vocal; Dwight Diller, bass. Note: Dwight played bass and occasionally clawhammer banjo for the band during the early 1970s. Tunes: Gold Rush, Last Old Dollar, East Virginia Blues, Midnight Storm, Mother's Not Dead, Forked Deer, Lonesome Reuben, A Million Lonely Days, Lonesome River, Sittin' on Top of the World, Muddy Road, Along the Way, These Old Blues, Walk Softly on This Heart of Mine, Thinking About You, The Memory of Your Smile, I Believe in You Darlin,' Mill Point, A Million Lonely Days, Blue and Lonely, Send Me Angels, Working on a Building, You're Not Easy to Forget, Say Old Man Can You Play the Fiddle.

Banjo Legacy: Traditional Music of West Virginia. 2001. Augusta Heritage Center, Elkins, WV. 18 tracks, various artists. Dwight Diller plays two tunes: Sail Away Ladies, Gospel Plow. Availability: https://www.murfie.com/albums/various-artists-banjo-legacy-traditional-music-of-west-virginia.

Fabulous Festival Favorites: Volume 1, Field Recordings. 2002. Yew Pine Music (YP-FF1). Musicians: Dwight Diller, banjo; Bo Hughes, fiddle; Dave Keller, fiddler; Doug Van Gundy, fiddle; John Morris, fiddle; Larry Combs, guitar. Tunes: June Apple, Sugar Hill, Tempy, Julie Ann Johnson, Forked Deer, Cotton-Eyed Joe, Liberty, Hawks and Eagles, Hang Me, The 8th of January, Mississippi Sawyer, Ducks on the Millpond, Year of Jubilo, Blue Eyed Girl, Sweet 16, Lost Indian. Availability: https://dwightdiller.bandcamp.com/album/fabulous-festival-favorites-volume-1-field-recordings.

Jericho Road. 2005. Yew Pine Music (YP-JRD). Tunes: Sally Ann, Sweet 16, Washington's March, Yellow Rose of Texas, Lost Girl, Angeline, Fall of Richmond, Horny [Horned] Ewe, Sandy Boys, New Castle/Texas, Callaway [Lee Hammons], Callaway [Maggie, Burl, Sherman Hammons], Old Joe Clark, Sugar Babe, Quince Dillon's Hi-D, Chicken Reel, Sally's A-Siftin Sand, Big Eyed Rabbit, Green Willis, Diamond Joe, Boll Weevil, Old Molly Hair, Soldier's Joy, Waterbound, Frosty Morn.

Trouble on Spring Creek. 2007. FR#16. Musicians: Dwight Diller, fiddle; Darin Gentry, banjo. Tunes: Elz[w]ick's Farewell; Shakin' Down the Acorns; Baby-O; Patty on the Turnpike; Greasy String; Boatin' Up Sandy; Calloway; Sourwood Mountain; Camp Chase; Abe's Retreat; Kitty Snyder; Greasy Coat; Frosty Morn; Come Back, Boys, and Let's Feed the Horses; Trouble on Spring Creek; Three Forks of Cheat; Shakin' Down the Acorns; Pretty Little Dog.

Mountain Voices: Authentic Appalachian Singing from Central WVa and Eastern KY. By Dwight Diller and Gail Hatton. 2008. Tunes: Jack Monroe, Silk Merchant's Daughter, Young Hennerly, Little Black Train, Sister Thou Was Mild and Lovely, Pretty Saro, Hiram Herbert, Crossing the Rocky Mountains, Wicked Polly, The Parting Hand, Last May Morning, Holy Manna, Shiloh's Hill, Lady Margaret (Liddy Morgie), The House Carpenter, Beautiful Hills of Galilee, Conversation with Death, When I Can Read My Title Clear.

CD accompanying the book Andrew Diamond, et al., *Yew Piney Mountain: Obscure Underground Clawhammer Banjo from Mysterious Central West Virginia.* Revised, produced and printed in Pocahontas County, volume one. 2006. Tunes: Big Scioty, Greasy String (Burl's), Greasy String (Lee's), Kitchen Girl, Old Christmas Morning, Sandy Boys, Shelvin Rock, Sugar in My Coffee, Waynesboro, Wild Hog in the Red Brush, Kitty Snyder, More Pretty Girls Than One, Walkin' in the Parlor, West Fork Girls, Come Back Boys and Let's Feed the Horses, Fall of Richmond, Patty on the Turnpike, Santa Anna's Retreat, The Old Drake, Abe's Retreat, Abe's Retreat, Yew Piney Mountain, Piney Woods, Low D Blues, Washington's March, Calloway (Burl, Maggie and Sherman's), Dead Man's Piece. Availability: http://dwightdiller.com/wp-content/uploads/2013/12/C.-DLLR-TabBook-2006_07_31-page-numbers-correct.pdf.

Music Videos

The Old Drake: Traditional Music from the Mountains of East Central West Virginia Played on the Banjo and Fiddle: Visiting Dwight Diller with Jimmy Triplett. AFC 1996/041: Don Patterson/Mountain Music Video Collection. 1996. Tunes:

Shelvin Rock, Lost Girl, Pretty Little Dog, Shippinsport, Elsick's Farewell, Elk River Blues, Three Forks of Reedy, Houston, Big Scioto, Piney Woods, Greasy String, Shakin Off the Acorns, The Old Drake, Abe's Retreat, Lovely Nancy, The Fall of Richmond.

Instructional Videos

Just Rhythm: West Virginia Clawhammer Banjo Instruction—First Volume. Thornapple Productions, Bates and Jody Littlehales. 2000. Tunes: Mole in the Ground, Sally Ann, Boil Them Cabbage Down, Cripple Creek, Frosty Morning, Black-Eyed Suzie/Cindy, Arkansas Traveler, Shelvin Rock, Jimmy Johnson/Cluck Ol Hen/Lisa Jane Chicken Reel, Shakin Down the Acorns, S.A.D., Sail Away Ladies, Black-Eyed Suzie, Abe's Retreat.

More West Virginia Clawhammer Banjo Instruction—Second Volume. Thornapple Productions, Bates and Jody Littlehales. 2000. Tunes: Walking in the Parlor, Cripple Creek, Groundhog, Cluck Old Hen, Greasy String, Frosty Morning, Black-Eyed Susie, Blue Eyed Girl (Fly Around My Pretty Little Miss).

Intermediate Level Clawhammer Banjo Instruction—Third Volume. Thornapple Productions, Bates and Jody Littlehales. 2000. Tunes: Kitchen Girl (not taught), Jimmy Johnson, Muddy Roads, Old Mother Flannagan, John Brown's March, Blue Eyed Girl, Angeline the Baker, John Henry Blues, Greasy String (not taught).

Modal Clawhammer Banjo Instruction—Fourth Volume. Thornapple Productions, Bates and Jody Littlehales. 2000. Tunes: The Old Drake (not taught), Boatin Up Sandy, Greasy Coat, Texas/Newcastle, Shakin Down the Acorns, Pretty Little Dog, Abe's Retreat, Falls of Richmond (not taught), Yew Piney Mountain (not taught).

YouTube Videos

Dwight Diller, banjo, on all tunes, unless otherwise noted.

Abe's Retreat. Dwight Diller, fiddle. https://www.youtube.com/watch?v=6y-qA0BZDMI.
Abe's Retreat. https://www.youtube.com/watch?v=8QNJPmFADjo.
Angeline Baker. Darin Gentry, fiddle. https://www.youtube.com/watch?v=9RsqmK-zlO8.
Arkansas Traveller. https://www.youtube.com/watch?v=xVLankVTdKY.
Arkansas Traveller. https://www.youtube.com/watch?v=yz8ddzsnwlM.
Big Scioty. https://www.youtube.com/watch?v=C96gDdF-uv4.
Black Eyed Susie. https://www.youtube.com/watch?v=ZOaZmTMP7Wk.
Black Eyed Susie. https://www.youtube.com/watch?v=qqPWIOFU7go.
Black-Eyed Susie. https://www.youtube.com/watch?v=-m7BSZX9l8Q&index=5&list=PL26DCBEB012AD82F2.
Blue Eyed Girl. https://www.youtube.com/watch?v=WFT4CF8Uf3o.
Bonaparte Crossing the Rhine. https://www.youtube.com/watch?v=MKmkDUG0B4I.
Burl Hammons' Cranberry Rock. Darin Gentry, fiddle. https://www.youtube.com/watch?v=6fJxqe4MP2I.
Burl Hammons' Greasy String. Darin Gentry, fiddle. https://www.youtube.com/watch?v=kO9lhOHbjWg.
Burl Hammons' Greasy String. https://www.youtube.com/watch?v=NmdzZeieXQE.
Burl Hammons' Shelvin' Rock. https://www.youtube.com/watch?v=XihXmoXfJ5o.
Cindy (in slow motion). https://www.youtube.com/watch?v=d74bynKGYkM.
Cindy Harris. https://www.youtube.com/watch?v=L8hAdE2K9bI.
Come Back Boys, Let's Feed the Horses. https://www.youtube.com/watch?v=17iMdbwtmxw.
Cranberry Rock. Darin Gentry, fiddle. https://www.youtube.com/watch?v=4Zw85IE107o&list=PL26DCBEB012AD82F2&index=2.
Cumberland Gap. https://www.youtube.com/watch?v=u8S6NxlYIi0.
God Gave Noah the Rainbow Sign. https://www.youtube.com/watch?v=FwKjJsPK5uI.
Hang Me. https://www.youtube.com/watch?v=XhqeQfXauEo.
Jake Gilley. https://www.youtube.com/watch?v=gDyfc1KQD1Y.
Jimmy Johnson. Larry Combs, guitar. From *Intermediate Level Clawhammer Banjo Instruction* DVD. https://www.youtube.com/watch?v=FUkO4nv81fk.
John Brown's March. https://www.youtube.com/watch?v=0bEIcucshFk.
John Henry Blues. https://www.youtube.com/watch?v=T8zfL9qMDs4.
John Lover's Gone. https://www.youtube.com/watch?v=KJdOdKMiITU.
John Lover's Gone and Cindy. https://www.youtube.com/watch?v=FZH-OzQGQrA.
John Lover's Gone, Cindy # 2. https://www.youtube.com/watch?v=p7Eqvxjdtr8.
Kitchen Girl. From *Intermediate Level Clawhammer Banjo Instruction* DVD. https://www.youtube.com/watch?v=-ioh0XRO80Q.
Lee Hammons' Callaway. https://www.youtube.com/watch?v=A1sn3U26bzI.
Lee Hammons' Callaway. https://www.youtube.com/watch?v=VWf_NK9Dx3U.
Lee Hammons Calloway (#2). https://www.youtube.com/watch?v=P1xDZ2p8ejQ.
Mole in the Ground. https://www.youtube.com/watch?v=1lHiWR-pF6M.
Mole in the Ground, Sally Ann. From *Just Rhythm* DVD https://www.youtube.com/watch?v=ePhSsBpeTW0.
More Pretty Girls Than One. https://www.youtube.com/watch?v=-hktP-amllE&index=3&list=PL26DCBEB012AD82F2.
Old Drake, Boatin Up Sandy. From *Modal Clawhammer Banjo Instruction* DVD. https://www.youtube.com/watch?v=L9SeH8Zsqv0.

Old Mother Flanagan. https://www.youtube.com/watch?v=1d8IySI-Rxk.
Old Mother Flanagan (Slow Motion). https://www.youtube.com/watch?v=tf4VVvSlD4k.
Piney Woods, Arkansas Traveller, Chicken Reel. From *West Virginia Mountain Music with Dwight Diller*. https://www.youtube.com/watch?v=Jk8Q3ZXPatk.
Put Your Hand on the Plow. https://www.youtube.com/watch?v=P9ZVxofPYaU.
"SAD." https://www.youtube.com/watch?v=cq5cIOl14ps.
Sally Ann. https://www.youtube.com/watch?v=YdUPyz6p2l8.
Sally Ann. https://www.youtube.com/watch?v=G9LTjH_1vbA.
Shakin Down the Acorns. Dwight Diller, fiddle. https://www.youtube.com/watch?v=746pWbsLK_Q.
Shakin Down the Acorns. Dwight Diller, fiddle. https://www.youtube.com/watch?v=ARG8tih_ojI.
Shelvin Rock. Darin Gentry, fiddle. https://www.youtube.com/watch?v=-hktP-amllE&index=3&list=PL26DCBEB012AD82F2.
Walkin in the Parlor. https://www.youtube.com/watch?v=WFT4CF8Uf3o.
Walkin in the Parlor and Cripple Creek. From *More West Virginia Clawhammer Banjo Instruction* DVD. https://www.youtube.com/watch?v=3an1gkR-FzQ.
Washington's March. https://www.youtube.com/watch?v=R8OZtGpsDos.
Waynesboro. https://www.youtube.com/watch?v=0-sS5CVdxkY.
Wild Bill Jones. https://www.youtube.com/watch?v=rjxQMq_bfhM.
Yeller Rose. Darin Gentry, fiddle. https://www.youtube.com/watch?v=Ua34SE3LSXk&index=1&list=PL26DCBEB012AD82F2.
Yellow Rose of Texas. Darin Gentry, fiddle. https://www.youtube.com/watch?v=aKqF3uO3fP4.
Yew Piney Mountain. Dwight Diller, fiddle. https://www.youtube.com/watch?v=zeLMxGPQ9jY.
Yew Piney Mountain. https://www.youtube.com/watch?v=PFHwnXaIyl0.

Miscellaneous

Dwight Diller's music can be heard on the following videos:

Several West Virginia documentaries produced by Patchwork Films, including:

-30- Cal Price and "The Pocahontas Times" (www.patchworkfilms.com/pocahontastimes.htm), *Mountain Mourning* (www.patchworkfilms.com/mm_dvd.htm), *Look What They've Done!* (www.patchworkfilms.com/maria.htm), *Keeper of the Mountains* (www.patchworkfilms.com/larry.htm) and *A Sense of Values*.

Perfect Porch: A Banjo Camp with Dwight Diller and Ken Perlman. Taped at Cass, Pocahontas County, West Virginia, during the week of 13 July 1998.

West Virginia Mountain Music, with Dwight Diller. By Bates and Jody Littlehales, 2009.

The Fifth String. Feature length film starring Dwight Diller and John Morris. Front Porch Entertainment/American Film Partners, 2004.

Chapter Notes

Introduction

1. My Hosting Experience, 28 January 2002, http://dwightdiller.com/camp/lowdown-i/lew-sterns-hosting-experience/.

2. Dwight pointed out the Yew Piney Mountains were made up of Black, Cranberry, Kinnison, Viney, Caesar, and Droop Mountains. Dwight grew up at the base of these mountains. See Andrew Diamond, et al., *Yew Pine Mountain: Obscure Underground Clawhammer Banjo From Mysterious Central West Virginia* (revised, produced and printed in Pocahontas County, WV, 2006), p. 41. http://dwightdiller.com/wp-content/uploads/2013/12/C.-DLLR-TabBook-2006_07_31-page-numbers-correct.pdf.

3. *Across the YewPines*, http://dwightdiller.com/across-yew-pines-dvd/.

4. Alan Jabbour and Gerald Parsons recorded an interview with Dwight in December 1980. See Dwight Diller interview conducted by Alan Jabbour, 18 December 1980 (AFC 1986/060), American Folklife Center, Library of Congress. I am grateful to Carl Fleischhauer for facilitating access to this recorded interview. Jack Bernhardt conducted a 180-minute interview in 1983 at the Augusta Heritage Center in Elkins, West Virginia. See: University of North Carolina at Chapel Hill, Collection Number: 20061, Collection Title: Jack Bernhardt Papers, 1943–2011, Dwight Diller Interview, Elkins, WVA, 3 August 1983, Tape 1 of 2. Dwight Diller Interview, Elkins, WVA, 3 August 1983, Tape 2 of 2. In 1996 Dwight was interviewed by Bates Littlehales: "Dwight Diller," *Banjo Newsletter*, vol. 23, no. 8, June 1996, pages 10–17. In 1997, Dwight sat down with Ken Perlman, and that interview was published as: "Dwight Diller and the Music of Pocahontas County," *Sing Out!*, vol. 42, no. 1, May/June/July 1997, pp. 52–63. Also see: Carrie Osborne, "Killer Diller," *Folk Roots* (United Kingdom), no. 180, June 1998, pp. 17–18. Pat Costello conducted an interview in 2000: see Interview with Dwight Diller, conducted in Cass, WV, published on 22 July 2012, from *The Down Neck Gazette*. https://www.youtube.com/watch?v=zujNF7MCKro. On 22 February 1999, Dwight and Dave Bing were interviewed by BBC Radio Derby, and in March, the two sat for an interview with BBC Radio Scotland in Edinburgh. I have not been able to locate audio recordings of those radio interviews. In 2000 or so, Dwight was interviewed on Seattle radio. I am grateful to Bob Thornburg for providing an audiocassette of that broadcast. It is possible that the Seattle interview captured much of what Dwight said in the interviews with the BBC in that period. In 2013 Craig Evans conducted a video interview made available as: "A Piece of Living History: A Conversation with Teacher—Dwight Diller," Conversations with North American Banjo Builders, vol. 3, Conversations with Banjo Historians, Frailinflix Productions.

5. John Brian said of his family's West Virginian way of talking: "For me, coming home always had to do with language. [...] To my ear, Appalachian speech is music." *At Home in the Heart of Appalachia* (New York: Random House, 2001), p. 13.

Chapter One

1. John Diller left Germany and settled in York County, Pennsylvania, around 1823. Henry Diller, Vernon's grandfather, was born in 1839 and arrived in American after John. Henry died in 1894. Dwight talked about a Casper Diller who settled in New Holland, Pennsylvania, in 1739, and a Francis Diller who arrived in the United States in 1752. "Diller Concert—12/03," tape 4. The concert took place in Pittsburgh, Pennsylvania, in December 2003 at the home of Cindy Harris.

2. Red Lick Mountain is a 4,685-foot mountain peak near Marlinton, West Virginia, that ranks as the seventh highest mountain in West Virginia. http://peakery.com/red-lick-mountain-west-virginia/.

3. See Carl Fleischhauer and Alan Jabbour, *The Hammons Family: A Study of a West Virginia Family's Traditions* (Washington, D.C.: Library of Congress, 1973), page 32. The 40-page booklet accompanying the records set was reissued in 2011 as an online version for the Archive of Folk Culture sound recording. http://www.loc.gov/folklife/LP/AFSL65andL66_Hammons.pdf.

4. 25 November 2014 (5:28 p.m.) email from Dwight Diller to Lew Stern. Also see William F. Bailey, ed., "A.A. Cutter Shoe Factory," in *History of Eau Claire County, Wisconsin, 1914, Past and Present*, pp. 474–476. http://eauclaire.wigenweb.org/histories/1914ecco/chapter34/aacuttershoefactory.htm. Luther Flynn described his experience in a West Virginia lumber camp in 1912 in *Beyond the Mountains: An Autobiography* (Virginia: McClure, 1979), chapter 2, page 8. Also see *The Pocahontas Times*, 8 November 1979, p. 5.

5. 25 November 2014 (5:28 p.m.) email from Dwight Diller to Lew Stern.

6. Dwight learned these things about his grandmother from his Aunt Betty in 2011. 25 November 2014 (5:28 p.m.) email from Dwight Diller to Lew Stern, and 15 October 2014 (3:30 p.m.) email from Dwight Diller to Lew Stern. D. W. Stubblefield, a chemical company official, Charleston, West Virginia, retired sometime in the later 1940s. From 1949 to 1950 he was president of the Rotary Club of Charleston, West Virginia. See: https://www.charlestonrotary.com/Goverance/Past-Presidents.aspx and http://www.newspapers.com/newspage/42489654/.

7. 15 October 2014 (3:30 p.m.) email from Dwight Diller to Lew Stern.

8. 15 October 2014 (3:30 p.m.) email from Dwight Diller to Lew Stern.

9. William Thomas Price, *Historical Sketches of Pocahontas County, West Virginia* (Marlinton, WV: Price Brothers, 1901), pp. 16–17.

10. Author's notes, 17 October 2014 (10:00 a.m.–12:00 p.m.) telephone conversation with Dwight Diller.

11. Catherine Rowe told me: "In the beginning stages of finding out about ourselves, and therefore the search for God who is 'within,' we identify ourselves with our ego, then our behavior, then our feelings and emotions, then our searching and insights, then our newly discovered negative side, before beginning to accept who we really are with all the contradictions. It is possible to remain at an early stage and believe that, for example, our behavior influences whether God loves us. God can't have a change of heart. God is constant in love, and is not internally divided. It is this knowledge [that] creates the confidence to act, and to keep trying, 'perfect love casts out fear.' It is the opposite of how things are normally done: approval and acceptance is dependent upon what we do. Dwight is very firmly rooted in the New Testament, in which God is a loving Father, always on our side. However, I do feel that he believes this, yet at the same time regards the working out of it like being in the military, with no choice and a lot of discomfort." 16 October 2014 (10:16 p.m.) email from Catherine Rowe to Lew Stern. I owe a great debt to Ms. Rowe, who on my behalf spent considerable time and energy untangling the complexities of Dwight's beliefs, and did so in a straightforward, articulate manner.

12. 25 November 2014 (5:28 p.m.) email from Dwight Diller to Lew Stern.

13. Dwight recalled that Vernon's job with the Civilian Conservation Corps "was to help start the reclaimation of the acreage in Pocahontas County that had been stripped of timber by the lumber companies. Hot cinders from the Shay Locomotives' engines that were used to haul the logs out of the mountains ignited the dry tree tops that caused forest fires in the area." That, together with the significant soil runoff from deforestation, further contributed to the degradation of the environment." 25 November 2014 (5:28 p.m.) email from Dwight Diller to Lew Stern.

14. Before World War II, Faith worked at Belle Alkali, later Diamond Alkali, located adjacent to the DuPont plant in Belle. 25 November 2014 (5:28 p.m.) email from Dwight Diller to Lew Stern.

15. 27 August 2014 (9:47 a.m.) email from Dwight Diller to Lew Stern.

16. Dwight stated: "When [Faith] brought my sister and I back to her home area, Pocahontas County, from Kanawha County, in January 1952, her five sisters lived or soon after moved back here. Over the years they each took a turn, large or small, rescuing me from my mother. My sister, Nancy, was left with her, but there was the Kellison family, Roy and Mamie, who provided a place to stay during the day many times over those early years. The Lord saw to it that she had a haven where there was never one cross word in that household in all the years Nancy stayed there. They were older and Nancy was treated as a very special granddaughter." 25 November 2014 (5:28 p.m.) email from Dwight Diller to Lew Stern.

17. Author's notes, 23 March 2015 (10:30–11:45 a.m.) telephone conversation with Dwight Diller, Marlinton, West Virginia.

18. In 1991, while organizing his father's possessions before moving him from Toledo, Ohio, back to Pocahontas County, Dwight found notes, messages, and a short diary, and reflected on their contents: "Beginning when he had to leave, the emptiness set in and finally having to give up hope that he would ever have a relationship with his children even when they became adults. There was nothing but a shell in later years until the end in 1993." Dwight added, in what could have been an elliptical reference to his own situation, "This kind of story keeps getting played out over and over more and more it seems." 25 November 2014 (5:28 p.m.) email from Dwight Diller to Lew Stern.

19. 25 November 2014 (5:28 p.m.) email from Dwight Diller to Lew Stern, and 15 October 2014 (3:30 p.m.) email from Dwight Diller to Lew Stern. In one of the notes that Dwight came upon in his father's possessions, after Vernon had passed away, his father had written: "What I have regretted the most was to have to leave Dwight behind with Faith. I know how she is going to treat him because he is so much like me." 25 November 2014 (5:28 p.m.) email from Dwight Diller to Lew Stern.

20. 25 November 2014 (5:28 p.m.) email from Dwight Diller to Lew Stern.

21. 25 November 2014 (5:28 p.m.) email from Dwight Diller to Lew Stern.

22. John O'Brien describes the rough-edged way of his West Virginia family in *At Home in the Heart of Appalachia*, pp. 9–26. Also see Truman Fields, *Remembering the 40's in the Heart of Appalachia: School Days, 1942–43* (Bloomington, IN: AuthorHouse, 2009), chapter one, and Flynn, *Beyond the Mountains*, chapters 1–3.

23. 25 November 2014 (5:28 p.m.) email from Dwight Diller to Lew Stern.

24. Dwight recalled the number of annual visits his father made to West Virginia after the divorce to spend time with him and his sister Nancy. In late November 2014, he remembered his father traveling to Pocahontas County five or six times a year. In early March 2015, Dwight recalled four visits a year. 25 November 2014 (5:28 p.m.) email from Dwight Diller to Lew Stern; 6 March 2015 (1:16 a.m.) email from Dwight Diller to Lew Stern.

25. Terry Lauer and his wife visited Dwight in the veterans hospital in Salem, West Virginia, after his car wreck in November 2005. 6 March 2015 (1:16 a.m.) email from Dwight Diller to Lew Stern.

26. 6 March 2015 (1:16 a.m.) email from Dwight Diller to Lew Stern.

27. The 1932 Official Code of West Virginia contained explicit language that should have left no doubt about the right of a teacher to remain in the classroom after marriage: "Marriage Not Ground for Removal: Marriage is not covered by the grounds of removal named in this section, and does not constitute in and of itself ground of removal. Jameson v. Board, 74 W. Va. 389, 398, 81 S. E. 1126, L. R. A. 1916C, 795n." As Robert J. O'Brien pointed out: "With the clear language of the Code and of the annotation, teachers who married should have realized they were protected from dismissal, and school board members should not have been in doubt about the matter. However, the law was ignored, and for years in many parts of the state, women were persecuted for getting married." See "Persecution and Acceptance: The Strange History of Discrimination Against Married Women Teachers in West Virginia," *West Virginia History* 56, (1997), pp. 56–75. I would like to thank Ms. Betty Jordan, executive assistant to the state superintendent, Board of Education of the State of West Virginia, for helping me understand the laws governing the dismissal of teachers in West Virginia during the 1930s.

28. 25 November 2014 (528 p.m.) email from Dwight Diller to Lew Stern. John O'Brien offers a poignant picture of grade schooling in Marlinton during the mid–1970s in *At Home in the Heart of Appalachia*, pages 215–228. Also see Truman Fields, *Remembering the 40's in the Heart of Appalachia*, chapters one and eight, on an elementary school experience in Berea, Kentucky, during the 1940s, and Flynn, *Beyond the Mountains*, chapters 1–2.

29. 25 November 2014 (5:28 p.m.) email from Dwight Diller to Lew Stern.
30. 25 November 2014 (5:28 p.m.) email from Dwight Diller to Lew Stern.
31. 25 November 2014 (5:28 p.m.) email from Dwight Diller to Lew Stern. In early March Dwight observed: "You see where I get my banjo style. To push the beat. Double clutch and split shift and keep the proper RPM on that V8 good enough to keep it rolling and safe. That is my playing technique." 6 March 2015 (1:16 a.m.) email from Dwight Diller to Lew Stern.
32. 25 November 2014 (5:28 p.m.) email from Dwight Diller to Lew Stern.
33. 6 March 2015 (1:16 a.m.) email from Dwight Diller to Lew Stern; Author's notes, 31 March 2015 (10:00–11:00 a.m.) telephone conversation with Dwight Diller, Marlinton, West Virginia.
34. 25 November 2014 (6:05 p.m.) email from Dwight Diller to Lew Stern.
35. "Uncle Bill with no children of his own, he became my father who taught with almost no words, [I had] to pay close attention. And to be permitted to sit at the bar. These men trained me [in the way] boys need to [be taught] to become men." 6 March 2015 (1:16 a.m.) email from Dwight Diller to Lew Stern.
36. 25 November 2014 (5:28 p.m.) email from Dwight Diller to Lew Stern. Dwight drew a firm distinction between stories and tales.
37. 25 November 2014 (5:28 p.m.) email from Dwight Diller to Lew Stern.
38. Draft notes, untitled, dated 2013, provided by Dwight Diller to Lew Stern, 9 October 2014 (8:16 p.m.) email from Catherine Rowe to Lew Stern.
39. Draft notes, untitled, dated 2013, provided by Dwight Diller to Lew Stern, 9 October 2014 (8:16 p.m.) email from Catherine Rowe to Lew Stern.
40. Luther Flynn remembered Hillsboro (about ten miles from Marlinton) in the 1920s as a "little village situated in a large rural areas" where almost all the residents grew their own vegetables, the road system was rudimentary and horseback was the preferred means of transportation, chestnut trees and their abundant fruit were still very much a part of the landscape, squirrel hunting was an annual event, schools were crowded and often without heating systems, and the harshest weather came to the area after the Christmas holidays. See *Beyond the Mountains*, chapter 3, pp. 4–12.
41. 10 December 2014 (1:02 a.m.) email from Dwight Diller to Lew Stern.
42. 16 December 2014 (2:09 a.m.) email from Dwight Diller to Lew Stern.
43. 16 December 2014 (2:09 a.m.) email from Dwight Diller to Lew Stern. John O'Brien characterizes Cass, West Virginia, in *At Home in the Heart of Appalachia*, pp. 234–238.
44. Writing in 1955, Malvin Newton Artley stated that the fiddle music of the counties of the Allegheny mountain range of central West Virginia "has been handed down from generation by ear, but it is fast becoming extinct by virtue of the radio, television, and modern living habits. Few young people are today interested in preserving the fiddle tradition." See Artley, *The West Virginia Country Fiddler: An Aspect of the Folk Music Tradition in the United States*. Ph.D. dissertation, Chicago Musical College [Roosevelt University], 1955, p. 21.
45. University of North Carolina at Chapel Hill, Collection Number: 20061, Collection Title: Jack Bernhardt Papers, 1943–2011, Dwight Diller Interview, Elkins, West Virginia, 3 August 1983, Tape 1, Side 1; 3 November 2014 (2:05 p.m.) email from Walt Koken to Lew Stern.
46. "As to the music, my mother was without any extra cash, so there were no new 'rock and roll' records in our home. I did not have the friends who had the pop music that kids were listening to in the mid–1950s to the early 1960s." Draft notes, untitled, dated 2013, provided by Dwight Diller to Lew Stern, 9 October 2014 (8:16 p.m.) email from Catherine Rowe to Lew Stern.
47. 1 December 2014 (7:38 a.m.) email from Dwight Diller to Lew Stern.
48. 30 November 2014 (9:04 p.m.) email from Dwight Diller to Lew Stern; 30 November 2014 (11:52 p.m.) email from Dwight Diller to Lew Stern; 1 December 2014 (2:06 a.m.) email from Dwight Diller to Lew Stern. Dwight also recalled a brief and unsatisfying tryst with modern jazz in the mid–1960s, especially the music of Martin Denny, whose eccentric percussion and interpretations of popular tunes left Dwight cold.
49. https://www.youtube.com/watch?v=V2aj0zhXlLA.
50. https://www.youtube.com/watch?v=2Gn9A-kdsRo.
51. https://www.youtube.com/watch?v=4zRwze8_SGk.
52. 1 December 2014 (7:38 a.m.) email from Dwight Diller to Lew Stern.
53. https://www.youtube.com/watch?v=teJfuKdzbOo.
54. https://www.youtube.com/watch?v=O7umIJj8UBo.
55. https://www.youtube.com/watch?v=berL-80EPmg.
56. https://www.youtube.com/watch?v=lTzP7ecGQiw.
57. https://www.youtube.com/watch?v=pt-dfPnBeLE.
58. 30 November 2014 (9:04 p.m.) email from Dwight Diller to Lew Stern; 30 November 2014 (11:52 p.m.) email from Dwight Diller to Lew Stern; 1 December 2014 (2:06 a.m.) email from Dwight Diller to Lew Stern. Dwight notes that these were extremely small schools: "There were three high schools in this county back them days. We had by far the biggest graduating class that had been in the county. It was 67 students. I think the other schools [in 1963 graduated fewer students]; there were 43 from Marlinton, 23 from Green Bank, and 21 from Hillsboro." 30 November 2014 (9:04 p.m.) email from Dwight Diller to Lew Stern. Dwight appeared to be captivated by theatre and stage productions. One example: the senior members of the National Honor Society of Marlinton High School presented two one-act plays to the high school on 10 January and to the public on 11 January 964. Dwight staged managed the production of Thornton Wilder's play *The Happy Journey to Camden and Trenton*. The plays were directed by Mrs. Alice Moore, sponsor of the society. See *The Pocahontas Times*, 2 January 1964. http://pocahontastimes.com/fifty-years-ago-9/. In later years he continued an involvement in local theatre productions. Doug Van Gundy recalled being involved in a theatre production about the history of the town of Cass with Dwight. Van Gundy and Dwight provided the music for that production in the early 1990s. Author's notes, 15 June 2015 (7:00–7:30 a.m.) telephone conversation with Doug Van Gundy, from Elkins, West Virginia.
59. Draft notes, untitled, dated 2013, provided by Dwight Diller to Lew Stern, 9 October 2014 (8:16 p.m.) email from Catherine Rowe to Lew Stern.
60. https://www.youtube.com/watch?v=3EsBOhRwqE4; https://www.youtube.com/watch?v=u0Ujb6lJ_mM.
61. https://www.youtube.com/watch?v=6lnpkuEEljY; https://www.youtube.com/watch?v=j4NquCaWIQI.
62. https://www.youtube.com/watch?v=R24QLILwdHE
63. https://www.youtube.com/watch?v=Joo90ZWrUkU.
64. https://www.youtube.com/watch?v=J6xA-Tc7sb0.
65. https://www.youtube.com/watch?v=9ax0kLiGUAI; 30 November 2014 (11:52 p.m.) email from Dwight Diller to Lew Stern.
66. https://www.youtube.com/watch?v=8Xh3pwda0kc.
67. https://www.youtube.com/watch?v=wEV58ztuihs.
68. 30 November 2014 (11:52 p.m.) email from Dwight Diller to Lew Stern.

69. What Dwight heard in Jones' banjo playing won Grandpa a considerable following. As Greg Wright, a Kettering, Ohio, banjo player said in a Banjo Hangout forum in December 2014: "I've always loved the 'drive' that Grandpa put into his banjo pickin'. The timing, the brushes, just everything he puts into it ... well, that's just Grandpa, and he certainly caught my attention way back when…!!!" And Bill, a 34-year-old banjo player from the United Kingdom, makes very similar points in the same thread: "I think what makes Grandpa's playing so special lies in that right arm of his […] The fabulously meticulous action on the frail makes his playing sound dead right and his precision is what makes the whole thing carry you along. Grandpa's ending lick is always the same sort of notes but it always takes my breath away. It's all about that driving rhythm, it's the element of the music that makes us dance, whether listening to Fred Cockerham and Kyle Creed or Sun-Ra." Jones played a hypnotically rhythmic banjo, and he very clearly articulated his melody line." Dwight is not alone in his appreciation for Jones' straightforward, powerful clawhammer playing. See: http://www.banjohangout.org/topic/296823/2/#3752017.

70. 1 December 2014 (7:38 a.m.) email from Dwight Diller to Lew Stern.

71. Ron Mullennex remembered that Dwight studied Bill Monroe's music. "He listened to it, tried to understand what Monroe was pushing and why Monroe was who he was." 20 January 2015 (7:00–8:00 p.m.) telephone conversation with the author. I think people also believe Dwight's view is that learning bluegrass can kill old time musical instincts. I don't think that is true. In the early 2000s he encouraged my attempt to delve into bluegrass, warning only of the need to stick with the real, true, first bluegrassers. Dwight certainly believed that his own time on the road with the Morris Brothers made a difference for him as a musician.

72. Irving was diagnosed with leukemia in 1959 and died a year later. "Lonnie Irving," *Hillbilly Music*, http://www.hillbilly-music.com/artists/story/index.php?id=16518.

73. 1 December 2014 (7:38 a.m.) email from Dwight Diller to Lew Stern.

74. 1 December 2014 (7:38 a.m.) email from Dwight Diller to Lew Stern.

75. Official Transcript of Academic Record, Dwight Hamilton Diller, issued by Steve Robinson, University Registrar, West Virginia University at Morgantown, 26 February 2015; West Virginia University, 1964–1965 Catalog, West Virginia University Bulletin, Series 64, no. 12-3, June 1964, p. 425. https://archive.org/details/under6465west.

76. Official Transcript of Academic Record, Dwight Hamilton Diller, issued by Steve Robinson, University Registrar, West Virginia University at Morgantown, 26 February 2015; West Virginia University, 1964–1965 Catalog, West Virginia University Bulletin, Series 64, no. 12-3, June 1964, p. 449. https://archive.org/details/under6465west.

77. Dwight told me: "I'm not good at sports, but I was good at teaching." Dwight noted that "I got something out of it because it was a way for me to meet women." He eventually dropped the sport because he felt that fencing match judges were not paying attention to contests between opponents, and as a consequence they were scoring competitions wrongly, so he grew frustrated and eventually laid down his foil. Author's notes, 5 February 2015 (10:30–11:40 a.m.) telephone conversation with Dwight Diller. West Virginia musician Bob Smakula told me this anecdote, his favorite Diller related-story: "I was at a guitar show near Pittsburgh about 10 years ago. I was buying some vintage guitars from a husband and wife. They saw I was from West Virginia and asked if I knew someone by the name Diller. I asked: 'Dwight Diller?' expecting some sort of unusual story. 'Yes' they replied. 'We were in the fencing club with him when we went to WVU.' Never expected that." 16 January 2015 (2:49 p.m.) email from Bob Smakula to Lew Stern.

78. Author's notes, 27 October 2014 (10:00 a.m.–12:30 p.m., 3:30 p.m.–5:15 p.m.) telephone conversation with Dwight Diller.

79. See "Openings in Lodi for U.S. Navy 'Cache' Program," *Lodi News Sentinel*, 25 January 1969. http://news.google.com/newspapers?nid=2245&dat=19690125&id=jeAzAAAAIBAJ&sjid=VzIHAAAAIBAJ&pg=2760,2065272 Also see: http://www.leagle.com/decision/19801544484FSupp1060_11368.

80. 11 September 2014, telephone conversation with Dwight Diller.

81. 13 October 2014 (11.52 p.m.) email from Dwight Diller to Lew Stern.

82. 8 September 2014 email from Dwight Diller to Lew Stern.

83. 8 September 2014 email from Dwight Diller to Lew Stern; 13 October 2014 (11:52 p.m.) email from Dwight Diller to Lew Stern. Wayne Howard stated that after Dwight's hitch in the navy, even more than most young men, he was desperately trying to find himself. See "West Virginia's Hammons Family," *Goldenseal*, December 2014, p. 8; 15 September 2014 telephone conversation between Dwight Diller and Lew Stern.

84. Author's notes, 12 February 2015 (10:30 a.m.–12:00 p.m.) telephone conversation with Dwight Diller.

85. Official Transcript of Academic Record, Dwight Hamilton Diller, issued by Steve Robinson, University Registrar, West Virginia University at Morgantown, 26 February 2015.

86. Author's notes, 27 October 2014 (10:00 a.m.–12:30 p.m., 3:30 p.m.–5:15 p.m.) telephone conversation with Dwight Diller.

Chapter Two

1. 20 November 2014 (11:53 p.m.) email from Dwight Diller to Lew Stern. Also see Jerry Waters, "Don't Call 'em Bars or Taverns, They're Beer Joints," http://www.mywvhome.com/fifties/beer.htm

2. See Gerald Milnes, *Play of a Fiddle: Traditional Music, Dance and Folklore in West Virginia* (Lexington: University of Kentucky Press, 2009), pp. 35–44, on the Carpenter family's fiddling legacy.

3. "Sunday Folks," KCDS radio interview with Dwight Diller, Seattle, Washington, 1999.

4. Author's notes, 27 October 2014 (10:00 a.m.–12:30 p.m., 3:30 p.m.–5:15 p.m.) telephone conversation with Dwight Diller. John O'Brien described the wood hicks and their jobs in *At Home in the Heart of Appalachia*, pp. 195–196.

5. 3 August 2015 (1013 a.m.) email from Carl Fleischhauer to Lew Stern.

6. Draft notes, untitled, dated 2013, provided by Dwight Diller to Lew Stern, 9 October 2014 (8:16 p.m.) email from Catherine Rowe to Lew Stern.

7. 16 May 2005 (12:35 a.m.) email from Dwight Diller to Cindy Harris.

8. Author's notes, 12 February 2015 (10:30 a.m.–12:00 p.m.) telephone conversation with Dwight Diller; Author's notes, 28 May 2015 (10:00 a.m.–11:00 a.m.) telephone conversation with Nancy Burks, Dwight's sister, in Marlinton, West Virginia.

9. http://dwightdiller.com/2013/11/20/the-acknowledgements/

10. Author's notes, 12 February 2015 (10:30 a.m.–12:00 p.m.) telephone conversation with Dwight Diller.

11. http://www.lib.utexas.edu/taro/utcah/00276/cah-00276.html and http://fayfare.blogspot.com/2013/04/may-opry-highlights.html.
12. https://www.youtube.com/watch?v=PTr4Kb-TtGI Dwight saw a significant difference between Grandpa Jones' approach to the tune and Dave "Stringbean" Akeman's version: https://www.youtube.com/watch?v=CVHQM-ogU2U.
13. Author's notes, 27 October 2014 (10:00 a.m.–12:30 p.m., 3:30 p.m.–5:15 p.m.) telephone conversation with Dwight Diller.
14. Author's notes, 27 October 2014 (10:00 a.m.–12:30 p.m., 3:30 p.m.–5:15 p.m.) telephone conversation with Dwight Diller.
15. Milnes, *Play of a Fiddle*, p. 59, and Milnes, "The Hammonds Family of Randolph County," *Goldenseal*, Winter 2014, p. 13.
16. Wayne Howard noted: "Emmy married John Roberts, her first cousin, after she ran away from her first husband to go with John. Emmy lived with Burl and Maggie in the time when I visited them." 19 August 2015 (9:05 p.m.) email from Wayne Howard to Lew Stern.
17. See "Lee Hammons Banjo: Complete Recordings," *The Hammons Legacy: Field Recordings from Dwight Diller and Wayne Howard*," liner notes, no date, and "Happy Birthday, Lee Hammons!," *Fiddle Hangout*, 29 May 2010, http://www.fiddlehangout.com/archive/14903. Also see Wayne Howard, "Memories of the Hammons Family Part I: Lee Hammons," *The Old-Time Herald*, vol. 12, no. 2 (December 2009–January 2010), p. 32. Howard notes his year of birth as 1886, and records that he passed away at the age of 94 on Christmas Eve in 1980. Lee's sons threw their father a birthday party in 1971, marking his 85th year. 6 March 2015 (12:25 p.m.) email from Wayne Howard to Lew Stern.
18. See Wayne Howard, "West Virginia's Hammons Family," p. 12; Carl Fleischhauer, "'A History of the Hammons Family," in Fleischhauer and Jabbour, *The Hammons Family*, pp. 14–15.
19. Frank Hammons, a great-grandson of Lee Hammons, remembered Dwight asking Lee this question at the festival Pioneer Day. Author's notes, 26 May 2015 (10:23–10:36 a.m.) telephone conversation with Frank Hammons from Marlinton, West Virginia.
20. Carl Fleischhauer stated: "When Alan and I were visiting Sherman one year later, Sherman was living in a house that Dwight referred to as 'Maggie's house, where Sherman lives.' It was in a relatively flat area, with higher ground not far away." 3 August 2015 (1013 a.m.) email from Carl Fleischhauer to Lew Stern.
21. Wayne Howard stated: "Several members of Lee's family lived along the road that led up the hollow to his house, and Loy and his wife, Maisie, who was one of Lee's daughters, were among them." 19 August 2015 (9:05 p.m.) email from Wayne Howard to Lew Stern.
22. 20 November 2014 (11:53 p.m.) email from Dwight Diller to Lew Stern; Author's notes, 26 May 2015 (10:23–10:36 a.m.) telephone conversation with Frank Hammons from Marlinton, West Virginia; "Lee Hammons Banjo: Complete Recordings," *The Hammons Legacy: Field Recordings from Dwight Diller and Wayne Howard*," liner notes, no date, and "Happy Birthday, Lee Hammons!," *Fiddle Hangout*, 29 May 2010, http://www.fiddlehangout.com/archive/14903. Also see Wayne Howard, "Memories of the Hammons Family Part I: Lee Hammons," *The Old-Time Herald*, vol. 12, no. 2 (December 2009–January 2010), p. 32; and 6 March 2015 (12:25 p.m.) email from Wayne Howard to Lew Stern.
23. Author's notes, 27 October 2014 (10:00 a.m.–12:30 p.m., 3:30 p.m.–5:15 p.m.) telephone conversation with Dwight Diller.
24. Author's notes, 27 October 2014 (10:00 a.m.–12:30 p.m., 3:30 p.m.–5:15 p.m.) telephone conversation with Dwight Diller.
25. Author's notes, 27 October 2014 (10:00 a.m.–12:30 p.m., 3:30 p.m.–5:15 p.m.) telephone conversation with Dwight Diller.
26. In the late 1960s and early 1970s, small groups of musicians from a variety of old time music communities began seeking out older players to learn their repertoire. Most of the musicians who were building personal collections of taped music from festivals and jams and front porch parties were accumulating the music for their own learning purposes, to help them figure out how to play tunes and to document provenance for their own efforts to study the music. They had no intention of making these field recordings commercially available. As Mark Campbell recalled: "In fact the old guys used to ask us what we were going to do with the recordings and we would typically say that we were to use them to learn the tunes, to add to the collections in our heads." Many decades later, often after the recorded artist had passed on, such collectors were invited by the Field Recorders' Collective to make these recording commercial available. The Collective contacted the artist or next of kin for permission and paid royalties. Campbell remembered that during 1971–1972, when he was playing in Armin Barnett's Yellow Mountain String Band, there was an annual gathering of banjo and fiddle players who were keen on recording the music of the elders in Appalachia that met outside of Charlottesville, Virginia, near the base of the Blue Ridge, called "The Alternative Galax." Among those who attended were Carl Baron, Bill Hicks, Alan Jabbour, Gerry Milnes, Peter Hoover, Mark Gunther, Dave Milefski, and Dwight Diller. Armin Barnett hosted two such gatherings before he left Virginia. Dwight attended one of these and music he played with Armin Barnett itself survived on several field recordings made by attendees of one of these gatherings. 16 January 2015 (9:21 a.m.) email from Mark Campbell to Lew Stern. In Bill Hicks' memory, the event was referred to the Alternate Galax largely because it coincided with the "real" Galax festival. He also recollected that musicians from outside of the area were frustrated that at Galax, the contests were always won by insiders, people from the host region: "You couldn't go to Galax and play some other regional style and expect to win anything much, no matter how well you played," so the designation "Alternative Galax" served to underscore this sentiment. 18 January 2015 (10:31 a.m.) email from Bill Hicks to Lew Stern. On Barnett's field collection work, see Letter from Carl Fleischhauer to Armin Barnett, copied to Alan Jabbour, 16 August 1973, regarding tape of "Over 50" fiddle contest at the West Virginia State Folk Festival, Library of Congress, American Folklore Collection, AFS 14,481–14,485. Fleischhauer described the tape as an "aural glimpse" of Melvin Wine, Lester McCumbers and Delbert Hughes—who won the contest.
27. Author's notes, 27 October 2014 (10:00 a.m.–1230 p.m., 3:30 p.m.–5:15 p.m.) telephone conversation with Dwight Diller. Fiona Ritchie quoted David Holt as saying of "older people" like Tommy Jarrell, Bayard Ray, Zipporah Rice and Dellie Norton: "these were people almost from another world." Holt continued: "this generation of people that I was lucky enough to learn from, somebody said to me they were born before self doubt was invented. I think the media and just our modern world, the pace of it, creates this kind of unease inside of us. You wouldn't have found that in Tommy Jarrell, you wouldn't have found that in Dellie Norton. These people were just as centered as you could possibly get." Quoted in *Wayfaring Strangers: The Musical Voyage from Scotland and Ulster to Appalachia* (Chapel Hill: University of North Carolina Press, 2014), p. 173.

28. See Carl Fleischhauer collection of West Virginia and Ohio folk music (AFC 1974/011), American Folklife Center, Library of Congress, containing two 7-inch and four 5-inch tapes of instrumentals and interviews recorded in Ohio and West Virginia by Carl Fleischhauer and others, February 15, 1973–April 6, 1974. The collection includes 22 pages of concordances, correspondence, and lists. Notes regarding AFS 17,017 (also filed as 17,019), LWO 7976, Reel 5, characterize the Hammonses as people who did not work in a regular, conventional manner in formal or informal employment.

29. Author's notes, 27 October 2014 (10:00 a.m.–12:30 p.m., 3:30 p.m.–5:15 p.m.) telephone conversation with Dwight Diller. Other musicians who visited and recorded Lee Hammons did capture him talking about the old musicians (such as Edn Hammons) and telling stories. 5 July 2015 (11 45 a.m.) email from Wayne Howard to Lew Stern.

30. Author's notes, 27 October 2014 (10:00 a.m.–12:30 p.m., 3:30 p.m.–5:15 p.m.) telephone conversation with Dwight Diller.

31. Author's notes, 27 October 2014 (10:00 a.m.–12:30 p.m., 3:30 p.m.–5:15 p.m.) telephone conversation with Dwight Diller. Dwight has told this story numerous times, and the embellishments vary slightly from version to version. See, for example, Ken Perlman. "Dwight Diller and the Music of Pocahontas County," page 55, and University of North Carolina at Chapel Hill, Collection Number: 20061, Collection Title: Jack Bernhardt Papers, 1943–2011, Dwight Diller Interview, Elkins, WVA, 3 August 1983, Tape 1, Side 1.

32. Author's notes, 27 October 2014 (10:00 a.m.–12:30 p.m., 3:30 p.m.–5:15 p.m.) telephone conversation with Dwight Diller. Also see Craig Evans, "A Piece of Living History: A Conversation with Teacher—Dwight Diller," Conversations with North American Banjo Builders, Volume 3, Conversations with Banjo Historians, Frailinflix Productions. Through at least 2002, Artie Barkley was shop superintendent of the Cass Scenic Railroad, a state park in the Alleghenies about five hours from Baltimore. Barkley worked around loggers and locomotives from the time he was a teenager. Barkley managed Cass No. 5, an 80-ton Shay locomotive that came from the Lima, Ohio, factory in 1905 to pull red spruce logs off Cheat Mountain. See http://articles.baltimoresun.com/2002-04-28/travel/0204280394_1_locomotive-cass-scenic-railroad-steam.

33. http://dwightdiller.com/2013/11/20/the-acknowledgements/ According to Wayne Howard, Lee Hammons said that Hamp had once been pretty good, but "he got to playing in beer joints, and that ruined him. Lee, of course, was prejudiced against beer joints." 3 January 2015 (11:21 a.m.) email from Wayne Howard to Lew Stern, and Wayne Howard, *Mountain Lore Journal*, field notes from visits with Burl, Maggie, Sherman and Lee Hammons, 10 September 1971–2 May 1972, p. 47.

34. 6 November 2014 (2:44 a.m.) email from Dwight Diller to Lew Stern. In a September 1975 *Banjo Newsletter* column, Dick Kimmel wrote: "Dwight's banjo is an eleven inch 'Improved George Washburn' pot with a custom neck. The pot has been called 'air conditioned' because the tone rung sits up on ⅜" stilts: you have an open gap between the tone ring-head-tension hoop assembly and the rim. The brackets hold them together. The neck by Len Reiss of Collierstown, W.Va. is a 5 piece maple neck with engraved pearl flower inlays. Dwight says that Odell McGuire named this banjo 'Snotty Banjo' because it was so loud and crisp. Strings are medium gauge with a 2nd or 3rd string replacing the 5th. (5-star plastic head and an old Presto tailpiece.) The banjo is set up to have low action with a ½ inch bridge, but Dwight keeps a ⅝ inch pearl insert Grover on it so it plays hard and loud. The action is ½ inch above the last fret. Dwight first set it up this way to play loud with the Morris Brothers of Ivydale, W.Va. 'It's hard to play so you can bear down on it and it won't give out on you.' He keeps the banjo tuned up in A without a capo, unless he's playing with someone who's changing keys a lot. Dwight stresses the glove under the dowel stick. He says it cuts down the treble ring and seems to bring out the bass. It's also important where the glove is. Dwight rolls a woman's cashmere glove very tightly and puts it longways under the dowel close to the neck." See Kimmel, "Thumpin' For Clawhammer Pickers: Banjo Set Up," *Banjo Newsletter*, vol. 2, no. 11 (September 1975), pp. 4–5. Len Reiss confirmed that he built the neck for this banjo. Reiss, who at the time was living in Sinking Spring, Pennsylvania, about six miles west of Reading, said that the neck was carved out of a block of laminated maple with three veneers down the centerline. Reiss did the fingerboard inlay, which included some simple flowers. "Nothing fancy," he recalled, "as it was probably my third neck." The heavy gauge strings helped moderate the banjo's "raucous sound." 8 July 2015 (10:48 a.m.) email from Len Reiss to Lew Stern.

35. University of North Carolina at Chapel Hill, Collection Number: 20061, Collection Title: Jack Bernhardt Papers, 1943–2011, Dwight Diller Interview, Elkins, WVA, 3 August 1983, Tape 1, Side 1. Dwight added: "I had a lot of problems when I was in the Navy and I was looking for some alternative to middle class America but I wasn't looking for the drug culture. I didn't know anybody else was doing it. They were, but I didn't know." Also see Dwight Diller interview conducted by Alan Jabbour, December 18, 1980 (AFC 1986/060), American Folklife Center, Library of Congress, part one. Accessioned as: "AFS 26,768–26,769: Dwight Diller Collection of Reminiscences of the Hammons Family: Two 7-inch tapes of five instrumentals and an interview with Dwight Diller concerning his recollections of the Hammons family of Pocahontas County, West Virginia, his own religious awakening, and aspects of traditional music. Conducted by Alan Jabbour and recorded by Gerald E. Parsons at the Library of Congress, December 18, 1980. The collection includes four pages of collection entries, a concordance, and photocopies of tape boxes. (1 hour; RXA 4003–4004)." See: http://loc.gov/folklife/guides/WestVirginia.html. I am grateful to Carl Fleischhauer for making the digitized version of this interview available to me.

36. As Dwight told Jabbour and Parsons: "I don't know why I was interested in music, but it had something to do with something stable, and it seemed that the old things were more stable than the new. And I think a whole lot of other people have felt the same way. There's something about things in the past that seem to be more stable ... I guess we kind of slow life down a little bit, it's going by too fast. And the more I was around the music the more I wanted it. It became my whole life." Dwight Diller interview conducted by Alan Jabbour, December 18, 1980 (AFC 1986/060), American Folklife Center, Library of Congress, part one.

37. 6 March 2015 (1:16 a.m.) email from Dwight Diller to Lew Stern; "Sunday Folks," KCDS radio interview with Dwight Diller, Seattle, Washington, 1999.

38. Wayne Howard adopted the practice of calling Lee "Mr. Hammons," and referring to him that way in his field notes, in order to distinguish him from the Hammons family members (including Sherman, Burl and Maggie) but also to avoid the presumption of familiarity that using his given name would have represented. See Wayne Howard, *Mountain Lore Journal*, field notes from visits with Burl, Maggie, Sherman and Lee Hammons, 10 September 1971–2 May 1972.

39. Dwight Diller interview conducted by Alan Jabbour, December 18, 1980 (AFC 1986/060), American Folk-

life Center, Library of Congress, part one. Dwight also talked about how Lee constructed a tractor from a Model T truck frame and assorted other vehicle parts, and referenced Lee Hammons' explanation of this as the "cobble, piece and patch" approach to solving problems. "Diller Concert–12/03," tape 4. Lee's great-grandson, Frank Hammons, remembered that Lee helped Dwight fix a badly damaged bass fiddle. Author's notes, 26 May 2015 (10:23–10:36 a.m.) telephone conversation with Frank Hammons from Marlinton, West Virginia.

40. Dwight's point was that Lee's hiatus from fiddling possibly preserved the archaic 1920s sound that represented his playing style when he shelved his fiddle and banjo. It would appear that when Lee decided to resume doing music, he reached for the skills and playing style that had served him until he put down the instruments. If it did not preserve the character of the sound, the fact that he had not played for many years certainly meant that he reverted to old habits and preferences in handling his instrument, and thus—in Dwight's assessment—produced the same sounds that old way. Gerry Milnes agreed with Dwight's assessment of these circumstances, and noted that Lester McCumbers started out with an old-time sound as a youngster: "He gradually started playing a more bluegrass style in mid-life, but later reverted back to his early archaic old-time style." 17 March 2015 (9:08 p.m.) email from Gerry Milnes to Lew Stern.

41. Wayne Howard took a different view. He pointed out that Lee Hammons definitely did not "shun the country music that was broadcast and recorded during those years. One tune he played for me on the fiddle was Roy Acuff's 'Fireball Mail.' He was familiar with, and seemed to revere, Jimmie Rodgers. He told me a story about seeing a television dramatization of 'Pretty Polly,' and he was a fan of Stringbean (he called him 'Stringbeans'), whom he had heard on *The Grand Old Opry*. Listening to commercial music doesn't necessarily corrupt anyone for life, of course. Lee and Sherman both were stubborn enough to play their music as it was *supposed* to be, in defiance of the lords of the music industry." 17 March 2015 (3:47 p.m.) email from Wayne Howard to Lew Stern.

42. 6 March 2015 (1:16 a.m.) email from Dwight Diller to Lew Stern.

43. 6 March 2015 (1:16 a.m.) email from Dwight Diller to Lew Stern.

44. Dwight says of these five tunes: "There are just the five tunes I still play with his non-syncopated rhythm. When I would try to play along with him on the fiddle and me on banjo, I would have to totally change my rhythm. I never knew why." 6 March 2015 (1:16 a.m.) email from Dwight Diller to Lew Stern.

45. 6 March 2015 (1:16 a.m.) email from Dwight Diller to Lew Stern.

46. In a December 1980 interview, Dwight recalled one of his last visits with Lee Hammons: "One of the last times I'd been to see him and he'd cut his thumb off on a bandsaw around 90, 91 ... was making a dulcimer and it was not a bandsaw, it was a table saw. I said, 'Mr. Hammons, what's about it?' and he said 'Thing just got in the way and I cut it off.' He was still able to take that stub and pick 'Walking in the Parlor' for me. His hands were really getting stiff and everything but there was still something about it and nobody else has it. And I don't know what it is. It's some kind of magic kind of thing." Dwight Diller interview conducted by Alan Jabbour, December 18, 1980 (AFC 1986/060), American Folklife Center, Library of Congress, part two.

47. Brad Leftwich stated: "Lee's music, both on fiddle and banjo, had worlds of depth and expressiveness. His banjo playing could almost send you into a trance, and his fiddling had an archaic, timeless quality that transported you to another time and place. It wasn't hard-driving dance music. He had a light, raspy touch on the fiddle that forced you to listen carefully, and listening carefully you could hear the craftsmanship and subtle ornamentation in each tune. It didn't bowl you over so much as it drew you in. Somehow I suspect that he would have played that way whether or not he'd stopped playing for so many years, but it's hard to know how that would affect someone's playing. Lee's fiddling was not as rough as Sherman's and not as polished as Burl's, but I'd say it was more elegant and subtle than either of the others. It's amazing how all three had such distinctive personal styles of playing. All were appealing in their own ways." 18 March 2015 (12:28 p.m.) email from Brad Leftwich to Lew Stern.

48. 6 March 2015 (1:16 a.m.) email from Dwight Diller to Lew Stern.

49. Jacqueline G. Goodwin, "'I've Always Loved Music': Champion Fiddler Glen Smith," *Goldenseal*, vol. 16, no. 2 (Summer 1990), page 20. Dwight played with the Glen Smith who was born in Woodlawn, Virginia, about seven miles away from Hillsville. Wade Ward's Glen Smith was born around Hillsville, another source of confusion. See: http://www.beebalmmusic.com/glen_smith.html; http://www.countysales.com/products.php?product=GLEN-SMITH-%27Mountain-State-Fiddler%27; and http://www.folkways.si.edu/wade-ward/conversation-between-wade-ward-and-glen-smith/arkansas-traveler/katy-hills-recollections-of-the-fiddlers-convention/old-time-oral-history-biography/track/smithsonian.

50. Author's notes, 12 February 2015 (10:30 a.m.–12:00 p.m.) telephone conversation with Dwight Diller. Dwight told Ken Perlman that in playing banjo behind Glen Smith "You have to play and make every note be exactly with his note without speedin' him up and without in the tiniest bit draggin' him down. If you drag him down the tiniest bit, he can't stand it." See Perlman, "Dwight Diller and the Music of Pocahontas County," p.58.

51. Author's notes, 12 February 2015 (10:30 a.m.–12:00 p.m.) telephone conversation with Dwight Diller.

52. "I was the first younger person for many miles as far as I know that was interested in the old traditional music. And for sure I was the first […] in my area who was interested." 20 November 2014 (11:53 p.m.) email from Dwight Diller to Lew Stern.

53. 18 September 2014 (5:06 p.m.) email from Dwight Diller to Lew Stern.

54. While some of the younger musicians were motivated by a love of the archaic regional music and the desire to learn repertoire from older musicians, some of the first visitors to the Hammons family had much more personal reasons for seeking out the family, akin to Dwight's driving effort to keep company with local elders who held him spellbound with their stories and offered the kind of embracing friendship he so very much wanted. In mid–January 2015, Wayne Howard told me: "When I started hearing the Hammonses' stories, I wrote them down with no thought of publishing them or doing anything in particular with them. It just seemed to me that they were *important* somehow—that they ought to be preserved. Their music took on the same aura for me. I recorded it to preserve it and learn it, but even learning it was a part of preservation. And not only the age of the people and the antiquity of their ways appealed to me but also their human kindness and goodness to me. They quickly became real friends, and who can explain the nature of friendship—why some people appeal to you and others don't? Dwight gets teary-eyed and starts to choke up when he talks about the Hammonses, and I am not far behind him. I just loved those old people." 17 January 2015 (1:51 a.m.) email from Wayne Howard to Lew Stern. In 2015, the Field Recorders' Collective produced a CD that captured the songs and

tunes of Maggie Hammons Parker, recorded by Wayne Howard in eight sessions, from December 1973 to September 1980. According to Howard, all the sessions took place at the home in Stillwell, Pocahontas County, West Virginia, where Maggie lived with her brother Burl and sisters Emma and Ruie. http://fieldrecorder.org/product/maggie-parker-hammons-family-songs-music-frc713/.

55. Dwight said in 1983: "First time I met Sherman he was down at the Tasty Freeze sitting out front, I think he was probably drunk the night before. I'd heard stories about Sherman Hammons for years. I knew who he was. People loved to get Sherman to gobble like a turkey, and to tell stories of something that walked like a man lived in the mountains which he called a 'Yahoo' based on the sound that it made—Sherman really likes people so he'd go along with all that stuff. [...] This was real exciting to me. [...] I could spend hours with these people. This was a way for me to escape, kind of go back and live in the past. The reason for me that I got into the old time music was I didn't like what Middle class America had to offer and I just started running headlong into this. Just got right in the middle of it. I was by myself. Nobody else that I knew of anywhere was doing this." University of North Carolina at Chapel Hill, Collection Number: 20061, Collection Title: Jack Bernhardt Papers, 1943–2011, Dwight Diller Interview, Elkins, WVA, 3 August 1983, Tape 1, Side 1.

56. Author's notes, 20 January 2015 (7:00–8:00 p.m.) telephone conversation with Ron Mullennex from Bluefield, West Virginia.

57. Author's notes, 26 January 2015 (11:00–11:45 p.m.) telephone conversation with Jimmy Costa, from Talcott, West Virginia.

58. Old time banjo and fiddle player Walt Koken remembered: "I roomed with Dwight at Augusta in 1994, where I heard him perform the Highwoods' version of 'Wild Bill Jones.' I was surprised to learn from him that he did not hear old time music nor begin playing until he was in college." 3 November 2014 (2:05 p.m.) email from Walt Koken to Lew Stern.

59. Kimmel stated: "I must give credit to Dwight Diller for kindling my interest in clawhammer banjo.... The purity and beauty of Dwight Diller's music made quite an impression. Dwight and I performed music together as 'The Black Mountain Bluegrass Boys' and later 'Mountain Grass' during the mid–1970's. I appreciate the many evenings listening to the beautiful sounds that Dwight has in his banjo." Dick Kimmel, *Fishing Creek Blues: 17 Clawhammer Tunes* (Missouri: Mel Bay, 2000), p. 4.

60. Author's notes, 27 October 2014 (10:00 a.m.–12:30 p.m., 3:30 p.m.–5:15 p.m.) telephone conversation with Dwight Diller.

61. Author's notes, 27 October 2014 (10:00 a.m.–12:30 p.m., 3:30 p.m.–5:15 p.m.) telephone conversation with Dwight Diller.

62. Dan Levenson, "Dick Kimmel," *Banjo Newsletter*, June 2001, p. 18. Also see http://www.dickkimmel.com/artist_profile/artist_profile.html.

63. Dick Kimmel, "Clawhammer Banjo, Part 6: 'Blue Eyed Gal,'" *Banjo Newsletter*, vol. 2, no. 2 (December 1974), p. 5. Kimmel thought back to that 1968 lesson in Morgantown, and remembered Dwight was wearing a baseball cap, embossed with the letters CAT for Caterpillar. Kimmel commented: "Morgantown isn't like Pocahontas County. The accent isn't as strong. It's more like Pittsburgh than West Virginia. I had never met anyone from the mountains. I remember visiting [Dwight] in his apartment [in Morgantown.] He was cooking squirrel brains. Someone had gone hunting, gotten some squirrel, and Dwight laid claim on the brains. He loved that [West Virginia mountain] culture. He lived the identity of a West Virginia person before he lived the identity of a West Virginia musician." Author's notes, 2 December 2014 interview with Dick Kimmel from New Ulm, Minnesota.

64. Dan Levenson, "Dick Kimmel," *Banjo Newsletter*, June 2001, p. 19.

65. Dan Levenson, "Dick Kimmel," *Banjo Newsletter*, June 2001, p. 20.

66. Littlehales, "Dwight Diller," *Banjo Newsletter*, p. 16; 29 October 2014 (10:04 a.m.) email from Dick Kimmel to Lew Stern.

67. "Henry Ossawa Tanner was born in 1859 in Pittsburgh into a middle class family. At the age of 13, after observing an artist at work at a neighborhood park, Turner decided to become an artist. Tanner's father, a bishop of the African Methodist Episcopal Church, discouraged his artistic pursuits, hoping that he would instead enter the ministry. However, at the age of 21, Tanner enrolled in the Pennsylvania Academy of Fine Arts. There his interest turned to landscapes. His teacher, Thomas Eakins, a noted genre painter, encouraged him to paint scenes from everyday life. In 1893, Tanner painted 'The Banjo Lesson,' a realistic study of African American life. By portraying an elder teaching a boy how to play the banjo, Tanner showed a positive and dignified image of African Americans. In 1895, believing he could not fulfill his artistic aspirations in America, Tanner settled in Paris. There, he focused on religious paintings, winning much critical acclaim for 'Daniel in the Lion's Den' and 'The Resurrection of Lazarus.'" See "Exploring Freedom: Henry O. Tanner (1859–1937)," http://www.pbs.org/wnet/aaworld/arts/tanner.html. Also see David Byron, "Evidence in Art: Tanner's The Banjo," Baroque Potion: Art, Belief, Context, 8 January 2008, http://www.baroquepotion.com/2008/01/evidence-in-art-tanner%E2%80%99s-the-banjo-lesson/.

68. 31 December 2014 (11:40 a.m.) email from Dick Kimmel to Lew Stern.

69. 4 September 2014 (10:57 p.m.) email from Dwight Diller to Lew Stern. Dwight added: "I don't think I have ever showed off once while playing the banjo since 1973."

70. 29 October 2014 (1004 a.m.) email from Dick Kimmel to Lew Stern. Kimmel added: "After taking his banjo and leaving for a period when he did learn the style and tunes from folks in southeast WV, especially the Hammonses, he came back to Morgantown, WV, for more college—thankfully, because he then taught me to play clawhammer and to develop a lifelong interest in old-time music. Dwight spent many evenings on my front porch in rural Morgantown playing for whomever was around and actually perked my interest in playing clawhammer rather than basic strum. I've played clawhammer ever since."

71. Dan Levenson, "Dick Kimmel," *Banjo Newsletter*, June 2001, p. 19.

72. 3 June 2015 (4:20 a.m.) email from Dick Kimmel to Lew Stern.

73. Howard, "West Virginia's Hammons Family," p. 8.

74. This is confirmed by Carl Fleishhauer, who added: "I think Dwight brought some of his tapes to that class—I would have heard a bit about this after the fact, from Dwight. I lived in Morgantown, working at West Virginia University at the time." 4 January 2015 (12:46 p.m.) from Carl Fleischhauer to Lew Stern. Dwight connected with Fleishhauer in 1970. Author's notes, 27 October 2014 (10:00 a.m.–12:30 p.m., 3:30 p.m.–5:15 p.m.) telephone conversation with Dwight Diller; 20 November 2014 (11:53 p.m.) email from Dwight Diller to Lew Stern.

75. Among Gainer's publications: *West Virginia Centennial Book of 100 Songs*, 1863–1963 (1963), *Witches, Ghosts and Signs* (1975), *Folk Songs from the West Virginia Hills* (1975), the "Music" chapter in B. B. Maurer's *Mountain Heritage* (1974), and a 1963 recording for Folk Heritage Recordings, *Folk Songs of the Allegheny Mountains*. See John H. Randolph, "Pat Gainer," e-WV: The West Vir-

ginia Encyclopedia. 23 October 2012. Accessed 10 October 2014. http://www.wvencyclopedia.org/articles/2077 Frank George credited Gainer with attracting state-wide attention to Appalachian music, largely through the Glenville festival that he first organized in 1950. George suggested that he had an influence on the Morris Brothers. See Michael Meador, "Grandpaw Got Me Started: Frank George and the Old Time Music," *Goldenseal*, vol. 9, no. 1 (Spring 1983), page 29. Also see Ivan Tribe, *Mountaineer Jamboree: Country Music in West Virginia* (Lexington, University of Kentucky Press, 1984), p. 155.

76. John Harrington Cox was the author of *Folk Songs of the South* (Cambridge, MA: Harvard University Press, 1925) and Louis Watson Chappell was the author of *John Henry: A Folklore Study* (Jena: Frommanische Verlag, 1933).

77. https://www.libraries.wvu.edu/collections/patrickgainer/.

78. In the late 1960s, early 1970s, the television station was licensed to West Virginia University and used the call letters WWVU. Fleischhauer was hired as a cinematographer in 1969, after he completed a graduate school degree in fine arts and filmmaking. He worked at WWVU until late October 1976 when he was offered a job at the Library of Congress. In 1983, the management of the public television station in Morgantown was merged with the other two state public TV stations with a new call sign, WNPB. The facility and staff stayed in Morgantown but the license was moved from the state university to the state broadcasting authority. 18 April 2015 (10:09 p.m.) email from Carl Fleischhauer to Lew Stern.

79. Fleischhauer recalled: "Gainer enjoyed performing. I remember him talking about some kind of radio gig (early radio!) he had in St. Louis at that time, where he performed as the Irish tenor Michael McCubbin (not sure of the spelling). And as his later record album demonstrates, he also performed the material he collected in West Virginia. This was (I think) entirely vocal music in contrast to Dwight's performances of the instrumental music he had collected. But both men enjoyed performing what they learned in the field." 6 April 2015 (9:23 p.m.) email from Carl Fleischhauer to Lew Stern.

80. Rice and Brown, *West Virginia, A History* (Lexington: University of Kentucky Press, 1985), p. 264. Regarding the use of the term "hillbilly," in liner notes to his record album, *Folk Songs of the Allegheny Mountains*, Gainer stated: "In recent years there has been much confusion of 'hillbilly' songs with genuine folk songs. There is, of course, no relation between the two. The various vocal and instrumental styles of the modern 'hillbilly' singers and musicians are a fairly recent development and were never known to the genuine mountaineers until they were heard on radio. Indeed, the word 'hillbilly' was until recent years considered a term of contempt by real hill dwellers." https://www.libraries.wvu.edu/collections/patrickgainer/.

Dwight shared Gainer's understanding of the term "hillbilly" and continued to acknowledge the extent to which it was "politically incorrect," culturally inappropriate, and outlandishly inaccurate as a depiction of West Virginians. Actually, Dwight used the term in his discussions of West Virginia music, but he used it as a reference point that spoke to what "outsiders" knew of or had learned about the music, specifically the caricatures promoted in film and television. Carl Fleischhauer observed that Gainer shared with Dwight, the Morris brothers, and others a deep resentment of the hillbilly stereotype: "At times, although to a lesser degree and with far less intensity, Dwight and the Morris brothers also echoed Gainer's unhappiness with the infernal bad influence of modern media and country and western music on mountaineer culture." Fleischhauer felt that Gainer displayed a "passion to correct wrong-headed ideas about his home state." 7 January 2015 (8:59 p.m.) email from Carl Fleischhauer to Lew Stern and 6 April 2015 (9:23 p.m.) email from Carl Fleischhauer to Lew Stern. Also see Tribe, *Mountaineer Jamboree*, pp. 154–155.

81. See "Pat Gainer." The West Virginia Encyclopedia. http://www.wvencyclopedia.org/articles/2077. *Also see:* https://www.libraries.wvu.edu/collections/patrickgainer/

82. Ken Perlman. "Dwight Diller and the Music of Pocahontas County," pp. 54–55; Carl Fleischhauer, "A History of the Hammons Family," in *The Hammons Family, p. 53*.

Also see John A. Cuthbert, "The Music," in *The Edden Hammons Collection, Volume Two: The Legendary West Virginia Fiddler from 1947 Field Recordings* (Morgantown, WV: West Virginia University Press, 2000), p. 18; and Alan Jabbour, "The Recordings," in *The Edden Hammons Collection, Volume One: The Legendary West Virginia Fiddler from 1947 Field Recordings*, Morgantown, WV: West Virginia University Press, 1999, p. 18. Wayne Howard notes: "Among themselves, [the Hammonses] did not jam. Sometimes Maggie would start to sing while Burl played fiddle [...] Burl would sometimes play guitar backup; sometimes he would back his cousin James on banjo; but there was no inclination for everybody to join in. It was just solo playing or *a capella* singing, as a rule." Howard, "Memories of the Hammons Family Part III: Maggie Hammons Parker," *The Old-Time Herald*, vol.12, no. 4 (April—May 2010), p. 34. Sherman Hammons confirmed that he had never known any of the "Old People" to play and sing at the same time. See Wayne Howard, "Transcript, Session 13—Recorded 07/29/1973 at the home of Sherman Hammons, Marlinton, WV. Original Reel Tape: Tapes 14–15." Howard noted that this session probably resumed the morning of 30 July 1973.

83. Maggie Hammons said of the old time music of her youth in Pocahontas County: "Well, you see they used to have dances. They'd go and have dances and people didn't care a bit around—the neighbors wouldn't—they'd clean out a room and everything fixed for 'em to come to their house and have a dance. That's the truth. Have music there, have good—have a fiddle and banjo, that's what they played on. They never played on, they never, you never, you hardly ever did see anybody a-playing on a guitar, back then. No sir, it was a banjo and a—a banjo and a fiddle, that's what they used." See Carl Fleischhauer, "A History of the Hammons Family," in *The Hammons Family*, p. 52, http://www.loc.gov/folklife/LP/AFSL65andL66_Hammons.pdf.

84. Gerry Milnes documented a "legitimate, long-standing and unaffected dulcimer heritage" in southern and central West Virginia prior to the mid–20th century national revival of the instrument. See Milnes, *Play of a Fiddle*, pp. 134–135, 151. Carl Fleischhauer offered some thoughtful views of this matter of the place of dulcimers in folk culture: "[The] dulcimer may have been seen as a true home made instrument of the mountains (easier to build than fiddle or banjo), and free of the connections between the guitar and what were deemed to be non-folk or semi-folk musical genres. It was also an appropriate, non-overpowering accompaniment for the ballad singer. [...] except for not-so-West-Virginia-rooted folk musicians (including the coffee-house subcategory), the dulcimer was not that common in the 1970s. And compared to the fiddle or banjo, the dulcimer was less expressive in the performance of instrumental music, although, as noted, it made for good accompaniment for vocals." 6 April 2015 (9:23 p.m.) email from Carl Fleischhauer to Lew Stern.

85. Alan Jabbour and Carl Fleischhauer, "Letter to the Editor," *Goldenseal*, Spring 2015, pp. 3 and 4. Regarding the published photographs, Fleischhauer stated: "[The]

original booklet for the Library of Congress album contains 27; Dwight took 3 of them. In the redone PDF booklet, there are 46 photos, 2 by Dwight. [...] [In] both versions of the booklet, the largest number of photos are historical. Most of these are copies I made from the family's collection of snapshots and portraits." 6 April 2015 (9:23 p.m.) email from Carl Fleischhauer to Lew Stern.

86. Carl Fleischhauer, "A History of the Hammons Family," in *The Hammons Family*, pp. 40–41.

87. 26 April 2015 (6:10 p.m.) email from Carl Fleischhauer to Lew Stern.

88. 6 April 2015 (9:23 p.m.) email from Carl Fleischhauer to Lew Stern. Also see Fleischhauer, "Revisiting West Virginia Folk Culture: The Hammons Family Album Thirty Years Later," *Folklife Center News*, vol. 25, no. 4 (Fall 2003), pp. 13–14.

89. 6 April 2015 (9:23 p.m.) email from Carl Fleischhauer to Lew Stern.

90. 6 April 2015 (9:23 p.m.) email from Carl Fleischhauer to Lew Stern; Author's notes, 14 March 2015 (2:00–4:00 p.m.) conversation in Staunton, VA, with David Winston from Lexington, Virginia; Author's notes, 28 May 2015 (10:00 a.m.–11:00 a.m.) telephone conversation with Nancy Burks, Dwight's sister, from Marlinton, West Virginia; Author's notes, 8 May 2015 (12:00 p.m.–3:30 p.m.) conversation in Staunton, Virginia, with Al Tharp from Lexington, Virginia.

91. Dwight recalled that he told Fuzzy Mountain String Band members and some others about his field recordings of the Hammonses and played some recorded tunes for them and other musicians at the old time festivals at Hillsville or Ivydale in June and July 1970. It would appear that Dwight made the decision to share the field recordings in a matter of weeks, possibly between the June date for the Hillsville festival and the 4th of July weekend festival in Independence, Virginia. By then, to some extent, he had taken on the role of gatekeeper for the Hammonses and was probably, to some extent, concerned with the disruption, inconvenience, and discomfort—as well as the importance of arranging for financial dividends for events, performances and appearance—that a constant stream of inquisitive outsiders seeking to visit and record the Hammonses might mean for the family. 31 December 2014 (1:03 p.m.) email from Tom Mylet to Lew Stern.

92. 4 January 2015 (12:46 p.m.) from Carl Fleischhauer to Lew Stern; "In Scotland Town Where I Was Born" (Child 17, "Hind Horn") in Patrick Gainer, *Folk Songs from the West Virginia Hills* (Grantsville, WV: Seneca, 1975), pp. 22–23. On the disc, a version of the song from one recording session is combined with conversation about the song recorded at another. The album notes provide two dates and two AFS numbers for the two parts of the selection on the disc (see PDF booklet, p. 56). 7 January 2015 (11:07 a.m.) email from Carl Fleischhauer to Lew Stern; 6 April 2015 (9:23 p.m.) email from Carl Fleischhauer to Lew Stern.

93. *The Hammons Family*, page 90.

94. 7 January 2015 (11:07 a.m.) email from Carl Fleischhauer to Lew Stern; 7 January 2015 (8:59 p.m.) email from Carl Fleischhauer to Lew Stern.

95. Patrick Gainer, *Folk Songs from the West Virginia Hills* (Grantsville, WV: Seneca, 1975). The first edition of Gainer's *Witches, Ghosts and Signs: Folklore of the Southern Appalachians*, published in 1975 (and reprinted by West Virginia University Press in 2008) was intended as a companion volume to the *Folk Song* book. Fleischhauer noted that the ballad itself, is discussed here: http://www.bluegrassmessengers.com/17-hind-horn.aspx.

96. 7 January 2015 (8:59 p.m.) email from Carl Fleischhauer to Lew Stern. On ethnographic research, see Christine Ballengee Morris, "Roots, Branches, Blossoms, and Briars: Cultural Colonialsm of the Mountain Arts in West Virginia," a Thesis in Art Education, Submitted in Partial Fulfillment of the Requirements for the Degree of Doctor of Philosophy, the Graduate School, Department of Art Education, Pennsylvania State University (UMI Number: 9531992), 1995, pp. 20–21.

97. 7 January 2015 (8:59 p.m.) email from Carl Fleischhauer to Lew Stern.

98. 6 April 2015 (9:23 p.m.) email from Carl Fleischhauer to Lew Stern.

99. 4 January 2015 (12:46 p.m.) email from Carl Fleischhauer to Lew Stern.

100. University of North Carolina at Chapel Hill, Collection Number: 20061, Collection Title: Jack Bernhardt Papers, 1943–2011, Dwight Diller Interview, Elkins, WVA, 3 August 1983, Tape 1, Side 1; 4 January 2015 (12:46 p.m.) from Carl Fleischhauer to Lew Stern.

101. Christine Ballengee Morris, "Roots, Branches, Blossoms, and Briars: Cultural Colonialism of the Mountain Arts in West Virginia," in *Marilyn Zurmuehlen Working Papers in Art Education*, vol. 13, issue 1, Article 17, 1995. Available at: http://ir.uiowa.edu/mzwp/vol13/iss1/17

102. 18 September 2014 (12:40 a.m.) email from Dwight Diller to Lew Stern.

103. The only documented use of the "Edn" spelling is Cal Price's 1906 newspaper story. Carl Fleischhauer, who wrote the Hammons family history for the 1973 Library of Congress project, stated: "How did the family itself spell the name? The authority Alan [Jabbour] and I used when we re-did the booklet for the Rounder CD set was Edden's gravestone." 6 April 2015 (9:23 p.m.) email from Carl Fleischhauer to Lew Stern. On that gravestone, under a banner of the name "Hammons," the name "Edden" and the dates 1876–1955" appear on the left, and his wife's name, Elizabeth D., and the dates "1876–1954" appear on the right. See: http://www.findagrave.com/cgi-bin/fg.cgi?page=pv&GRid=13238873 Fleischhauer observed that the name Edden in some etymological sense is a descendant of Edwin. The silent W appears often but not always in Britain. For the family, it was indeed pronounced "Edin." Fleischhauer continued: "This headstone must date from the 1950s after Edden and his wife had died, and this seems to be how his children preferred to render his name as they remembered him. If Alan and I had run into this stone prior to 1973, we would have used this spelling from the start. This is the spelling that John Cuthbert used for the reissue of the Chappell recordings, which came along later." Dwight never met Edn but heard much about him from family members, and Edn was a character in many of their stories, complete with dialog and voice-imitation. Dwight himself always spelled this Hammons fiddler's name as "Edn," and delighted in mimicking Edn's high pitched voice and unusual locution, and quoting the fiddler repeatedly reminding folks that he was "E-D-N, just Edn." Dwight's view is that when Edn was "discovered" in the 1970's "they carried on the tradition of refusing to show him respect by spelling his name exactly as he said it was." The assumption, Dwight mused, was that Edn, "like all hillbillies, was far too ignorant to know how to spell his own name or to know anything about the world except in their hovel and two miles in every direction. And they get away with it because they are the 'experts,' but how do we know they are the 'experts'? They tell us, of course." 25 October 2014 (10:51 a.m.) email from Dwight Diller to Lew Stern. An interesting parallel regarding the spelling of Roscoe Holcomb's name is discussed in Scott L. Matthews, "John Cohen in Eastern Kentucky: Documentary Expression and the Image of Roscoe Halcomb During the Folk Revival," *Southern Spaces*, 6 August 2008. http://southernspaces.org/2008/john-cohen-eastern-kentucky-documentary-expression-and-image-roscoe-halcomb-during-folk-revival

104. In field notes compiled during his visits to the Hammons family members in 1977, Wayne Howard noted that Lee Hammons said two things about Edn Hammons (recorded as "Uncle Edwin") that "are still matters of pride to him": Uncle Edwin would come and leave his own fiddle and take Lee's homemade black birch one with him when he went to play somewhere. He also would take a fiddle Lee tuned and not have to change one string before he played." Wayne Howard, "Notes of 1977 Field Trip, June 26, 1977."

105. John A. Cuthbert, "Louis Watson Chappell." e-WV: The West Virginia Encyclopedia. 04 October 2012. Accessed 26 October 2014. http://www.wvencyclopedia.org/articles/1058

106. John Cuthbert noted that Chappell recalled a law had been passed that Edn "could not play in any towns at all" because "he was that much of a nuisance." Cuthbert quotes George Parkinson, folklorist and curator of the West Virginia and Regional History Collection: "In this particular recording session in Richwood, Chappell says the people gathered all the way up the stairs of the hotel, in the lobby of the hotel and out in the road, and he had to quit recording. But later on he went back and had a second recording session with Ed where he took Ed to a hotel, no—it was a motel out in the country someplace—not only was it out in the country but one of the cabins was back off the main road where nobody could hear the playing." John S. Cuthbert, "The Chappell-Hammons Recordings," in *The Edden Hammons Collection, Volume One: The Legendary West Virginia Fiddler From 1947 Field Recordings*, Morgantown: West Virginia University Press, 1999, pp. 9–10.

107. In the early 1990s, Dwight recounted the story this way: "In fact, the family was given one of those disks whenever [Chappell] made those recordings of Edn. That's how I found out that there was something more going on because nobody knew anything about it. They said 'Yeah, they've got a record down there with Edn on it. He's playing "Washington's March."' Chappell had given Edn one of those—I guess—aluminum disks. So I found that out and then I told this person and this person told the next person and they got all that stuff back. So, undoubtedly ['Washington's March'] was a real popular [tune] with the Hammons family. But I don't think I've heard anybody else play it [who was not] a member of the Hammons family." Audiocassette of a Banjo Camp conducted on the shore of the Greenbrier River, Seneca Park, 1991, tape provided by Bob Thornburg. Also see Danny Williams, "Preface to the CD Edition," in *The Edden Hammons Collection, Volume One: The Legendary West Virginia Fiddler from 1947 Field Recordings*, Morgantown: West Virginia University Press, 1999, p. 3. Carl Fleischhauer confirmed that Chappell made aluminum discs, noting that the 1940s were well past the era of wax cylinders. Fleischhauer photographed Chappell's recording apparatus and some discs in 1975 or 1976; several of those photographs were used to illustrate some of John Cuthbert's writings about the recordings. 6 April 2015 (9:23 p.m.) email from Carl Fleischhauer to Lew Stern.

108. Thomas Spencer Brown (1930–) received a Ph.D. in music from Northwestern University in 1968, and taught instrumental and vocal music in schools in Kansas, Nebraska, and Louisiana. In 1967, Brown took a position as an assistant professorship in Music Education at West Virginia University. In the 1970s, Brown attended folk festivals and made field recordings of traditional music in West Virginia. Professor Brown's field recordings have become part of the folk music archives of the West Virginia and Regional History Center. https://wvrhc.lib.wvu.edu/research/collections/folkmusic.

109. Cuthbert, "The Chappell-Hammons Recordings," pages 8–9. Dwight recalled that he had learned from Edn's son Smith that the recording session took place on 16 and 17 August 1947; the second day of that session took place a year before Dwight's 17 August 1946 birthday, which anchored this memory in Dwight's mind. Author's notes, 27 October 2014 (10:00 a.m.–12:30 p.m., 3:30 p.m.–5:15 p.m.) telephone conversation with Dwight Diller.

110. Dwight recalled, erroneously, that Jabbour lived in North Carolina at the time, and was associated with the University of North Carolina. Author's notes, 27 October 2014 (10:00 a.m.–12:30 p.m., 3:30 p.m.–5:15 p.m.) telephone conversation with Dwight Diller. In fact, in September 1969 Jabbour was appointed head of the Archive of Folk Song—now the Archive of Folk Culture—at the Library of Congress. Jabbour held that position until April 1974 when he moved to the National Endowment for the Arts to become founding director of that agency's grantgiving program in folk arts. http://www.alanjabbour.com/Bio_and_bibliography.html.

111. Cuthbert, "The Chappell-Hammons Recordings," p. 9. Dwight recalled that a woman schoolteacher (whose name he did not remember) told him in 1989 that she had visited Chappell in North Carolina and that Chappell had told her about his field recordings of Edn Hammons and others. The woman returned to West Virginia after that visit and told John Cuthbert about Chappell's field recordings of Edn Hammons. Dwight suggested that Thomas Brown brought the story regarding Edn Hammons 1947 recordings to the attention of John Cuthbert in 1973, after Dwight told Brown about them. Author's notes, 27 October 2014 (10:00 a.m.–12:30 p.m., 3:30 p.m.–5:15 p.m.) telephone conversation with Dwight Diller. Also see Jabbour-Cuthbert correspondence on the project in "Edden Hammons Collection album project (AFC 1985/034)." The Library of Congress file includes three cassettes of instrumentals and interviews performed on fiddle and guitar and spoken by Edn and James Hammons. Originally recorded on discs in Pocahontas County, West Virginia, by Louis Watson Chappell, August 14–23, 1947. The collection also includes one linear inch of manuscripts, and was donated by John A. Cuthbert of West Virginia University. (4 hours and 30 minutes; RYB 0701–0703). Also see Gerald Milnes, *Play of a Fiddle*, chapter 4 (pp. 45–60). on the Hammons family.

112. Carl Fleischhauer, "A History of the Hammons Family," in *The Hammons Family*, pp. 40–41. In January 2015, Carl Fleischhauer stated: "to some degree, Dwight did some connecting between the family and visitors. But except for nearby and low-key festivals like Ivydale, he did not bring family members to bigger and more distant venues. The archetype of that kind of connecting—with its attendant problems—is John Cohen and Roscoe Holcomb/Halcomb." 4 January 2015 (12:46 p.m.) from Carl Fleischhauer to Lew Stern. Also see Matthew, "John Cohen in Eastern Kentucky," 6 August 2008.

113. Fleischhauer stated: "Dwight's observation of all of the players […] led him to think about what his relationship with the family should be. He sought a relationship that was passionate and personal. In terms of his own personal development his effort to shape his relationship to the family played out even as he was finding his own self-identity. This dynamic may provide a context for his recollections and assessments of the people and the time, and may also account for things like him veering from being (a) the evangelist telling the world about these wonderful people and their art to [him playing the role of] (b) the gatekeeper, trying to control access to the family and, later, to their meaning and their art." 6 April 2015 (9:23 p.m.) email from Carl Fleischhauer to Lew Stern.

Chapter Three

1. Bill Hicks stated that the Fuzzy Mountain String Band, a loose "conglomeration of Chapel Hill/Durham musicians," started in 1967. Hicks joined that band in 1970; the Fuzzy Mountain String Band recorded its two albums in 1971 and 1973. Hicks recalled that the second album was recorded after Tommy Thompson's first wife, Bobbie Thompson—who was the original guitar player in the Fuzzy Mountain String Band—was killed in a car accident in February 1972. 28 January 2015 (8:18 a.m.) email from Bill Hicks to Lew Stern.

2. Author's notes, 16 December 2014 (10:30 a.m.–12:49 p.m.) telephone conversation with Dwight Diller. In early January 2015, Wayne Howard told me: "I had heard that Len Reiss was making some beautiful banjos. After I reconnected with Dwight [in the 1990s] he told me that Len had moved on to something else—said he was always like that: totally into something until he had mastered it, then dropping it altogether for a new obsession. He didn't say whether Len was still playing, and he would be my only source for information about these musicians." 5 January 2015 (7:11 p.m.) email from Wayne Howard to Lew Stern. Len Reiss, a retired computer maintenance expert and a banjo builder of note who was credited with roughly 30 to 35 banjos through the 1970s, was living in Lexington, Virginia, when I tracked him down in mid–2015, and was still doing some banjo repair work. Reiss made contact with Thren possible. Author's notes, 24 July 2015 conversation (12:00–3:00 p.m.) with Len Reiss and Bob Thren from Lexington, VA. Varela surfaced later, in mid–October 2015, thanks to the assistance of Barry Poss. Varela played music in Chapel Hill with Barry and Sharon Poss, and sometimes with Cece Conway. Varela made a small banjo for the young son of Tommy Thompson and Professor Conway, named Tom Ashley. Conway stated that Varela learned a lot of Thompson's music indirectly. 11 July 2015 (11:05 p.m.) email from Cece Conway.

3. At a banjo retreat held in Cass, West Virginia, in 1989 (attended by Diane Jones, Howard Zane, Tom King, and Ben Carr, among others), Dwight told the class that he learned "Santa Ana's Retreat" from Bob Thren, the same person from whom he learned the tune "Texas." Dwight explained that he taught the tune the way Thren taught it to him "except for that one small part of the low part I've forgotten." Dwight recollected that Thren taught him Lee Triplett's "West Folk Girls" and "Kitchen Girl," in standard G tuning, but played in a "modal" fashion, and that Thren's way of playing those tunes was complicated and, as he thought back on it, a bit too complex since Dwight had only been playing banjo for about about nine months at that point. Alex Varela taught Dwight "Frosty Morn," a different tune than the one Melvin Wine played so famously. Len Reiss showed Dwight some of the fiddler Henry Reed's tunes that Alan Jabbour had recorded. Audiotape cassette of Dwight Diller's banjo retreat taught at Cass, West Virginia, 1989, provided by Bob Thornburg; 27 August 2015 (8:31 p.m.) email from Dwight Diller to Lew Stern; Author's notes, 27 October 2014 (10:00 a.m.–12:30 p.m., 3:30 p.m.–5:15 p.m.) telephone conversation with Dwight Diller.

4. 13 June 215 (9:27 a.m.) email from Bill Hicks to Lew Stern; 11 July 2015 (11:05 p.m.) email from Cece Conway; Mike Craver, "Memorial Tribute to Tommy Thompson," http://www.mikecraver.com/tommy.html; Mark Greenberg, "Tommy Thompson: High Energy Clawhammer Banjo," *Frets, The Magazine of Acoustic String Instruments*, November 1980, http://www.earlyblurs.com/fretsTT.htm.

5. 20 December 2014 (10:53 a.m.) email from Walt Koken to Lew Stern.

6. Jimmy Sutton identified "Monkey on a String" as a Charlie Poole tune. See http://www.banjohangout.org/topic/296265.

7. The audiotape of the Hillsville, Virginia, clawhammer banjo contests, provided to me by Kilby Spencer, recorded the performances of Mutt Worrell, contestant number one, from Pulaski, Virginia, who played "John Henry"; Blanton Owen, contestant number two, from Swannee, Tennessee, who played "John Henry"; Noel Redderick, contestant number three, from Bristol, Tennessee, who played "Over the Waterfall"; Russell Worrell, contestant number four, from Virginia, who played "Monkey on a String"; Jimmy Edmonds, contestant number six, from Galax, Virginia, played "Here Rattler"; Bambi Walsh, contestant number seven, from Chapel Hill, North Carolina, who played a tune the name of which was not captured on the audiotape; Tommy Thompson, contestant number eight, from Chapel Hill, North Carolina, who played "Devil on a Stump"; Dwight Diller, contestant number nine, from Sally Hollow, West Virginia, who played "Sixteen Horses Was My Team"; Tom Walsh, whose place of residence and lineup in the contest were not captured on the audiotape, who played "Cluck Old Hen." The audiotape captured a contestant playing "Sally Ann," but the lineup number and the name of the banjo player were not recorded. Audiotape of competitions at the 11th Annual Old Time Fiddlers and Bluegrass Convention, June 1970, Hillsville, Virginia, provided by Kilby Spencer of Whitetop, Virginia, on 18 December 2014. Katie Lundy Golding, sister of the late banjo player Ted Lundy (http://julianwinston.com/music/ted_lundy.php), told Kevin Fore that she and Kyle Creed were judges at the 1970 Hillsville competitions, but she did not remember Dwight playing in the banjo contest. 26 December 2014 (9:15 a.m.) email from Kevin Fore to Lew Stern.

8. Dwight lived at the mouth of Sally Hollow. Using spelling that captured the local pronunciation, Dwight stated in a December 2014 email: "According to Amos McCarty who was born just before 1870 and lived half mile up the road from my house, there was an old horse name Sally who stayed up in this holler. Plus Amos said that 'A bunch of Georgia Regulars camped out in that holler and about froze out.' This is exactly true about there being confederates in hollers on this road, now Route 28. And there is actual evidence that some did die. But for unknown reasons. Nothing has showed up in my holler. But there was a sawmill right where I am living so any evidence would be gone." 19 December 2014 (2:25 p.m.) email from Dwight Diller to Lew Stern.

9. In a mid–December 2014 email exchange, Dwight stated that "Sixteen Horses" was Maggie Hammons' name for the tune called "Angeline," and that he used these words with the same melody as "Angeline": "Sixteen horses was my team/ The old grey went before/ Almost broke Angeline's ear to hear the wagons roar." Another verse he recalled being sung by Maggie: "Bought Angeline a brand new dress/Neither black nor brown/ It was the color of a stormy cloud/ Before the rain pours down." 19 December 2014 (2:25 p.m.) email from Dwight Diller to Lew Stern. After being told about the audiotapes of the Hillsville banjo contest, in that same email exchange, Dwight stated that he had never heard of a tune named "Old Folks Comin' Down the Road" and that he did not recall playing "Soldier's Joy" at the contest. 19 December 2014 (2:25 p.m.) email from Dwight Diller to Lew Stern.

10. Walt Koken stated: "Devil on a Stump was a tune I learned in California from Bert Levy about 1971, who played with Alan Jabbour and Tommy and Bobbie Thompson in the Hollow Rock String Band, from the Durham/Chapel Hill area in the late sixties. Alan may have collected it from Henry Reed of Glen Lynn VA." 20 December 2014 (10:53 A.M) email from Walt Koken to Lew

Stern. Alan Jabbour stated: "'Devil on a Stump,' which I recorded from Ross Miller, and 'Hell up Cole Holler,' which I recorded from Henry Reed, are at least kindred tunes, arguably versions of the same tune, though Henry Reed's version is more complex. 'Devil on a Stump' is published on our original Hollow Rock String Band LP, published in 1968 (Kanawha 311) and still in print on County CO-CD-2715." 25 July 2015 (12:34 a.m.) email from Alan Jabbour to Lew Stern. Also see: Fiddle Tunes of the Old Frontier: The Henry Reed Collection, Library of Congress, http://www.loc.gov/item/afcreed000182/.

11. University of North Carolina at Chapel Hill, Collection Number: 20061, Collection Title: Jack Bernhardt Papers, 1943–2011, Dwight Diller Interview, Elkins, WVA, 3 August 1983, Tape 1, Side 1. In a mid–December 2014 conversation, Dwight said: "I still have that red ribbon hanging on a wall. It was a hinge that flipped my life in another direction." 19 December 2014 (225 p.m.) email from Dwight Diller to Lew Stern.

12. University of North Carolina at Chapel Hill, Collection Number: 20061, Collection Title: Jack Bernhardt Papers, 1943–2011, Dwight Diller Interview, Elkins, WVA, 3 August 1983, Tape 1, Side 1.

13. Author's notes, 27 October 2014 (10:00 a.m.–12:00 p.m., 3:30–5:15 p.m.) telephone conversation with Dwight Diller.

14. Dwight took first place in the July 1982 Pioneer Days gathering in Marlinton, West Virginia. Jim Costa placed second, and Woody Simmons placed third. Ron Parks, "1982 Pioneer Days Fiddle and Banjo Contest," *The Pocahontas Times*, 22 July 1982, page 3. http://pch.stparchive.com/Archive/PCH/PCH07221982P03.php.

Dwight took third place in the old time banjo category in the Banjo Pickers competition at the 1998 Vandalia Gathering in on 29 May 1988. Tim Bing won first place at the competition, held at the Cultural Center in Charleston as part of the 12th annual Vandalia Gathering. "Banjo Contest Winners," *The Pocahontas Times*, 9 June 1988, p. 4. http://pch.stparchive.com/Archive/PCH/PCH06091988P04.php. By the late 1980s, Dwight had come to see festival-hosted banjo contests as a homogenizing influence that rewarded speed and agility instead of graceful playing of archaic tunes learned from the source musicians. Contestants were judged on their picking prowess, singing was separated from the music; rules evolved to require contestants to compete on the basis of their banjo playing alone. In his own account, he entered fewer and fewer of them in subsequent years. See Dwight Diller, with Bing Brothers and Tom King, workshop on the banjo in string bands, Augusta Heritage Center, Elkins, West Virginia, 1988. Audiocassette provided by Bob Thornburg. However, there were exceptions. For example, Dwight entered the senior old time banjo competition at the 39th Annual Vandalia Gathering held at the West Virginia State Capitol in Charleston on Memorial Day weekend in 2015. "Local Musicians Perform, Compete at Vandalia Gathering," *The Pocahontas Times*, 11 June 2015, p. 6.

15. 23 January 2015 (1:03 p.m.) email from Brad Leftwich to Lew Stern. Leftwich made it clear that his memory of the event was inexact: "The time I played 'Sugar Hill' at Independence with Dwight was later, probably 1974 although I wouldn't swear to it. Also, although I think it was Independence, I couldn't swear to that either. Memory is a funny thing, isn't it? I remember so clearly playing with him on stage, even the tune, but I can't recall the place or year with any certainty." 23 January 2015 (1:03 p.m.) email from Brad Leftwich to Lew Stern and 23 January 2015 (11:24 p.m.) email from Brad Leftwich to Lew Stern.

16. Dwight Rogers recalled standing in front of the stage with a tape recorder, but by 2015 that tape was lost. Gail Gillespie presumed that Dwight Diller was not the contest winner. In her recollection: "The winners of almost everything at Independence were members of the band the New River Ramblers. Their banjo player Buck Perry had a huge 'large motor' style of claw hammer and usually won something. Another 'big lick' claw hammer player, Enoch Rutherford, also from the area, might have won a ribbon if he was there." 27 January 2015 (1:18 p.m.) email from Gail Gillespie to Lew Stern; 27 January 2015 (1:22 p.m.) email from Gail Gillespie to Lew Stern; 27 January 2015 (1:25 p.m.) email from Gail Gillespie to Lew Stern. A 2013 article memorializing Rutherford stated: "Enoch took a hiatus from playing while raising a family; he would attend conventions, but never enter, just jam out in the field. But in 1972, Enoch got dragged up on the stage by a friend, Harold Ward, at the Independence Fiddlers' Convention. Enoch tore into 'Banjo Picking Girl,' won first place, and after that, he kept going, never looked back, winning countless old time banjo competitions." Martha Spencer and Erika Godfrey, "Remembering Enoch Rutherford," *Mountain Music Magazine*, 18 June 2013, http://mountainmusicmagazine.weebly.com/mountain-music-legacies/remembering-enoch-rutherford.

17. Carl Fleischhauer's photographs of the October 1970 "get-together" at the schoolhouse in Buckeye include images of Hamp Carpenter, Mose Coffman, and one or another of the Hammonses. "I remember this evening as a nice round of jam sessions and friendly social sharing." 4 January 2015 (12:46 p.m.) email from Carl Fleischhauer to Lew Stern; 12 April 2015 (5:23 p.m.) email from Carl Fleischhauer to Lew Stern. Also see: "A List of Banjo Recordings in the Archive of Folk Culture, Acquired Through 1978," The American Folklife Center, Library of Congress, http://www.loc.gov/folklife/guides/Banjo.html.

18. See Wayne Howard, "Memories of the Hammons Family Part III: Maggie Hammons Parker," *The Old-Time Herald*, vol. 12, no. 4 (April—May 2010), p. 26; "Memories of the Hammons Family Part IV: Burl Hammons," *The Old-Time Herald*, vol. 12, no. 5 (June—July 2010), p. 37. Also see Gilbert Wayne Howard Collection of Hammons Family Recordings (AFC 1999/023). This Library of Congress file contains nineteen 7-inch tapes of fiddle and banjo tunes, played by Burl Hammons and others; folk songs, riddles, and narration performed and told by members of the Hammons Family recorded by Gilbert Wayne Howard from 1971 to 1980.

19. Bill Hicks remembered: "At some point in the late 1960s or possibly 1970, Blanton Owen (of the Fuzzies) and Bertram Levy went to visit Burl Hammons and recorded a long session of him playing and talking. This tape was amongst the music sources that, during my initiation into the Fuzzy Mountain Band, I spent a lot of time listening to. It's possible Dwight introduced Blanton and Bert to the Hammonses, but I wasn't aware of that fact back then. I was so struck by Burl's music that I undertook a trip up to visit him myself, I believe in the summer of 1971, but it could have been 1970. I sat and played a lot of music with Burl, some with Sherman, also a great long morning with Maggie Hammons. I'm pretty sure Dwight was there for some of that. I also went up to that Buckeye school session, which was in the fall of '70 or '71. Dwight organized that. Burl and Sherman were there, [along with] some other local fiddlers. Carl Fleishhauer was there recording on a serious field recording machine, probably a Nagra." 15 January 2015 (720 a.m.) email from Bill Hicks to Lew Stern. Nagra-brand tape recorders, a series of mostly battery-operated portable professional audio recorders produced by Kudelski SA, based in Cheseaux-sur-Lausanne, Switzerland, were "the de facto standard sound recording systems for motion picture and (non-video) single-camera television production from the 1960s until the 1990s." http://en.wikipedia.org/wiki/Nagra. Cece Conway re-

called that the Library of Congress allowed fieldworkers such as herself, Tom Carter and Blanton Owen, to borrow its Nagra. 11 July 2015 (11:05 p.m.) email from Cece Conway.

20. 6 April 2015 (9:23 p.m.) email from Carl Fleischhauer to Lew Stern.

21. Author's notes, 8 August 2015 conversation (3:00–4:00 p.m.) with James Leva in Verona, VA.

22. 11 August 2015 (1:11 p.m.) email from James Leva to Lew Stern.

23. I have heard only one recording of McGuire playing banjo, courtesy of Al Tharp, who captured McGuire and Andy Williams playing "Magpie" at what Tharp recalled was a Breaking Up Christmas party at McGuire's home in Lexington, Virginia. Tharp told me that McGuire played in G out of Sawmill tuning; Tharp learned that approach from McGuire and adapted that for probably 90 percent of the G tunes he played. McGuire's general approach, Tharp observed, involved a kind of "loping backbeat with an accentuated brush," clawhammer style, but with a fair amount of inside thumbing. Of McGuire, Tharpe said that he was at once "inspirational, brilliant, exasperating, cantankerous, impossible. [His wife] Mata nicknamed him 'Ordeal' [but he] really made so much happen, his legacy is immeasurable. I do miss him." 8 May 2015 (9:16 p.m.) email from Al Tharp to Lew Stern. McGuire passed away in 2008.

24. http://www.fieldrecorder.com/docs/notes/plank road.htm.

25. 23 January 2015 (1:03 p.m.) email from Brad Leftwich to Lew Stern.

26. The Highwoods String Band, Benford noted, telegraphed the idea that "young folks, regardless of where they were raised, could perform the music for money, with skill and depth, without harming the spirit of the music, and in fact, helping spread the music along towards the days when the 'Old People' were gone." 11 January 2015 (11:39 a.m.) email from Mac Benford to Lew Stern.

27. 6 November 2014 (2:44 a.m.) email from Dwight Diller to Lew Stern; 26 October 2014 (10:50 a.m.) email from James Leva to Lew Stern; and Author's notes, 24 July 2015 conversation (12:00–3:0 p.m.) with Len Reiss and Bob Thren from Lexington, Virginia. Len Reiss recalled that Breaking Up Christmas was a West Virginia tradition and on that basis suggested that Dwight might have had a hand in shaping the event organized in Lexington in the early 1970s. John Bealle, writing about the community and folk revival in Bloomington, Indiana, in the early 1970s, spoke of the emergence of the tradition of organizing a weeklong celebration of old time music and dance commencing right after Thanksgiving. Bealle suggested that there were older practices in places such as Lexington, Virginia, where the community organized a Breaking Up Christmas event that was in fact a schedule of interlocking parties running through the New Year celebration, patterned loosely on the mountain communities' tradition of Old Christmas. John Bealle, *Old-Time Music and Dance: Community and Folk Revival* (Bloomington: Indiana University Press, 2005), pp. 212–215.

28. 26 October 2014 (1050 a.m.) email from James Leva to Lew Stern. Dwight met Sheila Adams in Kentucky when he went to set up the old time festival there on behalf of the Morris Brothers, funded by a Rockefeller grant in 1972 and 1973. Dwight said: "Sheila Rice, Sheila Adams, she's from Sodom over in Asheville she got to be a very good banjo player. I went down in 1972 and set up for the Morris Brothers Festival. She got to be a really crackerjack banjo player. Far and away the best woman banjo player I've ever heard and can really sing. When got there in 1972 she was 19, been married and divorced, had a child and was just really hurting, kind of like I had been in earlier years. I helped her some with the banjo and she took it and learned it on her own. Really, really made a musician out of herself. She did all the work." University of North Carolina at Chapel Hill, Collection Number: 20061, Collection Title: Jack Bernhardt Papers, 1943–2011, Dwight Diller Interview, Elkins, WVA, 3 August 1983, Tape 1, Side 2. Also see Sheila Kay Adams, *Come Go Home with Me*, (Chapel Hill: University of North Carolina Press, 1995), pages ix, x. Adams writes about her pilgrimage to Ivydale in *Come Go Home with Me*, p. 85.

29. 15 October 2014 (3:30 p.m.) email from Dwight Diller to Lew Stern.

30. http://www.fieldrecorder.com/docs/notes/plank road.htm. Dick Kimmel recalled that "Frosty Morn,'" played by a few fiddlers and clawhammer banjo players, was used as the processional for Dwight and Molly Diller's wedding: "The tune played in a small backwoods church, complete with a slave-loft and wood stove, along with the older Hammons being present, created quite a mood out of the past." See Kimmel, "Claw-hammer Banjo: 'Frosty Morn,'" *Banjo Newsletter*, vol. 2, no. 4 (February 1975), page 9. Wayne Howard recalled: "My wife and I were both at Dwight's wedding. It was held in an old log church not far from where Sherman Hammons was living. I think it was at Woodrow, a Methodist church. Lee Hammons was the best man, and he wore a necktie! I took a picture of him. I took a lot of pictures, and I was heartsick when I found that I hadn't stuck the end of the film far enough into the reel. It didn't pass through the camera, and not one picture turned out. There were scads of old-time musicians there, and music was a prominent part of the wedding. I'm pretty sure Bill Hicks was one of those who played, and I think his entire band was there. I have a memory of the bride and groom passing between two files of attendees, under arches of their extended arms. I don't know if this was during their exit from the ceremony or just a figure in the square dance that followed." 5 January 2015 (7:11 p.m.) email from Wayne Howard to Lew Stern.

31. http://www.fieldrecorder.com/docs/notes/plank road.htm.

32. 26 October 2014 (10:50 a.m.) email from James Leva to Lew Stern.

33. Bob Carlin commented: "I'm not so sure that all of this was 'planned' out. It just seemed a natural attraction of outcasts interested in an arcane music looking to belong to a group of liked minded individuals. This turned into a traveling circus of musicians, dancers and spouses that went from festival to festival, event to event, especially during the summers when school was out." 29 October 2014 (9:57 a.m.) email from Bob Carlin to Lew Stern.

34. 29 October 2014 (9:57 a.m.) email from Bob Carlin to Lew Stern. Also see Bill C. Malone, *Music from the True Vine: Mike Seeger's Life and Musical Journey* (Chapel Hill: University of North Carolina Press, 2011), pp. 147–148.

35. 25 July 2015 (1234 a.m.) email from Alan Jabbour to Lew Stern.

36. Author's notes, 5 March 2015 (5:22–5:48 p.m.) telephone conversation with Gary Ruley; 6 March 2015 (8:38 a.m.) email from Gary Ruley to Lew Stern.

37. Author's notes, 15 July 2015 telephone conversation (10:46–11:20 a.m.) with Olin Bare from Lexington, VA.

38. Dwight disseminated the music and stories of the Hammons family to a much wider audience in the early 1970s. According to Mark Campbell, "It was Dwight who was instrumental in getting the Charlottesville people exposed to the Hammons family. I remember going to the Marlinton festival with Armin [Barnett] when I was a teenager, and seeing the three Hammons siblings taking turns playing tunes and songs in what was probably Dwight's driveway. The Lexington folks were more Tommy Jarrell/Kyle Creed-oriented it seems to me. I remember

the first time contests opened up at Clifftop, the south western Virginia and North Carolina musicians were chagrined at being beaten by West Virginia musicians and vice versa. The styles they had evolved were still fairly regional." 12 January 2015 (3:59 p.m.) email from Mark Campbell to Lew Stern. Armin Barnett was a fiddler and a friend of William Franklin "Frank" George, who was born in 1928 in Bluefield, Mercer County, and was a respected fiddler and an authority on the history of West Virginia traditional music. George had a particular interest in the Irish and Scottish roots of mountain culture, and played the Scottish bagpipes, the pennywhistle, the fife, the mountain and the hammered dulcimer, and the old-time banjo. He frequently performed Celtic music with the band "Poteen." http://www.wvculture.org/goldenseal/Vandalia2k/frankgeorge.html

39. Ken Perlman. "Dwight Diller and the Music of Pocahontas County," p. 54. On the West Virginian fiddler Jack MacElwayne see Milnes, *Play of a Fiddle*, pp. 22–24.

40. One good example of this: Wayne Howard recounted that in those days, in the early 1970s, "People were into their heritage, and one West Virginia University professor, Patrick Gainer, had been harping on the notion that old-time fiddle style and the mountain dulcimer employed drone strings in imitation of bagpipes. Accordingly, a number of would-be old-timers took up bagpiping." Howard continued: "One year, when we got to Ivydale, an enormous young man had taken a strong position on a hilltop above the stage. He was about six-foot-eight and at least 250 pounds, had on kilts, garters, a tartan cap—the works—and his name was Angus Miller. He was playing the bagpipes for all he was worth, and he kept on playing for what seemed like hours and hours. I love the bagpipes, myself, but they are loud. After the contests started, nobody could hear a thing from the stage, but nobody dared to climb up and ask Angus to cool it. I don't remember what finally got him to quit, but the next day the Charleston Gazette had a front-page article on the festival. It mentioned that 'bagpipes were played by Anus Miller.' We thought at first that this was a typo. On reflection, though, we decided that, after all, the reporter had been there, too ." 5 January 2015 (7:11 p.m.) email from Wayne Howard to Lew Stern.

41. 11 January 2015 (12:27 p.m.) email from Brad Leftwich to Lew Stern. In early January 2015, Wayne Howard told me: "I did happen to meet up with O'Dell McGuire seven or eight years ago, at Clifftop. It was the year when we were selling CD's of the Hammonses for Dwight's benefit. A fellow came up to me and said that he was there with an old man who had known Lee Hammons and was dying to get hold of one of his CD's. I took one to their camp, and the purchaser was O'Dell McGuire, then in his mid-eighties. He and Lee Hammons had been very close friends. They had many common interests apart from the music and just liked each other." 5 January 2015 (7:11 p.m.) email from Wayne Howard to Lew Stern. Howard explained that Lee Hammons and McGuire would often just sit and talk, without playing music. McGuire had concocted a "better mousetrap," a human means of live trapping uninvited visitors who found their way into his cabin in the woods. (See http://rockbridgeadvocate.com/mousex.htm.) McGuire's invention is something that would have captured Hammons' attention, inveterate tinkerer that he was. Howard continued: "Lee Hammons [had] a mind that appreciated technical details. He once described to me how automated lathes could turn out pieces with threads or spiral patterns on them, for example. I think things of that nature probably fascinated both of them. But again, I'm speculating. Another thing Lee told me once, and I think this is on tape, was that [the man who wrote the ballad of Jay Legg] looked a lot like Odell McGuire." 12 July 2015 (11:41 p.m.) email from Wayne Howard to Lew Stern.

42. 16 January 2015 (9:21 a.m.) email from Mark Campbell to Lew Stern.

43. Author's notes, 15 July 2015 telephone conversation (10:46–11:20 a.m.) with Olin Bare from Lexington, VA.

44. 11 January 2015 (11:39 a.m.) email from Mac Benford to Lew Stern.

45. Carlin noted the lengths to which some were prepared to go to attain authenticity: wearing elements of camouflage hunting gear, living in unheated houses, working hard to to "connect" with the culture by living in the South, drinking homemade alcohol. "This is what people were talking about." Author's telephone conversation with Bob Carlin, 11 January 2015.

46. Author's notes, 15 July 2015 telephone conversation (10:46–11:20 a.m.) with Olin Bare from Lexington, VA.

47. Author's notes, 5 March 2015 (5:22–5:48 p.m.) telephone conversation with Gary Ruley; 6 March 2015 (8:38 a.m.) email from Gary Ruley to Lew Stern; 7 March 2015 (11:36 a.m.) email from Gary Ruley to Lew Stern; and 8 March 2015 (10:48 a.m.) email from Gary Ruley to Lew Stern.

48. 11 January 2015 (12:27 p.m.) email from Brad Leftwich to Lew Stern. Also, Author's notes, 17 June 2015 (2:00–2:36 p.m.) telephone conversation with Andy Williams, from Natural Bridge, Virginia.

49. "I was frankly disappointed in Odell, because I know from personal experience that there is immense depth to Tommy's music and didn't understand how Odell could have missed it." 23 January 2015 (1:03 p.m.) email from Brad Leftwich to Lew Stern.

50. 25 August 2014 email from Dwight Diller to Lew Stern; 25 July 2014 email from Dwight Diller to Matthew Evans.

51. 23 January 2015 (1:03 p.m.) email from Brad Leftwich to Lew Stern.

52. Author's notes, 8 August 2015 conversation (3:00–4:00 p.m.) with James Leva in Verona, VA.

53. Brad Leftwich stated: "In those early years, the early 1970s, Lexington was very much in its formative years. There were many talented musicians, but most of them were just learning and didn't have much experience or knowledge of traditional music. Dwight was a much more experienced, developed musician and was in a position to have an influence on the scene there. He has a great deal of charisma for people who are just getting started in old-time music and who want a mentor who can spell out in no uncertain terms what's right and wrong, good and bad, what they should like, and how they should play. It's a very complex world to pick your way through, and people want the certainty that a guru can provide. And Dwight has always liked the role of mentor, molding and shaping younger or less experienced musicians. But as the Lexington scene grew and developed, many of its musicians became respected in their own right and developed tastes and views that Dwight was no longer able to influence and which may have been at odds with his own. Pure speculation, but he may have been disappointed by his loss of influence on the scene." 23 January 2015 (1:03 p.m.) email from Brad Leftwich to Lew Stern.

54. See Ken Perlman, "Dwight Diller and the Music of Pocahontas County," pages 53 and 57. Ken Perlman stated: "In the mid-to-late '70s, Diller became disillusioned with the direction taken by the old-time revival scene and withdrew from participation." Dwight dated this disillusionment earlier than that. In a 1983 interview, Dwight said: "Lexington and the whole Lexington sound degenerated after the alcohol got a hold of it [....] There was some really really, really good music came out of there but there's almost a hedonist scene and I backed out of that scene in 1974. For me I had to find something else. Not the music,

I had to find something else. But I feel like we took the music and gave it a kick. Each step was very important starting with the NLCR, Alan Jabbour, Fuzzy Mountain Boys, and then what happened in Lexington." University of North Carolina at Chapel Hill, Collection Number: 20061, Collection Title: Jack Bernhardt Papers, 1943–2011, Dwight Diller Interview, Elkins, WVA, 3 August 1983, Tape 1, Side 1. Also see 15 October 2014 (3:30 p.m.) email from Dwight Diller to Lew Stern. Some who were familiar with Lexington's old time community in the early 1970s had a very different memory. "It was the 1970s and folks were young," James Leva recalled. "There was a lot of partying, always centered around music. I don't remember drugs being very much in the mix, but maybe it just wasn't obvious. There was a good bit of drinking. Beer, whiskey, often moonshine, were at most every music party and the White Column Inn was a restaurant that served alcohol." Leva concluded: "Things could get wild, but I didn't see degeneration or disintegration in the community." 30 November 2014 (9:26 a.m.) email from James Leva to Lew Stern. Bill Wellington, an old time fiddler and banjo player familiar with Lexington in the late 1970s, described the old time community as a "party scene" where the old time music was "hot, fast" and had a bit of an "acidy sound." The music, Wellington remembered, was "louder and faster," electric in its effect, and energetic in the extreme. Wellington recorded eight West Virginia musicians and singers in the late 1970s in a project sponsored by the Grant County Arts Council with funding by the West Virginia department of Culture and History. In 2009, he assembled a two-part slide show that featured ballad singer Florena Duling and fiddlers Blaine Likens, Israel Welch, and Tom Welch. Author's notes, 21 April 2015 (10:00 a.m.–12:00 p.m.) conversation with Bill Wellington, in Staunton, Virginia.

55. 15 January 2015 (7:20 a.m.) email from Bill Hicks to Lew Stern. Hicks stated that the Red Clay Ramblers was formed in the fall of 1972 when he, Tommy Thompson and Jim Watson teamed up. Mike Craver joined in the spring of 1973, thus "completing" the sound. "The original Red Clay Rambler 'musical idea' is embodied in the 'Stolen Love'" CD," the band's second record, recorded in 1974 and released in 1975. 13 June 2015 (9:27 a.m.) email from Bill Hicks to Lew Stern.

56. Perlman, "Dwight Diller and the Music of Pocahontas County," p. 57. Tellingly, Hicks observed the impact of contemporary social and political developments on the old time music scene: "The Union Grove festival itself, as it became an overly popular phenomenon in the late 1960s, had its own influence on culture. Union Grove, by 1973, was not very different from the free Rolling Stones concert at the Altamont Raceway, in California, in 1969. [...] The whole evolution of a 'modern' old-time music 'scene' is actually part of the social phenomenon that made gigantic 'stars' of Bob Dylan and the Rolling Stones, although it's also kind of an eddy at the edge of the great pyroclastic events of the late 1960s, which were set off by Vietnam, the murder of Martin Luther King, Watergate, etc. Here's a great double feature: 'Harlan County, USA' [and] 'Gimme Shelter.'" 15 January 2015 (7:20 a.m.) email from Bill Hicks to Lew Stern. Hicks's point was that elements of that story—the confluence of real world events that changed American youth, and impacted on public venues for music, social behavior, and the relevance of archaic music and musicians—form at least the backdrop for Dwight's dwindling interest in what was going on in Lexington, Virginia. 15 January 2015 (7:20 a.m.) email from Bill Hicks to Lew Stern. Also see John Bealle, *Old-Time Music and Dance*, pp. 55–56.

57. 4 February 2015 (11:23 p.m.) email from Dwight Diller. Also see 30 December 2014 (1:22 p.m.) email from Dwight Diller to Lew Stern.

58. 29 October 2014 (10:04 a.m.) email from Dick Kimmel to Lew Stern. Also see Ivan Tribe, *Mountaineer Jamboree*, pages 164–165.

59. After Irvine left the band, guitarist Bill Hefner also played mandolin.

60. http://www.traveling219.com/stories/marlinton-lewisburg/the-black-mountain-bluegrass-boys/.

61. The band continued to play through at least 2015 with two sons of the original members. Richard Hefner, born in 1946, the only surviving original member, began to learn bluegrass banjo in the late 1960s, around the time Dwight was pursuing old time banjo. Richard Carpenter, the son the late Harley Carpenter—Hamp Carpeter's son—who played guitar and was the lead singer for the band, died after a struggle with cancer in 1998. Richard's brother, Bill Hefner, was on the guitarist for the group in 1968, and provided baritone vocals. Richard and Bill's uncle, Glenn "Dude" Irvine, born in 1920, played the mandolin. He had always been in a wheelchair. He was on the group's first recording in January 1972. http://mountainmusictrail.com/the-black-mountain-bluegrass-boys/ Also see "Opera House Welcomes Back Black Mountain Bluegrass Boys," *The Pocahontas Times*, 1 August 2014. http://pocahontastimes.com/opera-house-welcomes-back-black-mountain-bluegrass-boys-2/.

62. 29 October 2014 (10:04 a.m.) email from Dick Kimmel to Lew Stern.

63. University of North Carolina at Chapel Hill, Collection Number: 20061, Collection Title: Jack Bernhardt Papers, 1943–2011, Dwight Diller Interview, Elkins, WVA, 3 August 1983, Tape 1, Side 2.

64. There are numerous accounts of the Morris Brothers festivals. See: Bob Heyer, Ivydale: "The Morris Family Old Time Festivals," *Goldenseal*, Summer 1998, http://www.wvculture.org/goldenseal/Summer98/ivydale.html. Also see http://www.mudcat.org/thread.cfm?threadid=69009#1166757; http://www.der.org/films/morris-family-festival.html; http://www.earlyblurs.com/pics/ivydale.htm.

65. In 1971, Howard and his wife took Lee and Sherman Hammons with them to Ivydale. 5 January 2015 (7:11 p.m.) email from Wayne Howard to Lew Stern.

66. 6 November 2014 (2:44 a.m.) email from Dwight Diller to Lew Stern and Dwight Diller, Tom King and Glen Smith at Augusta Heritage Center, Elkins, West Virginia, 1991, audiocassette provided by Bob Thornburg.

67. 19 September email from Dwight Diller to Lew Stern; 20 September 2014 email (10:20 a.m.) from Dwight Diller to Lew Stern.

68. 13 October 2014 (11:04 a.m.) email from Dwight Diller to Lew Stern. Dwight continued: "Along with John and Dave Morris and Glen Smith in 1972 and 1973, Lee Triplett would invite me on stage with him even when I usually did not know many [of the tunes] and often did not have a clue of any the melody notes. But they let me charge on." On Dave Morris, see Sue Rock, "Music," *The Baltimore Grotto News*, National Speleological Society, Baltimore, Maryland, vol. 11, no. 10 (November 1971), p. 5. Rock related her experience at Ivydale in 1971: "Dave can do almost anything and he did. He recited beautiful poetry (Dylan Thomas), strummed his Martin guitar, played a song which he composed himself on the autoharp, danced jigs, and told jokes that he laughed at harder than anybody else—which made everybody laugh at him laughing." http://www.karstportal.org/FileStorage/Baltimore_Grotto/1971-v011-n010.pdf.

69. In Dwight's words: "The Morris Brothers [...] was a crazy time. It was hard at that time for me. Dave Morris said on stage that was some of the hardest years he's ever had." University of North Carolina at Chapel Hill, Collection Number: 20061, Collection Title: Jack Bernhardt Pa-

pers, 1943–2011, Dwight Diller Interview, Elkins, WVA, 3 August 1983, Tape 1, Side 2.

70. https://www.youtube.com/watch?v=pLX5PRfVa2s Dwight recalled: "John Morris was the vocal lead on 'Yonder Come the Hog Eyed Man' and fiddle and harmony vocal. Dave was guitar and lead vocal. John Martin was the snarl and harmonicas. I had banjo and squeal. Our first take was a beauty and the recording machine was not switched on. On our third take Dave broke a string but we kept going. Some good memories of the kindness and graciousness of those folks [....] That banjo was the one I played for quarter century and recently it went to a hidden extended care ward in a banjo nursing home. That banjo never had a name. That was the one used in the studio for the 45 rpm ['Hog Eyed Man'] release." 22 September 2014 (12:21 a.m.) email from Dwight Diller to Lew Stern. On *Dwight Diller's Modal Clawhammer* video, at the very end of the instructional video there is a clip of Dwight playing banjo and John Morris on fiddle, pounding away at "Yew Piney Mountain." The clip, in black and white, might be forty years old or so. They are playing the tune under a big natural rock ledge in Pocahontas County.

71. 20 September 2014 (10:14 a.m.) email from Dwight Diller to Lew Stern.

72. "I am always wary of dealing with people. Always try to not have a photograph with me holding a banjo. If there is a group picture, I will try to always be without a banjo." 6 October 2014 (10:33 a.m.) email from Dwight Diller to Lew Stern.

73. At some point, perhaps during his stage performance years, Dwight took exception to his music ever being played for enjoyment, especially by students. In later years he would explain that he figured that playing music for this purpose engaged the mind, not the heart and the soul. Thinking about his music would ruin any effort to get the students' instincts sharpened so as to focus on the rhythmic core of the music instead of the satisfying components that made it easy, infectious listening music. 6 November 2014 (9:27 p.m.) email from Dwight Diller to Lew Stern.

74. Kilby Spencer, originally from Whitetop, Virginia, made available to me recordings of the banjo contest taped at the 4th Annual Old Time Fiddlers and Bluegrass Convention in Hillsville, Virginia, in June 1970. Kilby learned old-time music from his parents, Thornton and Emily, who have been in the Whitetop Mountain Band for over 40 years. He collects and digitizes rare local recordings, and serves on the board of the Field Recorders' Collective, whose mission is to preserve and release rare field and home recordings of old time music. Dwight was amazed that his contest tunes had survived, and was deeply grateful to hear himself playing, so soon after he had solidified what became his signature banjo sound.

75. 19 December 2014 (2:25 p.m.) email from Dwight Diller to Lew Stern.

76. 19 December 2014 (2:25 p.m.) email from Dwight Diller to Lew Stern.

77. "It was a memorable event, we still talk about it occasionally." 6 February 2015 (11:42 p.m.) email from William Talley to Lew Stern. Carl Baron told me: "Anyway, come August, 1972, Mark [Campbell] (who grew up just across the Blue Ridge in Waynesboro, Virginia) said he'd heard of some festival out near the airport. So, in essence, Mark and I crashed Armin's Alternate Galax festival. The only person I knew there was Trina Milefsky." Baron recalls meeting Bill Hicks, Alan Jabbour, Gerry Milnes, Peter Hoover, probably Mark Gunther from Chicago, Dave Milefsky. He also recalls that most members of the Fuzzy Mountain String Band, Tommy Thompson, other Philadelphia area folks such as Phip Cressman, Doug Linton, Bill Talley, Tom Mylet, and Miles Krassen were at the gathering. 7 February 2015 (10:18 a.m.) email from Carl Baron to Lew Stern. Dwight and Armin Barnett performing "Sally Ann": wtalley.com/diller/A15 Armin—Dwight Sally Ann.wav.

78. "Angeline the Baker," "Quince Dillon's High D," "Jaybird," "Fine Times at Our House" (two cuts), "Locklaven Castle," "Sally Ann," "Frosty Morn," "The Route," "Boatin Up Sandy," "Greasy Coat," "Falls of Richmond," "Sugar Grove Blues" (two cuts), "Old Mother Flannigan," "All Christmas Morn," "Camp Chase" (two cuts, Burl's version and Emmet Bailey's version), "Three Forks of Cheat," "Washington's March," "Pigeon on a Gate," "Miller's Reel," "Rocky Mountain Goat," "Forked Deer," "Paddy on the Turnpike" (two cuts, one in the key of D), "Sally Johnson," "Cuffy," and "Miss McLeod's Reel." 5 February 2015 (3:27 p.m.) email from William Talley to Lew Stern.

79. 14 February 2015 (11:12 a.m.) email from Wayne Howard to Lew Stern. Howard's tape captures 26 tunes, and according to his notes Dwight plays banjo on these: "Jimmy Sutton," "Birdie," "Billy in the Low Ground," "Soldier's Joy," and "Sally Goodin," and may have played "Ragtime Annie." Dwight played banjo for a portion of Burl's fiddling the tune "Leather Breeches," a difficult four-part piece. Howard also provided a tune list for a session at Sherman Hammon's home on 20 April 1973, at which Dwight and Andy Williams played fiddle, and Brenda Williams played banjo. The session does show the basic constancy of repertoire shared by Dwight and Sherman. The three musicians played "John Henry," "Dinah, "Greasy String," "Boatman," "Eliza Jane," "Old Jimmy Johnson," "Sally Ann, "Pretty Little Miss," "Angeline," and "Pretty Little Dog." 3 February 2015 (6:14 p.m.) email from Wayne Howard to Lew Stern.

80. University of North Carolina at Chapel Hill, Collection Number: 20061, Collection Title: Jack Bernhardt Papers, 1943–2011, Dwight Diller Interview, Elkins, WVA, 3 August 1983, Tape 1 of 2.

81. Author's notes, 4 February 2015 (11:00 a.m.–12:00 p.m.) telephone conversation with Dan Levenson. Also see Levenson, "Playing Half-Fast," *Old Time Herald*, vol. 10, no. 7 (October—November 2006).

82. Wayne Howard visited Sherman Hammons at his home in Marlinton, West Virginia, on 6 May 1973, and asked Sherman what he listened for in a fiddler, what made a fiddle good. Sherman's reply spoke to the fact that he did not much care for music played at breakneck speed, as this excerpt from Howard's transcript of that discussion shows. In Sherman's words: "It's the bow. The way he handles that bow. You take a fellow whenever he [ain't]—starts fiddling and he's just a-cutting it all to pieces just as fast—I don't like to hear that at all. [...] I like to hear a [fellow]—you see, you know—time with music's what makes music. You see, when you cut it up like that, it ain't got no time to it. [...] It can't have. It's like singing. Say for instance singing. You can't just start out there singing, just singing just as fast as you can sing. You can't follow a tune, can you?" Wayne Howard, "Transcript, Session 12, Recorded 05/06/1973 at the home of Sherman Hammons, Marlinton, WV, Original Reel Tape: Tape 1, page 2."

83. Author's notes, 1 February 2015 (10:30 a.m.– 11:52 a.m.) telephone conversation with Dwight Diller.

84. Author's notes, 1 February 2015 (10:30 a.m.–11:52 a.m.) telephone conversation with Dwight Diller.

85. Dan Levenson, "Review: 'Just Banjo '99,'" *Banjo Newsletter*, February 2000, pages 6–7.

86. Andrew Diamond, David Dry and Stewart Seidel, "Yew Pine Mountain: Obscure Underground Clawhammer Banjo from Mysterious Central West Virginia," revised, produced and printed in Pocahontas County, West Virginia.

87. Lew Stern, "Review: 'Just Rhythm': West Virginia

Clawhammer Banjo," *Banjo Newsletter*, February 2004, p. 6.

88. Dwight remembered seeing James stop in his aunt and uncle's beer joint in Hillsboro when he was a boy growing up there. "He never owned an automobile and I saw him walking the roads right often." Edn died in 1955. James lived with his parents until his father died. 6 November 2014 (2:44 a.m.) email from Dwight Diller to Lew Stern.

89. "Wanted it far, far more than eat when I was hungry. But it has been a constant fight. Never could get it." 6 November 2014 (2:44 a.m.) email from Dwight Diller to Lew Stern. In a 1997 interview with Ken Perlman, talking of growing up in Pocahontas County, Dwight said: "I got the feelin' that every home had a banjo. Or more homes had banjos than fiddles. It was easier to make.... You could have a banjo real easy. So lots of people had banjos when they didn't have fiddles. The fiddle just demanded a whole lot more investment all the way around.... There weren't many tunes that were really worked out (on banjo) compared to the fiddle. There were hundreds of tunes on the fiddle, just so few on the banjo." See Ken Perlman. "Dwight Diller and the Music of Pocahontas County," p. 55.

90. 6 November 2014 (2:44 a.m.) email from Dwight Diller to Lew Stern.

91. According to Gerald Milnes, Ralph Roberts was born on Poplar Creek of Birch River. His Uncle Jesse played fiddle. Ralph's late brothers were musical. His nephew, Rick Roberts, of Cox's Mills, plays fiddle and mandolin. Milnes states that Ralph "plays a more laid back, Wilson Douglas style. I don't know if they knew each other although they lived in the same county. Ralph knows old tunes, but he is also agreeable to learning tunes he hears that are new to him. His wife, Charlie, is a great fan and encourages Ralph in his music." See 30 December 2014 (10:43 a.m.) email from Gerald Milnes.

92. Regarding Dwight's banjo playing, Roberts told me: "I usually play [fiddle] in DGDG and [Dwight] plays in G, but he has a different style than anyone I've ever heard. He plays more old time stuff, and he plays more like Lee Hammons. He knew Lee and that's where he got his style." Roberts concluded: "The way I see it, Lee played his music from the heart. He played how the song sounded." Author's notes, 5 February 2015 (9:39 a.m.–10:00 a.m.) telephone conversation with Ralph Roberts.

93. 6 November 2014 (2:44 a.m.) email from Dwight Diller to Lew Stern.

94. 9 June 2013 email from Dwight Diller to Lew Stern.

95. 6 September 2014 (2:28 a.m.) email from Dwight Diller to Lew Stern.

96. 5 August 2013 (7:07 p.m.) email from Dwight Diller to Lew Stern; 9 June 2013 email from Dwight Diller to Lew Stern.

97. *"Lee Hammons Banjo: Complete Recordings," "The Hammons Legacy: Field Recordings from Dwight Diller and Wayne Howard,"* liner notes, no date.

98. Dwight explained that Burl Hammons' father, Parris, came from the real frontier in Kentucky but it in mid–1800s that frontier was receding, so elements of the Hammons family migrated to the last frontier in middle–eastern United States, Webster and Pocahontas Counties, in central West Virginia. Dwight recalls that Parris said to Burl, "You are going to play the fiddle or you are going to work but you can't do both." As Dwight reflects on that, the choice, in Parris' mind, was to elect a situation where, in labor, your life was not totally within your control, or to elect a life in which playing the fiddle becomes the central force. 7 September 2014 (1:29 p.m.) email from Dwight Diller to Lew Stern.

99. 6 September 2014 (2:28 a.m.) email from Dwight Diller to Lew Stern.

100. Ivan Tribe, *Mountaineer Jamboree*, pp. 110–137.

101. University of North Carolina at Chapel Hill, Collection Number: 20061, Collection Title: Jack Bernhardt Papers, 1943–2011, Dwight Diller Interview, Elkins, WVA, 3 August 1983, Tape 1, Side 1.

102. University of North Carolina at Chapel Hill, Collection Number: 20061, Collection Title: Jack Bernhardt Papers, 1943–2011, Dwight Diller Interview, Elkins, WVA, 3 August 1983, Tape 1, Side 1. Old time music communities across the country organized themselves in different ways. In early January 2015, Mark Campbell, a traditional musician who grew up in the Shenandoah Valley of Virginia, told me: "The Lexington crowd was good at spreading the word and playing in bands with hot energy, while we in Charlottesville were focused on learning the music. It was a scholarly approach, yes, but has paid off in the long run as the idea of studying each old musician one crossed path with results in a deep understanding of the music. We would go to West Virginia and North Carolina as well as South West Virginia for our sources. It was difficult at first since one week we would be listening to Melvin Wine and the musicians in Glenville, and two weeks later we would be hanging around Tommy Jarrell. It took some time to figure out that one had to learn different styles to spread that far." 12 January 2015 (3:59 p.m.) email from Mark Campbell to Lew Stern.

103. University of North Carolina at Chapel Hill, Collection Number: 20061, Collection Title: Jack Bernhardt Papers, 1943–2011, Dwight Diller Interview, Elkins, WVA, 3 August 1983, Tape 1, Side 1.

104. 17 June 2015 (847 a.m.) email from Bill Hicks to Lew Stern.

105. University of North Carolina at Chapel Hill, Collection Number: 20061, Collection Title: Jack Bernhardt Papers, 1943–2011, Dwight Diller Interview, Elkins, WVA, 3 August 1983, Tape 1, Side 2.

106. In Dwight's words: "The music was very important at that time but at times there wasn't much music being played. Old Man Lee Hammons. I'd go in I'd go up there I may be up there once or twice a week, we'd go in and play five or six or seven or eight tunes we'd fool with them every day. We'd be out working in his shop on some building a dulcimer or something and we'd be laughing and talking and he'd be telling me stories. The man was a mechanical genius too. All this was going on. It was really helping me be saturated." University of North Carolina at Chapel Hill, Collection Number: 20061, Collection Title: Jack Bernhardt Papers, 1943–2011, Dwight Diller Interview, Elkins, WVA, 3 August 1983, Tape 1, Side 2.

107. "Because of this saturation, and because I'm not built that way—I'm too lazy I have to study things in a different way, and it's studied by feeling rather than breaking things down by notes." University of North Carolina at Chapel Hill, Collection Number: 20061, Collection Title: Jack Bernhardt Papers, 1943–2011, Dwight Diller Interview, Elkins, WVA, 3 August 1983, Tape 1, Side 2.

108. University of North Carolina at Chapel Hill, Collection Number: 20061, Collection Title: Jack Bernhardt Papers, 1943–2011, Dwight Diller Interview, Elkins, WVA, 3 August 1983, Tape 1, Side 2. Old time banjo player David Winston who, with Brad Leftwich, played music in the Lexington, Virginia area in the early 1970s, was familiar with the music gatherings at Odell McGuire's home during those years. In early January 2015 Winston told me: "The Lexington scene to me was distinguished by the fact that its 'core value' was to play 'powerfully' either to make the tipsy party-goers flatfoot or with the West Virginia tunes, to channel the 'power' of the haunting old music. I leaned away from the latter as in my mind, at that time, it tended toward the 'sensitive preciousness' sometimes affected by singer-songwriter types. Obviously, my interests were

more in the dancer camp. The 'scene' did seem to have a shared identity that embraced the power, drive and party aspects of the music and sometimes felt superior to the derisively labeled 'tune museum' approach of say, the Fuzzy Mountain String Band, who had their own scene in the Triangle area. This of course was narrow and childish, but not uncommon to zealous new converts to a sect." 10 January 2015 (9:13 a.m.) email from David Winston to Lew Stern.

109. University of North Carolina at Chapel Hill, Collection Number: 20061, Collection Title: Jack Bernhardt Papers, 1943–2011, Dwight Diller Interview, Elkins, WVA, 3 August 1983, Tape 1, Side 2.

110. "I started going to Odell's in 1971. We were looking for something more. He and I would sit up all night long arguing over how to play a tune. I started inviting people from North Carolina. Alex was the only one to show up, Odell would invite [visitors] and we'd gather in for a weekend at his place and play music, and me and him were going head to head. He'd say this is in that tune, this is the way to play that tune, I'd so no, he'd say yes, and well we just keep on and on and on. [...] First of all I grown up in the mountains, growing up poor not dirt poor but I had a feeling. I hunted and fished all the time since I was 6 or 7, I had a feeling for the mountains that you can't get if you live in the city. You can't say that don't mean nothing. It means something." University of North Carolina at Chapel Hill, Collection Number: 20061, Collection Title: Jack Bernhardt Papers, 1943–2011, Dwight Diller Interview, Elkins, WVA, 3 August 1983, Tape 1, Side 2.

111. University of North Carolina at Chapel Hill, Collection Number: 20061, Collection Title: Jack Bernhardt Papers, 1943–2011, Dwight Diller Interview, Elkins, WVA, 3 August 1983, Tape 1, Side 2.

112. Cece Conway made the case that the New Lost City Ramblers were not a significant influence on the Hollow Rock String Band; if anything, the reverse was the case. In Professor Conway's words: "In fall of 1967, Tommy Thompson was thrilled to play the Southern fiddle tunes, which he had learned mostly from Alan [Jabbour], for and with the New Lost City Ramblers while jamming at Herb David's in Ann Arbor, Michigan, before the New Lost City Ramblers' gig that night. It was a lot of fun and I was hearing the New Lost City Ramblers live for the first time. John Cohen was amazed and charmed that our baby son was named Tom Ashley. This was when I got to know the New Lost City Ramblers well enough to later invite them to play a concert at Western Michigan University where I taught." Interestingly, Professor Conway speculated that the New Lost City Ramblers may have been an influence on Tommy Thompson and may have contributed to shaping his repertoire with the Red Clay Ramblers, although Thompson, according to Conway, was also influenced by local North Carolina singers such as Tom Turner who sang a lot of songs that were "early bluegrass," a "somewhat blurred category." 13 July 2015 (1:45 p.m.) email from Cece Conway to Lew Stern.

113. University of North Carolina at Chapel Hill, Collection Number: 20061, Collection Title: Jack Bernhardt Papers, 1943–2011, Dwight Diller Interview, Elkins, WVA, 3 August 1983, Tape 1, Side 2. Bill Hicks dissented from this depiction of the Chapel Hill old time community: "I think Dwight and possibly Odell and the whole Lexington scene constructed a strange and unnecessary strawman to push against, namely the 'Chapel Hill way.' I was part of the Chapel Hill old-time music community from 1966 until 1974, at which point I was solidly entrenched in the Red Clay Ramblers, i.e., had become a working musician, which means you have to find gigs to play and don't hang out so much at home. I can't say who actually "was" this Chapel Hill music scene after 1974. Hit warn't me. Alan Jabbour had moved away. So had the Owens, Malcolm and Blanton, and Tom Carter, though Blanton and Tom had become musicologists doing academic collecting projects during this period of time. The Fuzzy Mountain band hardly existed except as a little group around Barry and Sharon Poss (nee Sandomirsky) who played at home in Durham and backed up Fred Cockerham some. So I can't say with any clarity who or what the Lexington people were describing." 14 June 2015 (9:28 a.m.) email from Bill Hicks to Lew Stern.

114. University of North Carolina at Chapel Hill, Collection Number: 20061, Collection Title: Jack Bernhardt Papers, 1943–2011, Dwight Diller Interview, Elkins, WVA, 3 August 1983, Tape 1, Side 2.

Chapter Four

1. 25 November 2014 (5:28 p.m.) email from Dwight Diller to Lew Stern.

2. 25 November 2014 (5:28 p.m.) email from Dwight Diller to Lew Stern.

3. 26 August 2014, Dwight Diller Email to Lew Stern.

4. See John Lilly, "The Morris Brothers Music from the Head of the Holler," *Goldenseal*, Spring 2011, vol. 37, issue 1, p. 52.

5. 26 August 2014, Dwight Diller Email to Lew Stern.

6. 25 November 2014 (5:28 p.m.) email from Dwight Diller to Lew Stern. At least two pastors provided some guidance to Dwight in this period: Eugene Ten Brink and David Rittenhouse. Ten Brink was a missionary of the Reformed Church in America who served in partnership with the Church of South India from 1946 to 1967. In 1967, he and his family returned to the United States, and sometime after that he was admitted to the priesthood in the Episcopal Church. He served as an Episcopal priest in West Virginia. Bruce Molsky remembered visiting Reverend Ten Brink at his house that may have been in Marlinton. It was a cold house, Molsky recalled, and Ten Brink was wearing layers of clothing. Molsky also remembered that the visit took place during a time when Dwight was having an intense religious experience, suggesting that it could have been in the mid–1970s, or early 1980s. 25 September 2015 (7:35 a.m.) email from Bruce Molsky to Lew Stern; 29 September 2015 (11:14 a.m.) email from Victoria Fanning, Eerdmans Publishing House, relaying information from Eugene Heideman, author of *From Mission to Church: The Reformed Church in America Mission to India* (Eerdmans, 2001). David Rittenhouse, a Church of the Brethren pastor, recalled that he baptized Dwight in August 1976, in Knapp's Creek, Pocahontas County. He remembered that Dwight often talked to Ten Brink about matters of faith, and that Ten Brink himself was a brilliant man, a good pastor—he served in an Episcopal church in Marlinton—and was an important source of encouragement for Dwight. Rittenhouse also remembered Dwight as a man possessed of an inquisitive mind who used to come by to visit, and sit and talk through all manner of philosophical issues. In the end, Rittenhouse observed, he worked his way through these thoughts and questions, and made a "simple commitment to Christ." Rittenhouse recalled that Dwight embraced the way of the Church of the Brethren because he liked the idea of a church that was not so wrapped up in doctrine but focused instead on life. Rittenhouse said of Dwight: "In a time in his life when he was unsure of who he was, his Grandmother's prayers meant a lot to him."

7. Allen Johnson observed that Dwight "had disapproval from some in the Mennonite Church for his divorce from his first wife, Molly, and marriage to Elaine. But overall I think he was accepted for his faith." 20 October 2014 (2:55 p.m.) email from Allen Johnson to Lew Stern. David

Rittenhouse, a Church of the Brethren member from Dunmore, West Virginia, knew that Dwight felt that what happened to his marriages was enough to disqualify him from continued service to the church. Rittenhouse believed that both the Brethren and the Mennonites, while they did not approve of divorce, understood the complexities of life and reasoned that the circumstances that impacted on an individual should not interrupt that person's ability to continue as a servant to Christ. Author's notes, 5 October 2015 (9:58–1010 a.m.) telephone conversation with David Rittenhouse from Dunmore, West Virginia.

8. 3 October 2014 (5:35 a.m.) email from Dwight Diller to Lew Stern.

9. 5 October 2014 (1:54 p.m.) email from Dwight Diller to Lew Stern. "I basically know nothing about the Mennonites. The Lord used them to help me get some concentrated help in my constant searching." 5 October 2014 (1:54 p.m.) email from Dwight Diller to Lew Stern.

10. Official Transcript of Academic Record, Dwight Hamilton Diller, issued by David A. Detrow, University Registrar, Eastern Mennonite University, Seminary Division, 5 January 2015.

11. Professor Brunk earned his bachelor of arts degree from Eastern Mennonite University in 1961, and a bachelor of divinity in 1964. In 1975 he was awarded a theological doctorate by Union Theological Seminary in Virginia. http://www.emu.edu/seminary/about/retired-faculty/.

12. Official Transcript of Academic Record, Dwight Hamilton Diller, issued by David A. Detrow, University Registrar, Eastern Mennonite University, Seminary Division, 5 January 2015.

13. 21 January 2015 (3:43 p.m.) email from George Brunk to Lew Stern.

14. Official Transcript of Academic Record, Dwight Hamilton Diller, issued by David A. Detrow, University Registrar, Eastern Mennonite University, Seminary Division, 5 January 2015.

15. A. Donald Augsburger was a pastor in the North Goshen Mennonite Church, established in 1936 in Goshen, Indiana, as an outpost of College Mennonite Church. He was also a high school principal for a number of years in Goshen. Between 1974 and 1980 he served as a permanent lead pastor at Park View Mennonite Church (PVMC), a congregation founded in 1953 as the campus church of Eastern Mennonite College, now Eastern Mennonite University. Professor Augsburger focused his ministry on biblical preaching and identified himself as a topical preacher. In the 1980s he served as a pastor at the Bahia Vista Mennonite Church (formerly known as Tuttle Avenue Mennonite Church), located in Sarasota, Florida. His brother Myron was appointed president of Eastern Mennonite University (EMU) in 1965. See: http://www.northgoshenmc.com/information/history.html; http://findingharmonyblog.com/2014/04/03/finding-home-and-harmony-the-first-preacher-i-ever-heard/; http://www.pvmchurch.org/congregational-history.html; and Don Augsburger, "Focus on Church Renewal," *The Seminarian* (Eastern Mennonite Seminary, Harrisonburg, Virginia, February, 1979), p. 1; Author's notes, 29 September 2014 telephone conversation with Donald Augsburger from Harrisonburg, Virginia.

16. 7 September 2014 (1:29 p.m.) email from Dwight Diller to Lew Stern.

17. http://www.emu.edu/personnel/people/show/yoderlm.

18. Official Transcript of Academic Record, Dwight Hamilton Diller, issued by David A. Detrow, University Registrar, Eastern Mennonite University, Seminary Division, 5 January 2015.

19. Author's notes, 17 October 2014 (10:00 a.m.–12:00 p.m.) telephone conversation with Dwight Diller.

20. 11 September 2014, telephone conversation with Dwight Diller.

21. http://www.newmarkethistoricalsociety.org/Bethlehem_Stone_Church4.web.pdf.

22. Author's notes, 22 October 2014 (1:00 p.m.–3:00 p.m.) telephone conversation with Dwight Diller.

23. Author's notes, 17 October 2014 (10:00 a.m.–12:00 p.m.) telephone conversation with Dwight Diller.

24. Author's notes, 17 October 2014 (10:00 a.m.–12:00 p.m.) telephone conversation with Dwight Diller.

25. 15 September 2014 telephone conversation between Dwight Diller and Lew Stern.

26. Author's notes, 21 October 2014 (1:00–3:00 p.m.) telephone conversation with Dwight Diller.

27. Author's notes, 22 October 2014 (1:00 p.m.–3:00 p.m.) telephone conversation with Dwight Diller.

28. 6 August 2013 email from Dwight Diller to Lew Stern.

29. *See* http://www.banjohangout.org/archive/160312 *and* http://www.fiddlehangout.com/archive/30272.

30. http://www.banjohangout.org/reviews/search.asp?m=m&v=9735&redir=true

31. Author's notes, 21 October 2014 (1:00–3:00 p.m.) telephone conversation with Dwight Diller.

32. 3 March 2–15 (8:49 a.m.) email from Dwight Diller to Lew Stern. As West Virginia fiddler Bobby Taylor put it, people who are there for the party are wasting their time. Author's notes, 1 June 2015 (11:10 a.m.–12:12 p.m.) telephone conversation with Bobby Taylor from St. Albans, West Virginia.

33. 3 March 2015 (8:49 a.m.) email from Dwight Diller to Lew Stern.

34. Author's notes, 3 March 2015 (9:30–10:30 a.m.) telephone conversation with Dwight Diller.

35. Author's notes, 23 February 2015 (10:30–11:30 a.m.) telephone conversation with Dwight Diller.

36. 10 December 2014 (1:02 a.m.) email from Dwight Diller to Lew Stern; 12 December 2014 (5:50 p.m.) email from Dwight Diller to Lew Stern; 5 February 2015 (3:40 p.m.) email from Dwight Diller to Lew Stern.

37. Author's notes, 23 February 2015 (10:30–11:30 a.m.) telephone conversation with Dwight Diller.

38. Author's notes, 23 February 2015 (10:30–11:30 a.m.) telephone conversation with Dwight Diller.

39. Author's notes, 23 February 2015 (10:30–11:30 a.m.) telephone conversation with Dwight Diller.

Chapter Five

1. Dwight kept no systematic records of his teaching over time. He does remember travelling to the Midwest and the West for classes, and there is ample documentation of his retreats in the form of personal cassettes recorded during the course of numerous workshops of his by banjo and fiddle students. Such records indicate, for example, that Dwight, the Bing Brothers and Tom King conducted a workshop on the banjo in string bands at the Augusta Heritage Center, in Elkins, West Virginia, in 1988. Dwight taught banjo at Cass, West Virginia, from late the late 1980s through at least the late 1990s. In 1991 he conducted a banjo workshop and evening concert in Seneca Park, on the Greenbrier River, in West Virginia. He conducted numerous banjo workshops at the homes of friends and students, such as the one Bob Thornburg hosted in Bishop, California, in 1995. Dwight organized a banjo camp at D Base Camp near the Virginia Lakes in Bishop, California, in September 1997, and in 1997 he conducted a banjo camp in Port Ludlow, Washington. Dwight held a banjo workshop at the home of Tersh McCracken near Red Lodge, Montana, in September 2000, and during the summer of 2001 he conducted a banjo retreat in Vancou-

ver, British Columbia, that was hosted by Stewart Seidel. In 2002 and 2003 he conducted long weekend sessions at my home in northern Virginia.

2. See University of North Carolina at Chapel Hill, Collection Number: 20061, Collection Title: Jack Bernhardt Papers, 1943–2011, Dwight Diller Interview, Elkins, WVA, 3 August 1983, Tape 1, Side 2. Also see Sheila Kay Adams, *Come Go Home with Me*, pp. ix, x.

3. 3 January 2015 (11:21 a.m.) email from Wayne Howard to Lew Stern.

4. 19 February 2015 (4:42 p.m.) email from Rock Garton to Lew Stern.

5. AFS 17,016 (LWO 7976 Reel 3) contains a cassette tape of Ward Jarvis of near Gaysville, Ohio, recorded 1 September 1973 by Bob Buhl. The third cut on side two of the tape included a spoken comment by Jarvis on Becky Williams' "skills at pounding the banjo."

6. 19 February 2015 (4:42 p.m.) email from Rock Garton to Lew Stern. Ron Mullennex's recollection is slightly different than Garton's memory. Mullennex explained: "When I was in Morgantown I ran into Dwight Diller. [...] We had a mutual interest in music. He had only been playing a year or two. I had been playing three-finger style [banjo]. I liked what he was doing. He took the time to show me [his clawhammer playing style]. We were pretty good friends for a while, went through a lot of things together. The semester when he did teach there he remembers me [being] in that class, but that summer [of 1972] I was in Basic Training, [and in the fall of 1972] I was working construction. I did travel to Morgantown [and] helped [Dwight] with six or eight people teaching guitar." Author's notes, 12 January 2015 (6:00–6:30 p.m.) telephone conversation with Ron Mullennex from Bluefield, West Virginia.

7. Audiocassettes made of some of these sessions show that Dwight kept the sessions focused on tunes with similar structure, overlapping licks, and that he played fairly sparse and rhythmic. Andy Williams, playing "Leather Britches," and the A.A. Cutters playing "Lisa Jane," "Jimmy Johnson," and "Boatman," audiocassette made by Rock Gorton in Morgantown, West Virginia, early 1970s; A.A. Cutters String Band, audiocassette made by Rock Gorton in Morgantown, West Virginia, early 1970 (side one); Dwight Diller and Andy Williams, Cindy Hutchinson, jam tape, audiocassette made by Rock Gorton in Morgantown, West Virginia, early 1970 (side two); Rock Gorton playing dulcimer and fiddle; Jack Ramsey playing banjo; Ron Mullennex, Jack Ramsey, Rock Garton, et al., audiocassette made by Rock Garton in Morgantown, West Virginia, early 1970 (sides one and two).

8. Author's notes, 25 May 2015 (12:30–12:40 p.m.) telephone conversation with Jackie Horvath, from Mount Morris, Pennsylvania. Dick Kimmel said of the A.A. Cutters: "I was impressed with how serious they were about old-time fiddle music, which helped foster that serious approach to old-time music in me. From my observations, this might have been the first time I saw Dwight being the 'task master' making sure the people were playing old-time music the 'right' way. It worked, as the band sounded great together. I don't think I ever heard these folks do a formal performance, but just heard them around Dwight's apartment." 3 June 2015 (4:20 a.m.) email from Dick Kimmel to Lew Stern.

9. Author's notes, 14 March 2015 (2:00–4:00 p.m.) meeting in Staunton, Virginia, with David Winston, from Lexington, Virginia.

10. 21 May 2015 (7:46 p.m.) email from David Winston to Lew Stern. Charlie Trimble was the father of Dwight's first wife, Molly. Winston recalled: "Dwight had taught a bunch of people to play very much in his style and there could be six or seven banjo players surrounding one fiddle." See Steve Arkin, "David Winston," *Banjo Newsletter*, April 2015, online edition: https://banjonews.com/2015-04/david_winston_interview_by_steve_arkin.html.

11. 31 October 2014 (11:46 a.m.) email from Carl Baron to Lew Stern.

12. Author's notes, 2 December 2014 interview with Dick Kimmel.

13. See Dwight Diller, banjo classes taught as Cass, West Virginia, 1988, 1989, 1990 and 1991: Fourteen audiocassettes provided by Bob Thornburg; "Perfect Porch: A Banjo Camp with Dwight Diller and Ken Perlman," taped at Cass, Pocahontas County, West Virginia, during the week of 13 July 1998. Also see Michael Brooks, "North—South Banjo Camp—July 12–18 1998 in Cass, West Virginia: Rhythm by Dwight Diller and Several Notes by Ken Perlman," *Mississippi Old-Time Music Society Newsletter*, vol. 3, no. 8 (September 1998).

14. Lee Talmadge stated: "My understanding is he began coming up to Michigan in the early to mid-1990s and conducted banjo camps in the Portland Michigan area. Doug Van Gundy and Paul Gartner also came up with Dwight, probably from about 1997 to 2002 and/or made contacts up here because of the connection with him. There still exists up here a small group of folks, I can think of six or seven who I play music with, who were his students and his influence and the music he taught them, is foundational to their love for old time music, and in some cases maybe their lives." 3 August 2015 (9:46 a.m.) email from Lee Talmadge to Lew Stern.

15. http://chestertownspy.org/2014/10/05/mainstays-fallfest-concludes-with-celebrating-the-banjo/ 26 January 2015 (11:34 a.m.) email from Dwight Diller to Lew Stern. Peter Irvin organized U.K. tours for the band Cordelia's Dad, whose members introduced Irvin to Dwight's music. Irvin ended up arranging a couple of U.K. trips for Dwight, and chauffeuring him around during his visits to England; as Irvin puts it, he "spent quite a lot of time with him in close confinement!" 26 February 2015 (5:12 a.m.) email from Phil Tyler to Lew Stern. 10 April 2015 (3:01 p.m.) email from Nick Pilley to Lew Stern.

16. 10 April 2015 (3:01 p.m.) email from Nick Pilley to Lew Stern. Dwight attended the 4th National Festival of American Old Time Music and Dance in Gainsborough, Lincolnshire, in 1998. See Carrie Osborne, "Killer Diller," *Folk Roots* (United Kingdom), no. 180 (June 1998), pages 17–18. Keith Johnson, the founder of FOAOTMAD and the driving force behind the Gainsborough Festival, passed away on 2 May 2015. See: http://foaotmad.org.uk/wordpress/news/?p=1488; http://www.mudcat.org/thread.cfm?threadid=157139; and http://www.banjohangout.org/topic/303551.

17. 10 May 2015 (759 p.m.) email from Phil Tyler to Lew Stern.

18. 1 May 2015 (1:23 p.m.) email from Betty Vornbrock to Lew Stern; 1 May 2015 (7:29 a.m.) email from Billy Cornette to Lew Stern.

19. Teri Hayes hosted banjo workshops in Pittsburgh, Pennsylvania, from 1996 to 1999. Beginning in 2000, Cindy Harris organized the workshops in her living room in Pittsburgh, and Hayes helped recruit attendees, and was herself a banjo student. In 2005, the December visit to Pittsburgh was cancelled; Dwight was recuperating from the car accident in Marlinton. In 2006 and 2007 Hayes attended the workshops as a fiddle student, and Harris undertook the organizing and hosting responsibilities herself. Hayes did not participate in the Pittsburgh workshops after 2007, but she did attend the house concerts; the workshops and concerts were held in Harris' home from December 2006 through December 2014. 10 May 2015 (2:56 p.m.) email from Cindy Harris to Lew Stern.

20. http://dwightdiller.com/camp/lowdown-i/lew-sterns-hosting-experience/.

21. http://dwightdiller.com/2013/11/20/the-acknowledgements/.
22. https://www.banjohangout.org/reviews/search.asp?m=m&v=9735&redir=true.
23. http://www.imdb.com/title/tt0432285/plotsummary?ref_=tt_ov_pl.
24. Author's notes, 13 July 2015 (3:52–4:20 p.m.) telephone conversation with John Phelan, from northern Los Angeles, California; Author's notes, 31 August 2015 telephone conversation (11:00 a.m.–11:36 a.m.) with Joseph Rizzi, from San Francisco, California.
25. http://www.banjohangout.org/archive/83414.
26. http://www.banjohangout.org/archive/83414 In August 2015 Rizzi made the point that there was little in the way of any "Hollywood" interest in the film project that from the beginning was a decidedly local, personal and small scale venture based on both his enthusiasm for the music and his son-in-law's embrace of the concept for a film that captured elements of Dwight's personal story, suggesting that the reference Dwight made to Hollywood was more of a metaphor than a recollection of the production and distribution issues involved in making *The Fifth String*. Author's notes, 31 August 2015 telephone conversation (11:00 a.m.–11:36 a.m.) with Joseph Rizzi, from San Francisco, California.
27. "That's the main role I see for myself, not as a musician but as a teacher, a person who has ability with words and feeling to push people. [...] it gives my life meaning [....] That gives my life meaning, keep on keeping on, you're on the right track, don't make it any more than it is, just be the vehicle." University of North Carolina at Chapel Hill, Collection Number: 20061, Collection Title: Jack Bernhardt Papers, 1943–2011, Dwight Diller Interview, Elkins, WVA, 3 August 1983, Tape 1, Side 1.
28. Bates Littlehales, "Dwight Diller," p. 13.
29. University of North Carolina at Chapel Hill, Collection Number: 20061, Collection Title: Jack Bernhardt Papers, 1943–2011, Dwight Diller Interview, Elkins, WVA, 3 August 1983, Tape 2, Side 1. Also see University of North Carolina at Chapel Hill, Collection Number: 20061, Collection Title: Jack Bernhardt Papers, 1943–2011, Dwight Diller Interview, Elkins, WVA, 3 August 1983, Tape 2, Side 2.
30. Early in his teaching experience, Dwight resolved not to confront these accusations. As he explained: "I've been letting these stories just go along because you can't really stop them. If people want it to where they'll beat their way through that kind of fear, they will be dead serious about learning. We can then relax and have fun too. I like to build a level of trust and then teach from that foundation. If I give all I got then I can expect that from my student also." See Bates Littlehales, "Dwight Diller," page 13. Bobby Taylor, a fourth generation West Virginia fiddler, seemed to teach in a similar fashion, and suggested that older fiddlers followed a similar recipe in their own informal teaching sessions. Kentucky fiddler J.P. Fraley, Sam Jarvis, and John Summers zeroed in on one favorite tune, urged students to drill down on that tune and "get it perfectly," resist the urge to play five thousand tunes, play one "favorite tune" over and over until all the elements of that tune become clear. Taylor stated "Once you've got it pieces of it and basic technique will lead you to other tunes." Author's notes, 1 June 2015 (11:10 a.m.–12:12 p.m.) telephone conversation with Bobby Taylor from St. Albans, West Virginia. Dwight spoke to these issues in a 1999 interview, "Sunday Folks," KCDS radio interview with Dwight Diller, Seattle, Washington, 1999.
31. Pat Costello, Interview with Dwight Diller, Published 22 July 2012, *From the Down Neck Gazette*. Filmed in 2000. https://www.youtube.com/watch?v=zujNF7MCKro.
32. The first step, to Dwight, was always this: "Quit trying to learn the banjo so you can learn the music." As he put it, "I don't see myself as a teacher of banjo tunes. [I do not] teach you how to play tunes, [I teach] how play the banjo." University of North Carolina at Chapel Hill, Collection Number: 20061, Collection Title: Jack Bernhardt Papers, 1943–2011, Dwight Diller Interview, Elkins, WVA, 3 August 1983, Tape 1, Side 1.
33. 25 August 2014 email from Dwight Diller to Lew Stern. Vivian Wagner quotes the fiddler Johnny Gimble as saying: "There's a lot of notes in that song, but they're not saying anything," in *Fiddler: One Woman, Four Strings, and 8,000 Miles of Music* (New York: Citadel, 2010), p. 130.
34. Lesson tapes, 28 January 1996, Brevard, North Carolina, digitized courtesy of Carroll Smith.
35. University of North Carolina at Chapel Hill, Collection Number: 20061, Collection Title: Jack Bernhardt Papers, 1943–2011, Dwight Diller Interview, Elkins, WVA, 3 August 1983, Tape 2, Side 1. Twelve years later, in his 1996 *Banjo Newsletter* interview, Dwight underscored the continued importance of these elements: "You have to ask yourself whether you're doing the music for your sake or for the music's sake. That's a question that we all as musicians have to ask all the time. Am I trying to get attention? Am I using it for my own gain? That kind of selfishness shows disrespect for the music." Littlehales, "Dwight Diller," p. 14. Dwight reiterates substantially the same message in a 2000 interview with Pat Costello. See Pat Costello, Interview with Dwight Diller, published on 22 July 2012, from *The Down Neck Gazette*. Filmed in 2000. https://www.youtube.com/watch?v=zujNF7MCKro.
36. University of North Carolina at Chapel Hill, Collection Number: 20061, Collection Title: Jack Bernhardt Papers, 1943–2011, Dwight Diller Interview, Elkins, WVA, 3 August 1983, Tape 2, Side 1.
37. Littlehales, "Dwight Diller," p. 13.
38. Pat Costello, Interview with Dwight Diller, Published 22 July 2012 *From the Down Neck Gazette*. Filmed in 2000. https://www.youtube.com/watch?v=zujNF7MCKro.
39. University of North Carolina at Chapel Hill, Collection Number: 20061, Collection Title: Jack Bernhardt Papers, 1943–2011, Dwight Diller Interview, Elkins, WVA, 3 August 1983, Tape 1, Side 1.
40. A beginner "knows little to nothing about the banjo and/or old time music. [...] Needs to get started properly on the 'rhythm hand' [usually right] using drill. This is the frustrating work but pays the most dividends in the long run. Get it right in the beginning and you don't have to go back and unlearn and relearn. Unlearning the poor, limiting habits and then relearning for good rhythm is the most tedious and most frustrating part of the process. Get it right the first time. To unlearn and relearn is when the real tears flow, real anger and frustration surfaces, and everything in the student says 'I'm gonna walk away or totally quit. I'll never get it.'" http://dwightdiller.com/camp/learning-levels/
41. In Dwight's words, the student "Begins to understand medium sized and larger 'jams' are killers for learning and proper playing the Music. Recognizes that the best way to play this music, in ensemble, is a banjo and fiddle w/ fiddle leading and banjo giving maximum support underneath. Has come to understand that speed rounds off the corners of each individual tune thus making it a 'festival' tune which is to be avoided at all costs for the sake of the music. Treating it in 'festival' way, a jam 'session' way is literally almost always an insult to the old time mountain Music." http://dwightdiller.com/camp/learning-levels/.
42. "Starting to be able to articulate the notes so the sound of each note has its own individual shape. This is extremely hard to learn. Takes years of listening, absorbing, cogitating before actually setting out to do this on the

instrument. If it is not inside so a person can, as Mose Coffman—the old fiddler from nearby said, "you have to be able to whistle, hum, or sing the tune before you can just begin to play it." Is willing to play honest music. Moving away from trying to grab the glory. Grabbing for glory, again, is an insult to the Music." http://dwightdiller.com/camp/learning-levels/.

43. http://dwightdiller.com/camp/learning-levels/.

44. The "rifle" metaphor interestingly connects to the fact that guns were, as Dwight recalls, prominent in his life: "When a young boy I had no father around. My uncle took me under his wing. Hunting and fishing. [...] But those times with that family and another up the road at Cass were good times. Much of my life has been a mess. Finally realized the other day, guns are my way of reconnecting with those good times I had as a boy." 25 August 2014 email from Dwight Diller to Lew Stern; 25 July 2014 email from Dwight Diller to Matthew Evans.

45. James Yeager, "Scientist vs Caveman—"Why I Cannot Train You," 30 December 2013, https://www.youtube.com/watch?v=pJ6HubpLSVM. Yeager argues that "Skills not learned in an adrenalized state cannot be replicated in an adrenalized state." Also see: http://www.TacticalResponse.com.

46. 22 September 2014 (12:57 p.m.) from Dwight Diller to Lew Stern.

47. 22 September 2014 (12:57 p.m.) from Dwight Diller to Lew Stern. There was in what Dwight was saying here something very much akin to what the philosopher and educator Jean Jacques Rousseau had to say in the mid-1700s about learning and about knowing. Rousseau suggested that the human *esprit* might be able to perceive matter directly, without reflection. That is to say, if "the idea that strikes the brain does not penetrate to the heart, it is nothing [nulle]." In many ways, this is what Dwight was getting at in saying that one will never quite grasp and internalize the old music by relying on brainpower exclusively. Tracy Strong has pointed out, "For something to 'penetrate to the heart' means, then, for it to become part of the way a person thinks, reasons, acts, and feels, rather than being entailed by those qualities. It is to become part of the constitution of a person rather than an acquired predicate. Why, without this, is an idea *nulle*? Because it remains unincorporated; it has not been made flesh and given real existence in and through a human being." In short, "Rousseau wants his understandings to penetrate beneath assessment to become a part of the assessment itself." See Tracy Strong, "Music, the Passions, and Political Freedom in Rousseau," 2010, page 2. Also see Philip Kennicott, "How to View Art: Be Dead Serious About It, But Don't Expect Too Much," *Washington Post*, 1 October 2014, http://www.washingtonpost.com/entertainment/museums/how-to-view-art-be-dead-serious-about-it-but-dont-expect-too-much/2014/10/01/28f7cdba-459a-11e4-b47c-f5889e061e5f_story.html?wpisrc=nl-eve&wpmm=1.

48. Dick Kimmel, "Thumpin' for Clawhammer Pickers–'An Appalachian Banjo Lesson, by Charles Kimmel,' and 'Marching Through Georgia,'" *Banjo Newsletter*, vol. 3, no. 2 (December 1975), p. 8.

49. 4 November 2014 (9:54 a.m.) email from Dwight Diller to Lew Stern.

50. Dwight found an online version of a kind of metronomic exercise that went beyond the "dull" tick-tock of the standard metronome that did not force the player to fight back against the rhythm, or coax the player to anticipate the beat. [See: https://www.youtube.com/watch?v=4wEilxoIGtg.] Dwight instructed: "This 160bpm is the correct speed for me on the fiddle. Best save up a bunch of that liquor money and buy good set head phones. Play up against drum beat with strings dead [suppressed by the left hand]. Drive the beat really hard up against the wall of the beat. Make the drum rhythm 'jump really hard.' This is important because there is no left hand working. [...] The human mind can only pick out melody notes. [...] All the human mind can do, once again, is beat out some kind of melody notes in a string. It has nothing alive within it. Dull, dead, dead as a doornail." 4 November 2014 (9:54 a.m.) email from Dwight Diller to Lew Stern.

51. Dwight suggested: "Now try this one and get the right hand doing exactly what fits with this: https://www.youtube.com/watch?v=Iowsqj3utbs This will keep you up again the wall. This will require you to slow down but you cannot, cannot, cannot play straight: https://www.youtube.com/watch?v=e2oXv8l0zg8" 4 November 2014 (9:54 a.m.) email from Dwight Diller to Lew Stern.

52. 4 November 2014 (9:54 a.m.) email from Dwight Diller to Lew Stern.

53. "Finally, on May 23rd last year after 28 years or maybe a little longer than that I finally had a breakthrough on the fiddle so I have really only been playing the fiddle for about a year. Cause I've never been a fiddler. I just run up against a wall and run up against it and just kept fighting through it through all these years and finally oh it's been awful, I understand about my students having a hard time, I really understand. Cause I couldn't do it myself. I could do it on the banjo but I couldn't do it on the fiddle." "Sunday Folks," KCDS radio interview with Dwight Diller, Seattle, Washington, 1999. Also see Dwight Diller house concert, Pittsburgh, Pennsylvania, December 2011. Seven digital audio files provided by Teri Hayes; http://www.fiddlehangout.com/archive/19878; *and* Cindy Harris, "Accepting Your Babble," 15 July 2011. http://dwightdiller.com/links/accepting-your-babble/.

54. Author's notes, 14 March 2015 (2:00–4:00 p.m.) meeting in Staunton, VA, with David Winston, from Lexington, Virginia; Author's notes, 8 May 2015 (12:00 p.m.–3:30 p.m.) conversation with Al Tharp, in Staunton, Virginia; Author's notes, 17 June 2015 (2:00–2:36 p.m.) telephone conversation with Andy Williams, from Natural Bridge, Virginia.

55. Lesson tapes, 28 January 1996, Brevard, North Carolina, digitized courtesy of Carroll Smith.

56. On Currance Hammonds, see Milnes, "The Hammonds Family of Randolph County," p. 13. On Woody Simmons, see Tribe, *Mountaneer Jamboree*, p. 134.

57. Author's notes, 15 June 2015 (7:00–7:30 a.m.) telephone conversation with Doug Van Gundy, from Elkins, West Virginia. Interestingly, Van Gundy made the point that Dwight's thinking about all this had a very cerebral dimension to it, while Dwight himself long believed that most of this learning about the old music and its practitioners needs to be conducted outside of the brain, in a spiritual manner using other, non-analytical resources. Van Gundy—and others—have pointed out that that Dwight "spent a lot of time in his head," thinking profound and enduring thoughts about the music and many other things. He was "deeply philosophical" in his approach to many of these issues, especially about the traditional music. He had "thought about it so much" that it had become a "spiritual" process. Van Gundy stated that it was unlikely this kind of intensive contemplation could be started in the spirit, and that he himself needed to have these things "in his head," addressed intellectually and analytically, before he could go beyond the physicality of the music. Regarding the "physicality of playing," Bill Hicks observed that music, or specifically fiddling, is "a combination of physicality and mental accuracy or focus." He argued that this combination was essential, and that "muscle memory" described a concept that included both the physical and mental." 14 June 2015 (9:238 a.m.) email from Bill Hicks to Lew Stern.

58. Littlehales, "Dwight Diller," page 13. In a 1999 interview, Dwight said: "My dad said once you've got to eat a pack of salt with somebody before you really get to know them. That takes a little while. You gotta eat a pack of salt before you really start catching onto what this music is really about. And that's why what troubles me is bouncing from one kind of music to another or this or that." "Sunday Folks," KCDS radio interview with Dwight Diller, Seattle, Washington, 1999.

59. 25 August 2014 email from Dwight Diller to Lew Stern.

60. *Flat Foot in the Ashes: Harvey Sampson and the Big Possum String Band*, CD, no date.

61. Lesson tapes, 28 January 1996, Brevard, North Carolina, digitized courtesy of Carroll Smith.

62. Lesson tapes, 28 January 1996, Brevard, North Carolina, digitized courtesy of Carroll Smith. Also see Milnes, *Play of a Fiddle*, p. 29.

63. 9 June 2015 (12:58 p.m.) email from Howard Zane to Lew Stern; 9 June 2015 (1:51 p.m.) email from Scott Prouty to Lew Stern; 9 June 2015 (4:43 p.m.) email from Ken Perlman to Lew Stern; 11 June 2015 (9:28 a.m.) email from Ron Mullennex to Lew Stern.

64. Dwight Diller, Jam tapes, Celestial Mountain Music Store, Brevard, North Carolina, 27 January 1996, audio digitized by Carroll Smith; Dwight Diller, Lesson tapes, Celestial Mountain Music Store, Brevard, North Carolina, 28 January 1996, audio digitized by Carroll Smith; Dwight Diller, Lesson tapes, Celestial Mountain Music Store, Brevard, North Carolina, January 1997, audio digitized by Carroll Smith; Dwight Diller. Banjo camp, D Base Camp, Virginia Lakes and Bishop, California, September 1997, two audiocassettes provided by Bob Thornburg; Dwight Diller, recording session, Cass, West Virginia, 1998, one audiocassette provided by Bob Thornburg; Dwight Diller, Banjo Camp, Port Ludlow, Washington, 1999, one audiocassette, "practice tape," provided by Bob Thornburg; Dwight Diller, Seattle, Washington, radio interview, circa 2000, one audiocassette provided by Bob Thornburg; Dwight Diller, banjo workshop, held at Tersh McCracken's summer home near Red Lodge, Montana, September 2000, two audiocassettes provided by Bob Thornburg; Dwight Diller, banjo workshop, held at Tersh McCracken's summer home near Red Lodge, Montana, September 2000, video by Stewart Seidel.

65. 8 June 2015 (7:14 p.m.) email from Cindy Harris to Lew Stern.

66. Lee Talmadge recalled his first fiddle lessons at a banjo retreat hosted by Rex and Karen Wambaugh in Portland, Michigan, in the late 1990s: "for most of the tunes Dwight was teaching the fiddle tuned GDGD, in tandem with the open G tuning on the banjo. So I don't know if I was already aware of that at the time or not but I got into GDGD and was encouraged to play along with Karen, just the two of us. Well I didn't know the tune and was trying to concentrate on the notes and her fingering to such an extent that I became literally frozen—playing nothing. Then I heard Dwight's voice just behind me. He leaned over and spoke clearly just above a whisper in my ear, "just move your bow." In time I understood this was the best thing he could tell me. Don't worry about fingering the notes, you are in cross G, focus on the rhythm. Well the sun went down, the room darkened and more people began to arrive a join the camp students till there may have been twenty-five, thirty people, all playing together with Dwight right in the middle, leading the jam on fiddle. It was a special experience for me which I had the fortune to repeat a few more times with Dwight over the next few years." 3 August 2015 (9:46 a.m.) email from Lee Talmadge to Lew Stern.

67. Jam tapes, 27 January 1996, Brevard, North Carolina; Lesson tapes, January 1997, Celestial Mountain Music Store, Brevard, North Carolina, digitized courtesy of Carroll Smith; Lesson tapes, 28 January 1996, Brevard, North Carolina, digitized courtesy of Carroll Smith.

68. "Lee Hammons played most of these tunes in cross tuning. Cross tuning is a relative thing. The Old People, they did not have tuners. They tuned it to where they thought it was at, it was all relative. So they never thought in terms of notes. Fiddle was either tuned in flat key which a lot of them didn't like very well—DADG." Lesson tapes, 28 January 1996, Brevard, North Carolina, digitized courtesy of Carroll Smith.

69. The fiddler Bill Hicks explained that the "high bass, high counter" reference is a common name for the AEAE cross tuning (low to high pitch). The ADAE tuning would be high bass, low counter, and works well for tunes in D. 5 July 2015 (12:15 p.m.) email from Bill Hicks to Lew Stern and 5 July 2015 (7:56 a.m.) email from Bill Hicks to Lew Stern. I'm indebted to Bill Hicks for taking the higher mathematics that fiddling concepts represent and rendering them as simple arithmetic ideas accessible to this banjo player. Also see Gerald Milnes, *Play of a Fiddle*, pp. 7–8, and Drew Beisswenger, *Fiddling Way Out Yonder: The Life and Music of Melvin Wine*, (Jackson: University of Mississippi Press, 2002), pp. 123–124.

70. Lesson tapes, 28 January 1996, Brevard, North Carolina, digitized courtesy of Carroll Smith.

71. Bill Hicks made the point that some traditional fiddlers disdained changing the strings, intimating that somehow tuning out of standard was "cheating," or evidence of a weaker player. Hicks noted: "Emmett Lundy said things like that. He played a tune in standard (on the Rounder record) that directly illustrated how a good player could do octave double stops without retuning to make that easier. [...] The handful of old masters I was lucky enough to meet did use tunings. Tommy Jarrell more than the Hammons. [John] Summers, the old master I didn't meet but have listened to extensively, did not use tunings at all that I can tell. I think the cross tuning feature is particularly notable amongst Appalachian players. Jabbour would probably say this reflects the more isolated and archaic aspect of deep mountain fiddling—that we're hearing to some extent a kind of time capsule of how people maybe even the first settlers were playing in the 1800s or 1700s. There is also the factor of individual taste and even genius to account for." 5 July 2015 (12:15 p.m.) email from Bill Hicks to Lew Stern.

72. See Drew Beisswenger, *Fiddling Way Out Yonder*, pp. 122–123 for a discussion of West Virginia fiddler Melvin Wine's use of various "non-standard" tunings. Also see Malvin Newton Artley, *The West Virginia Country Fiddler: An Aspect of the Folk Music Tradition in the United States*. (Ph.D. dissertation, Chicago Musical College [Roosevelt University], 1955), p. 25, on "discord tunings" in West Virginia fiddling.

73. Lesson tapes, 28 January 1996, Brevard, North Carolina, digitized courtesy of Carroll Smith.

74. Lesson tapes, 28 January 1996, Brevard, North Carolina, digitized courtesy of Carroll Smith.

75. Dwight Diller, banjo workshop, held at Tersh McCracken's summer home near Red Lodge, Montana, September 2000. Video by Stewart Seidel. Darin Gentry, who studied both banjo and fiddle with Dwight, recalled: "I remember the first workshop of Dwight's I attended in the late spring of '99. Was working on the banjo but some time prior to that I had a dream one night that I was playing the fiddle and it was really fun. So when I woke up after the dream I was set on learning. I don't remember exactly the timing of those two events but they were close on the time line. Both occurred in the spring of '99. The analogies that stuck in my head and have influenced my

banjo and fiddle playing were these: think of the motion of packing a can of dip, or trying to fling snot off your hand. Or be like a wet dish rag, keep your arm loose and relaxed and use the weight of your hand to snap and kick the rhythm along." 23 August 2015 (1:47 p.m.) email from Darin Gentry to Lew Stern.

76. Lesson tapes, 28 January 1996, Brevard, North Carolina, digitized courtesy of Carroll Smith.

77. Dwight Diller, banjo workshop, held at Tersh McCracken's summer home near Red Lodge, Montana, September 2000, video by Stewart Seidel.

78. Diane Jones commented that older musicians who played both fiddle and banjo in the traditional way often had two very different approaches to the same tune on the two instruments. Sometimes, the banjo and the fiddle versions were almost unrecognizable as the same tune. Jones pointed to Clyde Davenport as a good example of this. "Davenport is a master at fiddle and banjo, and a great singer. He'd play a tune on fiddle and then get the banjo out, but sometimes the banjo version would be really, really different. A lot of tunes he was a master at playing came out differently on each instrument." Author's notes, 11 June 2015 (3:30–4:10 p.m.) telephone conversation with Diane Jones, from the Eastern Shore, Maryland. Dwight made this point in a 2000 radio interview: "Old fiddlers like Edn Hammons and all those fiddlers they'd sit down and swap tunes all night and just tune after tune after tune after tune just playing back and forth. But they didn't play together, they played separately because they played them different. The same tune would be played a little different." KCDS radio interview with Dwight Diller, "Sunday Folks," Seattle, Washington, 1999, audiocassette provided by Bob Thornburg.

79. Diane Jones took this one step further, and studied fiddling briefly, but with the goal of improving her listening capabilities and becoming a better banjo player, not achieving capability as a fiddler. Author's notes, 11 June 2015 (3:30–4:10 p.m.) telephone conversation with Diane Jones, from the Eastern Shore, Maryland.

80. Lesson tapes, 28 January 1996, Brevard, North Carolina, digitized courtesy of Carroll Smith.

81. http://greghooven.org/biography.

82. https://www.youtube.com/watch?v=Tbk313RNZWw.

83. https://www.youtube.com/watch?v=baYoQMkXXRY.

84. https://www.youtube.com/watch?v=LR8_p5PQoqI.

85. Dwight Diller, banjo workshop, held at Tersh McCracken's summer home near Red Lodge, Montana, September 2000, video by Stewart Seidel.

86. 18 September 2014 email from Dwight Diller to Lew Stern; 18 September 2014 email from Dwight Diller to a new fiddle student.

87. http://en.wikipedia.org/wiki/T%27ai_chi_ch%27uan.

88. 18 September 2014 email from Dwight Diller to Lew Stern; 18 September 2014 email from Dwight Diller to a new fiddle student.

89. Petar Ramadanovic observed: "Too much past precludes action, happiness, and further development." As an antidote to this predicament he suggests a critical discourse on the past that would be attentive to the needs of the present and able to distinguish between what in the past is advantageous and what is disadvantageous for life. Thus, "active" forgetting is selective remembering, the recognition that not all past forms of knowledge and not all experiences are beneficial for present and future life. Active forgetting is then part of a more general attempt to rationalize the relation to the past and to render conscious—in order to overcome—all those haunting events that return to disturb the calm of a later moment." Petar Ramadanovic, "From Haunting to Trauma: Nietzsche's Active Forgetting and Blanchot's Writing of the Disaster," University of New Hampshire, 2001, http://pmc.iath.virginia.edu/text-only/issue.101/11.2ramadanovic.txt Also see "The Importance of Forgetfulness for Nietzsche," 4 February 2012, http://timlshort.wordpress.com/2012/02/04/the-importance-of-forgetfulness-for-nietzsche/. For Rousseau, "Forgetting is at least as important an element as is understanding. In traditional accounts one does not find a bad memory this high on the list of qualities necessary for philosophical contemplation." See Christopher Kelly, "Rousseau and the Case Against (and for) the Arts," in *The Legacy of Rousseau*, edited by Clifford Orwin, et al., p. 327 (Chicago: University of Chicago Press, 1997).

90. Jam tapes, 27 January 1996, Brevard, North Carolina, Lesson tapes, January 1997, Celestial Mountain Music Store, Brevard, North Carolina, digitized courtesy of Carroll Smith; Lesson tapes, 28 January 1996, Brevard, North Carolina, digitized courtesy of Carroll Smith; Dwight Diller, banjo classes taught as Cass, West Virginia, 1988, 1989, 1990 and 1991, fourteen audiocassettes provided by Bob Thornburg; Dwight Diller, banjo workshop and evening concert, Seneca Park, on the Greenbrier River, West Virginia, 1990 and 1991, eight audio cassettes provided by Bob Thornburg; Dwight Diller, banjo workshop, conducted at the home of Bob Thornburg, Bishop, California, 1995; audiocassettes provided by Bob Thornburg; Dwight Diller, Banjo camp, D Base Camp, Virginia Lakes and Bishop, California, September 1997, two audiocassettes provided by Bob Thornburg; Dwight Diller, Banjo Camp, Port Ludlow, Washington, 1999, one audiocassette, "practice tape," provided by Bob Thornburg; Dwight Diller, banjo workshop, held at Tersh McCracken's summer home near Red Lodge, Montana, September 2000, two audiocassettes provided by Bob Thornburg; Dwight Diller, Banjo Camp, Vancouver, British Columbia, summer 2001, hosted by Stewart Seidel, four audiocassettes provided by Bob Thornburg; Dwight Diller, banjo camp, Hood Canal, near Seattle, Washington, (no date), two audiocassettes provided by Bob Thornburg; Video of Dwight teaching at Tersh McCracken's summer home in Red Lodge Mountain, September 2000, provided by Stewart Seidel.

91. "What I want to say as I'm pushing you forward to play and come out, I want you to on the other hand to count the cost. I have to remind you that this stuff that I'm asking of you is expensive and just go ahead and expect it, and then decide how much of a price you want to pay. If you are going to play the music then you have a responsibility to it. You be real careful about playing this music for your glory. If you play it for your glory it will turn on you. Keep your hands off of it. You play it for the sake of the music rather than what you can get out of it." Lesson tapes, 27 January 1996, Brevard, North Carolina, (Diller 01.27.96 Tape 2B.mp3), digitized courtesy of Carroll Smith, who attended the class.

92. "So you don't have to move your body in order to play but I'm insisting you do it right now because that's a tool that you can use. Normally the white middle class folks, we just don't have any kind of rhythm going on inside of us, so when I'm teaching I have to try and bring it out. What it's doing is it is making you bring your soul out and put it right there on the stool and you don't like that. I can pick out those of you who find it harder to do this, because if you don't lay your soul out here then you're just playing notes, you're going to keep hearing me say over again it's the difference between notes and music." Lesson tapes, 27 January 1996, Brevard, North Carolina, (Diller 01.27.96 Tape 2A.mp3), digitized courtesy of Carroll Smith, who attended the class. Also, Jam tapes, 27 January 1996, Brevard, North Carolina, Lesson tapes, January 1997, Celestial Mountain Music Store, Brevard, North Carolina, digitized courtesy of Carroll Smith; Lesson tapes,

28 January 1996, Brevard, North Carolina, digitized courtesy of Carroll Smith.

93. Audiocassette of a Dwight Diller Banjo Camp conducted on the shore of the Greenbrier River, Seneca Park, 1991, tape provided by Bob Thornburg. The fiddler Vivian Wagner notes: "Sometimes the wrong note is perfect. You have to allow yourself to make mistakes." Wagner, *Fiddler*, pp. 146–147.

94. On nicknames as a long-standing tradition in rural West Virginia, see Milnes, *Play of a Fiddle*, pp. 93–94.

95. As Dwight said in a 1996 retreat: "I'm going to be asking more out of you than what you can give or what you think you can give, and that's alright. The important thing is to try and relax and go with it rather than getting your back up, getting angry and so on. People get angry and that's normal but it just wastes their time and my time. If you feel like you need to cry go ahead and cry. That's also normal in my classes […] I don't ever want it to be a put-down or anything like that. The tears when they've come over the years, it has been the frustration. Not being able to get it. But I can't back away from, but I can't afford tears because I might not be able to get anywhere." Lesson tapes, 28 January 1996, Brevard, North Carolina, (Diller 01.25.96 Tape 1A.mp3), digitized courtesy of Carroll Smith, who attended the class. His goal was to encourage the "grit, tenacity and fearlessness" that Vivian Wagner identifies as crucial for anyone pursuing the goal of learning to play music. See Wagner, *Fiddler*, p. 194.

96. Dwight apparently tried all manner of learning devices to communicate the nature of the right arm movement he was trying to teach. Michael Brooks described an innovation that made an appearance at a retreat conducted in Cass, West Virginia, in 1998: "Dwight starts again on rhythm: damp the strings, then try to rip out the fifth string!, keep that thumb stiff so you can pop the fifth sting immediately after you accelerate through the brush strum by a small rotation from the elbow (identified by the medical doctor in the class as 'pronation'), all the while being relaxed, not leaning the arm against the banjo rim. A little more practice I think for me. *Dwight constructed a lower-arm and wrist splint from a piece of rolled-up cardboard for several of us to use to decrease the wrist action in the strum* [emphasis added]. The strum should come from a motion like shaking down a thermometer, not waving like a wimpy wrist." Brooks, Michael. "North-South Banjo Camp—July 12–18, 1998 in Cass, West Virginia: Rhythm by Dwight Diller and Several Notes by Ken Perlman," *Mississippi Old-Time Music Society Newsletter*, 23 August 1998.

Conclusion

1. Drew Beisswenger, *North American Fiddle Music: A Research and Information Guide* (New York: Routledge, 2001), pp. 373–374. This is echoed in the Appalachian State University guide to the special collections at the Belk Library: "The traditional folk music of rural West Virginia is not well represented in halls of fame or by platinum record sales. West Virginia does not boast a Nashville, Bristol or Atlanta or the early commercial recording successes of these epicenters of commercial southern music. Nor has it been at the forefront of the more recent old-time music revival. The influence of West Virginia's traditional folk music has spread more subversively. It has continued to be transmitted orally and preserved locally through legendary families like the Carpenters, the Hammons, the Georges, the Kessingers and the Wines. The music has also been recorded by a growing number of unusually dedicated and passionate folklorists and ethnomusicologists such as Alan Jabbour, Gerald (Gerry) Milnes, Ray Alden, Ken Sullivan and Carl Fleischhauer." Published Field Recordings of West Virginia, http://collections.library.appstate.edu/research-aids/published-field-recordings-west-virginia Gerald Milnes stated: "The spotlight has never illuminated West Virginia as a pivotal area for traditional folk music (early recordings and performance centers in Bristol, Atlanta, Nashville and elsewhere have brough recognition to other states). Nor was the state in the forefront of a more recent old-time music revival." See *Play of a Fiddle*, p. 3.

2. Beisswenger, *North American Fiddle Music*, pp. 373–374; Brittany R. Hicks, "Exploring 'Nostalgia for the Future: A History of the Augusta Heritage Center in Elkins, West Virginia," Master's Thesis prepared for the Center for Appalachian Studies, May 2014. https://augustaheritagecenter.org/wp-content/uploads/BR-Hicks-Augusta-Thesis-2014.pdf.

3. http://www.oldtimeherald.org/archive/back_issues/volume-12/12-2/hammons.html.

4. Dwight did not retain any of the slides that composed this project, nor did he have any of the scripts or notes from which he worked in making his presentations to the various audiences that, between 1988 and at least 2000, had the opportunity to see the show and hear Dwight's narrative about the Hammons family. The *Across the YewPines* project incorporated elements of the original slide show, especially the photographs. An audiotape of a practice run of the "second revision" of the slide show, presented to a select audience of his friends at his Hillsboro, West Virginia, home in 1989, provided some sense of Dwight's earliest organized thinking about the Hammonses. Dwight Diller, audiotape of narration of the Hammons Slide Show, second revision, taped at Diller's home in Hillsboro, West Virginia, 1989, provided by Bob Thornburg.

5. In July 2015, Dwight was the recipient of the Legacy Award for his contributions to old time music at the Fourth Annual Highland County Old Time Fiddlers Convention in Monterey, Virginia. "Fiddlers Convention Names Contest Winners," *The Recorder*, 23 July 2015, page 5; Lewis M. Stern, "Dwight Hamilton Diller: Working to Preserve the Old Tunes," Program, 4th Annual Old Time Fiddlers Convention, Highland County, Virginia, 16–19 July 2015.

6. A scan of the 1996 flyer for the event, provided by Scott Prouty, shows the proper name for the event, and indicates that the event was sponsored by Pocahontas County Dramas, Fairs and Festivals with the assistance of the Pocahontas County Tourism Commission.

7. Author's notes, 23 February 2015 (10:30–11:30 a.m.) telephone conversation with Dwight Diller.

8. http://chestertownspy.org/2014/10/05/mainstays-fallfest-concludes-with-celebrating-the-banjo/ ; 26 January 2015 (11:34 a.m.) email from Dwight Diller to Lew Stern; 26 February 2015 (5:12 a.m.) email from Phil Tyler to Lew Stern; 10 April 2015 (3:01 p.m.) email from Nick Pilley to Lew Stern.

9. http://dwightdiller.com/2013/11/20/the-acknowledgements/.

10. "The Hammons legacy, Volumes 1 to 3," http://www.mustrad.org.uk/reviews/ham_leg3.htm.

11. 10 December 2014 (12:21 p.m.) email from Dwight Diller to Lew Stern; Dwight Diller banjo workshop, held at Tersh McCracken's summer home near Red Lodge, Montana, 2002, audiocassette provided by Bob Thornburg.

12. 10 December 2014 (12:21 p.m.) email from Dwight Diller to Lew Stern.

13. "For a couple of years I lived, ate, slept the music of the Hammons and Hamp Carpenter. I lived it until it became me. At that point I didn't have access to anyone else but them. Looking back, I'm glad." Littlehales, "Dwight Diller," p. 11.

14. 10 December 2014 (9:21 p.m.) email from Dwight Diller to Lew Stern.

15. Dwight related a story that John Morris told him about Wilson: "You know how Wilson was about fiddling, [John said]. It was first week of June, [and] he went in to the boss' office and said he wanted some time off. Boss asking him what for. Wilson told him that the Glenville festival [a few miles up the road] was coming up on the third weekend of June [around June 20th, West Virginia Day.] So the boss said that it would be ok for him to take a couple days off at that time. Wilson said he would need two weeks off to get ready. The boss blew up over that so Wilson just quit and walked off. John said Wilson knew it would take two weeks to get himself quieted down inside enough so he could play the fiddle at all. All that constant shaking and jarring [on the road grader] made the body so dull that he couldn't feel the strings or work the bow." John Morris told Dwight that Wilson went back after Glenville and asked for his job back. "They took him on but gave him a road grader that was totally wore out. He stuck with it until they gave him a good one again." 10 December 2014 (9:21 p.m.) email from Dwight Diller to Lew Stern.

16. Littlehales, "Dwight Diller, pp. 11, 12. Also see: http://www.traveling219.com/stories/marlinton-lewisburg/the-black-mountain-bluegrass-boys/.

17. "I am right sure that was the first place I went on stage with the Morris Brothers. They were well known as THE band in the country around. Dave and John in the middle. Me on the left and John Martin on the right." 10 December 2014 (921 p.m.) email from Dwight Diller to Lew Stern. Dwight played with the Black Mountain Bluegrass Boys at the Droop Mountain Festival in late July 1973. Wayne Howard attended, and recalled: "The location was Tommy Hills' farm on Droop Mountain. A hard rain had fallen—before I got there, I think—and the cars messed up Tommy's field so bad that (as I heard) he wouldn't let his land be used for another festival. It was only held that one year. [...] I saw quite a few people that I knew, including Lee Hammons, Len Reiss and others in Dwight's circle." 5 January 2015 (7:11 p.m.) email from Wayne Howard to Lew Stern. Also see Emma Eisenberg, "Hippies, Cops and Log Cabins: An Interview with Wayne Erbsen," 24 October 2010, http://emma-eisenberg.com/?page_id=22.

18. 10 December 2014 (9:21 p.m.) email from Dwight Diller to Lew Stern.

19. Littlehales, "Dwight Diller," p. 11; 4 January 2015 (12:46 p.m.) from Carl Fleischhauer to Lew Stern; 31 March 2015 (9:59 a.m.) email from Wayne Howard to Lew Stern.

20. 26 January 2015 (6:36 a.m.) email from Bill Hicks to Lew Stern.

21. Brad Leftwich, Al Tharp and Odell McGuire, "The Complete History of the Plank Road String Band and the Lexington, VA Music Scene," http://www.fieldrecorder.com/docs/notes/plankroad.htm. James Leva, "Final Notes: Odell McGuire," *Old Time Herald*, http://www.oldtimeherald.org/here+there/final-notes/odell-mcguire.html; http://www.fieldrecorder.com/docs/collectors/alden.htm.

22. Speaking of festivals in the mid–1970s, Dwight put it this way: "I saw the direction Galax was going. Galax went bad there for a while and now it has rolled back around. Police. Clamp down. Cleaned it up. I'm pretty sure it was 1970. Dave Morris was there and had stuff stolen out of his tents. I remember drunks. Port-a-pottie flipping." University of North Carolina at Chapel Hill, Collection Number: 20061, Collection Title: Jack Bernhardt Papers, 1943–2011, Dwight Diller Interview, Elkins, WVA, 3 August 1983, Tape 1, Side 1.

23. University of North Carolina at Chapel Hill, Collection Number: 20061, Collection Title: Jack Bernhardt Papers, 1943–2011, Dwight Diller Interview, Elkins, WVA, 3 August 1983, Tape 1, Side 1.

24. Brad Leftwich commented, in late February 2015: "I remember his stint with the Black Mountain Bluegrass Boys—he introduced me to one of them, named Harley Carpenter, I think, some distant relation of French Carpenter. I was really surprised when Dwight said he joined that band, he didn't seem like the kind to join a bluegrass band. He told me, maybe not in exactly these words, that there was something he felt inside that he was looking for a way to express, and thought maybe he could find it in bluegrass. But I had the impression that, whatever it was, he didn't find it there." 19 February 2015 (10:25 a.m.) email from Brad Leftwich to Lew Stern.

25. Dwight said in 1983: "I wasn't impressed at all with Jimmy Martin, Ralph Stanley and Bill Monroe but I was really impressed with Doc Watson. I just didn't believe that anyone could be that good. Doc Watson is a very pleasant person to watch and he plays a very pleasant music." University of North Carolina at Chapel Hill, Collection Number: 20061, Collection Title: Jack Bernhardt Papers, 1943–2011, Dwight Diller Interview, Elkins, WVA, 3 August 1983, Tape 1, Side 1. Interestingly, Ron Mullennex remembers that Dwight studied Bill Monroe's music: "He listened to it, tried to understand what Monroe was pushing and why Monroe was who he was." Author's notes, 20 January 2015 (7:00–8:00 p.m.) telephone conversation with Ron Mullennex from Bluefield, West Virginia.

26. Ron Mullennex remembered that Odell McGuire was a significant influence on Dwight, and he had very strong opinions on how to learn old time music, and how to play it. Mullennex himself took the position that there was not one right way of playing the music: "The banjo is a rhythm instrument. That part has to be right, but there's not only one way to get to the rhythm." Author's notes, 20 January 2015 (7:00–8:00 p.m.) telephone conversation with Ron Mullennex from Bluefield, West Virginia.

27. Dwight likened music to language, and suggested that a quick and dirty "study" of the visible part of a foreign language sacrificed understanding of the rhythm of speech, and the depth of nuance that inflection, aural eccentricities and complex layers of vocabulary. That is, a study that was not careful and respectful would miss the special stuff that made languages complex. Dwight's point was that linguists required a tenderness of analytical care in looking closely and critically at what languages represented. In Dwight's words: "Think about how important learning the rhythm of a 'foreign language' is. It is the nuances that catch you up. It is the tiny 'hold back' or 'drive forward' that changes the world within a language." 10 October 2014 (4:38 p.m.) email from Dwight Diller to Lew Stern.

28. After a late November 2014 visit to Ralph Roberts, the last of that line of Hammons/Roberts fiddlers, Dwight related that Roberts had said that he had listened to all manner of West Virginia fiddlers and fiddlers from other states who gathered at various old time festivals, and concluded that Dwight is "the only one with the 'old WAY.'" 29 November 2014 (8:30 p.m.) email from Dwight Diller to Lew Stern.

29. In a 1983 interview, Dwight stated: "I became a purist. Purist of the pure. No guitar. Just banjo and fiddle. I've looked back on that and if you're going to do anything like this it pays to be a purist, really zero in, but if you stay that way too long you become stagnant. Can't be purist to the exclusion of everything around you. I became a purist at that time." University of North Carolina at Chapel Hill, Collection Number: 20061, Collection Title: Jack Bernhardt Papers, 1943–2011, Dwight Diller Interview, Elkins, WVA, 3 August 1983, Tape 1, Side 1. During 1976–1977, when he worked as a substitute grade school music teacher in Marlinton, West Virginia, Dwight taught himself enough guitar to be able to use the instrument in class to get his elementary school classes, from the first to the sixth grade, to sing songs as a class. Author's notes, 20 April

2015 (10:41–11:05 a.m.) telephone conversation with Dwight Diller in Marlinton, West Virginia.

30. This is probably very similar to the arc of Benton Flippen's musical creativity that Paul Brown described this way: "Benton is a reflection of the changing times in which he grew up, but he's also a uniquely gifted musician who took what he heard around him and molded it to suit himself. His music, on banjo and fiddle, owes a debt to early bluegrass and an equally large debt to the powerful old-time musicians in the area." Brown continues: "He listened to clawhammer banjo picker Kyle Creed and bluegrass innovator Earl Scruggs then followed neither of them past a certain point. And when he decided to play fiddle again after a lapse of about a decade, Benton began visiting his older neighbor Tommy Jarrell, whose archaic, bow-rocking style was worlds different from Benton's in technique, yet remarkably similar in energy and overall drive." Paul Brown, "Through the Flippen Filter: The Life, The Times and Tunes of Benton Flippen," *Old Time Herald*, vol. 5, no. 1 (Fall 1995), pp. 16–22, 60.

31. Dan Levenson stated: "One of those families whose music Dwight studied was the Hammons family. He gives much of the credit of his style to them, but rest assured—Dwight has a pure mountain style all his own." See "Review: 'Just Banjo '99,'" *Banjo Newsletter*, February 2000, p. 6.

32. 29 December 2014 (11:00 a.m.–12:00 P.M) telephone conversation with Dwight Diller.

33. Kilby Spencer learned old-time music from his parents, Thornton and Emily, who have been in the Whitetop Mountain Band for over 40 years. He collects and digitizes rare local recordings, and serves on the board of the Field Recorders' Collective.

34. 29 December 2014 (11:00 a.m.–12:00 p.m.) telephone conversation with Dwight Diller.

35. 25 February 2015 (1:07 a.m.) email from Dwight Diller to Lew Stern.

36. 25 February 2015 (1:45 p.m.) email from Len Reiss to Lew Stern.

37. 25 February 2015 (1:07 a.m.) email from Dwight Diller to Lew Stern.

38. 30 April 2015 (3–58 p.m.) email from Ron Chacey to Lew Stern.

39. 4 March 2015 (9:17 p.m.) email from Dwight Diller to Lew Stern.

40. 26 February 2015 (10:18 p.m.) email from Dan Dagget to Lew Stern; 22 April 2015 (6:33 p.m.) email from Dan Dagget to Lew Stern.

41. 25 February 2015 (1:07 a.m.) email from Dwight Diller to Lew Stern.

42. 25 February 2015 (1:07 a.m.) email from Dwight Diller to Lew Stern. Also see: http://www.cedarmtnbanjos.com/About-Us.html. In an April 2015 *Banjo Newsletter* interview with Tim Gardner, who took over Cedar Mountain Banjos when Le Gordon retired in 2013, Gardner was asked when Cedar Mountain started using rosewood for the rims. Gardner's answer: "That started when Lo was working with Dwight Diller. Lo and Dwight developed the Diller model, which had steam-bent rims that he put a rosewood tone ring on. That model got discontinued in the late '90s but Lo thought that the rosewood tone ring seemed to add to the sound quality—why not build an entire rim out of rosewood? That's when the Vintage line was born. So, on Vintage models, the rim is rosewood. The woody was a sound that lots of folks were going for back then. Nowadays, they aren't as popular; most of my orders have the rolled brass tone ring." Knight Martorell, "Cedar Mountain Banjos and Tim Gardner," *Banjo Newsletter*, April 2015, https://banjonews.com/2015-04/cedar_mountain_banjos_and_jim_gardner.html. According to an August 1999 flyer from Cedar Mountain Banjos, featuring Diller Model, L Model, and including testimonials from John McEuen and Mac Benford, Gordon's "first generation rims" were three ply maple, measuring 11 inches by ⅝ inch with a rosewood tone ring and cap matching the neck and dowel stick. The "second generation" rims were "multilayered rosewood 'tone rims' capped to match neck and dowel stick." Also see Bob Buckingham, "Cedar Mountain Banjos—The Lo Gordon Story," *Banjo Newsletter*, December 2004, pp. 8–11.

43. 26 February 2015 (9:14 a.m.) email from Dwight Diller to Lew Stern. I know Dwight could play fretless banjo because one was thrust into his hands (I think it might have been one of my George Wunderlich banjos) while Dwight was visiting us in our northern Virginia home in January 2002. Don Rusnak, George Wunderlich, and John Huerta were among the guests that night. See: http://dwightdiller.com/camp/lowdown-i/lew-sterns-hosting-experience/.

44. 7 January 2015 (12:59 p.m.) email from Bates Littlehales to Lew Stern; 2 January 2015 (12:20 p.m.) email from Jeff Kramer to Lew Stern; 7 January 2015 (4:45 p.m.) email from Jeff Kramer to Lew Stern.

45. 25 February 2015 (1:07 a.m.) email from Dwight Diller to Lew Stern.

46. Author's notes, 17 March 2015 (3:40–4:14 p.m.) telephone conversation with Chuck Lee, Ovilla, Texas. I am grateful to Chuck Lee for making photographs of these banjos available to me, and for providing me with access to his internet records containing information on banjos built and sold.

47. This banjo, called a "Granbury Custom" in Lee's inventory, had a maple neck, 25.5 inch scale, and laminations up the center of the neck, under the fingerboard and peghead overlay in the form of a sandwich of three pieces of wood veneer dyed red, green, and red. The neck measured 1.5 inches at the nut. The fingerboard, peghead overlay and heel cap were ebony. Lee used a 12 inch Tony Pass sunken birch rim that was 0.75 inch thick, with a wood tone ring. The Granbury Custom model came with a Renaissance head, a No-Knot tailpiece, and Five-Star tuners with white knobs. 25 March 2015 (10:08 p.m.) email from Chuck Lee to Lew Stern; https://web.archive.org/web/20040614080036/http://www.leebanjos.com/Banjos/Banjo006.htm.

48. Chuck Lee recalled that banjo number "006" was finished in 2003 and sold. It later ended up at Donald Zepp's music store, Zepp Music, in Wendell, North Carolina. 19 March 2015 (7:53 p.m.) email from Chuck Lee to Lew Stern. Zepp, who retired in January 2015 and closed the music store, sold "006" in late May 2004. The banjo was returned to the store, and resold in November 2004 to a gentleman in Hayden, Colorado. 20 March 2015 (4:01 p.m.) email from Donald Zepp to Lew Stern.

49. Chuck Lee's archived records show that the second banjo, serial number 003, listed as a Granbury custom project, was destroyed in shipping. https://web.archive.org/web/20040703093610/http://www.leebanjos.com/Banjos/Banjo003.htm.

50. Author's notes, 17 March 2015 (3:40–4:14 p.m.) telephone conversation with Chuck Lee from Ovilla, Texas.

51. 19 March 2015 (7:53 p.m.) email from Chuck Lee to Lew Stern; Author's notes, 12 February 2015 (10:30 a.m.–12:00 p.m.) telephone conversation with Dwight Diller.

52. Banjo 004 was listed as "The Granbury, Take Down—A Custom Project," and was annotated as a shop-owned prototype in Lee's archived internet records. https://web.archive.org/web/20040703123018/http://www.leebanjos.com/Banjos/Banjo004.htm.

53. Author's notes, 17 March 2015 (3:40–4:14 p.m.) telephone conversation with Chuck Lee from Ovilla, Texas. The necks and rims from two banjos, serial numbers 003 and 004, ended up in the burn barrel outside his shop.

The hardware used on these two banjos was resold. 21 March 2015 (12:19 a.m.) email from Chuck Lee to Lew Stern.

54. 25 February 2015 (1:07 a.m.) email from Dwight Diller to Lew Stern.

55. Author's notes, 12 February 2015 (10:30 a.m.–12:00 p.m.) telephone conversation with Dwight Diller. Dwight worked briefly at blacksmithing beginning in the mid-1970s. He had done some work for Larry Mann in Lexington, Virginia, in the summer of 1974, and that engendered enough of an interest in blacksmithing to prompt him to trade for an anvil and tools. However, his workshop setup was not ventilated properly and he managed to get himself in trouble with carbon dioxide poisoning at which point he basically closed down shop and moved on. Sometime in 2010 or so, he traded his anvil to a policeman in Florida for several yards of wool woven on a loom used during the Civil War to make uniforms for Confederate soldiers. Author's notes, 12 February 2015 (10:30 a.m.–12:00 p.m.) telephone conversation with Dwight Diller.

56. 25 February 2015 (1:07 a.m.) email from Dwight Diller to Lew Stern.

57. 2 January 2015 (12:20 p.m.) email from Jeff Kramer to Lew Stern. Sometime in 2006 or so I played one or two banjos build by Jeff Kramer that were designed specifically for Dwight Diller. Dwight wanted a travel banjo, a banjo that would break down easily and assemble with little trouble. I remember playing one of the clever, finely constructed prototypes that Jeff Kramer built for Dwight, who also wanted a more traditional banjo—as a replacement for the Cedar Mountain banjos that he had endorsed for so long. I also recall playing a deep pot banjo that Dwight had Kramer build. The rim was four or more inches in depth. I think Dwight found this uncomfortable, mused about having Kramer cut down the rim—at least until Dwight found a large tree-trunk of a student who loved the dimensions of that deep dish banjo and took it off Dwight's hands.

58. 3 January 2015 (9:30 a.m.) email from Jeff Kramer to Lew Stern.

59. 2 January 2015 (12:20 p.m.) email from Jeff Kramer to Lew Stern. Dwight reflects on some of the experiments, some of the challenges confronted: "Jeff offered different kinds of wood to use for necks on the Pass Lost Timbre rims. He was even able to offer a rosewood neck. One of the problems he discovered, but not to do with the necks, was there is a problem with rosewood. After a few years, it seems the large amount of oil in rosewood starts to get 'soggy' and the vibrations are lost. There were many experiments with the tone rings over the years. And there were experiments that were used to 'Trick up' the tone rings [such as adding] a scalloped ring like the old Electrics. But unlike the old Electrics these banjos turned out so powerful they were hard to play to keep them from becoming crashy." 25 February 2015 (1:07 a.m.) email from Dwight Diller to Lew Stern.

60. 25 February 2015 (1:07 a.m.) email from Dwight Diller to Lew Stern.

61. 25 February 2015 (1:07 a.m.) email from Dwight Diller to Lew Stern.

62. 25 February 2015 (1:07 a.m.) email from Dwight Diller to Lew Stern.

63. 31 December 2014 (4:57 p.m.) email from Andrew Fults to Lew Stern.

64. 25 February 2015 (1:07 a.m.) email from Dwight Diller to Lew Stern.

65. 31 December 2014 (5:27 p.m.) email from Andrew Fults to Lew Stern.

66. In July 2015, Dwight played one of Fults' hand built banjos on stage at the Fourth Annual Highland County Old Time Fiddlers Convention in Monterey, Virginia, in July 2015 where he performed after being honored with the Convention's Legacy Award. Fults fitted the 23 inch scale banjo with a 12 inch Sapele block rim and a homemade Whyte Laydie style tone ring. The neck was made of African walnut with a ⅜ inch maple center lamination. Fults explained: "I actually built it for myself, but when played by me it sounded like it was down in a well. Just a little too responsive for my heavy hand. I had it with me when I was in West Virginia during the first weekend of July, along with another I carried up there for Ralph Roberts. Dwight picked it up, tweaked on it a little, and started playing. He made it sound really good. I reckon it was just too much banjo for me, but he has control enough to bring the best out of it, so he and I swapped banjos, and I brought back one I made for him a couple of years ago." See Andrew Holmaas, "Dwight Diller Honored at Highland County Old Time Fiddlers Convention," Banjo Hangout Forum, 24 July 2015, http://www.banjohangout.org/pages/forum/topic.asp?topic_ID=306829&whichpage=#3886152; 3 August 2015 (8:30 a.m.) email from Andrew Fults to Lew Stern.

67. See, for example, John O'Brien, *At Home in the Heart of Appalachia*, pp. 246–251, and Barbara Ellen Smith and Stephen L. Fisher, "The Place of Appalachia," *Southern Spaces*, 31 January 2013. Excerpted from *Transforming Places: Lessons from Appalachia* (Chicago: University of Illinois Press, 2012). http://southernspaces.org/2013/place-appalachia#content_top Also see Milnes, *Play of a Fiddle*, p. 147.

68. John O'Brien argued: "The pattern of outside agents working hand in glove with politicians that began more than a century ago remains a fact of life in West Virginia." See O'Brien, *At Home in the Heart of Appalachia*, p. 274, and David S. Walls, "Internal Colony or Internal Periphery?" in *Colonialism in Modern America: The Appalachian Case*, edited by Helen Matthews Lewis, Linda Johnson and Donald Askins (Boone, NC: Appalachian Consortium Press, 1978). http://www.sonoma.edu/users/w/wallsd/internal-colony.shtml. Also see Walls, "Central Appalachia: A Peripheral Region within an Advanced Capitalist Society," *Journal of Sociology and Social Welfare*, vol. IV, no. 2 (November 1976), pp. 232–246; "Three Models in Search of Appalachian Development: Critique and Synthesis," presented at a joint session of the Rural Sociological Society and the Society for the Study of Social Problems, Montreal, Quebec, 25 August 1974, abstracted in *Research in Education*, November 1976, ERIC no. ED 125 806.

69. Pat Costello, Interview with Dwight Diller, *From the Down Neck Gazette*. Filmed in 2000. Published on YouTube 22 July 2012. https://www.youtube.com/watch?v=zujNF7MCKro.

70. Author's notes, 4 February 2015 (11:00 a.m.–12:00 p.m.) telephone conversation with Dan Levenson.

Bibliography

Books

Abrahams, Roger D. *Singing the Master: The Emergence of African-American Culture in the Plantation South.* New York: Penguin, 1992.

Adams, Sheila Kay. *Come Go Home with Me.* Chapel Hill: University of North Carolina Press, 1995.

Allen, Ray. *Gone to the Country: The New Lost City Ramblers and the Folk Music Revival.* Chicago: University of Illinois Press, 2010.

Artley, Malvin Newton. *The West Virginia Country Fiddler: An Aspect of the Folk Music Tradition in the United States.* Ph.D. dissertation, Chicago Musical College [Roosevelt University], 1955.

Bealle, John. *Old-Time Music and Dance: Community and Folk Revival.* Bloomington: Indiana University Press, 2005.

Beisswenger, Drew. *Fiddling Way Out Yonder: The Life and Music of Melvin Wine.* Jackson: University of Mississippi Press, 2002.

_____. *North American Fiddle Music: A Research and Information Guide.* New York: Routledge, 2011.

Cox, John Harrington. *Folk-Songs of the South: Collected Under the Auspices of the West Virginia Folklore Society.* Morgantown: West Virginia University, 1925. https://archive.org/details/folksongsofsouth00coxj.

Diamond, Andrew, et al. *Yew Pine Mountain: Obscure Underground Clawhammer Banjo from Mysterious Central West Virginia.* Revised, produced and printed in Pocahontas County, West Virginia, 2006. http://dwightdiller.com/wp-content/uploads/2013/12/C.-DLLR-TabBook-2006_07_31-page-numbers-correct.pdf.

Fields, Truman. *Remembering the 40's in the Heart of Appalachia: School Days, 1942–43.* Bloomington, IN: AuthorHouse, 2009.

Filene, Benjamin. *Romancing the Folk: Public Memory and American Roots Music.* Chapel Hill: University of North Carolina Press, 2000.

Flynn, Luther. *Beyond the Mountains: A Biography.* Virginia: McClure Printing, 1979.

Gainer, Patrick W. *Folk Songs from the West Virginia Hills.* Grantsville, WV: Seneca, 1975.

_____. *Witches, Ghosts and Signs: Folklore of the Southern Appalachians.* Morgantown: West Virginia University Press, 2008.

The Hammons Family: A Study of a West Virginia Family's Traditions. Based on fieldwork by Dwight Diller, Alan Jabbour and Carl Fleischhauer. Washington, D.C.: Library of Congress, 1973. http://www.loc.gov/folklife/LP/AFSL65andL66_Hammons.pdf.

Hicks, Bill. *Blurred Time.* 1999. http://www.earlyblurs.com/time.htm.

Howard, Wayne. *Fiddle Songs and Banjo Songs: A Descriptive Index.* 1981, Masters Theses and Specialist Projects, Paper 1430, http://digitalcommons.wku.edu/theses/1430.

Kimmel, Dick. *Fishing Creek Blues: 17 Clawhammer Tunes.* Missouri: Mel Bay, 2000.

Malone, Bill C. *Music from the True Vine: Mike Seeger's Life and Musical Journey.* Chapel Hill: University of North Carolina Press, 2011.

Marshall, Erynn. *Music in the Air Somewhere: The Shifting Borders of West Virginia's Fiddle and Song Traditions.* Morgantown: West Virginia University Press, 2006.

Milnes, Gerald. *Play of a Fiddle: Traditional Music, Dance and Folklore in West Virginia.* Lexington: University of Kentucky Press, 2009.

Morris, Christine Ballengee. "Roots, Branches, Blossoms, and Briars: Cultural Colonialism of the Mountain Arts in West Virginia." Thesis, Pennsylvania State University (UMI Number: 9531992), 1995.

Muller, Eric, and Barbara Koehler. *Frailing the 5-String Banjo.* Missouri: Mel Bay, 2002.

O'Brien, John. *At Home in the Heart of Appalachia.* New York: Random House, 2001.

Price, William Thomas. *Historical Sketches of Pocahontas County, West Virginia.* Marlinton, WV: Price Brothers, 1901.

Ritchie, Fiona, and Doug Orr. *Wayfaring Strangers: The Musical Voyage from Scotland and Ulster to Appalachia.* Chapel Hill: University of North Carolina Press, 2014.

Rosenberg, Neil V. *Transforming Tradition: Folk Music Revivals Examined.* Chicago: University of Illinois Press, 1993.

Schwab, John. *Old Time Back Up Guitar: Learn from the Masters.* Maryland: L-Century, 2012.

Strong, Tracy B. *Friedrich Nietzsche and the Politics of Transfiguration.* Chicago: University of Illinois Press, 2000.

Tribe, Ivan. *Mountaineer Jamboree: Country Music in West Virginia.* Lexington: University of Kentucky Press, 1984.

Wade, Stephen. *The Beautiful Music All Around Us: Field Recordings and the American Experience.* Chicago: University of Illinois Press, 2012.

Whisnant, David E. *All That Is Native & Fine: The Politics of Culture in an American Region.* Chapel Hill: University of North Carolina Press, 1983.

Articles

"About Dwight and the Music." http://dwightdiller.com/about-dwight-and-the-music/.

Arkin, Steve. "David Winston," *Banjo Newsletter*, April 2015, online edition. https://banjonews.com/2015-04/david_winston_interview_by_steve_arkin.html.

Bond, Helen K. "Paul: A Misunderstood Disciple." http://www.bbc.co.uk/programmes/articles/2YlQztFwm3NCXM2Cs5M23KG/paul-a-misunderstood-disciple.

Borchelt, Don. "Banj'r: Ralph Roberts." 2012. http://www.banjr.com/roberts.htm.

Brightwell, Eric. "Black Hillbilly—or—What You Really Know About the Upper South?" AMOEBLOG, 7 February 2015. http://www.amoeba.com/blog/2015/02/eric-s-blog/black-hillbilly-or-what-you-really-know-about-the-upper-south-.html.

Brooks, Michael. "North—South Banjo Camp—July 12-18 1998 in Cass, West Virginia: Rhythm by Dwight Diller and Several Notes by Ken Perlman." *Mississippi Old-Time Music Society Newsletter*, vol. 3, no. 8 (September 1998).

Brown, Paul. "Through the Flippen Filter: The Life, the Times and Tunes of Benton Flippen." *Old Time Herald*, vol. 5, no. 1 (Fall 1995), pp. 16-22, 60.

Bryan, Sara. "A Sea of Things to Learn: An Interview with Bill Hicks." *Old Time Herald*, vol. 14, no. 1 (July 2015), pp. 20-33.

Buckingham, Bob. "Cedar Mountain Banjos: The Lo Gordon Story." *Banjo Newsletter*, December 2004, pp. 8-11.

Buford, Kate. "Freddie Goodhart: A Thread in the History of Bluegrass." *Bluegrass Unlimited*, vol. 44, no. 8 (February 2010), pp. 34-38.

Burman-Hall, Linda C. "Southern American Folk Fiddle Styles." *Ethnomusicology*, vol. 19, no. 1 (January 1975), pp. 47-65. http://www.jstor.org/stable/849746.

Burns, Shirley Stewart. "Mountaintop Removal in Central Appalachia." Prepared for the 2008 Southern Spaces series "Space, Place, and Appalachia, "a collection of publications exploring Appalachian geographies through multimedia presentations," 30 September 2009. http://southernspaces.org/2009/mountaintop-removal-central-appalachia#sthash.nYJvTszd.dpuf.

Conway, Cecelia. "Banjo." In *Encyclopedia of Appalachia*, edited by Rudy Abramson and Jean Haskell, pp. 1121-1123. Knoxville: University of Tennessee Press, 2006.

_____. "Black Banjo Songsters in Appalachia." *Black Music Research Journal*, vol. 23 (Spring-Autumn 2003), pp. 149-166.

"Cordelia's Dad Interviewed by Auger/Anvil." Transcription of an interview 26 January 1998 by A. Tieger at Peter Irvine's house in Northampton, Massachusetts, for Auger/Anvil. http://www.cordeliasdad.com/antiqueSite/anvilinter.html.

Cuthbert, John A. "Edden Hammons." In the CD *Edden Hammons Collection, Volume Two: The Legendary West Virginia Fiddler from 1947 Field Recordings.* Morgantown: West Virginia University Press, 2000.

_____. "*Edden Hammons Collection* Offers Vintage Fiddle Music to Public." *West Virginia and Regional History Collection Newsletter*, vol. 1, no. 1 (Spring 1985), pp. 1-2.

_____. "Edden Hammons' Fiddle." *West Virginia and Regional History Collection Newsletter*, vol. 2, no. 1 (Spring 1986), p. 5.

_____. "The Music." In the CD *Edden Hammons Collection, Volume Two: The Legendary West Virginia Fiddler from 1947 Field Recordings.* Morgantown: West Virginia University Press, 2000.

_____. "Patrick W. Gainer Folklore Archives Donated to Collection." *West Virginia and Regional History Collection* Newsletter, no. 2 (Summer 1986), pp. 1-4.

Dixon, Glenn. "The Gift of Music: Old-Time Musicians Band Together for Banjoist Dwight Diller." *Express: A Publication of The Washington Post*, 12 January 2006, p. 40 (E12). http://www.alanjabbour.com/dwight_diller_benefit.html.

Diller, Dwight. "Chewing the Fat: To My Students and Friends in England." *The Friends of American Old-time Music and Dance News*, no. 47 (Autumn 2006), p. 3.

"Dwight Diller and John Morris Wrap Up Opera House '05-06 Season." *Mountain Messenger*, 20 May 2006, p. e 6.

"Edden Hammons." http://en.m.wikipedia.org/wiki/Edden_Hammons.

"Edden Hammons: Portrait of a West Virginia Fiddler." Old Time Party: An Archive of Mostly Southern American Vernacular Music, http://oldtimeparty.wordpress.com/.

"The Edden Hammons Collection, Volume 1—Review." Old Time Party: An Archive of Mostly Southern American Vernacular Music, http://oldtimeparty.wordpress.com/.

"The Edden Hammons Collection, Volume 2—Review." Old Time Party: An Archive of Mostly Southern American Vernacular Music, http://oldtimeparty.wordpress.com/.

Eisenberg, Emma. "Hippies, Cops, and Log Cabins: An Interview with Wayne Erbsen." *Journalism/Americana*, 24 October 2010. http://emma-eisenberg.com/?page_id=22.

Eulberg, Steve. "The Applachian Mountain Dulcimer: Examining the Creation of an 'American Tradition.'" CFA MU 755, manuscript, no date.

Evans, Craig. "How Many Tunes Should I Be Learning in a Year?" http://www.frailin.com/frailin/Banjo_Buying_Advice.html.

Fischer, Cindy. "Accepting Your Babble." *Fiddle Hangout*, 3 October 2012. http://www.fiddlehangout.com/archive/30272.

Fleischhauer, Carl. "Revisiting West Virginia Folk Culture: The Hammons Family Album Thirty Years Later." *Folklife Center News*, vol. 25, no. 4 (Fall 2003), pp. 13-14.

Gartner, Paul. "Review of 'Piney Woods.'" *The Charleston Gazette*, 5 August 1993, p. P3C.

Gibson, George. "Learning to Play Banjo: Emulation vs. Imitation." BanjoHistory.com, 1 December 2002. http://www.banjohistory.com/article/detail/6_learning_to_play_banjo_emulation_vs_imitation.

"Going Home to Appalachia: Larry Groce/Irene McKinney/Patsy Hatfield Lawson/Pinckney Benedict." *Living on Earth*, 24 December 2004. http://www.loe.org/shows/segments.html?programID=04-P13-00052&segmentID=2.

Goldfield, Steve. "The Music of the Cumberland Trail: An Interview with Bob Fulcher." *Fiddler Magazine*, Winter 2002/2003, pp. 19–24.

_____. "This One's Going to Be Trouble: A Chat with Franklin George." *Fiddler Magazine*, 23 May 2014.

Goodwin, Jacqueline G. "'I've Always Loved Music': Champion Fiddler Glen Smith." *Goldenseal*, vol. 16, no. 2 (Summer 1990), pp. 18–22.

"Hammons Family Celebration a Success." *The Pocahontas Times*, 29 September 2011, p.e 4. http://pch.stparchive.com/Archive/PCH/PCH09292011p04.php.

"The Hammons Family: The Traditions of a West Virginia Family and Their Friends." Old Time Party: An Archive of Mostly Southern American Vernacular Music, http://oldtimeparty.wordpress.com/.

Hansen, Rick. "Using the Mind to Change the Brain." Wellspring Institute for Neuroscience and Contemplative Wisdom, no date. https://www.youtube.com/watch?v=0EM45CpeQb4&sns=em.

Hanson, Bradley. "The Tennessee Jamboree: Local Radio, the Barn Dance, and Cultural Life in Appalachian East Tennessee." In "Space, Place, and Appalachia," a collection of publications exploring Appalachian geographies through multimedia presentations, 20 November 2008. http://southernspaces.org/2008/tennessee-jamboree-local-radio-barn-dance-and-cultural-life-appalachian-east-tennessee#sthash.9QmTZMX3.dpuf.

Hay, Fred J. "Black Musicians in Appalachia: An Introduction to Affrilachian Music." *Black Music Research Journal*, vol. 23 (Spring–Autumn 2003), pp. 1–19. http://www.jstor.org/stable/3593206.

Heaton, C.P. "The 5-String Banjo in North Carolina." *Banjo Newsletter*, vol. 3, no. 5 (March 1976), pp. 4–9.

"Helena Faust and Barnstorm." *Folk Music News*, Palmerston North Folk Music Club, August-November 2013, p. 2. http://pnfolkclub.weebly.com/uploads/1/9/5/5/19551375/2013_aug_-_nov_newsletter.pdf.

Heyer, Bob. "Ivydale: The Morris Family Old Time Festivals." *Goldenseal*, Summer 1998, http://www.wvculture.org/goldenseal/Summer98/ivydale.html.

Hicks, Bill, Blanton Owen, and Sharon Sandomirsky. "Roots of the Red Clay Ramblers: The Fuzzy Mountain String Band," 1994. http://www.earlyblurs.com/fmsb.htm.

Hicks, Brittany R. "Exploring 'Nostalgia for the Future': A History of the Augusta Heritage Center in Elkins, West Virginia." Master's thesis, May 2014. https://augustaheritagecenter.org/wp-content/uploads/BR-Hicks-Augusta-Thesis-2014.pdf.

Hoffman, Jan. "More Pastors Embrace Talk of Mental Ills." *New York Times*, 28 November 2014. A version of this article appears in print on 29 November 2014, on page A1 of the New York edition with the same headline. http://www.nytimes.com/2014/11/29/health/more-pastors-embrace-talk-of-mental-ills.html?emc=edit_th_20141129&nl=todaysheadlines&nlid=57603975&_r=0.

Howard, Wayne. "Memories of the Hammons Family Part I: Lee Hammons." *The Old-Time Herald*, vol. 12, no. 2 (December 2009–January 2010), pp. 32–39.

_____. "Memories of the Hammons Family Part II: Sherman Hammons." *The Old-Time Herald*, vol. 12, no. 3 (February–March 2010), pp. 24–33.

_____. "Memories of the Hammons Family Part III: Maggie Hammons Parker." *The Old-Time Herald*, vol. 12, no. 4 (April–May 2010), pp. 26–36.

_____. "Memories of the Hammons Family Part IV: Burl Hammons." *The Old-Time Herald*, vol. 12, no. 5 (June–July 2010), p. 26–37.

_____. *Mountain Lore Journal*. Field notes from visits with Burl, Maggie, Sherman and Lee Hammons, 10 September 1971–2 May 1972.

_____. "West Virginia's Hammons Family." *Goldenseal*, Winter 2014, pp. 6–12.

Jabbour, Alan. "American Fiddle Tunes from the Archive of Folk Song" (AFS L-62). http://www.loc.gov/folklife/LP/AmFiddleTunesLiner_opt.pdf.

_____. "The American Folklife Center: A Twenty-Year Retrospective." *Folklife Center News*, vol. 18, no. 1–2 (Winter-Spring 1996), pp. 3–19; vol. 18, no. 3–4 (Summer-Fall 1996), pp. 3–23. http://www.loc.gov/folklife/fcn/fcnhome.html.

_____. "Ben Botkin and the Archive of American Folk Song." Presented at the Conference Honoring Benjamin A. Botkin, Library of Congress, Washington, D.C., November 2001. http://www.alanjabbour.com/benbotkinarchiveamericanfolksong.pdf.

_____. "Cascading Tunes: On The Descending Contour in the Fiddle Tunes of the Upper South." Essay delivered as a paper for a panel on fiddling during an American Folklore Society meeting in Rochester, New York, October 2002. http://alanjabbour.com/cascading_tunes.html.

_____. "Fiddle Tunes of the Old Frontier." Joseph Schick Lecture at Indiana State University, Terre Haute, 6 December 2001. http://alanjabbour.com/fiddle_tunes_old_frontier.html.

_____. "Hammons Family." e-WV, the West Virginia Encyclopedia, http://www.wvencyclopedia.org/articles/149.

_____. "The Mystery Tune Story." Presented to a fiddle workshop, Person Hall, University of North Carolina at Chapel Hill, 28 April 1990. http://www.alanjabbour.com/mystery_tune.html.

_____. "The Recordings." In the CD *Edden Hammons Collection, Volume One: The Legendary West Virginia Fiddler from 1947 Field Recordings*. Morgantown: West Virginia University Press, 1999.

_____, and Carl Fleischhauer. "Letter to the Editor." *Goldenseal*, Spring 2015, pp. 3–4.

Jiordano, Angelo. "Have Banjo, Will Travel." *The Pocahontas Times*, 7 June 2013, pp. 1, 11. http://pch.stparchive.com/Archive/PCH/PCH06072012p01.php.

Johnson, Allen. "The Rhythm of Dwight Diller." *Goldenseal*, Winter 2014, pp. 14–19.

"Juanita Fireball and the Continental Drifters Play

Benefit for Radio Hillsboro." July 2015. http://www.publicbroadcasting.net/wvmr/arts.artsmain?action=viewArticle&id=1656620&sid=13.

Kennicott, Philip. "How to View Art: Be Dead Serious About It, But Don't Expect Too Much." *Washington Post*, 1 October 2014. http://www.washingtonpost.com/entertainment/museums/how-to-view-art-be-dead-serious-about-it-but-dont-expect-too-much/2014/10/01/28f7cdba-459a-11e4-b47c-f5889e061e5f_story.html?wpisrc=nl-eve&wpmm=1.

Kramer, Peter D. "Why Doctors Need Stories." *New York Times*, 18 October 2014. http://opinionator.blogs.nytimes.com/2014/10/18/why-doctors-need-stories/.

Kuntz, Andrew. "Queen of Earth, Child of the Skies: Southern Marvel # 2." Old Time Party: An Archive of Mostly Southern American Vernacular Music, 7 January 2012. https://oldtimeparty.wordpress.com/tag/edden-hammons/.

Langrall, Peggy. "Appalachian Folk Music: From Foothills to Footlights." *Music Educators Journal*, vol. 72, no. 7 (March 1986), pp. 37–39. http://www.jstor.org/stable/3396598.

Lattea, Charlene. "WVU Professor Collects West Virginia's 'Old Time' Music." F:/MUSIC1.TXT, 10 January 1997 (typescript).

Leftwich, Brad. "Tom Fuller: The Life and Times of a Fiddler from Indian Territory." *Old Time Herald*, vol. 13, no. 11, pp. 18–31.

_____, Al Tharp and Odell McGuire. "The Complete History of the Plank Road String Band and the Lexington, VA, Music Scene." http://www.fieldrecorder.com/docs/notes/plankroad.htm.

Levenson, Dan. "Dick Kimmel," *Banjo Newsletter*, June 2001.

_____. "Playing Half-Fast," *Old Time Herald*, vol. 10, no. 7 (October–November 2006).

_____. "Review: 'Just Banjo '99.'" *Banjo Newsletter*, February 2000, pp. 6–7.

Lewis, Lloyd D. "Tradition: Mountain Music Family Revered After Discovery." *Huntington Herald Dispatch*, 7 August 1977, p. 24.

Lilly, John. "The Morris Brothers Music from the Head of the Holler." *Goldenseal*, vol. 37, issue 1 (Spring 2011), p. 52. http://www.wvculture.org/goldenseal/spring11/Morris.html.

Lipton, Michael. "Tommy Thompson." e-WV: the West Virginia Encyclopedia. 19 December 2011. Accessed 2 December 2014. http://www.wvencyclopedia.org/articles/2367.

Limnios, Michalis. "Historian and Musician Scott Ainslie Speaks About the Blues the Way He Plays Them: With Authority And Passion." 21 October 2014. http://blues.gr/profiles/blogs/historian-musician-scott-ainslie-speaks-about-the-blues-the-way.

Littlehales, Bates. "Dwight Diller." *Banjo Newsletter*, vol. 23, no. 8 (June 1996), pp. 10–17.

Logan, Helen. "Old Time Four Day Workshops." *The Old Time News*, vol. 20 (December 1999), pp. 10–11.

Long, Lucy M. "A History of the Mountain Dulcimer." Sweet Music Index. http://www.bearmeadow.com/smi/histof.htm.

"Magazine Reviews Diller Tapes." *The Pocahontas Times*, 2 December 1993, p. 3. http://pch.stparchive.com/Archive/PCH/PCH12021993P03.php.

Matthew, Scott L. "John Cohen in Eastern Kentucky: Documentary Expression and the Image of Roscoe Halcomb During the Folk Revival." *Southern Spaces*, 6 August 2008. http://southernspaces.org/2008/john-cohen-eastern-kentucky-documentary-expression-and-image-roscoe-halcomb-during-folk-revival.

McCormick, Fred. "The Hammons: The Traditions of a West Virginia Family and Their Friends." Rounder 1504/1505. http://www.mustrad.org.uk/articles/hammons.htm.

Meador, Michael. "Grandpaw Got Me Started: Frank George and the Old Time Music." *Goldenseal*, vol. 9, no. 1 (Spring 1983), pp. 26–32.

"Mennoniite." Wikipedia. http://en.wikipedia.org/wiki/Mennonite.

Milnes, Gerald. "The Hammonds Family of Randolph County." *Goldenseal*, Winter 2014, p. 13.

Morris, Christine Ballengee. "Roots, Branches, Blossoms, and Briars: Cultural Colonialism of the Mountain Arts in West Virginia." *Marilyn Zurmuehlen Working Papers in Art Education*, vol. 13, issue 1 (1995), article 17. http://ir.uiowa.edu/mzwp/vol13/iss1/17.

Obermiller, Phillip J., and Michael E. Maloney. "The Uses and Misuses of Appalachian Culture." Urban Appalachian Council Working Paper no. 20, May 2011. http://uacvoice.org/pdf/workingpaper20.pdf.

O'Brien, John. "Looking for Sherman: The Search for a West Virginia Fiddler." Typescript provided to author by Dwight Diller. No date.

O'Brien, Robert J. "Persecution and Acceptance: The Strange History of Discrimination Against Married Women Teachers in West Virginia." *West Virginia History*, vol. 56 (1997), pp. 56–75. http://www.wvculture.org/history/journal_wvh/wvh56-4.html.

"Old Time Fiddlers Hall of Fame: Edwin 'Edden' Hammons, 1874–1955—West Virginia." http://www.oldtimemusic.com/FHOFEdn.html.

Old Time Party: An Archive of Mostly Southern American Vernacular Music. http://oldtimeparty.wordpress.com/.

Osborne, Carrie. "Killer Diller." *Folk Roots*, no. 180 (June 1998), pp. 17–18.

Perlman, Ken. "Art Rosenbaum." *Banjo Newsletter*, vol. 25, no. 1 (November 1997), pp. 8–15.

_____. "Dwight Diller and the Music of Pocahontas County." *Sing Out!*, vol. 42, no. 1 (May/June/July 1997), pp. 52–63.

_____. "Melodic Clawhammer: The Origins of Old-Time." *Banjo Newsletter*, March 2015. https://banjonews.com/2015-03/the_origins_of_old-time.html.

Pitts, Leon, Jr. "White Poverty Exists, Ignored," *Miami Herald*. 10 June 2014, http://www.miamiherald.com/opinion/opn-columns-blogs/leonard-pitts-jr/article2518087.html.

Potorti, David. "Didn't He Ramble: Family, Friends and Fellow Musicians Remember Tommy Thompson." *Old Time Herald*, vol. 8, no. 4 (Summer 2002), pp. 26–32.

Prouty, Scott. "The Hammons Legacy: Volumes 1–3." Old Time Party: Archive of Mostly Southern American Old Time Music, 11 December 2011. http://oldtimeparty.wordpress.com/2011/12/11/the-hammons-legacy-volumes-1-3/.

Randolph, John H. "Pat Gainer." e-WV: the West Virginia

Encyclopedia. 23 October 2012. Accessed 10 October 2014. http://www.wvencyclopedia.org/articles/2077.

Rock, Sue. "Music." The Baltimore Grotto News, National Speleological Society, Baltimore, Maryland, vol. 11, no. 10 (November 1971), p. 5 (regarding Pipestem Festival, Bob Thren). http://www.karstportal.org/FileStorage/Baltimore_Grotto/1971-v011-n010.pdf.

Roth, Daniel. "O Brother! Daniel Roth Goes to Banjo Camp and Learns to Play Along." *Fortune*, 21 January 2002. http://archive.fortune.com/magazines/fortune/fortune_archive/2002/01/21/316565/index.htm.

Sanabria, Diane. "Tommy Thompson, My Banjo Guru." No date. http://www.banjoqueen.com/rants/blog/archive/000005.html.

Schultz, Dan. "Woody Simmons: Randolph County Fiddler." 14 December 2014, http://www.traveling219.com/blog/woody-simmons-randolph-county-fiddler/.

Smith, Albert. "Dwight Diller Brings His Music and Country Humor to Colorado." *The Pocahontas Times*, 6 November 2003, p. 12. http://pch.stparchive.com/Archive/PCH/PCH11062003P12.php.

Smith, Barbara Ellen, and Stephen L. Fisher. "The Place of Appalachia," *Southern Spaces*, 31 January 2013. Excerpted from *Transforming Places: Lessons from Appalachia* (University of Illinois Press, 2012). http://southernspaces.org/2013/place-appalachia#content_top.

Smithers, Aaron. "SFC Spotlight: Jack Bernhardt Papers. Field Trip South: Exploring the Southern Folklife Collection." 21 May 2013, http://blogs.lib.unc.edu/sfc/index.php/2013/05/21/sfc-spotlight-jack-bernhardt-paper/.

Spencer, Martha, and Erika Godfrey. "Remembering Enoch Rutherford," *Mountain Music Magazine*, 18 June 2013. http://mountainmusicmagazine.weebly.com/mountain-music-legacies/remembering-enoch-rutherford.

"Stonewall Jackson Jubilee." e-WV: The West Virginia Encyclopedia. 5 November 2010. Accessed 24 October 2014. http://www.wvencyclopedia.org/articles/596.

Strucko, Jenna. "So You Think You Know the Banjo?" *The Bitter Southerner* (Atlanta, Georgia), 20 January 2015, http://bittersoutherner.com/history-of-the-banjo#.VL_ByMbWqxU.

Stern, Lewis M. "Dwight Hamilton Diller: Working to Preserve the Old Tunes." Program, 4th Annual Old Time Fiddlers Convention, Highland County, Virginia, 16–19 July 2015.

_____. "Review: 'Just Rhythm': West Virginia Clawhammer Banjo." *Banjo Newsletter*, February 2004, p. 6.

Strong, Tracy B. "Music, the Passions, and Political Freedom in Rousseau." University of California at San Diego, 2010. http://ebooks.cambridge.org/chapter.jsf?bid=CBO9780511712098&cid=CBO9780511712098A017.

_____. "Philosophy of the Morning: Nietzsche and the Politics of Transfiguration." *The Journal of Nietzsche Studies* 39 (Spring 2010), pp. 51–65.

Taylor, Bobby. "Final Notes, Woody Simmons." *Old Time Herald*, http://www.oldtimeherald.org/here+there/final-notes/woody-simmons.html.

Todd, Roxy. "Musician Who Couldn't Walk Created One of the Longest Running Bluegrass Bands in W.Va." WVA Public Broadcasting: Telling West Virginia's Story, 15 August 2014, http://wvpublic.org/post/musician-who-couldnt-walk-created-one-longest-running-bluegrass-bands-wva.

_____. "Tunes and Tales: Old Time and Bluegrass Musicians of Pocahontas County." 30 July 2013. http://www.traveling219.com/blog/tunes-and-tales-old-time-and-bluegrass-musicians-of-pocahontas-county/.

Tonini, Holly. "Home on the Road: House Concerts Open Doors for Traveling Musicians." *Triblive*, 3 January 2013. http://triblive.com/aande/music/3228771-74/says-hosts-concerts#axzz3MgBob8MN.

Tribe, Ivan M. "The Black Mountain Bluegrass Boys: Forty-Six Years of Mountain State Bluegrass." *Bluegrass Unlimited*, vol. 49, no. 5 (November 2014), pp. 34–36.

_____. "Glen Smith, Mountain State Fiddler." Bee Balm Music, November 2004. http://www.beebalmmusic.com/glen_smith.html.

"Tributes and Music Fill Pocahontas Opera House this Weekend." *The Pocahontas Times*, 29 September 2011, p. 4. http://pch.stparchive.com/Archive/PCH/PCH09292011p04.php.

"Vernon C. Diller." Obituary. *The Pocahontas Times*, 6 January 1994, p. 1. http://pch.stparchive.com/Archive/PCH/PCH01061994P01.php.

Walls, David S. "Action, Scholarship, Reflection, Renewal." Keynote Address to the 34th Annual Conference of the Appalachian Studies Association, Eastern Kentucky University, Richmond, 11 March 2011, *Journal of Appalachian Studies*, vol. 17, no. 1 and 2 (Spring/Fall 2011), pp. 9–13, 23–25.

_____. "Central Appalachia: A Peripheral Region within an Advanced Capitalist Society." *Journal of Sociology and Social Welfare*, vol. IV, no. 2 (November 1976), pp. 232–246.

_____. "Internal Colony or Internal Periphery?" In *Colonialism in Modern America: The Appalachian Case*, edited by Helen Matthews Lewis, Linda Johnson and Donald Askins. Boone, NC: Appalachian Consortium Press, 1978. http://www.sonoma.edu/users/w/wallsd/internal-colony.shtml.

_____. "On the Naming of Appalachia." From *An Appalachian Symposium: Essays Written in Honor of Cratis D. Williams*, edited by J. W. Williamson. Boone, NC: Appalachian State University Press, 1977. http://www.sonoma.edu/users/w/wallsd/on-the-naming-of-appalachia.shtml.

_____. "Three Models in Search of Appalachian Development: Critique and Synthesis." Presented at a joint session of the Rural Sociological Society and the Society for the Study of Social Problems, Montreal, Quebec, 25 August 1974, abstracted in *Research in Education*, November 1976, ERIC no. ED 125 806.

_____, and Dwight B. Billings. "The Sociology of Southern Appalachia," *Appalachian Journal*, vol. 5, no. 1 (Autumn 1977), special issue, "A Guide to Appalachian Studies," pp. 131–144.

Weidlich, Joseph. "A Brief Introduction to 'Old Time Music.'" *Old Time Country Guitar Backup Basics: Based on Commercial Recordings of the 1920s and early 1930s*. California: Centerstream, 2005, pp. 4–6.

Williams, Danny. "Preface to the CD Edition." In *The Edden Hammons Collection, Volume One: The Legendary West Virginia Fiddler from 1947 Field Recordings*. Morgantown: West Virginia University Press, 1999.

Wohlwend, Chris. "Where the Hills and Hollows Are Alive with Music." *New York Times*, 31 October 2014. http://www.nytimes.com/2014/11/02/travel/where-the-hills-and-hollows-are-alive-with-music.html?emc=etal.

Wyatt, Marshall. "Pockets of Eccentricity: An Interview with Terry Zwigoff." *Old Time Herald*, vol. 5, no. 1 (Fall 1995), pp. 24–32.

Yeager, James. "Scientist vs Caveman: 'Why I Cannot Train You.'" 30 December 2013. https://www.youtube.com/watch?v=pJ6HubpLSVM.

Zemach, Heidi. "Fill Your Home and Heart in Hillsboro: Visits Are Fun at Morningstar FolkArts Any Time of the Day." *The Pocahontas Times*, 29 May 2003, p. 15. http://pch.stparchive.com/Archive/PCH/PCH05292003P15.php.

Documentary Films, Videos, Audio Works and Interviews

Listed chronologically

"Morris Family Old Time Festival: Preview." Morris brothers' old time music festivals, Ivydale, WV, 1969 to 1973, posted 5 May 2011. https://www.youtube.com/watch?v=kV60741TJ5g.

The Hammons Family: A Study of a West Virginia Family's Traditions, based on fieldwork by Dwight Diller, Alan Jabbour and Carl Fleischhauer, 1973. Library of Congress issued a boxed two-LP set with a 40-page booklet. Reissued as an online version of the booklet for the Archive of Folk Culture sound recording AFS L65-L66, 2011. http://www.loc.gov/folklife/LP/AFSL65andL66_Hammons.pdf.

"Where the Twisted Laurel Grows." Series Pilot Number 1, WMUL TV, West Virginia Public Broadcasting, Huntington, 4 July 1976, West Virginia Archives and History. https://www.youtube.com/watch?v=9Ph6pU0mCOI.

"Sugar in the Gourd: Music from the Mountains—Sherman Hammons and the Bing Brothers." Created and produced by Larry R. Hall, directed by Jim Wysong, West Virginia State Archives, 1978. An interview with Hammons from the series *Sugar in the Gourd*, produced by West Virginia Public Broadcasting. https://www.youtube.com/watch?v=OCpkQAe02XU&feature=youtube_gdata.

"My Old Fiddle: A Visit with Tommy Jarrell in the Blue Ridge." By Cece Conway, Les Blank, and Maureen Gosling, 1979. https://www.youtube.com/watch?v=8g9zVz2pM2o.

Dwight Diller Interview. University of North Carolina at Chapel Hill, Collection Number 20061, Collection Title: Jack Bernhardt Papers, 1943–2011. Dwight Diller Interview, Elkins, WV, 3 August 1983, Tape 1 of 2. Dwight Diller Interview, Elkins, WV, 3 August 1983, Tape 2 of 2.

Flat Foot in the Ashes. Harvey Sampson and the Big Possum String Band. Augusta Heritage Records, AHR-004C, 1986.

Damron, Randy. Interview with old-time fiddler Wilson Douglas, Clay County, WV, filmed for the West Virginia Library Commission program *Man to Man*. 26 May 1989. https://www.youtube.com/watch?v=4UNby5iO1ko.

Lomax, Alan. *Appalachian Journey*. Video (56:26), 1991. https://www.youtube.com/watch?v=MXh8SDp0H-E.

The Old Drake: Traditional Music from the Mountains of East Central West Virginia Played on the Banjo and Fiddle: Visiting Dwight Diller with Jimmy Triplett. AFC 1996/041: Don Patterson / Mountain Music Video Collection.

"Transcription of an Interview with Diane Jones, August 9, 1997." Susan A. Eacker and Geoff Eacker Collection, Accession 666, Special Collections, Marshall University Libraries, Huntington, WV.

"Transcription of an Interview with Helena Triplett by Susan A. Eacker and Geoff Eacker, October 20, 1997." Susan A. Eacker and Geoff Eacker Collection, Accession 666, Special Collections, Marshall University Libraries Huntington, WV.

"Perfect Porch: A Banjo Camp with Dwight Diller and Ken Perlman." Taped at Cass, Pocahontas County, WV, during the week of 13 July 1998, including performances by Marc Perdue, Jackie Phelan, Dinah Ainsley, Doug Tursman, Alvin Hudson, Pam Lund, Larry Combs, and Doug Van Gundy.

Costello, Pat. Interview with Dwight Diller, filmed in 2000. Published 22 July 2012, *The Down Neck Gazette*. https://www.youtube.com/watch?v=zujNF7MCKro.

Davenport, Tom, and Barry Dornfeld. *Remembering the High Lonesome*, 2003 film from Folkstreams, http://www.folkstreams.net/film,42; "Transcript of *Remembering the High Lonesome*," Folkstreams, http://www.folkstreams.net/context,92.

The Appalachians. Evening Star Productions, presented by Nashville Public Television, executive producer Mari-Lynn C. Evans, written and produced by Phylis Geller. DVD from Home Video, Ltd., distributed by APT, 2005.

Madison County Project: Documenting the Sound. Film by Martha King and Rob Roberts. Produced by Martha King and Rob Roberts. Cinematographers: Martha King, Rob Roberts, Judd Williamson. Sound: Martha King, Rob Roberts. Editing: Martha King, Rob Roberts. 24 minutes, color. Original format: DV Mini. 2005. http://www.folkstreams.net/pub/FilmPage.php?title=120.

David Holt interviews Sheila Kay Adams, from *Our State TV*. Produced by UNC-TV in partnership with *Our State Magazine*. May 2007. https://www.youtube.com/watch?v=ge07tEY8Obw.

"The Vandalia Gathering, 2009." West Virginia Public Broadcasting. https://www.youtube.com/watch?v=3h0MQZtf7OQ.

Bill Hicks, Mike Graver, James Watson, Joe Newberry. Pocahontas Opera House concert, August 2009. CD version of a field recording of this concert provided to the author by Bill Hicks.

Folkways. "Music of Surry County." UNC-TV, North Carolina Arts Council, Folklife Program, 2010. https://www.youtube.com/watch?v=Rbcj-n3QecQ.

Suchet, David. *In the Footsteps of St. Paul*. CTVC

documentary in cooperation with BBC Jersusalem. 2012. http://www.bbc.co.uk/programmes/b01pq9h5.
Across the YewPines. Pocahontas Free Libraries and the Yew Pine Cultural Traditions. Contains 29 out of a total of 130 stories told by the Hammons family and transcribed in dialect by Gail Hatton, 2013. http://dwightdiller.com/across-yew-pines-dvd/.
"Hidden America: Children of the Mountains." A Diane Sawyer Special Report on the Half Million People Living in Poverty in Central Appalachia, 2013. https://www.youtube.com/watch?v=NBdu6uhrNno'.
Creative License: The Art of Banjo. Featuring Dan Knowles of Paris, TN. PBS Creative Instincts, February 2013. http://www.banjohangout.org/myhangout/videos.asp?memberID=44416.
Blosser, Kurtis, and Josh Kraybill. "Glendon Blosser Interview." 29 October 2013. https://www.youtube.com/watch?v=yAl3rsJJw3M and https://www.youtube.com/watch?v=A4VbbzoQp5w.
Todd, Roxie. "Musician Who Couldn't Walk Created One of the Longest Running Bluegrass Bands in W.Va." West Virginia Public Broadcasting, 15 August 2014. http://wvpublic.org/post/musician-who-couldnt-walk-created-one-longest-running-bluegrass-bands-wva.
"Born Old, in Concert: Doug Van Gundy and Paul Gartner." The Four Directions, A Center For The Arts and Healing, Gibsonia, PA, 29 August 2014. https://www.eventbrite.com/e/born-old-a-harvest-home-concert-music-of-traditional-cultures-82914-tickets-12597255731.
"Sheila Adams Explains How She Learned Banjo." Frank Islam Athenaeum Symposia Speaker Series, Montgomery College, 3 October 2014. http://insidemc.montgomerycollege.edu/details.php?id=56758.
Ainslie, Scott. "Hammons Banjo Tunes." DVD provided to the author by Scott Ainslie, 2014.
Evans, Craig. "A Piece of Living History: A Conversation with Teacher Dwight Diller." Conversations with North American Banjo Builders, vol. 3, Conversations with Banjo Historians. Frailinflix Productions, 2014.
"The Black Mountain Bluegrass Boys: Traveling 219, The Seneca Trail." No date. http://www.traveling219.com/podcast/ and http://www.traveling219.com/stories/marlinton-lewisburg/the-black-mountain-bluegrass-boys/.
"Tommy Thompson Vignette." No date. https://www.youtube.com/watch?v=DOONIiWzDdU.
"Touched with Fire: A Documentary about the Highwoods String Band." Producer/director Chris Valluzzo, Horse Archer Productions. No date. http://www.whyoldtime.com/.

Audio and Video Tapes of Dwight Diller: Public Performances, Jams and Banjo Workshops/Retreats

Listed chronologically

Andy Williams fiddling "Leather Britches"; A.A. Cutters. No date, possibly 1973. Audiocassette provided by Rock Garton.
Dwight Diller. No date, possibly 1973. Audiocassette provided by Rock Garton.
Jack Ramsey on banjo. No date, possibly 1973. Audiocassette provided by Rock Garton.
A.A. Cutters, Dwight Diller and Andy Williams, fiddle and banjo. No date, possibly 1973. Audiocassette provided by Rock Garton.
Dwight Diller, banjo contest, 4th Annual Old Time Fiddlers and Bluegrass Convention, Hillsville, VA, June 1970. Digitized by Kilby Spencer.
Ken Segal, Buell Kazee, J.P. Fraley, Lee Triplett, Wilson Douglas, Franklin Davies, Mountain Heritage Festival, Carter Cove, KY, May 1972. Audiocassette provided by Tom Mylet.
Armin Barnett and Dwight Diller, Charlottesville, VA, August 1972. Two audiocassettes provided by Tom Mylet.
Dwight Diller and Armin Barnett, jam tape, recorded by William Talley of West Chester, PA, at "Alternative Galax," hosted by Armin Barnett on his farm in Charlottesville, Virginia, 1972. Audio digitized by William Talley.
John Summers, field recording by Armin Barnett, Marion, Indiana, 1972.
Dwight Diller and Mike Seeger, workshop conducted on the steps of the Pocahontas County Courthouse in Marlinton, WV, featuring the music of Lee, Burl, Sherman and Maggie Hammons, 11 July 1975. Recorded by Wayne Howard.
Dwight Diller, parking lot jam at a festival (NFI), May 1976. Audiocassette provided by Bob Thornburg.
Dwight Diller, with Bing Brothers and Tom King, workshop on the banjo in string bands, Augusta Heritage Center, Elkins, WV, 1988. Audiocassette provided by Bob Thornburg.
Dwight Diller, audiotape of narration of the Hammons Slide Show, second revision, taped at Diller's home in Hillsboro, WV, 1989. Audiocassette provided by Bob Thornburg.
Dwight Diller, banjo classes taught at Cass, WV, 1988, 1989, 1990 and 1991. Fourteen audiocassettes provided by Bob Thornburg.
Dwight Diller, banjo workshop and evening concert, Seneca Park, on the Greenbrier River, WV, 1990 and 1991. Eight audiocassettes provided by Bob Thornburg.
Dwight Diller, Tom King and Glen Smith, Augusta Heritage Center, Elkins, WV, 1991. Audiocassette provided by Bob Thornburg.
Dwight Diller, banjo workshop, conducted at the home of Bob Thornburg, Bishop, CA, 1995. Audiocassette provided by Bob Thornburg.
Dwight Diller, jam tapes, Celestial Mountain Music Store, Brevard, NC, 27 January 1996. Audio digitized by Carroll Smith.
Dwight Diller, lesson tapes, Celestial Mountain Music Store, Brevard, NC, 28 January 1996. Audio digitized by Carroll Smith.
Dwight Diller, lesson tapes, Celestial Mountain Music Store, Brevard, NC, January 1997. Audio digitized by Carroll Smith.
Dwight Diller, Banjo Camp, D Base Camp, Virginia Lakes and Bishop, CA, September 1997. Two audiocassettes provided by Bob Thornburg.
Dwight Diller, recording session, Cass, WV, 1998. Audiocassette provided by Bob Thornburg.
Dwight Diller, Banjo Camp, Port Ludlow, WA, 1999.

Audiocassette "practice tape" provided by Bob Thornburg.

Dwight Diller, Seattle, WA, radio interview, 1999. Audiocassette provided by Bob Thornburg.

Dwight Diller, banjo workshop, at Tersh McCracken's summer home near Red Lodge, MT, September 2000. Two audiocassettes provided by Bob Thornburg.

Dwight Diller, banjo workshop, at Tersh McCracken's summer home near Red Lodge, MT, September 2000. Video by Stewart Seidel.

Dwight Diller, Banjo Camp, Vancouver, British Columbia, summer 2001, hosted by Stewart Seidel. Four audiocassettes provided by Bob Thornburg.

Dwight Diller, Banjo Camp, Hood Canal, near Seattle, WA, no date, possibly 2001. Two audiocassettes provided by Bob Thornburg.

"Diller Concert—12/03," Pittsburgh, PA, December 2003, transfer from Mini-DV Master (62 minutes), converted and duplicated by Colorlab Laboratory and Telecine Services, Rockville, MD.

"Diller Concert—12/03," in Pittsburgh, PA, December 2003, transfer from Mini-DV Master (44:25), converted and duplicated by Colorlab Laboratory and Telecine Services, Rockville, MD.

Dwight Diller house concert, Pittsburgh, PA, December 2011. Seven digital audio files provided by Teri Hayes.

Dwight Diller, house concert for workshop students, 13 December 2014, four videos provided by Cindy Harris.

Burl and Maggie Hammons. No date. Audiocassette provided by Tom Mylet.

Dave Milesky and Amin Barnett, and Bill Hicks, Armin Barnett, Dwight Diller, and the Hammons. No date. Audiocassette provided by Tom Mylet.

Dwight Diller, Gail Hatton, John Blisard, Betty Vornbroch, Billy Cornette, "Glenville Friday Concert." Transfer from Mini-DV Master (47:49), converted and duplicated by Colorlab Laboratory and Telecine Services, Rockville, MD, no date.

"Firehouse concert in Hillsboro, West Virginia—Dwight Diller, John Morris, Larry Combs." Transfer from Mini-DV Master (23:04), converted and duplicated by Colorlab Laboratory and Telecine Services, Rockville, MD, no date.

Manuscripts

Banks, Gordon. "Tablature for Dwight's Tunes," online compilation, 1998.

Smith, Carroll. "Why 'Old Time' Five String Banjo?" March 2015.

Documents

Official Transcript of Academic Record, Dwight Hamilton Diller, issued by David A. Detrow, University Registrar, Eastern Mennonite University, Seminary Division, 5 January 2015.

Official Transcript of Academic Record, Dwight Hamilton Diller, issued by Steve Robinson, University Registrar, West Virginia University at Morgantown, 26 February 2015.

2012 State of Well Being: Community, State and Congressional District Well-Being Reports—West Virginia. Gallup-Healthways, 2013.

"West Virginia Collections in the Archive of Folk Culture Acquired Through 1990." LC Folk Archive Finding Aid, American Folklife Center, Library of Congress, LCFAFA No. 20, June 1996 (ISSN 0736–4903).

West Virginia University, 1964–1965 Catalog, West Virginia University Bulletin, Series 64, no. 12–3, June 1964. https://archive.org/details/under6465west.

Websites

Dwight Diller: West Virginia Mountain Music. http://dwightdiller.com/.

Dwight Diller, YouTube Channel. https://www.youtube.com/user/dwightdiller.

West Virginia and Regional History Center, Guide to Field Recordings of Folk Music: Alphabetical List of Performers. https://wvrhc.lib.wvu.edu/collections/core/folkmusic/byperformer/.

WVU Press Edden Hammons site. http://www.as.wvu.edu/~sharris/EH/.

Interviewees

Scott Ainslie, a traditional musician with expertise in both the Southern Appalachian fiddle and banjo tradition, and Piedmont and Delta blues.

A. Donald Augsburger, dean of high school students (boys) in 1948 and 1949 at Eastern Mennonite University, who returned to EMU and served as pastor of students from 1958 to 1964, was a professor in EMU's seminary program from 1970 to 1989, and pastored in the college community church from 1975 to 1980.

Olin Bare, old time fiddler and banjo player from Lexington, Virginia.

Carl Baron, old time fiddler, banjoist, guitarist, and member of the southeastern Pennsylvania-based band Hobo Pie.

Gordon Banks, a clawhammer banjo enthusiast and early student of Dwight's, developed the online resource Tablature for Dwight's Tunes in the late 1990s.

Mac Benford, a clawhammer banjo player who with Walt Koken formed the Highwoods String band that toured extensively from 1972 until disbanding in 1979. From the early 1980s to 2002, Benford performed with a succession of bands including the Backwoods Band, the Woodshed Allstars, and The Haywire Gang.

Coleman "Cully" Blake was a continuous presence at old time events hosted by Odell and Mata McGuire in Lexington, Virginia, in the early 1970s. He met Dave Morris in Vietnam where both served in the U.S. Army, and attended the Ivydale festival hosted by the Morris brothers in the early 1970s. Blake played jew's harp in The Bird Forest Band with Odell McGuire, Scott Ainslie, Al Tharp, and Chris Murray in the early 1970s in Lexington.

Michael Brooks, a clawhammer banjo player from West Virginia, attended banjo retreats taught by Dwight in the late 1990s, wrote about the 1998 "North-South Banjo Camp" co-hosted by Dwight and Ken Perlman, and now teaches banjo at various banjo retreats.

Mark Campbell, a traditional musician who grew up in the Shenandoah Valley of Virginia, learned bowing and picking styles from some of the last generation of great musicians of North Carolina, Virginia and West Virginia. He was the 2001 Champion Fiddler at the Appalachian String Band Festival at Clifftop, West Virginia, and in 2008 he was named the Virginia Foundation for the Humanities' master fiddler.

Bob Carlin, noted old time banjo performer, and the author of *The Birth of the Banjo: Joel Walker Sweeney and Early Minstrelsy* and *String Bands in the North Carolina Piedmont*.

Ron Chacey, an extremely talented and well known inlay artist, did the fingerboard inlay on the banjo neck that Dan Dagget built for Dwight in the early 1970s.

Cece Conway, professor, Appalachian Literature and Culture, American Literature, Department of English, Appalachian State University, Boone, North Carolina.

Billy Cornette, from Winston-Salem, North Carolina, was the guitar player with the Reed Island Rounders Old Time Band from 1993 through 2013 when the band was reconfigured to include Kirk Sutphin, replacing Diane Jones. Cornette's wife, Betty Vornbrock, continued to play fiddle for that group through 2013. Since at least 2000, Cornette and Vornbrock, along with Kim Johnson have also played together as a trio.

Jimmy Costa, a fiddler and banjo player from Talcott, West Virginia, is an accomplished performer of Dock Boggs' repertoire, and a collector of traditional southern stringed instruments, as well as a preserver of old West Virginia tools and agricultural instruments, housed on his farmland.

Mark Crabtree, a West Virginian fiddler and devoted student of Wilson Douglas and Monongalia County fiddler Elmer Rich, was a photographer for the Augusta Heritage Center in Elkins, West Virginia, and a long-time participant in the old time community in Morgantown, West Virginia.

John A. Cuthbert, director and curator of the West Virginia and Regional History Collection at the West Virginia University Libraries. Cuthbert, the author of *Early Art and Artists in West Virginia*, was educated at Worcester State College, the University of Massachusetts, and West Virginia University.

Dan Dagget, who in the early 1970s worked for Kix Stewart and Bill McDonald, built banjo necks for Stewart-Macdonald in Athens, Ohio. Dagget put the neck on an old Lange banjo pot that would be Dwight's banjo of choice for many years.

Dwight Hamilton Diller, born to Faith and Vernon Diller in 1946.

Nancy Faith Diller, Dwight's sister, born to Faith and Vernon Diller in 1948.

Joe Dobbs, an old time fiddler, was owner of the music store Fret 'n' Fiddle in St. Albans, West Virginia, through at least 2015.

Brendan Doyle, who grew up in rural central Minnesota, started playing banjo there in 1974. Doyle moved to the San Francisco Bay Area in late 1975. He plays banjo in the Cliffhangers, with Mark Simos fiddling, a once-a-year band that assembles at Clifftop each summer. Doyle recorded Burl Hammons in August 1979 and in August 1980, and again in the last quarter of 1992, a few months before Burl died.

Carl Fleischhauer was working for a television station in Morgantown, West Virginia, in 1970 when he joined Alan Jabbour in the project that led to two recorded publications issued in 1973 by the Library of Congress featuring the traditions, music and stories of the Hammons family of West Virginia. Fleischhauer worked for the American Folklife Center of the Library of Congress from 1976 to 1987, and served as the project manager, Office of Strategic Initiatives, Library of Congress, where he focused on digitizing historical documents.

Andy Fitzgibbon, a West Virginia fiddler and banjo historian, is a member of the band the Iron Leg Boys and a talented stringed instrument repairman who works for Smakula Fretted Instruments of Elkins, West Virginia.

Andrew Fults of Tennessee attended one of Dwight's banjo retreats in 2011, hauling along a five string he had built for himself, and that led to a long-running discussion with Dwight about building banjos. Sometime in 2011, Dwight decided that he wanted a short scale banjo and asked Fults to do the work. That led to a series of projects including one focused on recreating the first banjo Dwight played, an old Washburn famously christened Old Snotty in the early 1970s because of its assertive, overwhelming sound.

John Gallagher, a West Virginia fiddler from Elkins, WV, who performed on Dwight's CD *Piney Woods* and in 2013 collaborated with Scott Prouty and Chris Coole to produce the CD *No Corn on Tygart*, playing tunes from West Virginia, Kentucky, North Carolina, Indiana and Virginia.

Paul Gartner, an Ohio native, has lived in West Virginia for much of his life. He is a copy editor for the *Charleston Gazette*, where he also writes book reviews, features, and articles on traditional music. Gartner, who attended West Virginia University, is a multi-instrumentalist who plays banjo, fiddle, guitar and sings. He is a two-time Ohio State claw hammer banjo champion, and took first in 2003 at the West Virginia State Folk Festival at Glenville.

Rock Garton, a West Virginia fiddler, joined the band that called itself the A.A. Cutters in 1973, participated in the lessons that Dwight taught in his apartment in Morgantown, West Virginia, and played in the band's first gig, a pre-game show at the old Mountaineer Stadium for Mountaineer Week Festivities. Dwight remained associated with that band through at least the mid–1970s. Garton played with the band through 1974, by which time the Cutters had come to include Norm Strouse playing banjo and bass, Pete Mineer on fiddle, and Jackie Horvath on banjo.

Darin Gentry is an old time banjo and fiddle player with roots in western North Carolina. His parents and the earlier generations of his family are from Ashe and Watauga Counties. He owns and plays his great-great-grandfather's banjo. Gentry completed a degree in environmental policy and management at the University of North Carolina at Asheville. He and Dwight Diller recorded the CD *Jerico Road* together in 2005.

Gail Gillespie, an old time music multi-instrumentalist, was part of the Bucksnort Barndance Band of Gainesville before relocating to North Carolina in 1986, where she played with the East Carolina Catbirds and the Walkertown Rangers (with fiddler Kirk Sutphin). In the mid–1990s, Gillespie played in the band called the Herald Angels with Alice Gerrard. Gillespie was editor of the *Old Time Herald* from 2002 to 2008, and is a studious historian of traditional music.

Freddie Goodhart, born in Maryland, a member of the first generation of bluegrass musicians, played mandolin and banjo professionally. He played mandolin with Lightnin' Hopkins in Cambridge, Massachusetts, before settling in Lexington, Virginia, where he owns and operates the Second Hand Shop and regularly performs on radio and television. Goodhart has played with Don Reno and Red Smiley, Vassar Clements, Chubby Wise, Leon Poindexter, Larry Rice, and members of the Seldom Scene.

Jaynell Graham is the managing editor of the *Pocahontas Times* in Marlinton, West Virginia.

Buddy Griffin, a 2001 recipient of the Vandalia Award, West Virginia's highest folklife honor, began performing on radio and television with his family in the early 1960s and later became the staff banjo and fiddle player for WWVA's Jamboree USA in Wheeling. Between 1995 and 2003, Griffin developed an old-time radio-style creative writing and production workshop, "Radio's Golden Memories," in conjunction with the WFMT Fine Arts Network in Chicago. In 1997, Griffin returned home to West Virginia, where he founded the nation's first degree-granting program in bluegrass music at Glenville State College.

Franklin F. Hammons, grandson of Lee Hammons, and a resident of Marlinton, West Virginia, where, as an IRS registered tax preparer, he operated Frank's Tax Service. Franklin's father was Lee's son Theodore.

Cindy Harris worked with Dwight as a part of the Yew Piney Mountain Non Profit. Beginning in 2000, Cindy Harris organized the workshops in her living room in Pittsburgh. Dwight held workshops and concerts in Harris' home from December 2006 through December 2014.

Beth Williams Hartness, a fingerstyle guitar player, performs duets of traditional music from the Appalachian South and elsewhere with Adam Hurt. She has taught workshops, played in concerts and performed on CDs with her musical partner Hurt.

Teri Hayes, a clawhammer banjo player, one-time

owner of a music store in Pittsburgh, Pennsylvania, and a student of Dwight's, hosted banjo workshops in Pittsburgh from 1996 to 1999.

Bill Hicks, the founding fiddler of the Red Clay Ramblers (1972–1981), was a member of the Fuzzy Mountain String Band from 1970 to 1981. After leaving the Ramblers in 1981 he began playing music with his wife, Libby, and working as a stone mason in Chatham County, North Carolina. Hicks taught on the same "faculty" with Dwight a few times, particularly at the Augusta Heritage Workshops in Elkins, West Virginia, and attended some of the "get-togethers" Dwight organized in the early 1970s featuring the Hammons family.

Jackie Horvath, a banjo student of Dwight's in 1973 during his days of teaching in Morgantown, West Virginia.

Wayne Howard is a retired computer programmer and analyst and a clawhammer banjo player. He was born in Owensboro, Kentucky, and earned a bachelor's degree in English from the University of Notre Dame and a master's degree in folk studies from Western Kentucky University where, in 1981, he completed a project titled *Fiddle Songs and Banjo Songs: A Descriptive Index*. His four-part feature about the Hammons family appeared in the *Old Time Herald* in 2009 and 2010, and in December 2012 he revisited the subject of the Hammons family for *Goldenseal*.

John Huerta, former general counsel, Smithsonian, long-time banjo player and vintage banjo collector, and resident of Elkins, West Virginia.

Adam Hurt, a performer and teacher of traditional music, is a concertizing banjo and fiddle player with several CDs in his name, and has conducted banjo workshops around the country and abroad. Hurt has placed in or won many major old-time banjo competitions including Clifftop, Mount Airy, and Galax, and won the state banjo championships of Virginia, West Virginia, and Ohio, as well as the state fiddle championships of Virginia and Maryland.

Peter Irvine has been a percussionist with Cordelia's Dad, a band that has for over twenty years experimented with early American hymns, ballads and fiddle and banjo tunes. Irvine, along with the band founders Tim Eriksen and Cath Oss, recorded on Dwight Diller's CD *New Plowed Ground*. Irvine also sings sacred harp music.

Alan Jabbour, former director of the American Folk Life Center at the Library of Congress, co-author with Carl Fleischhauer of *The Hammons Family: The Traditions of a West Virginia Family and their Friends*.

Allen Johnson, co-founder of Christians for the Mountains, West Virginia.

Kim Johnson, from Clendenin, West Virginia, has been playing old time banjo since about 1978. From 1981 until his death in 1999, Kim performed extensively with Clay County, West Virginia, fiddler Wilson Douglas. From the late 1990s, she played banjo with Calhoun County fiddler Lester McCumbers. Through at least 2015 she was an editor for Goldenseal, a quarterly magazine published by the state of West Virginia, Division of Culture and History.

Diane Jones, born in New Jersey, learned banjo playing in the style of Ola Belle Reed, Maggie Hammons of Pocahontas County, West Virginia, and Lily May Ledford. Jones taught banjo at the Augusta Heritage Workshops in Elkins, West Virginia. She recorded a CD with banjoist Hubie King titled *There Are No Rules*, and played banjo in the Reed Island Rounders with Billy Cornette and Betty Vornbrock.

Dick Kimmel, a professional musician from Ulm, Minnesota, has been associated with traditional bluegrass and old-time country music for more than 50 years as a performer, recording artist, workshop instructor, teacher, historian, writer, and songwriter. Dick, a vocalist and multi-instrumentalist usually playing mandolin, clawhammer banjo, and guitar, performed with the Black Mountain Bluegrass Boys in the early 1970s.

Walt Koken, Pennsylvania-born old time banjo and fiddle player, member of the Orpheus Supertones, the Highwoods String Band and the Fat City String Band. Co-author with Clare Milliner of *Milliner-Koken Collection of American Fiddle Tunes*.

Jeff Kramer decided to try his hand at banjo building in 2000 after attending a few of Dwight's banjo retreats in West Virginia in the 1990s. At a 2001 banjo retreat, Dwight pulled out "a unique old Lange banjo with an 11.5 inch rim and excellent tone," and asked Kramer to build a banjo that would duplicate the sound of this banjo. Kramer agreed to take a stab at it and established his Wisconsin-based banjo building workshop, Cloverlick Banjos.

Chuck Lee, a native of Ovilla, Texas, is the owner and operator of Chuck Lee Banjos.

Brad Leftwich, an old-time fiddle and banjo player and teacher originally from Oklahoma, was a founding member of the Plank Road String Band in the mid–1970s.

James Leva is a multi-instrumentalist, singer, and songwriter who learned much of his fiddle, banjo and vocal repertoire from traditional masters such as Tommy Jarrell and Doug Wallin. During the 1970s and 1980s he performed with Plank Road (with Al Tharp and Michael James Kott), Ace Weems and the Fat Meat Boys (with David Winston and Chad Crumm), and the Hellbenders (with Bruce Molsky and Dave Grant). In February 2011, his play, *A Kindly Visitation*, based on memories of visits to Tommy Jarrell, had its debut performance at the Lenfest Center, Washington and Lee University.

Dan Levenson, born and raised Pittsburgh, Pennsylvania, is an old time fiddle, clawhammer banjo, guitar, dance and song artist who performs and teaches old time music. He has published fiddle and banjo instructional books, and edits the quarterly old time banjo music section for *Banjo Newsletter*.

John Lilly, a guitar player, was the editor of *Goldenseal*, West Virginia's state magazine, published in Charleston.

Bates Littlehales, a staff photographer for the National Geographic Society for 37 years, is considered one of the pioneers of underwater photography. Littlehales is a long time practitioner of clawhammer banjo and an accomplished banjo builder. Littlehales produced Dwight's instructional videos.

Gerry Milnes, former folk arts coordinator at the Augusta Heritage Center at Davis and Elkins College, the author of *Play of a Fiddle: Traditional Music, Dance, and Folklore in West Virgin*ia, published by University Press of Kentucky, and a long-time member of the West Virginia old-time band Gandydancer.

Bruce C. Molsky was born in New York City in the mid–1950s, and grew up in the Bronx. His father, a mechanical engineer, was a first-generation American descendant of Jewish immigrants from Poland. Molsky became absorbed in old-time music while studying engineering at Cornell University in Ithaca, New York, in the early 1970s. He plays fiddle, banjo and guitar, and sings, and performs and records old time music of the Appalachian region, among other types of music.

Ron Mullennex of Bluefield, West Virginia, plays clawhammer banjo and mandolin in the band Gandydancer with Gerry Milnes, Dave Bing, Mark Payne and Jim Martin. He grew up in Harmon, West Virginia, an epicenter of traditional dancing and music. Mullennex plays with his son Rory at the West Virginia State Folk Festival in Glenville and at the Vandalia Gathering in Charleston. He is an experienced teacher of the old-time music.

Tom Mylet, a native of Philadelphia, moved to Grayson County, Virginia, in the early 1970s to be closer to the music that he loved. He spent a lot of his twenties playing music and hanging out in the banjo shop of Kyle Creed. Mylet took over Old Blue Records in the 2013 after its owner and founder, Charlie Faurot, passed away. Mylet played clawhammer banjo for the New Camp Creek Boys.

David Nemec, a sound engineer and musician, met Dwight in 1991 at Augusta Heritage Center in Elkins, West Virginia, where he participated as a student in one of Dwight's banjo workshops. They became friends, and Nemec produced many of Dwight's commercial recordings beginning in the early 1990s. Between 1997 and 1999, Nemec worked on digitizing the original field recordings of the Hammonses and other source musicians made by Dwight form 1969 to 1971.

Ken Perlman, an acclaimed teacher of folk-music instrumental skills, has written banjo and guitar instruction books, has been on staff at prestigious teaching festivals around the world, and served as director or co-director for several banjo and music-instructional camps. He has spent several decades collecting tunes and oral histories from traditional fiddle players on Prince Edward Island in Canada. In 2015 the University of Tennessee Press published his book, *Couldn't Have a Wedding Without the Fiddler: The Story of Traditional Fiddling on Prince Edward Island*.

Jack Gordon Phelan, writer and director of *The Fifth String*, a feature length film starring Dwight Diller and John Morris, released in 2004 by the production company Front Porch Entertainment and distributed in 2004 by American Film Partners.

Nick Pilley, a clawhammer banjo player in England, was the president of the Friends of American Old Time Music and Dance (FOAOTMAD) in the United Kingdom through at least 2015.

Scott Prouty, a West Virginian fiddler and banjo player, worked as an intern in the Library of Congress on the American Folklore Center's accessions list of Hammons recordings in the 1990s, and assisted on the *Across the Yew Pines* project in the early 2000s.

Len Reiss, a retired computer maintenance expert and a banjo builder of note who is credited with roughly 30 to 35 banjos through the 1970s. Reiss met Dwight at the 4th Annual Old Time Fiddlers and Bluegrass Convention in Hillsville, Virginia, in June 1970.

Joe Rizzi, executive producer of *The Fifth String*, a feature length film starring Dwight Diller and John Morris, released in 2004.

Ralph Roberts, a West Virginia fiddler, is a relative of the Hammons family from Pocahontas County, West Virginia.

Catherine Rowe, from England, worked on the *Across the YewPines* multiple DVD project about the Hammons family, from 2005 to 2013.

Gary Ruley, a guitar flatpicker who was born and raised in Lexington, Virginia, grew up surrounded by the serious concentration of old time and bluegrass musical talent in that city. His current band, Mule Train, features musicians who straddle various musical worlds including old time, blue grass, and jazz.

Don Rusnak, a banjo player from northern Virginia, took his first lessons in the late 1950s from his father, who was a professional tenor banjo player in Pittsburgh. He began to build banjos and teach music in the northern Virginia area in the late 1960s. In the early 1970s he opened a music store in Arlington, Virginia, and founded and played banjo in Home Brew, a traditional bluegrass band that was active from 1973 to 1977. He has taught banjo in Arlington for nearly forty years, and in that time built a significant collection of vintage banjos, sustained his interest in banjo building, and developed an interest in clever, innovative banjo design.

Stewart Seidel, a banjo student and videographer of one of Dwight's retreats held in Red Lodge, Montana, in late 2000, collaborated on the tab book *Yew Pine Mountain: Obscure Underground Clawhammer Banjo From Mysterious Central West Virginia*.

Robert Shafer, a native of West Virginia, has been a professional musician since graduating high school in 1981. Shafer is a two-time winner of the National Flatpicking Championship (1983 and 2000) held annually in Kansas; the contest draws competitors from all over the globe. In the mid–1980s, Robert began playing electric guitar professionally in and around his native West Virginia. In 2000, Shafer returned to his acoustic roots and continues to perform in duo, trio and full band formats on Mountain Stage, The Grand Ole Opry, and in countless venues across the United States, Canada and Europe.

Bob Smakula, a West Virginia fiddler and banjo player who has played old time music since the 1970s, is the owner of Smakula Fretted Instruments in Elkins, West Virginia, and has been making and repairing old-time instruments for more than 35 years.

Carroll Smith, a photographer and videographer, as well as a clawhammer banjo player from Florida, recorded some of Dwight's earliest public performances in West Virginia.

Bobby Taylor, a fourth generation West Virginia fiddler, plays several styles of old-time and contest fiddling, and studied fiddling with the legendary Clark Kessinger. He retired in 2014 after working for 37 years for the West Virginia Archives and History Library Section of the West Virginia Division of Culture and History.

Carter Allen "Al" Tharp is a Grammy award winning multi-instrumentalist and producer. He was one of the founding members of the Plank Road old time music band that emerged in the early 1970s in Lexington, Virginia. Tharp was the bassist and second fiddler with the Cajun band BeauSoleil and divides his time between New Orleans and his home in rural Virginia and remains active in performance and recording. He operates his private project recording studio in New Orleans. In the 2000s he performed as the banjo and bass player in the band Purgatory Mountain with James Leva, Danny Knicely and Matty Olwell.

Bob Thornburg, a clawhammer banjo player and a dedicated old time banjo music historian, is a noted builder of gourd banjos and the owner of Sierra View Instruments in Bishop, California.

Bob Threns, a clawhammer banjo player and an enthusiastic caver, met Dwight in the early 1970s and attended several old time music festivals in Virginia and West Virginia with him.

Douglas Van Gundy, who grew up in Elkins, West Virginia, was among Dwight Diller's first fiddle students in the early 1990s. In 1993 Van Gundy studied fiddle with the late Mose Coffman of Greenbrier County, West Virginia, through the National Endowment for the Humanities folk arts apprenticeship program of the Augusta Heritage Center. He performs as a solo act and with Paul Gartner in the duo Born Old. Van Gundy recorded *Born Old* with banjo player Paul Gartner and *Two Far Gone* with fiddler Jake Krack.

Stephen Wade began studying with Fleming Brown at Chicago's Old Town School of Folk Music in 1970. In 1972, Wade began an association with Brown's teacher, old-time Kentucky-born radio singer Doc Hopkins. Under the tutelage of these two mentors, Wade immersed himself in the banjo, traditional music, and American folklore. In 2012 Wade published *The Beautiful Music All Around Us: Field Recordings and the American Experience* (University of Illinois Press).

Josh Wanstreet, whose family has ties to Doddridge County, West Virginia, that date to the 1830s, began playing traditional old-time fiddle and banjo in 1995. He performs at regional festivals and events including dances sponsored by the Morgantown Friends of Old Time Music.

Bill Wellington, a multi-instrumentalist from Staunton, Virginia, recorded eight West Virginia musicians and singers in the late 1970s in a project sponsored by the Grant County Arts Council with funding by the West Virginia department of Culture and History. In 2009, he assembled a two-part slide show that featured ballad singer Florena Duling and fiddlers Blaine Likens, Israel Welch, and Tom Welch.

Andy Williams, a fiddler from Virginia, met Dwight at the Droop Mountain festival in 1970, played with him in the jam band the A.A. Cutters in Morgantown, West Virginia, in 1972 and 1973, and travelled with him to Lexington, Virginia, where Williams joined the Plank Road String Band in the 1970s, and frequented the old time gatherings at Odell and Mata McGuire's home.

David Winston, an old time banjo player closely familiar with the old time music scene in Lexington, Virginia, of the early 1970s. Winston was the subject of a feature length interview in *The Banjo Newsletter* in April 2015.

Howard Zane, who as a boy in New Hampshire learned banjo playing from Bob Pressley, who was born in 1871 and whose father was a regimental banjo and guitar player in an Alabama brigade during the Civil War. After a hiatus of about 30 years, during which he built a career as an airline pilot and owner of an industrial engineering firm, Zane returned to banjo playing in the mid–1980s. He met and learned from Dwight at Augusta Heritage Center in the mid–1980s, attended Dwight's first banjo camp, and hosted several banjo workshops at his home in Maryland. He and his wife Sandy play old time music together as the New Southern Cow Tippers.

Index

A.A. Cutters 102, 103, 159*ch1n*4, 179*n*7-8
Across the YewPines 4, 7, 108, 128, 131, 159*n*3, 184*Cn*4
Adams, Sheila Kay 63, 102, 172*n*28, 179*n*2
Aiwa recording machine 39
Akeman, Dave "Stringbean" 30-31
"Alternative Galax" 73, 163*n*26
Annual Old Time Fiddlers and Bluegrass Convention 58-59, 73-74, 135, 138, 140, 168*n*91, 171*n*15, 175*n*74; *see also* Hillsville, VA
Appalachian String Band Festival 38
Archive of Folk Culture, Library of Congress 53-54, 128, 159*Ch1n*3, 169*n*110, 171*n*17
Augsburger, Donald 87-90, 178*n*15
Augusta Heritage Center 93, 104, 105, 129, 131
Automobiles, first 24-25

Baker, Kenny 77
Baker, Thaddeus 77
Ballard, Wilson 47
Banjo: approach to teaching 3-5; fretless 145, 185*n*29; instruments 139-150; learning to play 41-45; retreats 49, 93, 96, 102; style 73-75; *see also* Clawhammer banjo; Playing style; Teaching experiences
Banjo contests: Glenville, WV 61; Hillsville, VA, 1970 58-61
Banjo Hangout 1
BANJO-L 1
"Banjo ministry" 94-96
Baron, Carl 73, 103, 105, 163*n*26, 175*n*77, 179*n*11
Beer joints 26-29, 33, 35, 37, 72, 100, 162*n*1, 164*n*33
Beisswenger, Drew 128, 182*n*69, 184*Cn*1
Belle Alkali Chemical Plant 15, 20
Benford, Mac 48, 172*n*26, 173*n*44
Bernhardt, Jack 79, 82, 83, 114, 159*I*4, 161*n*45, 164*n*35, 166*n*55, 171*n*11, 171*n*12, 172*n*28, 174*n*54, 63, 69, 175*n*80, 176*n*102, 179*n*2, 180*n*35, 185*n*25
Bing, Dave 75, 105, 107, 121, 155, 159*In*4

Bing, Tim 47
Birth 15
Black Mountain 44
Black Mountain Bluegrass Boys 31, 35-36, 47, 49, 69-71, 105, 129, 135-136, 155, 166*n*59, 174*n*61, 185*n*24
Blacksmithing 146
Blake, Norman 119
Blosser, Glendon 93-94, 194
Bowman, Richard 94
Brown, Fleming 48
Brown, Thomas 56, 169*n*108
Browns Creek, WV 31, 109, 131, 132
Brunk, George 87-89, 178*n*11
Buena Vista, WV 86
Burgess, Loy 38

Campbell, Mark 66, 73, 163*n*26, 172*n*38, 175*n*77, 176*n*102
Campbell Lumber Company 15
Carpenter, French 119, 120, 185*n*24
Carpenter, Hamp 35-37, 42, 45, 47, 58, 119, 129, 137-138, 150, 171*n*17, 174*n*61, 184*n*13
Carpenter, Harley 33, 35, 70, 155, 174*n*61, 185*n*24
Cash, Johnny 27, 29-30
Cass, WV 27, 58, 70, 72, 85, 93, 105, 109, 110, 119, 121, 159*In*4, 178*n*1
Chacey, Ron, inlay artist 140, 142-144, 186*n*38
Chappell, Louis Watson 50
Child, Francis 52
Christianity 81, 94, 100
Church of the Brethren, Dwight and 85, 87, 91, 92, 101, 177*n*6, 178*n*7
Clawhammer banjo 1, 2, 44, 47-49, 59, 69, 74-76, 82, 102, 103, 105, 115, 117, 125, 129, 131, 137-139, 140, 153, 162*n*69, 166*n*59, 170*n*4, 172*n*23, 175*n*70, 176*n*87, 186*n*30
Clifftop 38, 68, 109, 128, 129, 173*n*38
Coffman, Mose 63, 117, 119, 120, 171*n*17, 181*n*42
Cohen, Stu 49
Colonialism 55
Comstock, Jim 47
Conway, Cece 112, 170*n*2, 171*n*19, 177*n*112
Cordelia's Dad 107

Correctones 61
Costa, Jimmy 47, 119, 166*n*57
Cox, John Harrington 50, 56, 167*n*76
Cranberry Mountain 44
Creed, Kyle 162*n*69, 170*n*7, 172*n*38, 186*n*30
"Cultural messages" 6, 95, 112, 113, 115
"Cultural receptor" 27, 89, 107, 126, 151
Cuthbert, John 56, 167*n*82, 168*n*103, 169*n*106

Dagget, Dan, banjo builder 140, 143-145, 186*n*40
Dickens, Hazel 77
"Diller Recidivists" 5
"Diller versus 'dllr'" 11-12
Diller, Nancy (sister) 21-22
Diller, Vernon (father) 15; death 22; divorce 21-22; U.S. Army service 20
Dilley, Mary Lou 42
Douglas, Wilson 46, 115, 129, 134, 176*n*91
Droop Mountain Festival 61
Dulcimer 52
Durham/Chapel Hill, North Carolina, old time scene 64

Eastern Mennonite University 87-90, 178*n*15
Edray, Pocahontas County, WV 16
Elementary school 24
Elkins, WV 76, 93, 105, 119, 128
England 105-107
Eppley, Mabel (aunt) 23

Family life, memories of 21-23
Family tree 15-18
Fencing 32, 102, 162*n*77
Festivals 58-61
Fiddling 41, 75-78; learning to play 41
The Fifth String 109-111
Fleischhauer, Carl 46, 50, 52-55, 60, 103, 129, 140, 146, 159*Ch1n*3, 163*n*20, 26, 167*n*78-80, 168*n*103, 169*n*107, 113, 171*n*17, 184*C*1, 185*n*19; relationship with Hammons family 54
Friends of American Old Time

201

Music and Dance (FOAOTMAD) 105, 189
Fults, Andrew 76, 148, 149, 187n66
Fuzzy Mountain String Band 54, 59, 64, 67–68, 73, 80–83, 168n1, 170n1, 172n19, 175n77, 177n108

G.I. Bill 37
Gainer, Patrick W. 50–56, 168n92, 95, 173n40; and the Hammons family 54–56
Gainsborough Old Time Music and Dance Festival 105–107
Garton, Rock 102, 118, 179n6-7
George, Franklin 173n38
George Washburn banjo 42, 49
Glenville, WV 61, 167n75, 176n102
Goldenseal 128, 162n83, 163n15, 165n49, 167n75, 85, 174n64, 177n4
Goodman, Benny 30
Gordon, Lo 144
Grand Old Opry 78, 163n11, 165n41
Grandpa Jones *see* Jones, Louis Marshall
Green Giant Company 34
Green Grass Cloggers 64
Gretsch banjo 37, 42, 140

Haggard, Paul 58, 61, 140
Hamlin Church 16, 63
Hammons, Burl 37–38, 41, 43–44, 52, 54, 57–58, 61, 63, 73, 76, 78–79, 112, 119, 129, 156, 157, 163n16, 164n38, 165n47, 166n54, 167n82, 171n19, 175n78, 79, 176n98
Hammons, Edn 18, 38, 44, 56–57, 65, 75, 99, 119, 124, 128, 168n103; "Edden" versus "Edn" 169n104, 176n88, 183n78
Hammons, Frank 163n19, 197
Hammons, James 56, 61, 140, 142
Hammons, Lee 18, 37–40, 43–46, 58, 61, 63, 72–73, 78, 82, 113, 121, 128, 129, 131, 134, 137, 140, 142, 144, 149, 150, 156, 157, 165n48, 176n106, 182n68
Hammons, Maggie 37–38, 40, 43–44, 52, 54, 57–58, 61, 63, 73, 76, 112, 128, 131, 138, 156, 166n54, 167n82, 170n9, 171n19
Hammons, Paris 38
Hammons, Sherman 36–38, 39–40, 43–44, 57, 61–63, 73, 75, 76, 80, 112, 121, 124, 128, 156, 163n20, 164n38, 165n41, 166n55, 167n82, 172n30, 174n65, 175n79
Hammons, Trevor 131, 171n14
Hammons family 3–5, 18, 36–39, 44–47, 49, 52–55, 57, 61, 63, 65, 72–73, 75–76, 80–82, 99, 109–110, 119, 128–129, 134, 136, 137, 159n3, 162n83, 176n98, 184n4, 186n31; Dwight's visits to Hammons family homes; local jams and "get togethers" 52; photographs of 52; recording of 39, 40; relationship with Dwight 39–41, 54
The Hammons Family: A Study of a West Virginia Family's Traditions 52, 129, 159n3
Harmony banjo 39

Health issues 132–134
Hicks, Bill 28, 59, 68, 80, 170n1, 4, 171n19, 174n56, 175n77, 177n113, 181n57
Highwood String Band 67, 68, 172n26
Hillbilly 47, 52, 109, 167n80
Hillsboro, WV 27, 33, 42, 56, 61, 70, 83, 86, 87, 93, 105, 119, 135, 154
Hillsville, VA 58–59, 73–74, 135, 138, 140, 165n49, 168n91, 170n7, 175n74; *see also* Annual Old Time Fiddlers and Bluegrass Convention
"Hind Horn" 54
"Hog Eyed Man" 49, 72, 73
Hog fiddles 52
Hollow Rock String Band 59, 64, 79–80, 82–83, 171n10
Holt, David 163n27
Horvath, Jackie 102, 179n8
Howard, Wayne 50, 61, 71, 73, 102, 162n83, 169n104, 170n2, 185n17
Hunting and firearms 25, 26

"In Scotland Town" 54
Iota-Chi (I-X) Cross, importance to Diller 96
Ivydale, WV 61, 71, 102, 130, 134, 136, 140, 164n34, 168n91, 169n112, 172n28, 173n40, 174n64

Jabbour, Alan 52, 53, 54–55, 57, 64, 68, 79–80, 82, 109, 129, 159In4, 163n26, 164n35
Jarrell, Ben 79
Jarrell, Tommy 58–59, 61, 63, 65, 67–68, 79–81, 112, 145, 163n27, 172n38, 176n102, 182n71, 186n30
Jarvis, Ward 77
Jericho Road 15
Johnson, Keith 105, 107; *see also* Friends of American Old Time Music and Dance
Jones, Diane 124, 170n3, 183n78, 79
Jones, Louis Marshall ("Grandpa Jones") 29–30, 37, 47, 74, 139–140, 162n69, 163n12

Kentucky 37–38, 71, 77, 113, 137, 139, 160n28, 168n103, 172n28, 176n98, 180n30
Kimmel, Dick 47–50, 58, 105
Krack, Jake 121, 154
Kramer, Jeff 145–149, 187n57

Lacy, Marvin 47
Leather Bitches Band 64
Lee, Chuck 145, 186n46-49
Leftwich, Brad 60, 64–65, 67–68, 165n47, 171n15, 173n41, 177n108, 185n21, 24
Leva, James 56, 61, 64, 68, 172n27-28, 174n54, 185n21
Levenson, Dan 48–49
Lewis, Jerry Lee 30
Lexington, Virginia 49, 61–69, 79–86, 136–140; Adams, Sheila Kay 63; as a old time music crossroads 61; "authenticity" debate over 66–68; Bare, Olin, on 65; Breaking up Christmas 63; Campbell, Mark, on 66; Carlin, Bob, on 64, 66–67; Diller's comments on old time scene 63; Fix, William Henry (Olin Bare's grandfather) 65; Hicks, Bill, on 68; Highwood String Band 63; Jabbour, Alan, on the Lexington, VA, and the Durham/Chapel Hill, NC, old time scenes 64; Jarrell, Tommy, Odell McGuire's comments on 68; Leftwich, Brad, on 63, 165–166; Leva, James, on 64, 68; Mata McGuire 63; "Mongrel Horde" 63; Odell McGuire 61–69; old time scene's influence on Diller 68–69; Plank Road Band 64; Ruley, Gary, on 65; West Virginia old time music, Diller's contributions to 129–132; White Column Inn 64
Library of Congress, Hammons Family Project 52–56, 57, 109, 128–129, 159n3, 163n26, 164n35, 165n46, 171n10, 19
"Life Narratives" 9
Lisburn, Pennsylvania 23–24
Littlehales, Bates 1, 2, 7, 114, 137, 144–145, 156, 158, 159In4, 180n35
Local stories, absorption of 26–27
Long Hunters 96
Lund, Pam 121, 193

MacElwayne, Jack 65
Marlinton, WV 15–17, 19, 21–22, 24–25, 30, 33–34, 37–38, 40, 44, 60–61, 73, 109, 129, 131–132
Marriages 16, 63, 86–87, 178n7
McGuire, Mata 63
McGuire, Odell 61–69, 73, 82–83, 105, 135–136, 140, 164n34, 173n41, 176n108, 177n110, 113, 185n21, 26
McLaughlin, Ed 16
Medical challenges 5
Memories of music, early 28–31
"Message" 150–151
Methodist Church 16
Miller, Glenn 29–30
Milnes, Gerry 38, 45, 153, 163n26, 165n40, 167n84, 175n77, 184Cn4
Ministries 8, 13, 91–94
Monongahela National Forest Service job 34, 38
Monroe, Bill 31, 162n69
Morgantown, WV 34, 37, 47–50, 56, 69, 87, 102–103, 118, 138, 140, 162n75-76, 85, 166n63, 70, 179n6
Morris, Dave 71–73
Morris, John 47, 71–73
Morris Brothers 45, 61, 71–73, 129, 134–135, 139–141, 150, 162n71, 164n34, 167n75, 80, 185n15, 17, 188, 191, 193
Mount Airy Old Time Festival 60, 83, 112
Mullennex, Ron 47, 102, 103, 162n71, 179n6, 185n25-26
Music as a local dialect 6, 7
Music, youthful memories of 29–32
Musical influences 134–137

National Forest Service 18, 34, 38
Nemec, David 53, 154
New Lost City Ramblers 48, 64, 79, 80, 82, 177n112

O. B. Fawley Music Store 48
O'Dell, David 47
Old fiddle tunings 121–122
"Old People" 9–11, 35, 37, 41, 46–47, 50, 57, 63, 65, 68, 77, 79, 80, 94, 97, 114, 131, 135–137, 150–151, 165n54, 167n82, 172n26, 182n68
Old time music 11, 12, 39, 41, 43, 46, 47, 49, 54, 57–59, 60–69, 79–84, 94, 97, 98–99, 150–152

Penniman, Richard Wayne (Little Richard) 27, 29–30, 155
Perlman, Ken 65, 68, 105, 153, 158, 159*In*4, 164n31, 167n82, 173n39, 54, 176n89, 179n13, 182n63, 184n96
Phelan, Jack 109, 110
Pioneer Days, Marlinton, WV 61, 171n14
Plank Road Band 64, 82–83, 172n30, 185n21
Playing style (banjo), early 74–75
Pocahontas County, WV 1, 9, 15–18, 21–22, 24, 29, 35–36, 44–45, 47, 49, 50, 52–53, 56, 63, 65, 76–77, 85–86, 93, 102, 105, 108, 109, 116, 121, 128, 131, 132, 134, 135, 139, 150, 153, 156, 169n111, 171n14, 174n54, 177Ch4n6, 179n13, 184n6
"Power Brokers" 56
Presbyterian Church 16
Presley, Elvis 29
Price, William Thomas 17

Ramsey, Jack 103, 179n7
Red Clay Ramblers 64, 68, 174n54, 177n112
Redlick Mountain 15, 39
Reed, Henry 58, 63, 80, 139, 154, 156, 166, 170, 171
Reed, Worthy 42, 140
Reiss, Len 58, 63, 73, 83, 136, 141–142, 164, 168, 170, 172, 185n17
Religion, family and 15–18
Religious awakening 85–86; influence of Eugene Ten Brink and David Rittenhouse 177Ch4n6
"Responsibility to the music" 4–5
"Revivalists" 67, 136
Richardson's Hardware Store 44
Ritchie, Fiona 163n27
Rittenhouse, David 177Ch4n6
Rizzi, Joseph D. 109, 110, 180n26
Roberts, Ralph 38, 75, 76, 131, 176n91, 185n28, 187n66

Sampson, Harvey 121, 182n60
Sattler, Bob 109
Scott, Rob 35; *see also* Carpenter, Hamp
Seeger, Mike 73, 80, 172n34
Seeger, Pete 2, 47–49, 59, 73, 74
Seminary 87–90
Sharp, Geneva (grandmother) 15, 17, 19
Shields, Liz 63
Simmons, Woody 47, 119, 171n14, 181n56
Slaughter, Matokie 59
"Sledgehammer" 49, 82, 140, 166n59
Smith, Glen 45
Sound 138–140
Spencer, Kilby 73, 138, 170n7, 175n74, 186n33
Sports, participation in 24–25
Square dances 35, 74
Stearns, Richie 61
Stony Creek Church 16, 17, 18
Stories 27–28; importance of 26–27
Stubblefield, D. W. 15, 159n6

Tanner, Henry Ossawa 49
Taylor, Bobby 119, 178n32, 180n30
Teaching experiences 102–109, 112, 121, 124, 126, 127, 131, 132–134, 147, 150
Teaching music, retreats and workshops 105–111, 126–128; teaching banjo 114–118; teaching 114–126
Teaching philosophy 111–113
Ten Brink, Eugene 177n6
Tharp, Al 64, 168n90, 172n23, 181n54, 185n21
Thompson, Bobbie 64, 80, 170n1, 10

Thompson, Tommy 58–59, 60, 64, 80, 82, 135, 138, 170n1, 4, 7, 174n55, 177n112
Thornapple Productions 1, 156
Thren, Bob 58, 63, 73, 135, 138, 140, 170n2–3, 172n27
Trimble, Charlie 103, 179n10
Trimble, Molly (first wife) 16, 63
Triplett, Lee 45, 46, 72, 82, 119, 129, 134, 137, 150, 156, 170n3, 174n68
Trombone 30

U.S. Navy, service in 31–33

Van Gundy, Douglas 119–121, 154, 155, 161n58, 179n14, 181n57
Varela, Alex 58, 136, 139, 141, 170n2–3

Wade, Stephen 189, 200
Ward, Wade 59, 65, 111, 113, 135, 165n49
Watson, Doc 136, 185n25
Weil, Elizabeth 103
West Virginia 4-H club 58
The West Virginia Hillbilly 47
West Virginia musicians 47
West Virginia University 18, 31–34, 36, 48, 49, 50–51, 52, 54–55, 56–57, 58, 61, 63, 87, 102, 140
Williams, Andy 63, 102, 103, 118, 172n23, 175n79, 179n7, 181n54
Williams, Becky 64, 102, 103, 179n7
Wine, Melvin 119, 121, 163n26, 170n3, 176n102, 182n69, 72
Woodell, Edgar Bowd (grandfather) 15, 17
Woodell, Faith (mother) 15, 17; death 22; wartime service in WAVES 21
Woodell, Geneva 15, 16, 17, 19; *see also* Sharp, Geneva
Woodhicks 15, 28, 35, 39, 40
Workman, Nimrod 71, 77
Workman, Phyllis 71, 77
Worrell, Mutt 59
Writing style 9–10

Yew Pine Cultural Traditions, Inc. 108
Yoder, Lawrence 87, 90

www.ingramcontent.com/pod-product-compliance
Ingram Content Group UK Ltd.
Pitfield, Milton Keynes, MK11 3LW, UK
UKHW050526150426
5217IPUK00026B/1823